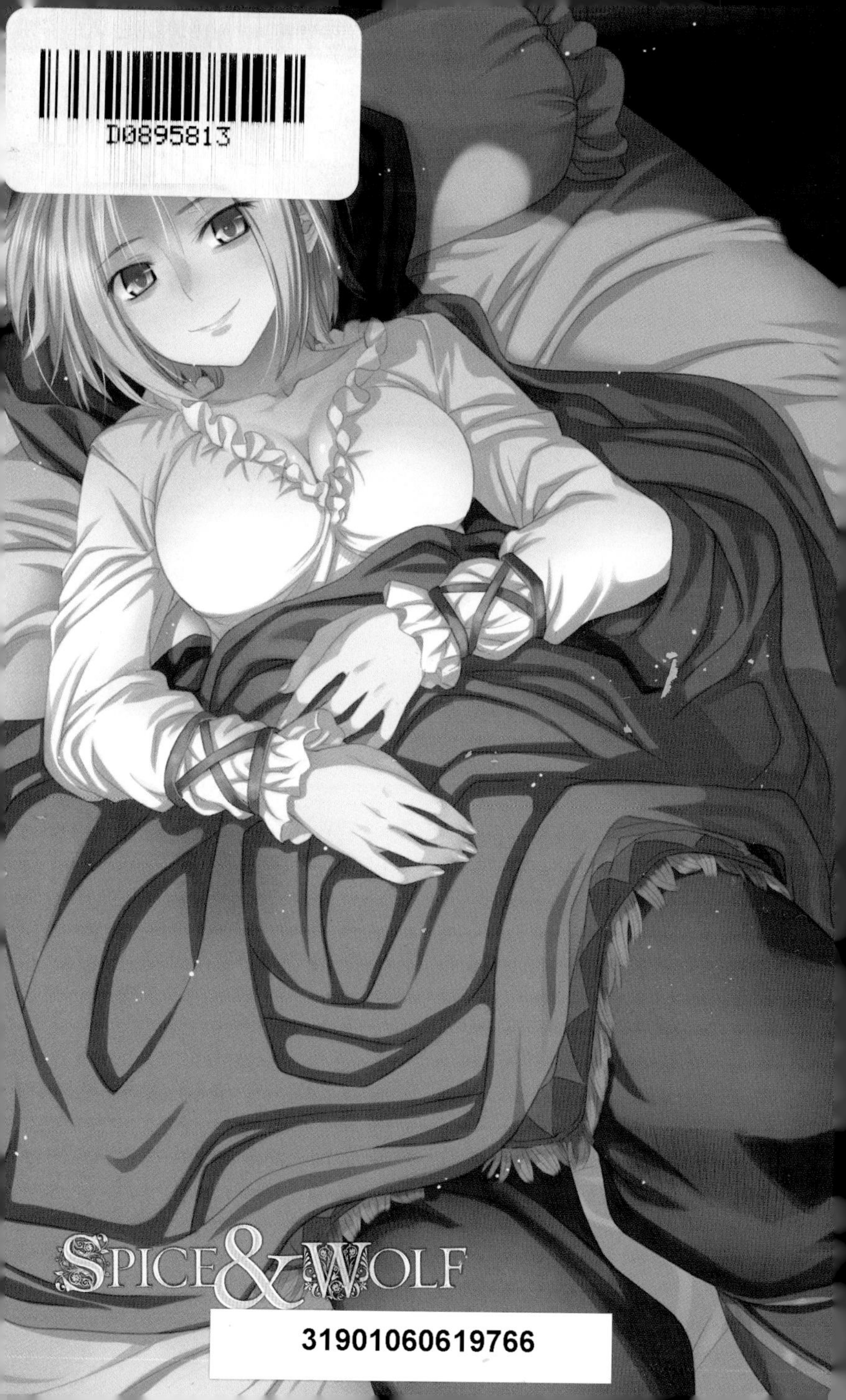
SPICE & WOLF

SPICE & WOLF

CONTENTS

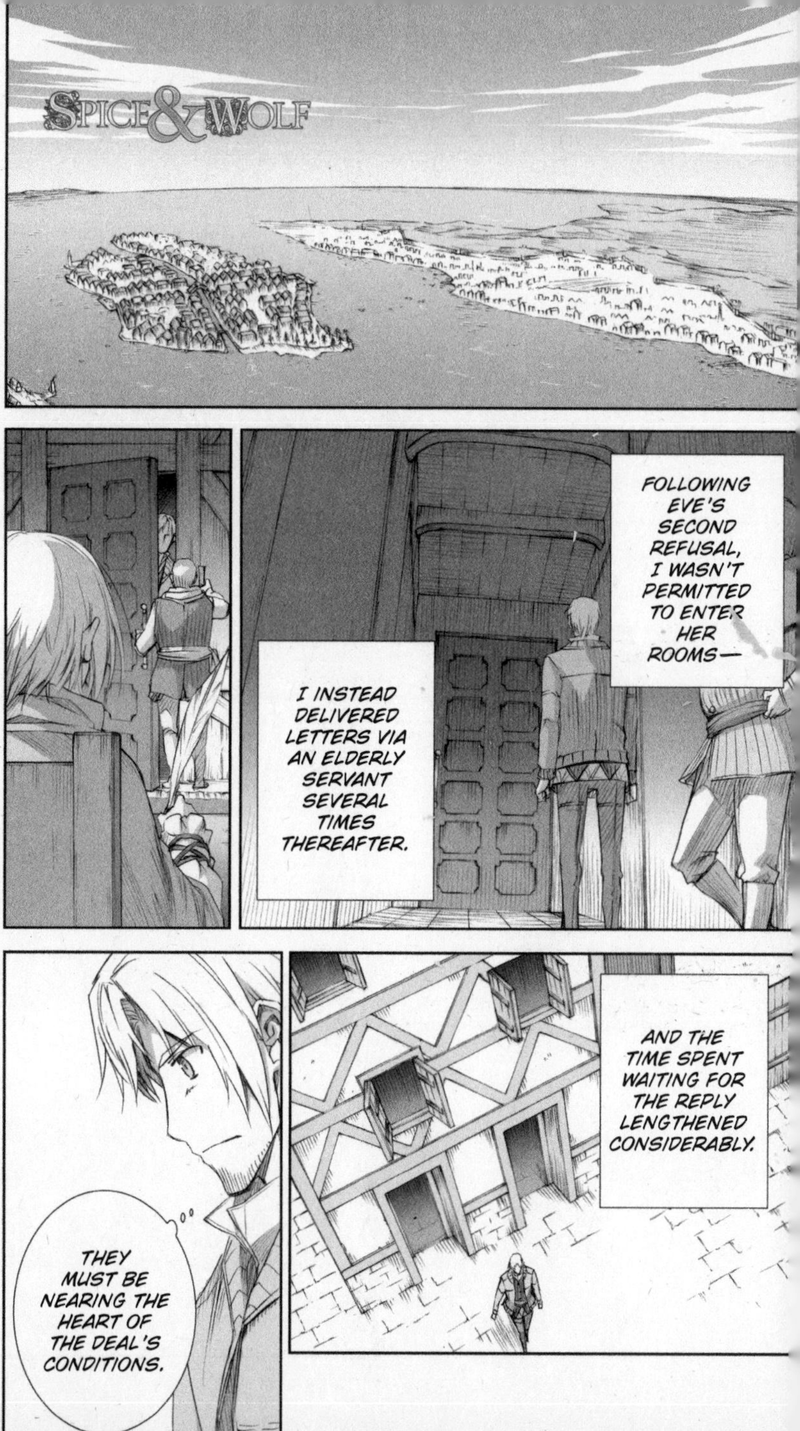
SPICE & WOLF
FOLLOWING EVE'S SECOND REFUSAL, I WASN'T PERMITTED TO ENTER HER ROOMS—
I INSTEAD DELIVERED LETTERS VIA AN ELDERLY SERVANT SEVERAL TIMES THEREAFTER.
AND THE TIME SPENT WAITING FOR THE REPLY LENGTHENED CONSIDERABLY.
THEY MUST BE NEARING THE HEART OF THE DEAL'S CONDITIONS.

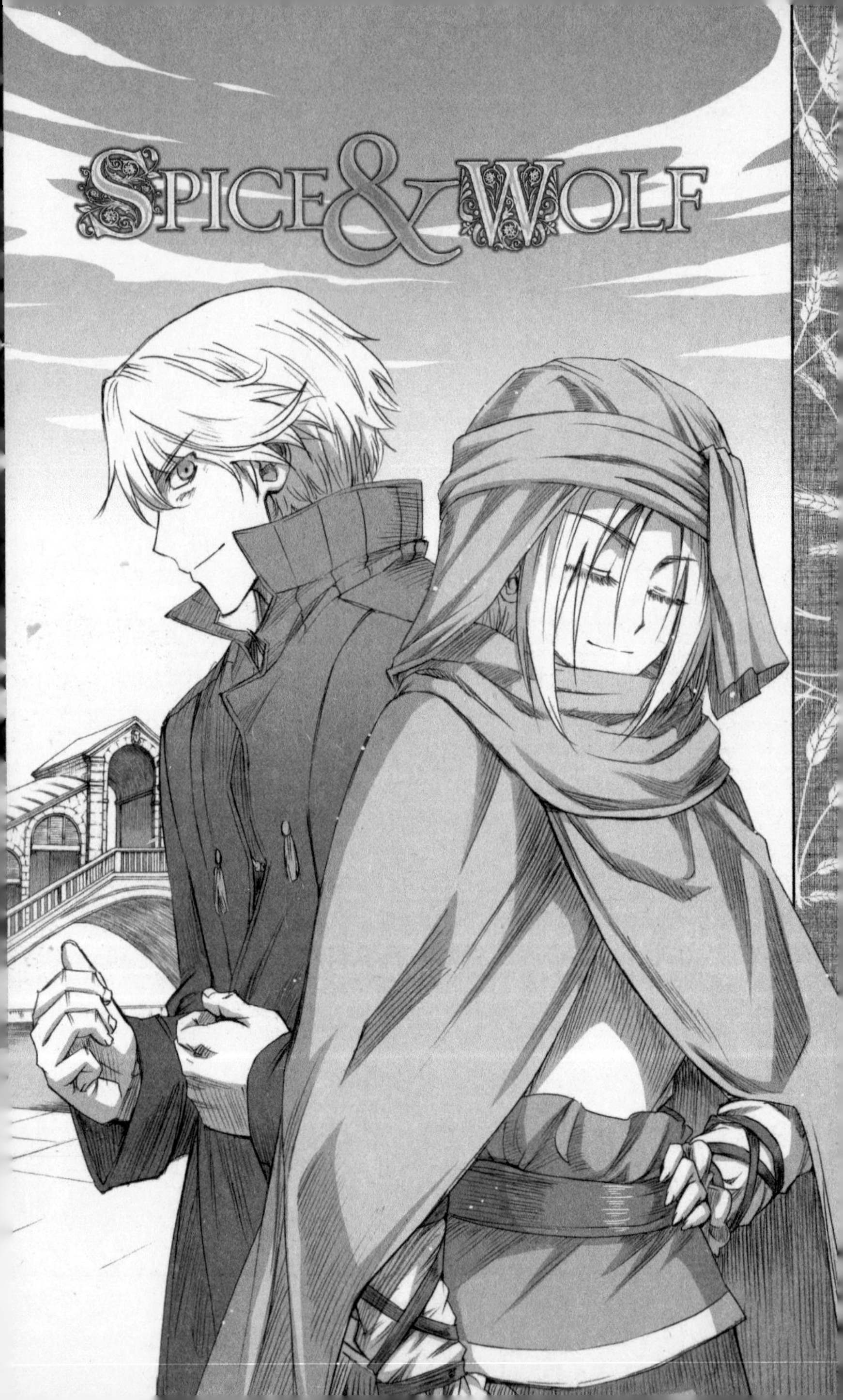
SPICE & WOLF

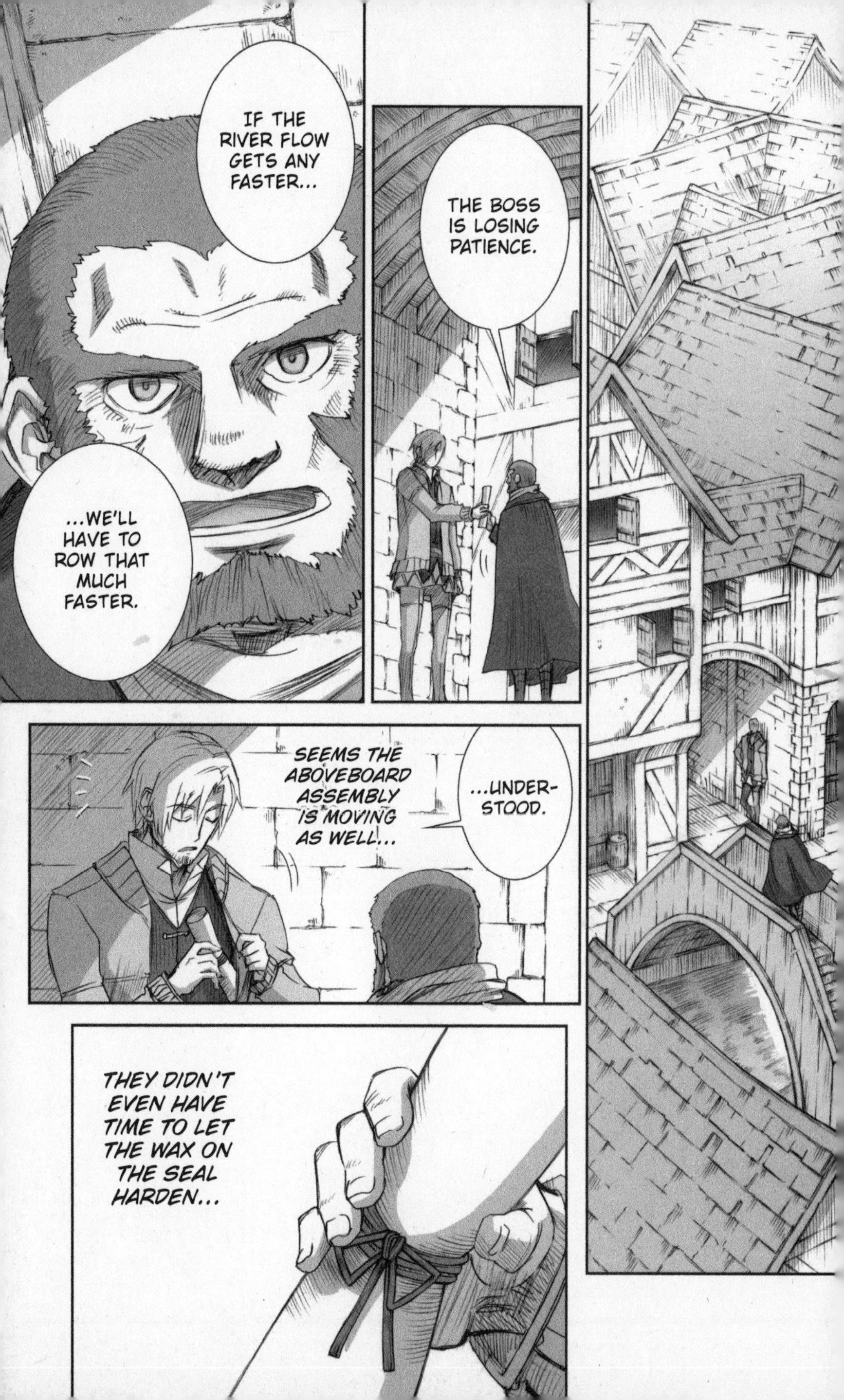
THE BOSS IS LOSING PATIENCE.
IF THE RIVER FLOW GETS ANY FASTER...
...WE'LL HAVE TO ROW THAT MUCH FASTER.
...UNDER-STOOD.
SEEMS THE ABOVEBOARD ASSEMBLY IS MOVING AS WELL...
THEY DIDN'T EVEN HAVE TIME TO LET THE WAX ON THE SEAL HARDEN...

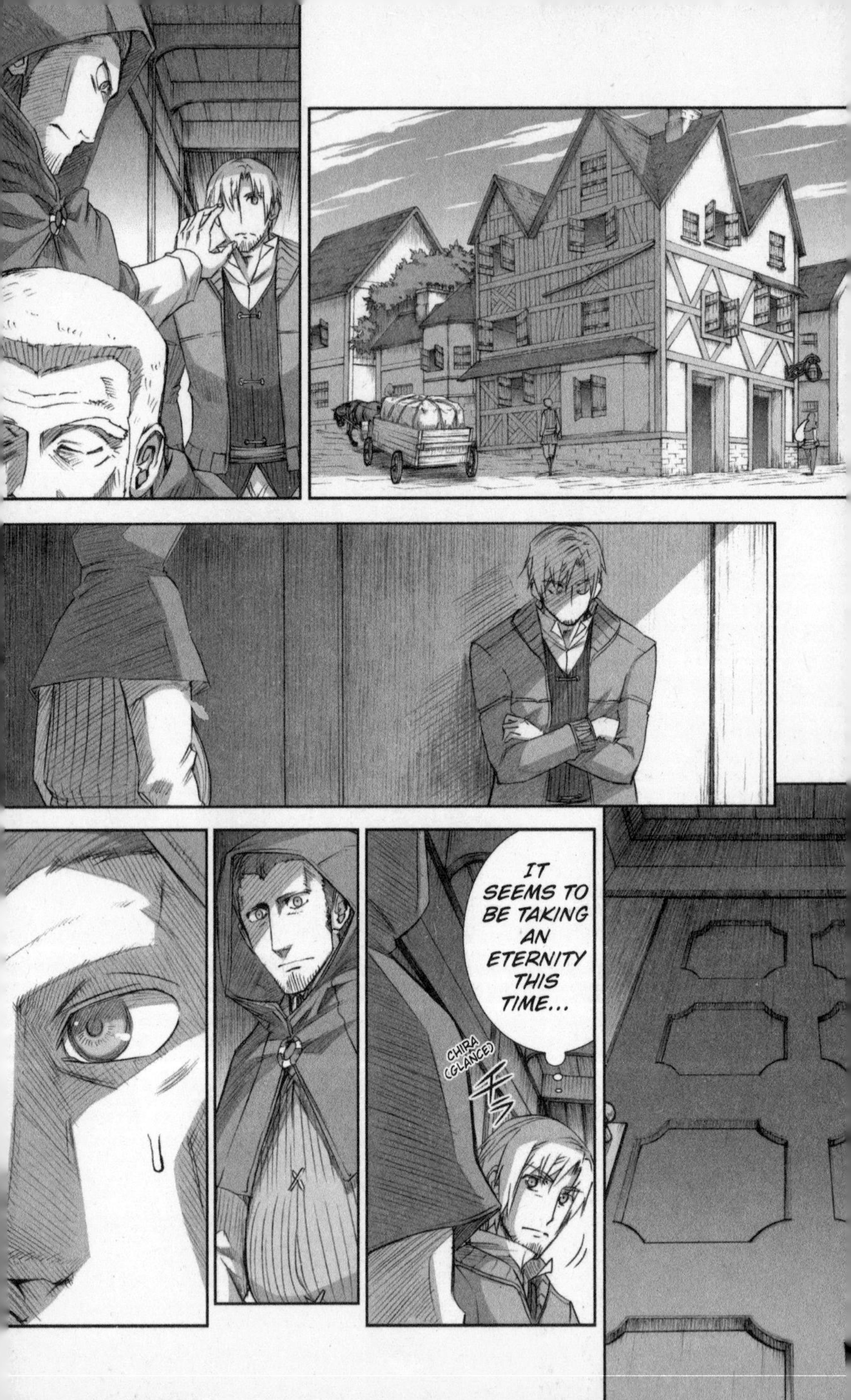
IT SEEMS TO BE TAKING AN ETERNITY THIS TIME...
CHIRA (GLANCE)

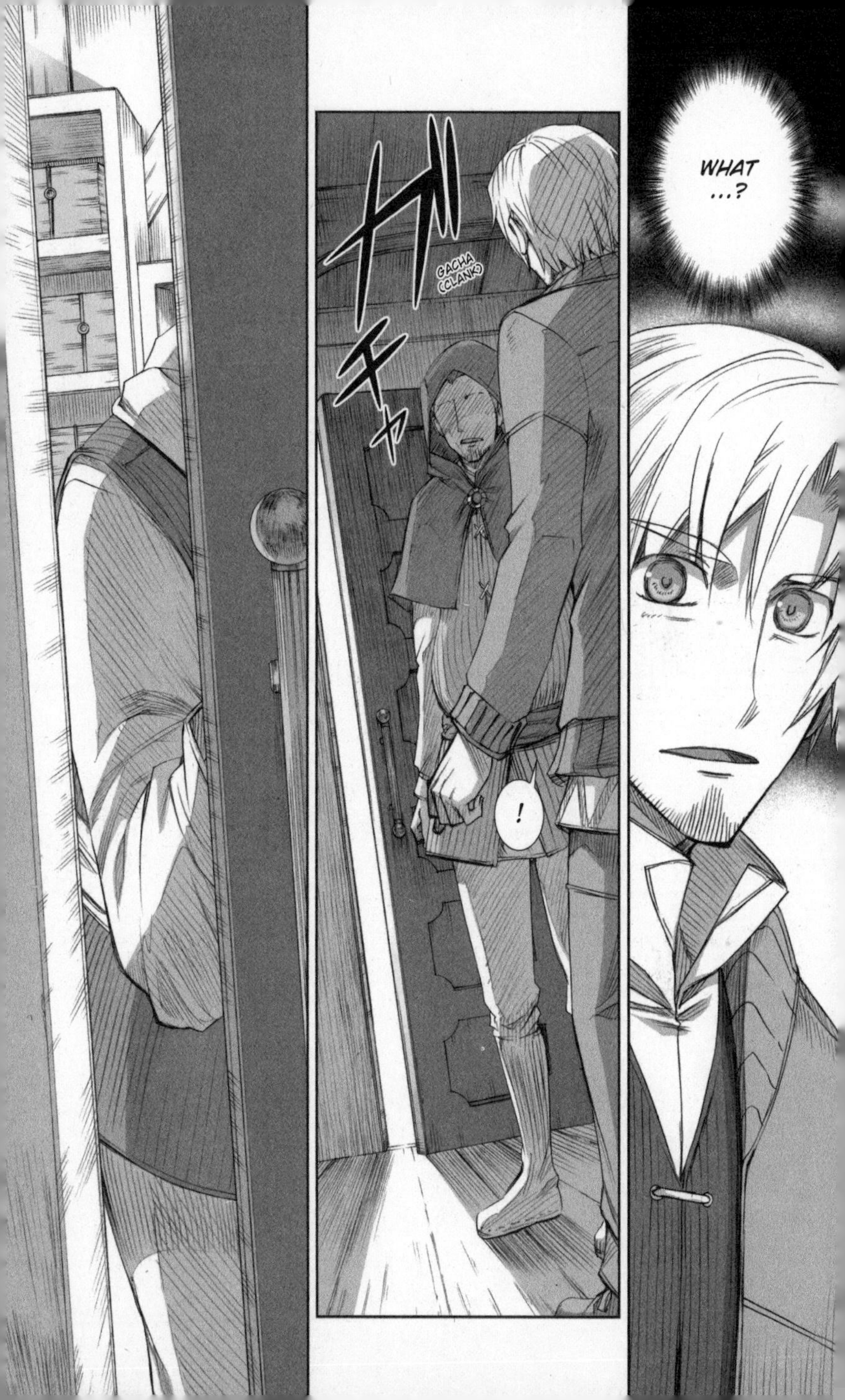
WHAT ...?
ガチャ
GACHA (CLANK)
!

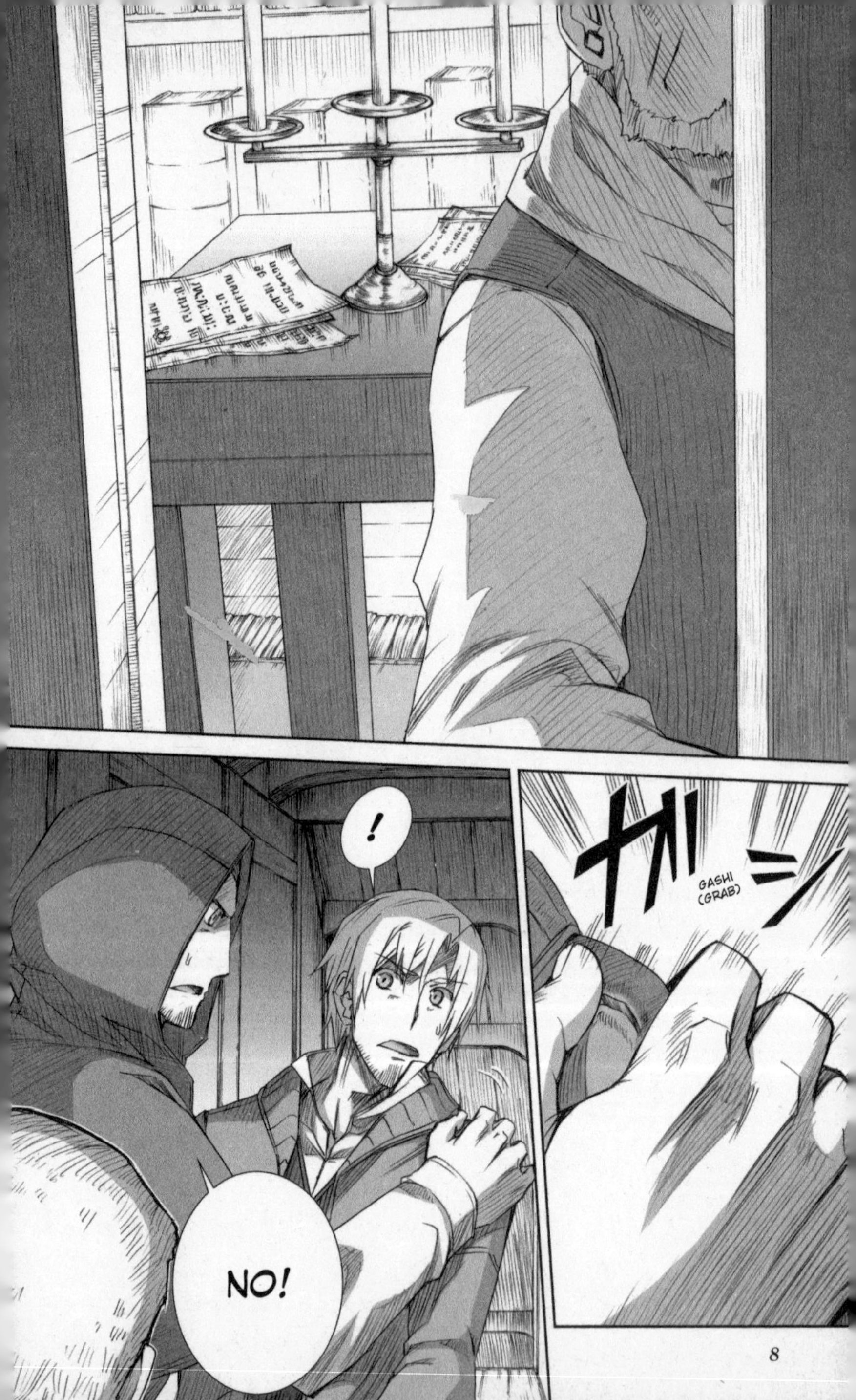
ガシッ
GASHI (GRAB)
!
NO!

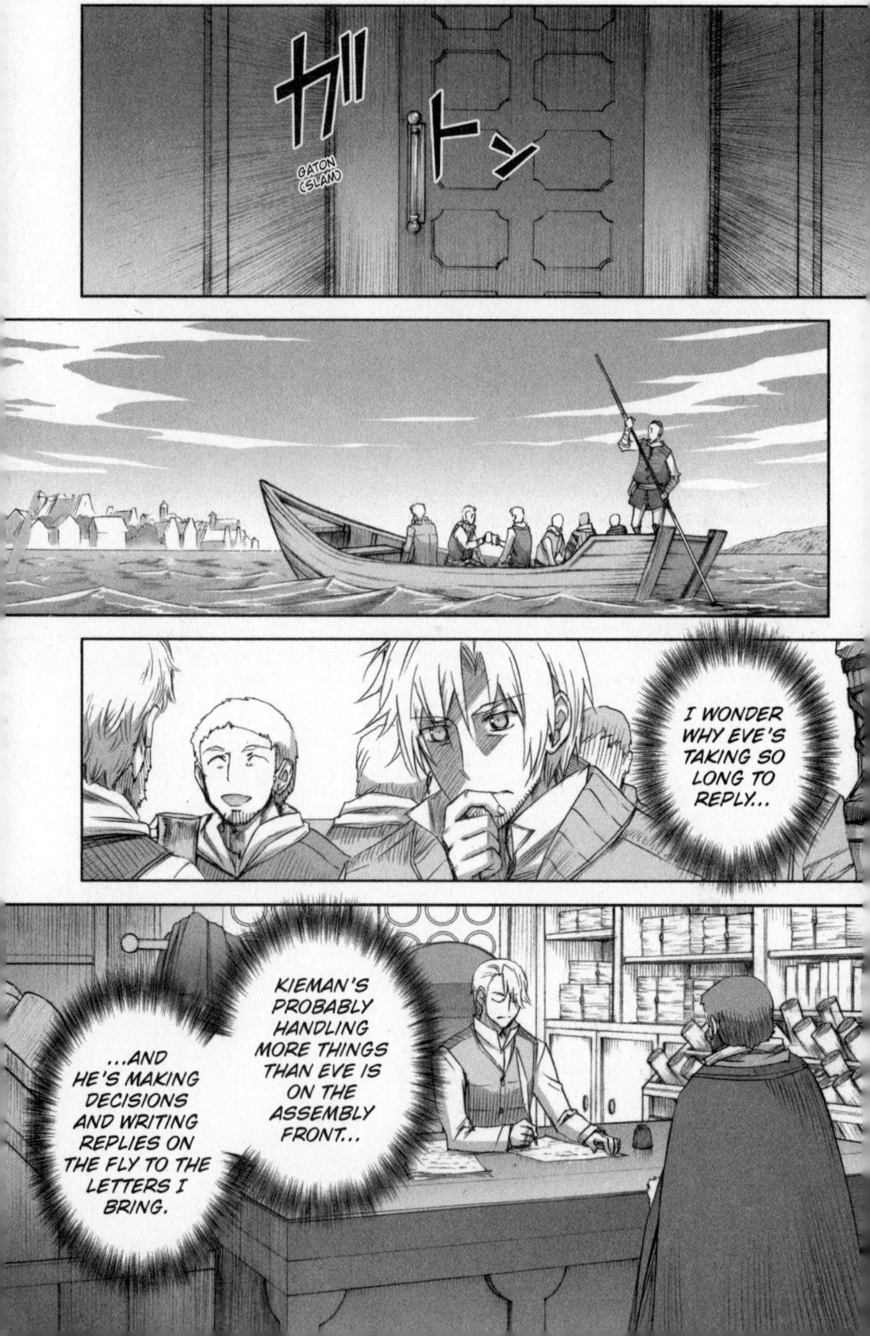
ガトン
GATON (SLAM)
I WONDER WHY EVE'S TAKING SO LONG TO REPLY...
KIEMAN'S PROBABLY HANDLING MORE THINGS THAN EVE IS ON THE ASSEMBLY FRONT...
...AND HE'S MAKING DECISIONS AND WRITING REPLIES ON THE FLY TO THE LETTERS I BRING.

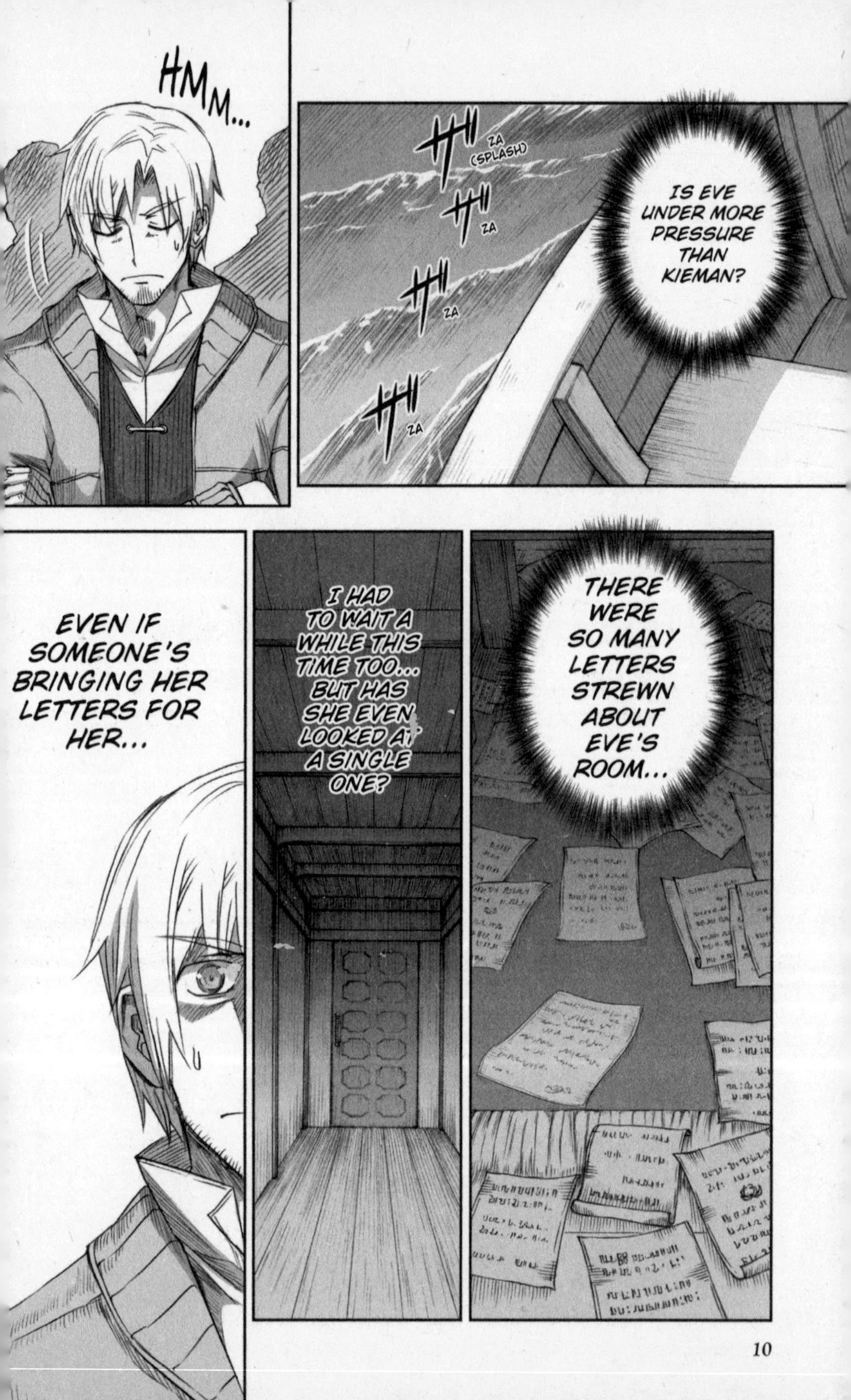
ZA (SPLASH)
ZA
ZA
ZA
IS EVE UNDER MORE PRESSURE THAN KIEMAN?
HMM...
THERE WERE SO MANY LETTERS STREWN ABOUT EVE'S ROOM...
I HAD TO WAIT A WHILE THIS TIME TOO... BUT HAS SHE EVEN LOOKED AT A SINGLE ONE?
EVEN IF SOMEONE'S BRINGING HER LETTERS FOR HER...

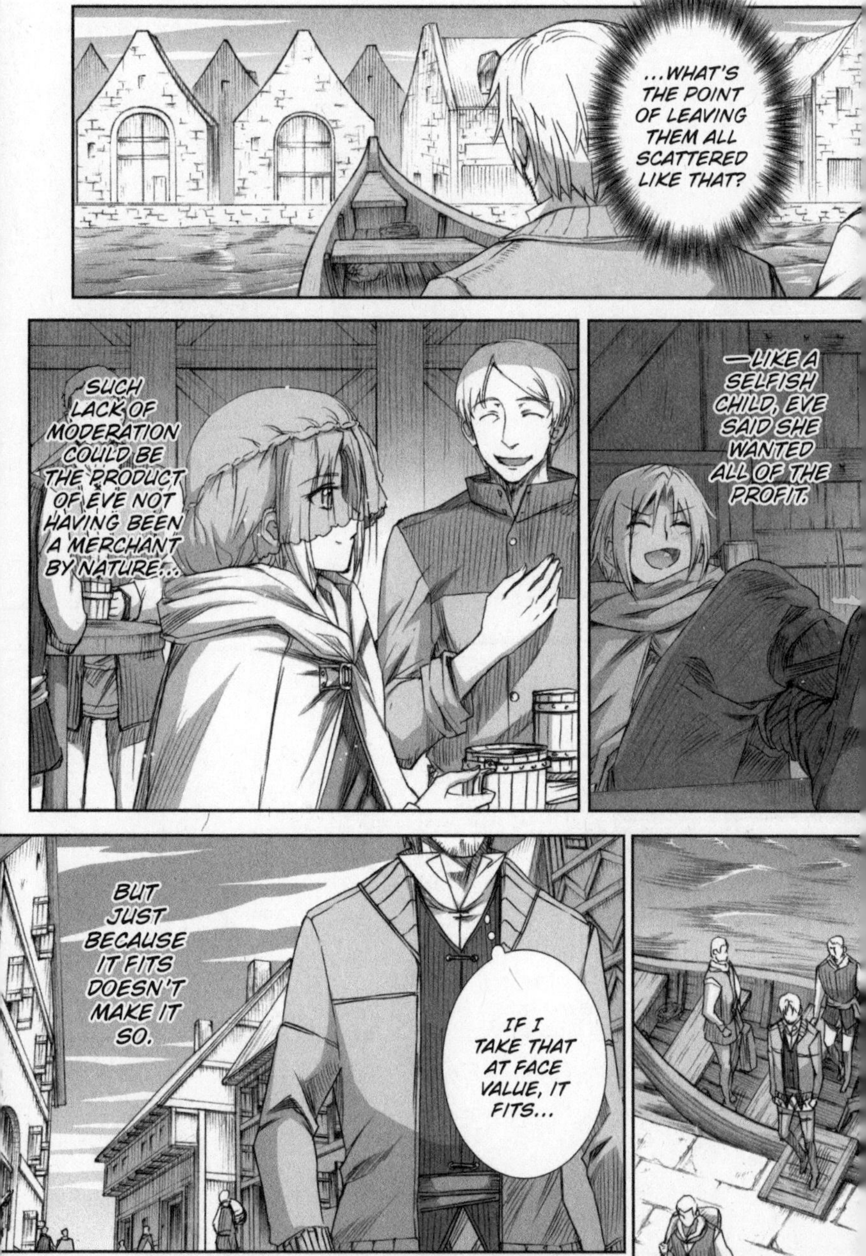
...WHAT'S THE POINT OF LEAVING THEM ALL SCATTERED LIKE THAT?
—LIKE A SELFISH CHILD, EVE SAID SHE WANTED ALL OF THE PROFIT.
SUCH LACK OF MODERATION COULD BE THE PRODUCT OF EVE NOT HAVING BEEN A MERCHANT BY NATURE...
IF I TAKE THAT AT FACE VALUE, IT FITS...
BUT JUST BECAUSE IT FITS DOESN'T MAKE IT SO.

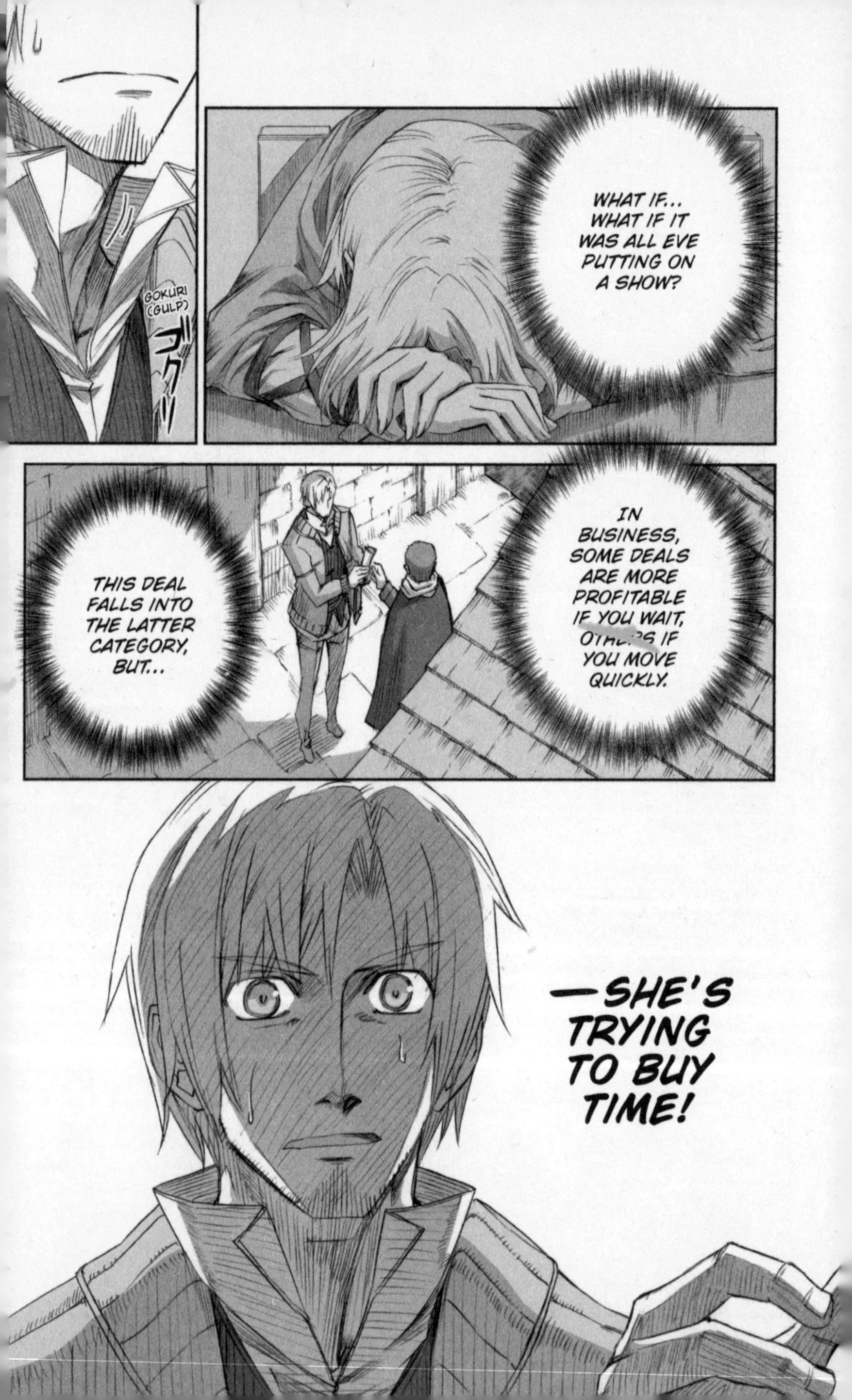
WHAT IF... WHAT IF IT WAS ALL EVE PUTTING ON A SHOW?
GOKURI (GULP)
ゴクッ
IN BUSINESS, SOME DEALS ARE MORE PROFITABLE IF YOU WAIT, OTHERS IF YOU MOVE QUICKLY.
THIS DEAL FALLS INTO THE LATTER CATEGORY, BUT...
—SHE'S TRYING TO BUY TIME!

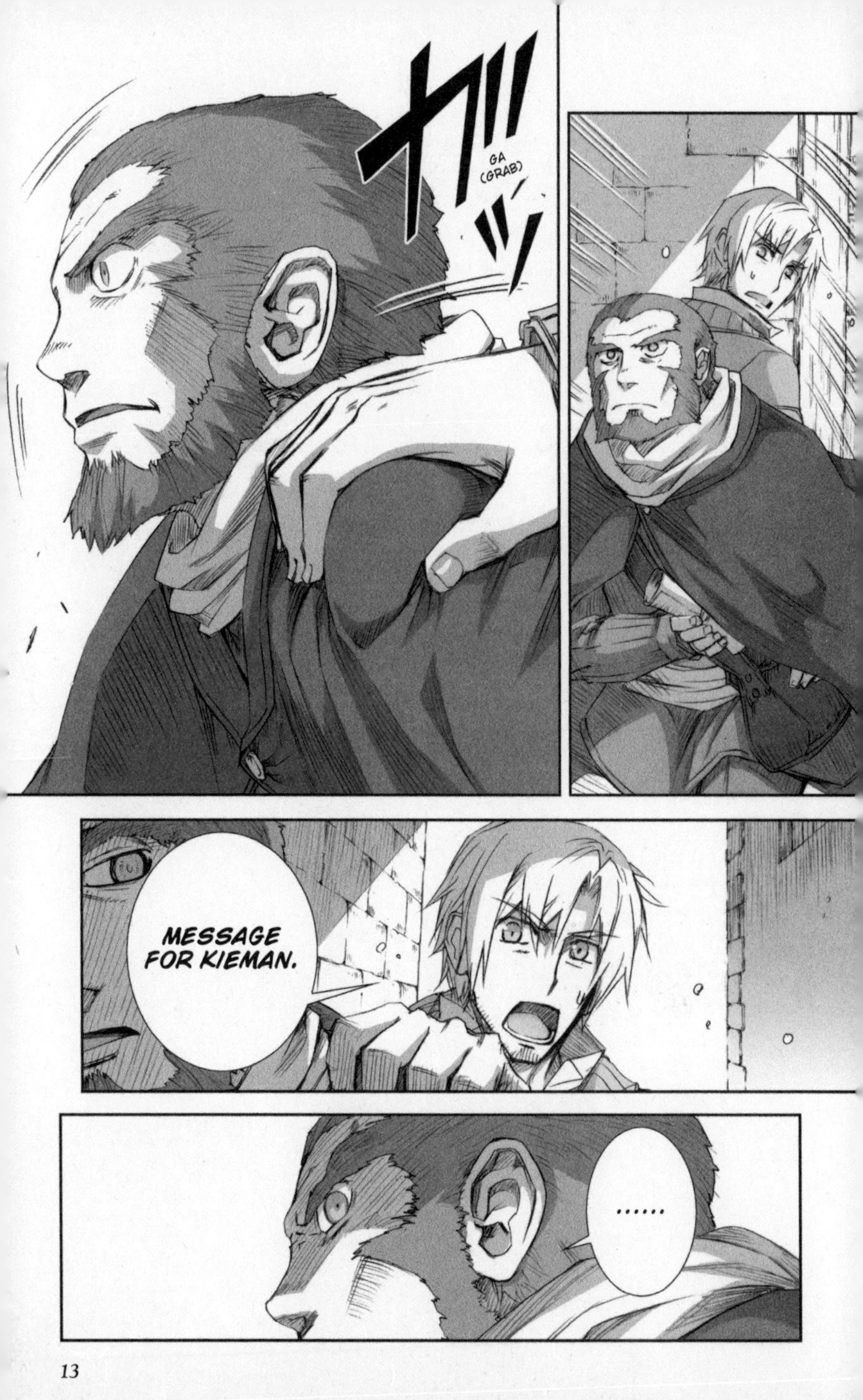
GA (GRAB)
MESSAGE FOR KIEMAN.
......

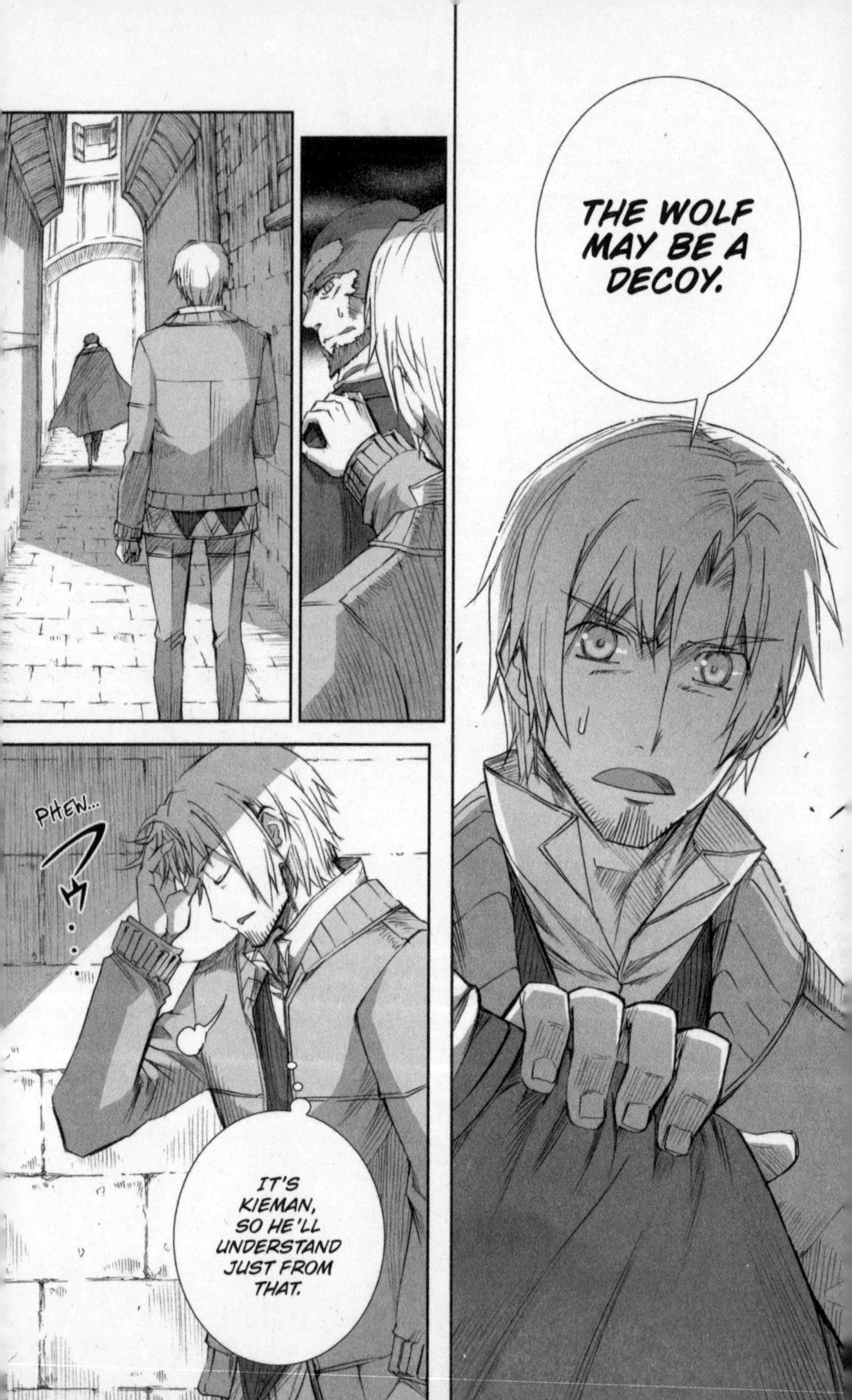
THE WOLF MAY BE A DECOY.
PHEW...
IT'S KIEMAN, SO HE'LL UNDERSTAND JUST FROM THAT.

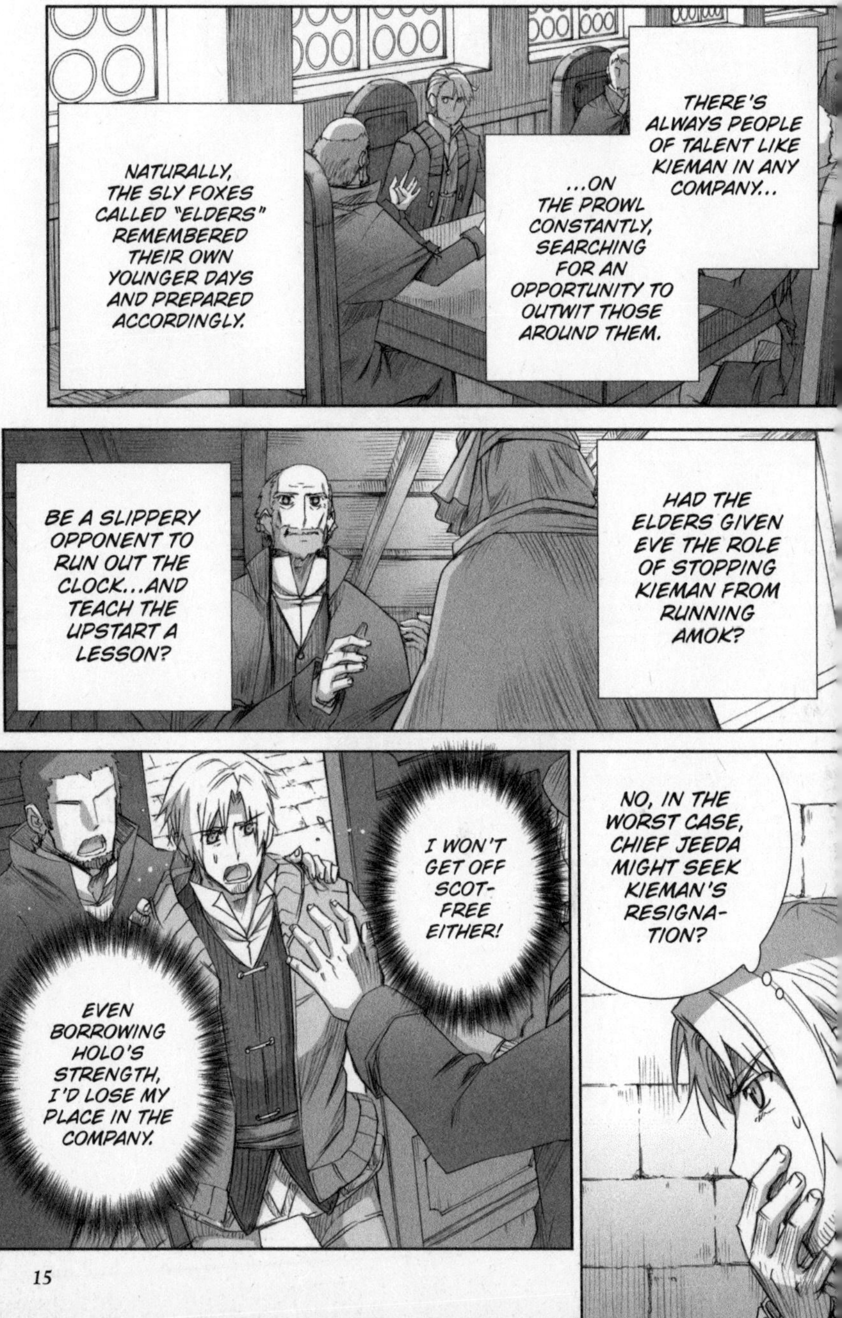
THERE'S ALWAYS PEOPLE OF TALENT LIKE KIEMAN IN ANY COMPANY...
...ON THE PROWL CONSTANTLY, SEARCHING FOR AN OPPORTUNITY TO OUTWIT THOSE AROUND THEM.
NATURALLY, THE SLY FOXES CALLED "ELDERS" REMEMBERED THEIR OWN YOUNGER DAYS AND PREPARED ACCORDINGLY.
HAD THE ELDERS GIVEN EVE THE ROLE OF STOPPING KIEMAN FROM RUNNING AMOK?
BE A SLIPPERY OPPONENT TO RUN OUT THE CLOCK...AND TEACH THE UPSTART A LESSON?
NO, IN THE WORST CASE, CHIEF JEEDA MIGHT SEEK KIEMAN'S RESIGNA-TION?
I WON'T GET OFF SCOT-FREE EITHER!
EVEN BORROWING HOLO'S STRENGTH, I'D LOSE MY PLACE IN THE COMPANY.

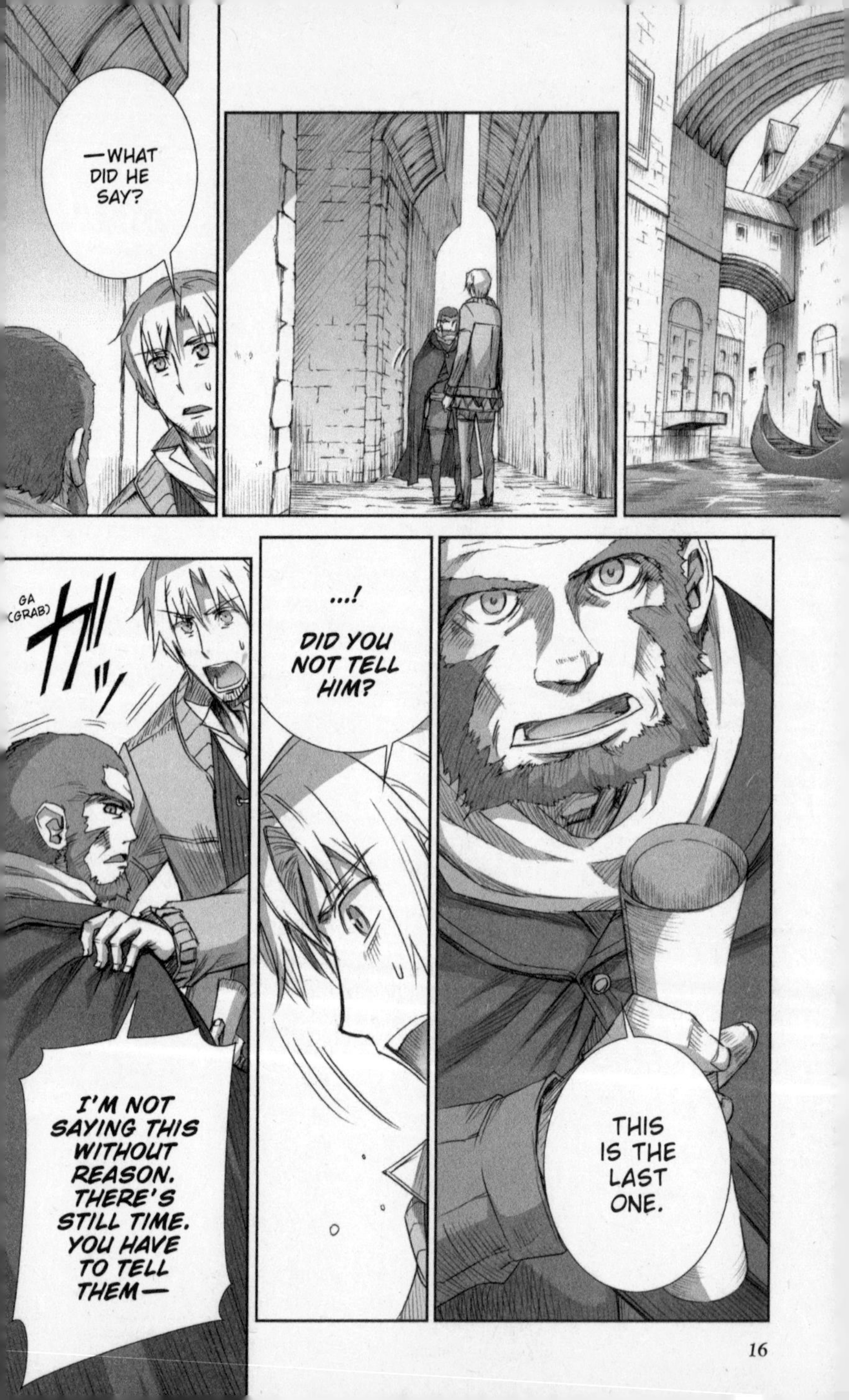
—WHAT DID HE SAY?
THIS IS THE LAST ONE.
...!
DID YOU NOT TELL HIM?
GA (GRAB)
I'M NOT SAYING THIS WITHOUT REASON. THERE'S STILL TIME. YOU HAVE TO TELL THEM—

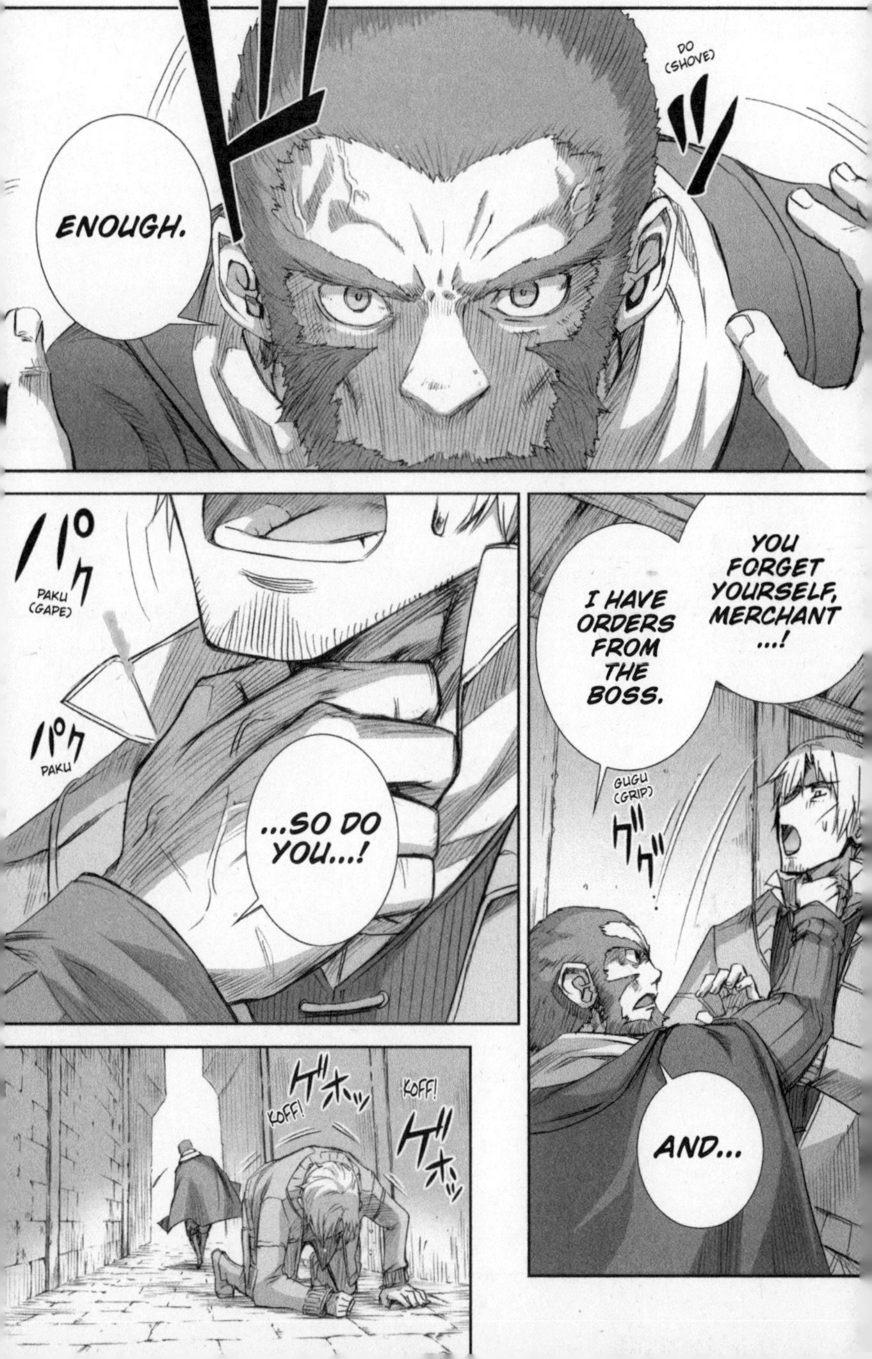
DO
(SHOVE)
ENOUGH.
YOU FORGET YOURSELF, MERCHANT ...!
I HAVE ORDERS FROM THE BOSS.
GUGU
(GRIP)
AND...
...SO DO YOU...!
PAKU
(GAPE)
PAKU
KOFF!
KOFF!

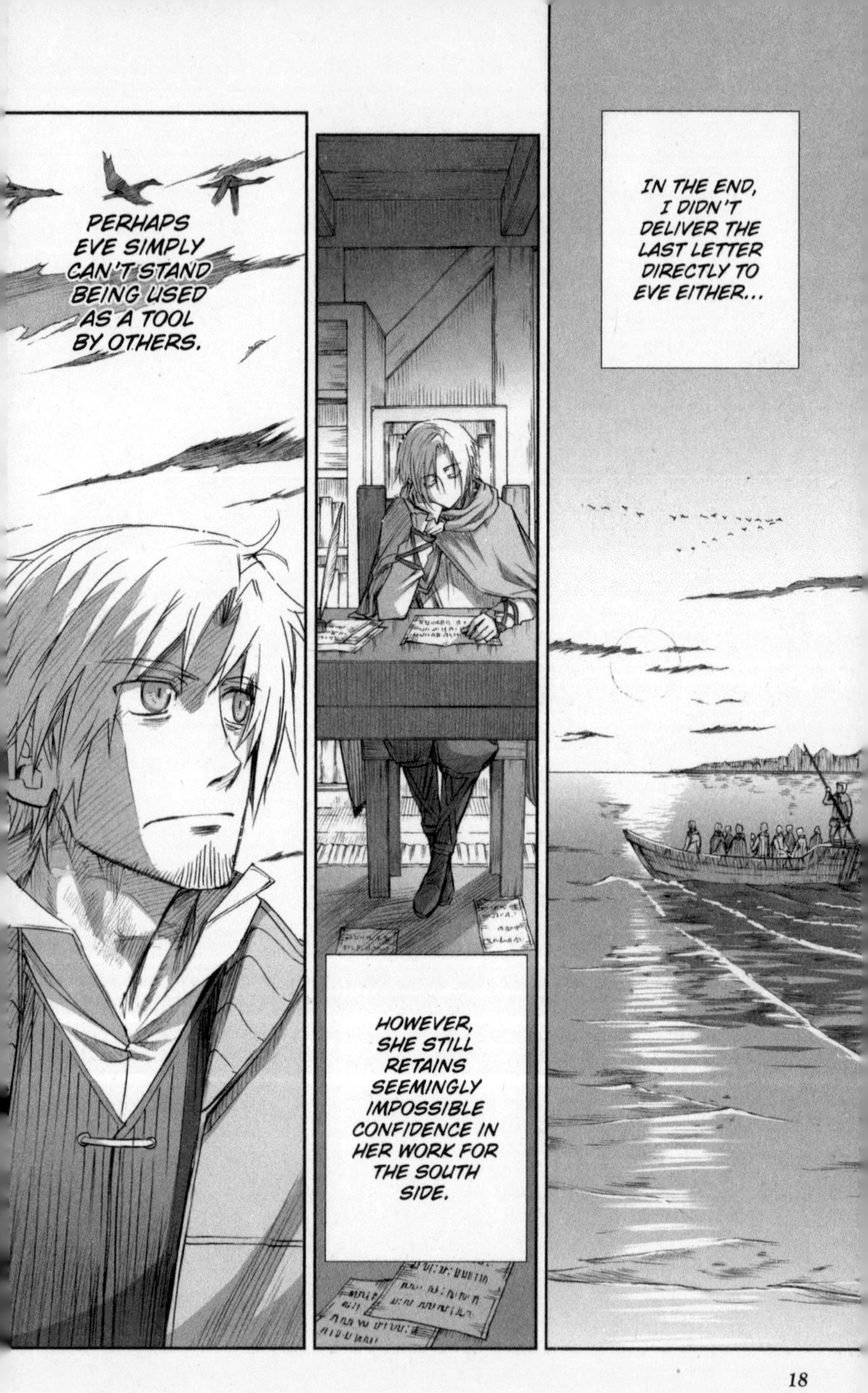

IN THE END, I DIDN'T DELIVER THE LAST LETTER DIRECTLY TO EVE EITHER...
HOWEVER, SHE STILL RETAINS SEEMINGLY IMPOSSIBLE CONFIDENCE IN HER WORK FOR THE SOUTH SIDE.
PERHAPS EVE SIMPLY CAN'T STAND BEING USED AS A TOOL BY OTHERS.

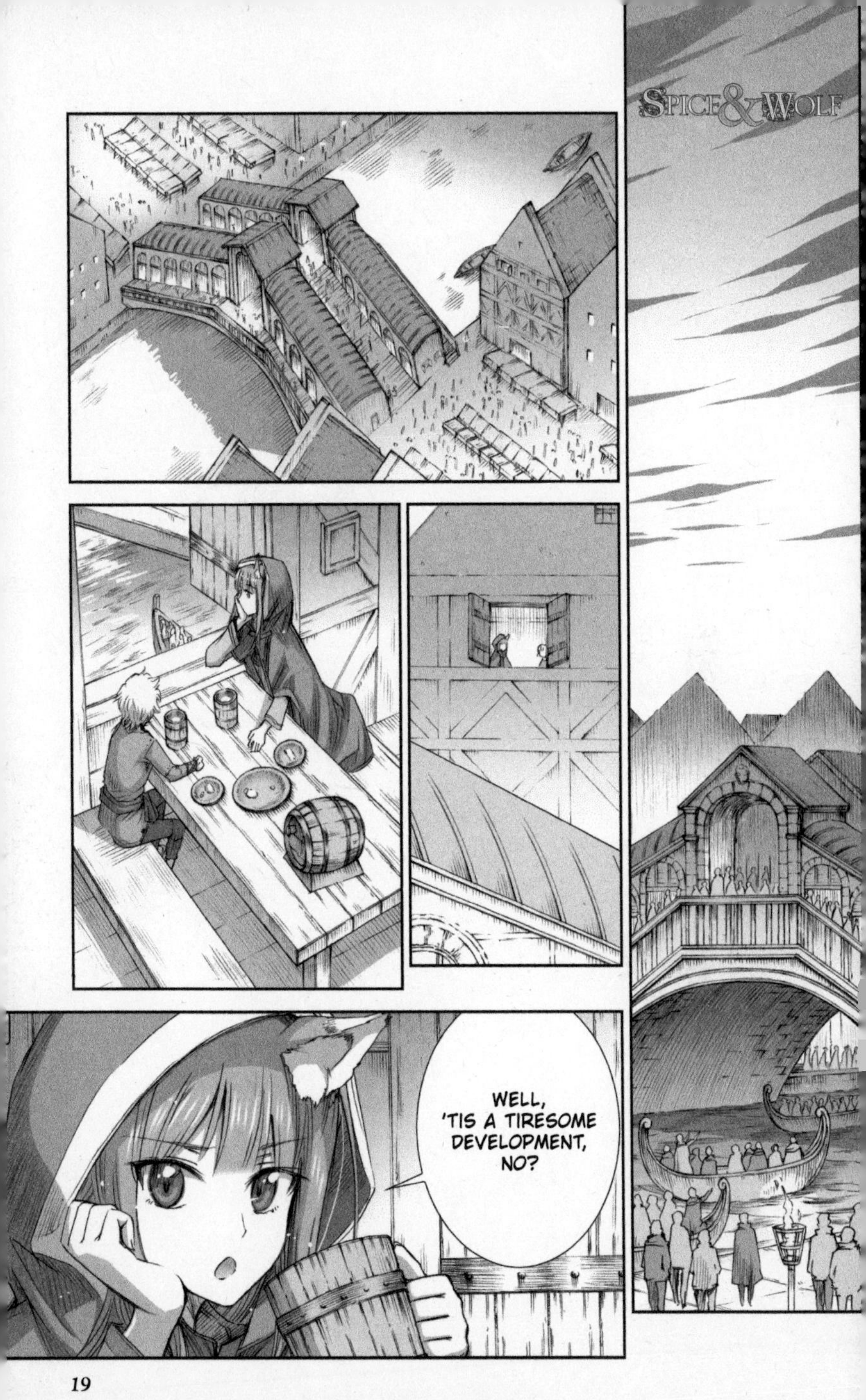
SPICE & WOLF
WELL, 'TIS A TIRESOME DEVELOPMENT, NO?

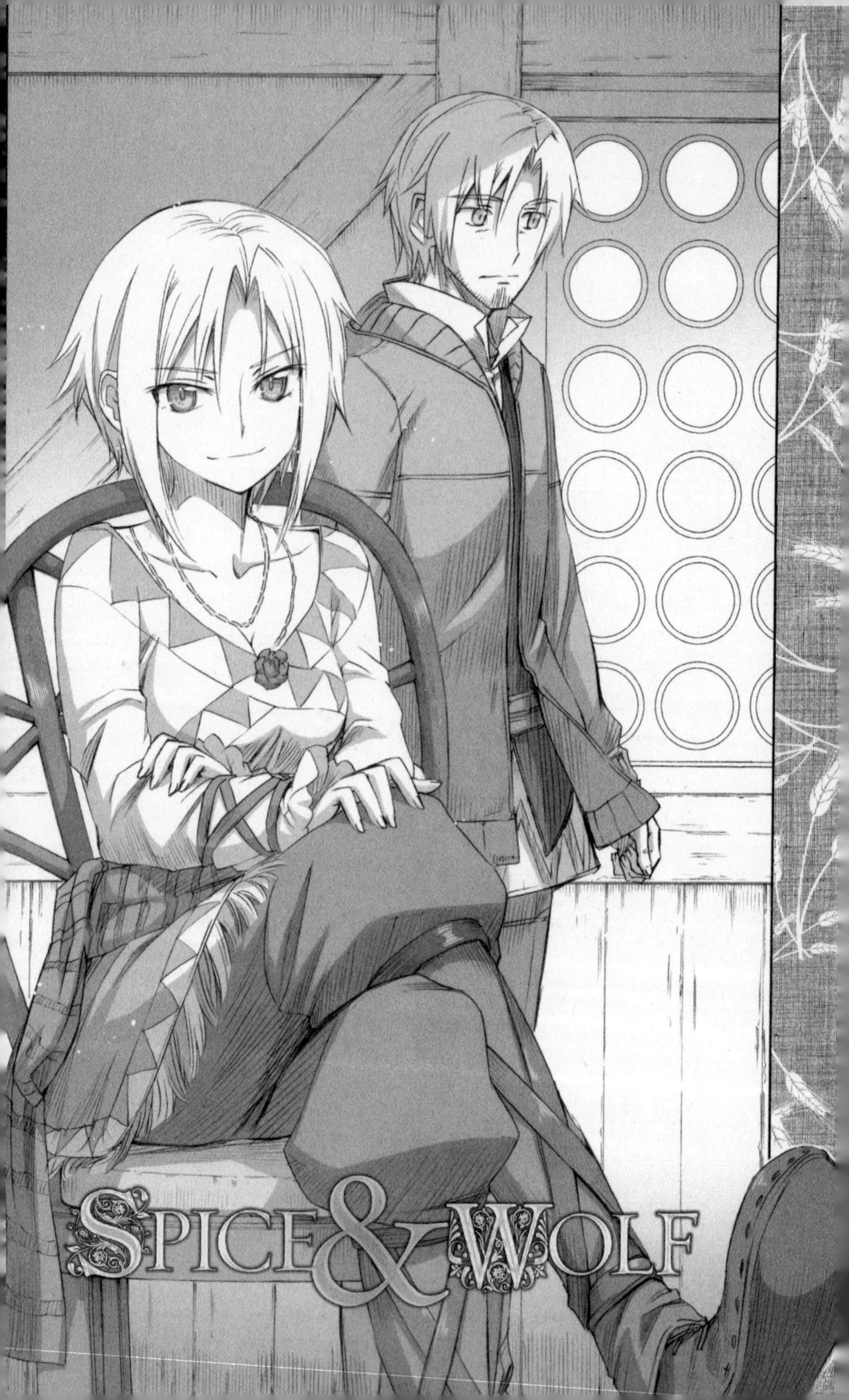
SPICE & WOLF

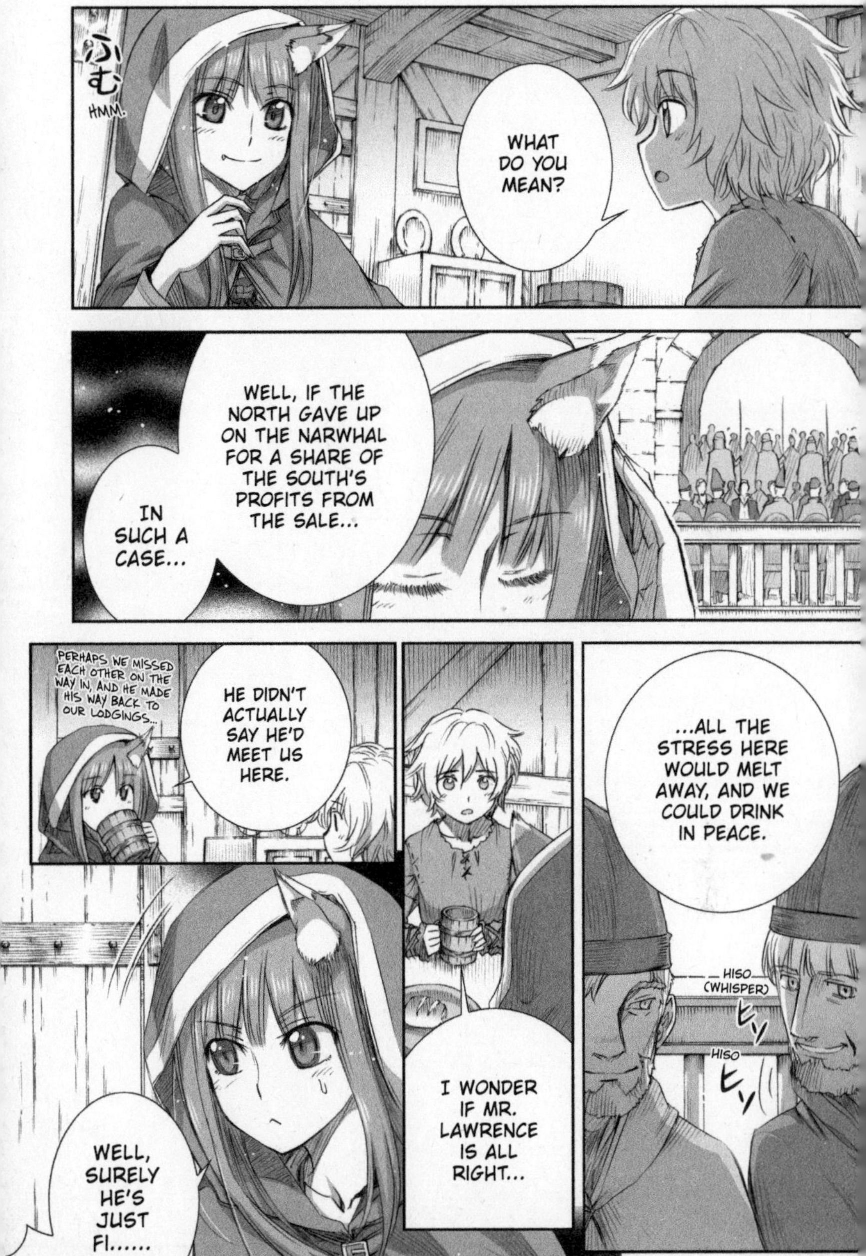
WHAT DO YOU MEAN?
ふむ
HMM.
WELL, IF THE NORTH GAVE UP ON THE NARWHAL FOR A SHARE OF THE SOUTH'S PROFITS FROM THE SALE...
IN SUCH A CASE...
...ALL THE STRESS HERE WOULD MELT AWAY, AND WE COULD DRINK IN PEACE.
HISO (WHISPER)
ヒソ
HISO
ヒソ
I WONDER IF MR. LAWRENCE IS ALL RIGHT...
HE DIDN'T ACTUALLY SAY HE'D MEET US HERE.
PERHAPS WE MISSED EACH OTHER ON THE WAY IN, AND HE MADE HIS WAY BACK TO OUR LODGINGS...
WELL, SURELY HE'S JUST FI......
!?

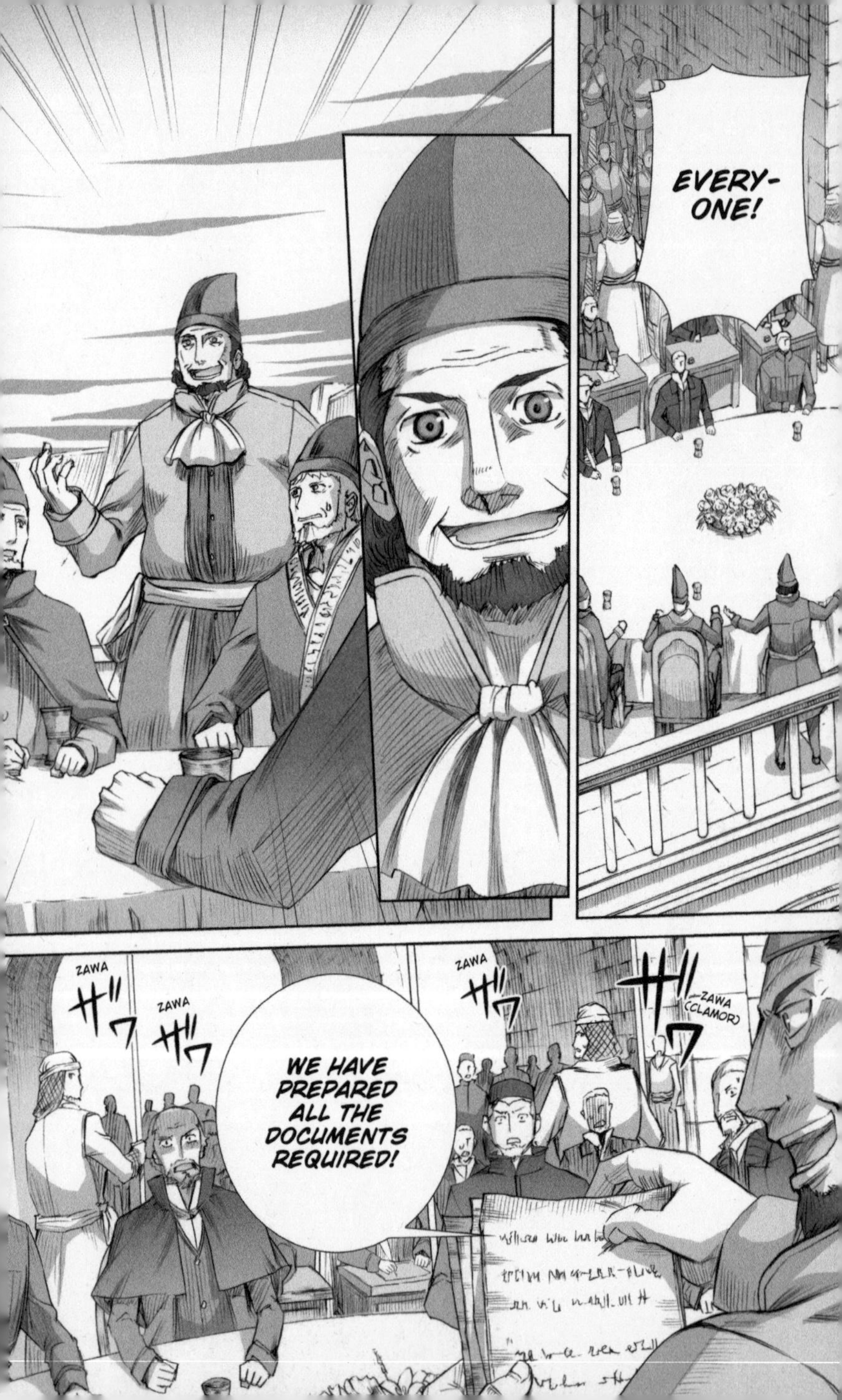
EVERY-ONE!
ザワ ZAWA (CLAMOR)
ザワ ZAWA
WE HAVE PREPARED ALL THE DOCUMENTS REQUIRED!
ザワ ZAWA
ザワ ZAWA

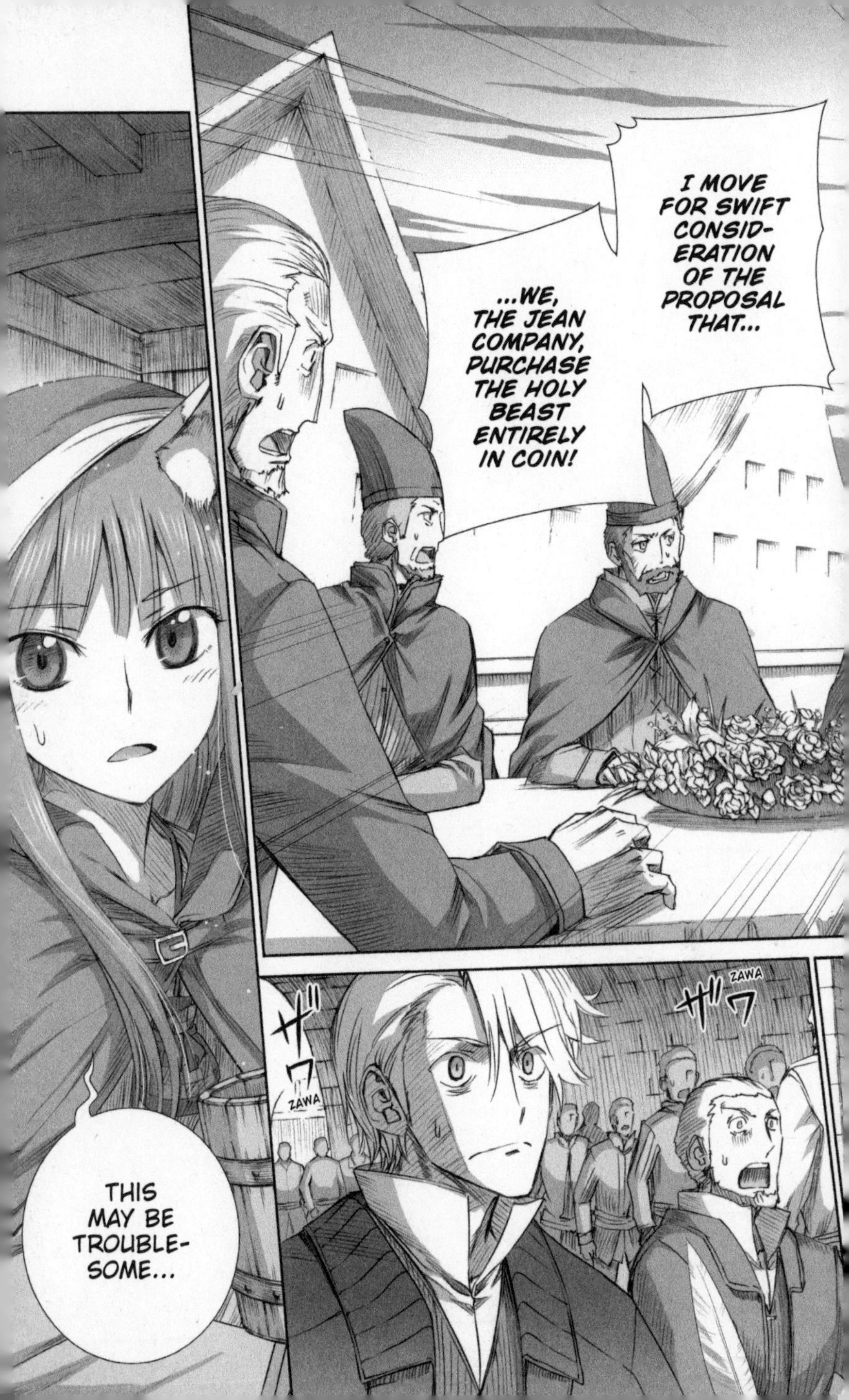
I MOVE FOR SWIFT CONSID-ERATION OF THE PROPOSAL THAT...
...WE, THE JEAN COMPANY, PURCHASE THE HOLY BEAST ENTIRELY IN COIN!
ザワ ZAWA
ザワ ZAWA
THIS MAY BE TROUBLE-SOME...

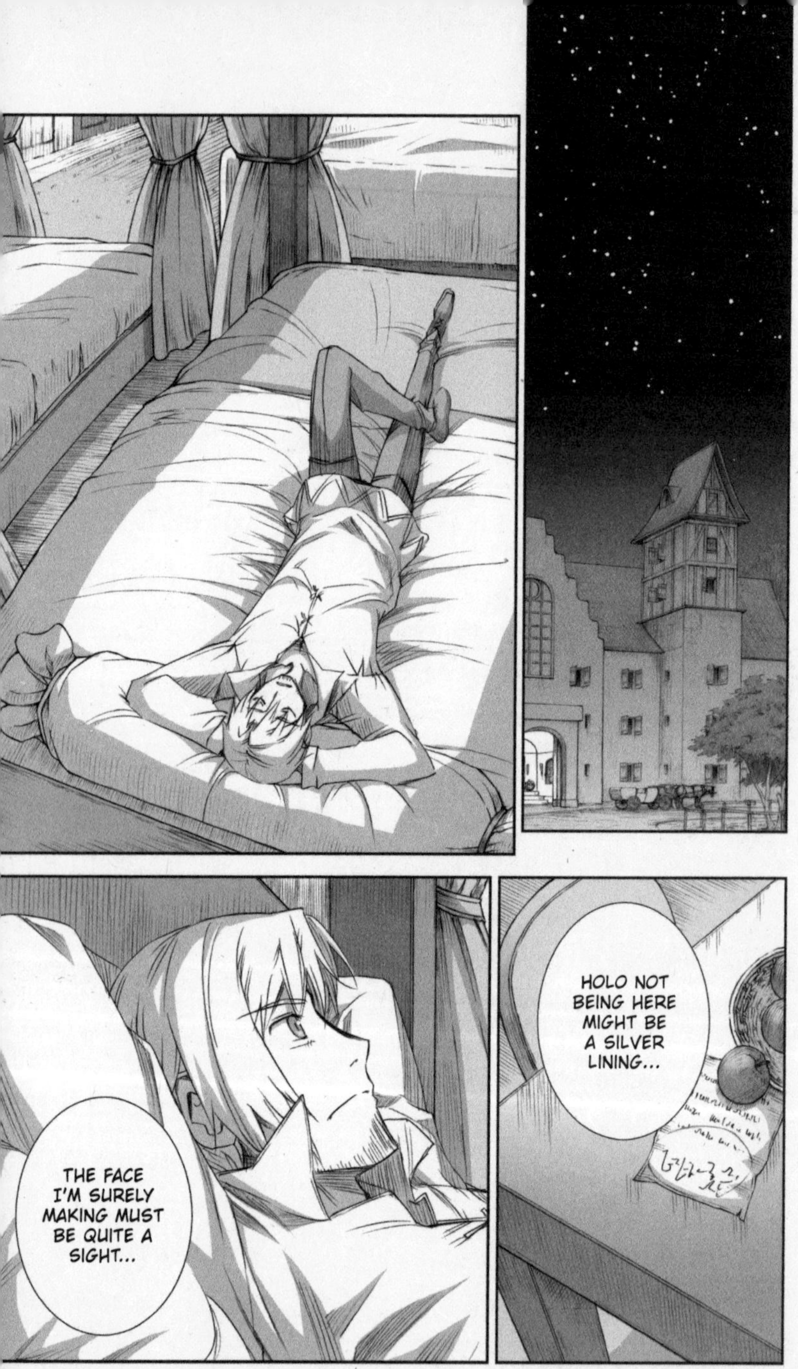
HOLO NOT BEING HERE MIGHT BE A SILVER LINING...
THE FACE I'M SURELY MAKING MUST BE QUITE A SIGHT...

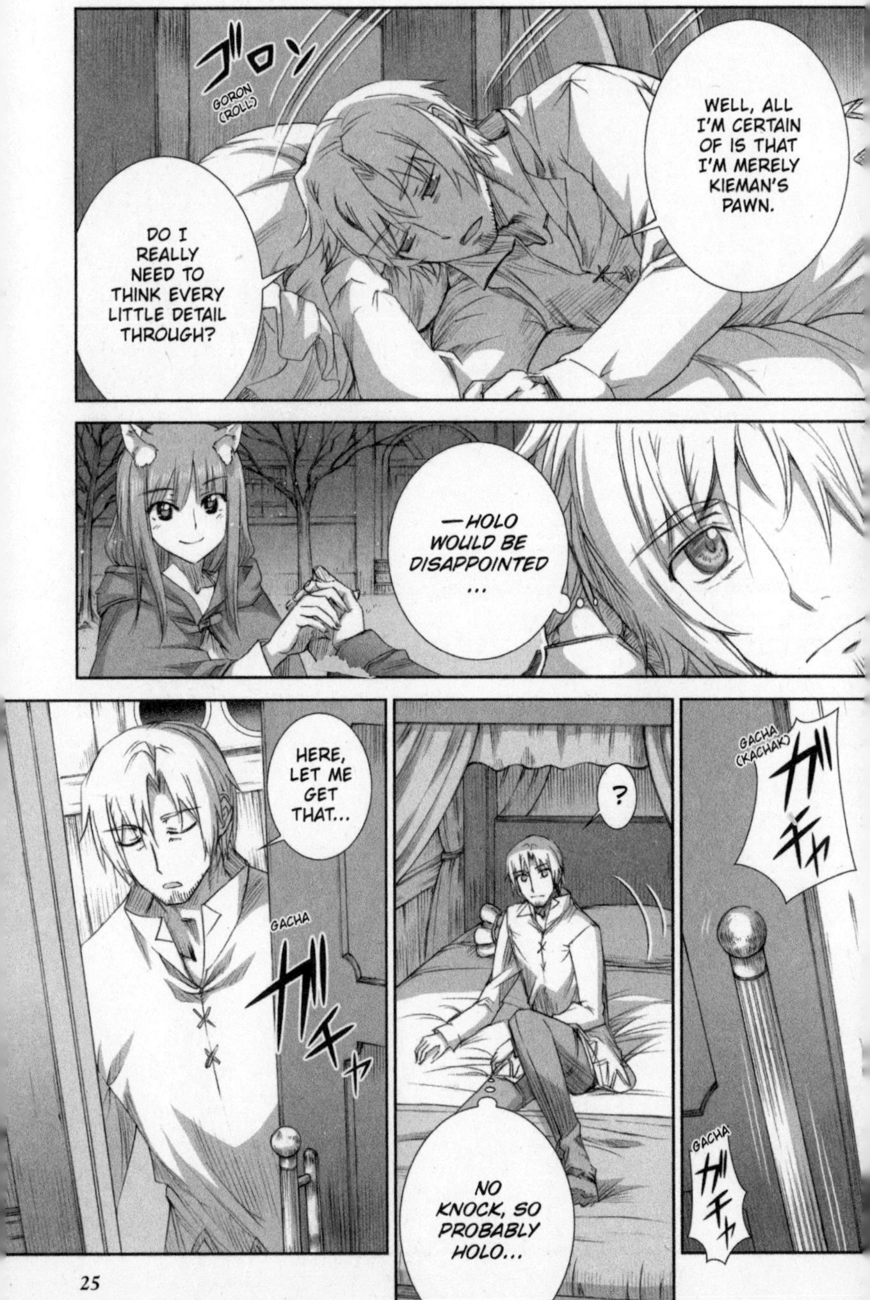
WELL, ALL I'M CERTAIN OF IS THAT I'M MERELY KIEMAN'S PAWN.
ゴロン
GORON (ROLL)
DO I REALLY NEED TO THINK EVERY LITTLE DETAIL THROUGH?
—HOLO WOULD BE DISAPPOINTED ...
GACHA (KACHAK)
ガチャ
GACHA
ガチャ
?
NO KNOCK, SO PROBABLY HOLO...
HERE, LET ME GET THAT...
GACHA
ガチャ

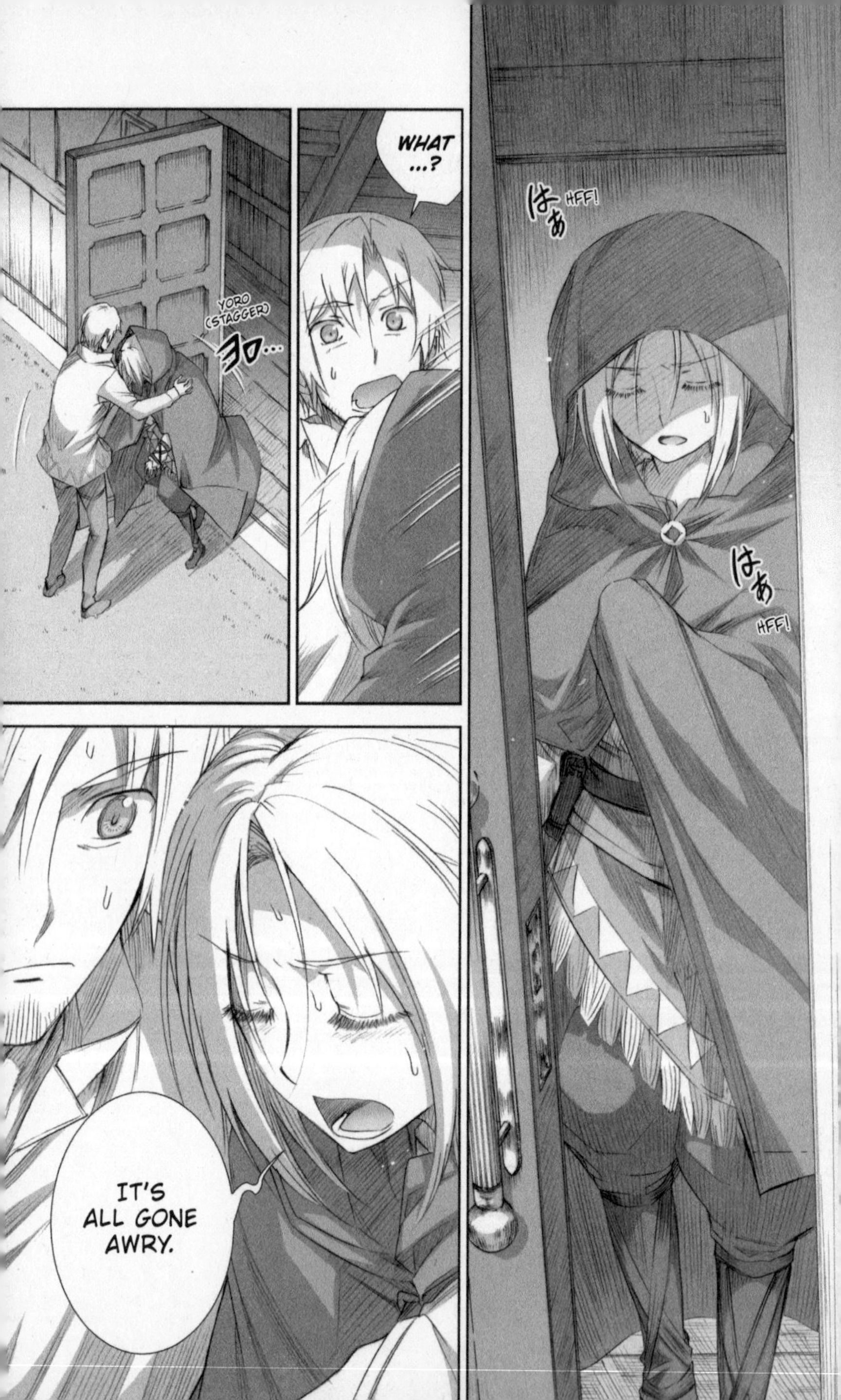
はぁ HFF!
はぁ HFF!
WHAT ...?
YORO (STAGGER)
ヨロ…
IT'S ALL GONE AWRY.

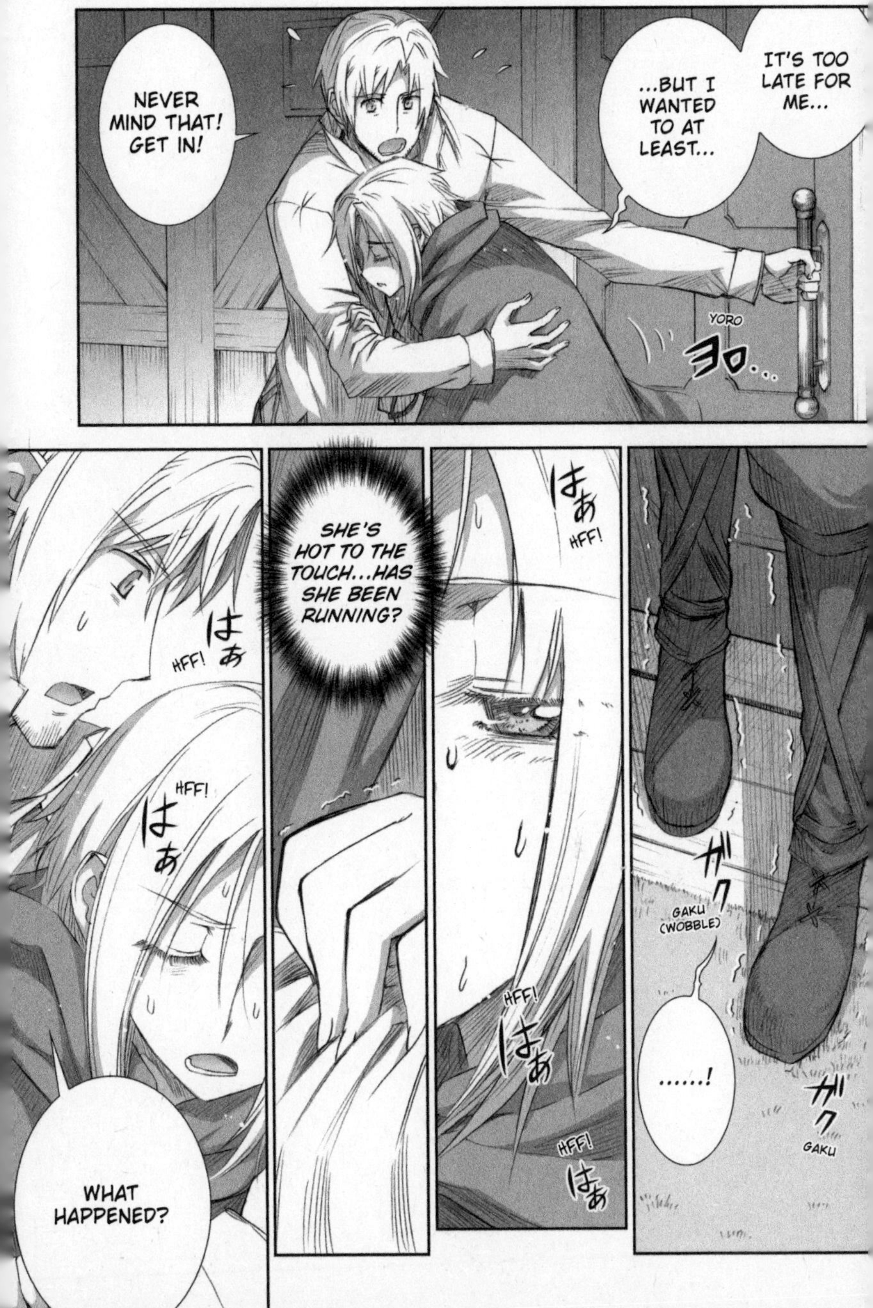
IT'S TOO LATE FOR ME...
...BUT I WANTED TO AT LEAST...
NEVER MIND THAT! GET IN!
ヨロ...
YORO
ガク
GAKU (WOBBLE)
......!
ガク
GAKU
はぁ
HFF!
はぁ
HFF!
はぁ
HFF!
SHE'S HOT TO THE TOUCH...HAS SHE BEEN RUNNING?
はぁ
HFF!
はぁ
HFF!
WHAT HAPPENED?

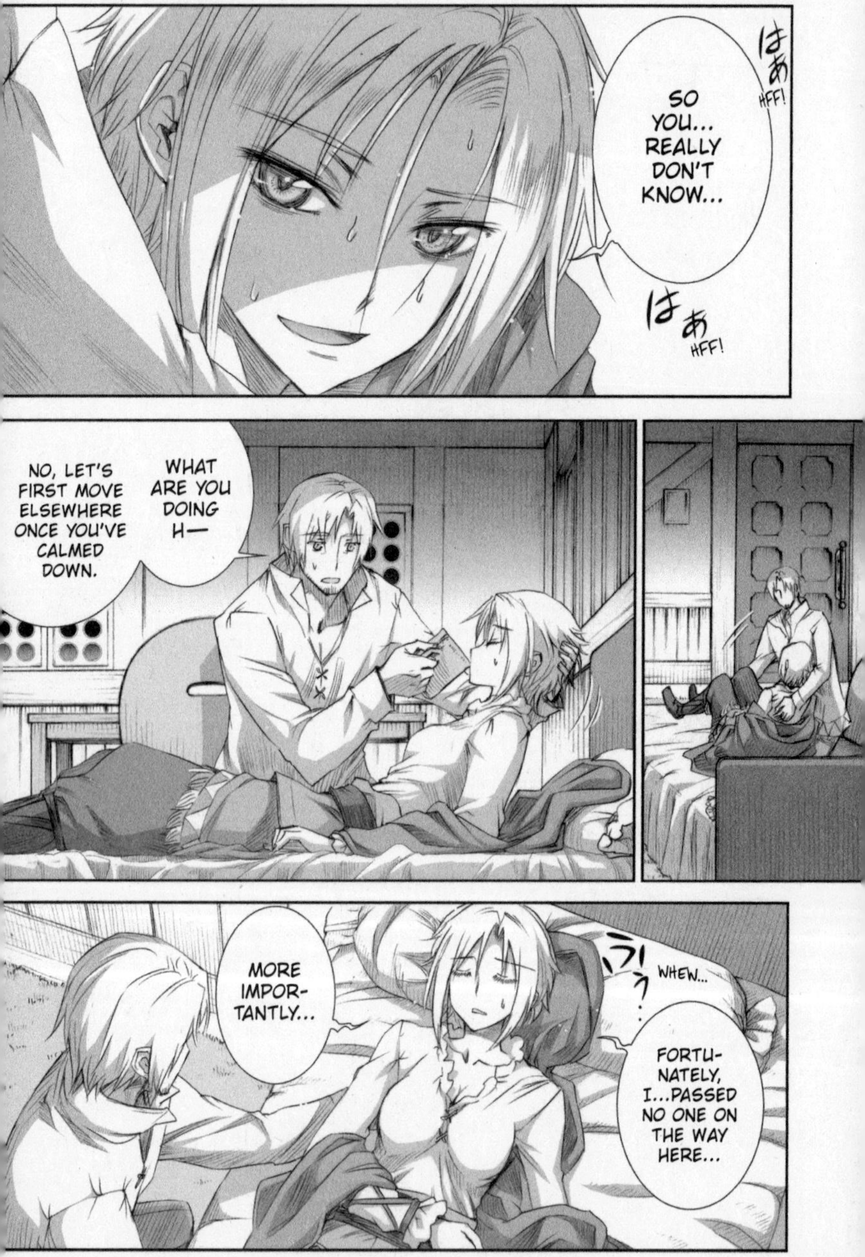
はあ
HFF!
SO YOU... REALLY DON'T KNOW...
はあ
HFF!
WHAT ARE YOU DOING H—
NO, LET'S FIRST MOVE ELSEWHERE ONCE YOU'VE CALMED DOWN.
WHEW...
FORTU-NATELY, I...PASSED NO ONE ON THE WAY HERE...
MORE IMPOR-TANTLY...

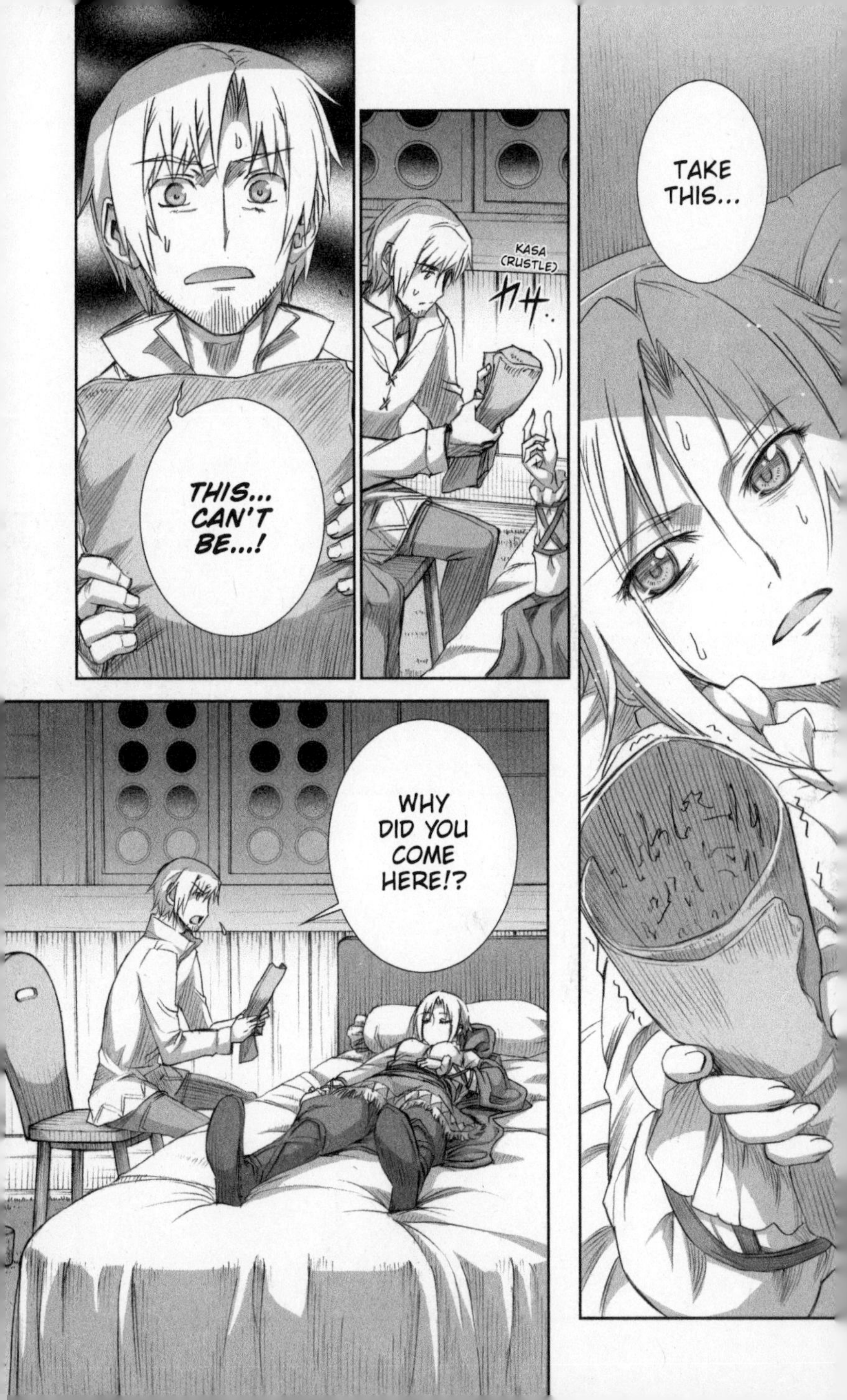
TAKE THIS...
KASA (RUSTLE)
カサ..
THIS... CAN'T BE...!
WHY DID YOU COME HERE!?

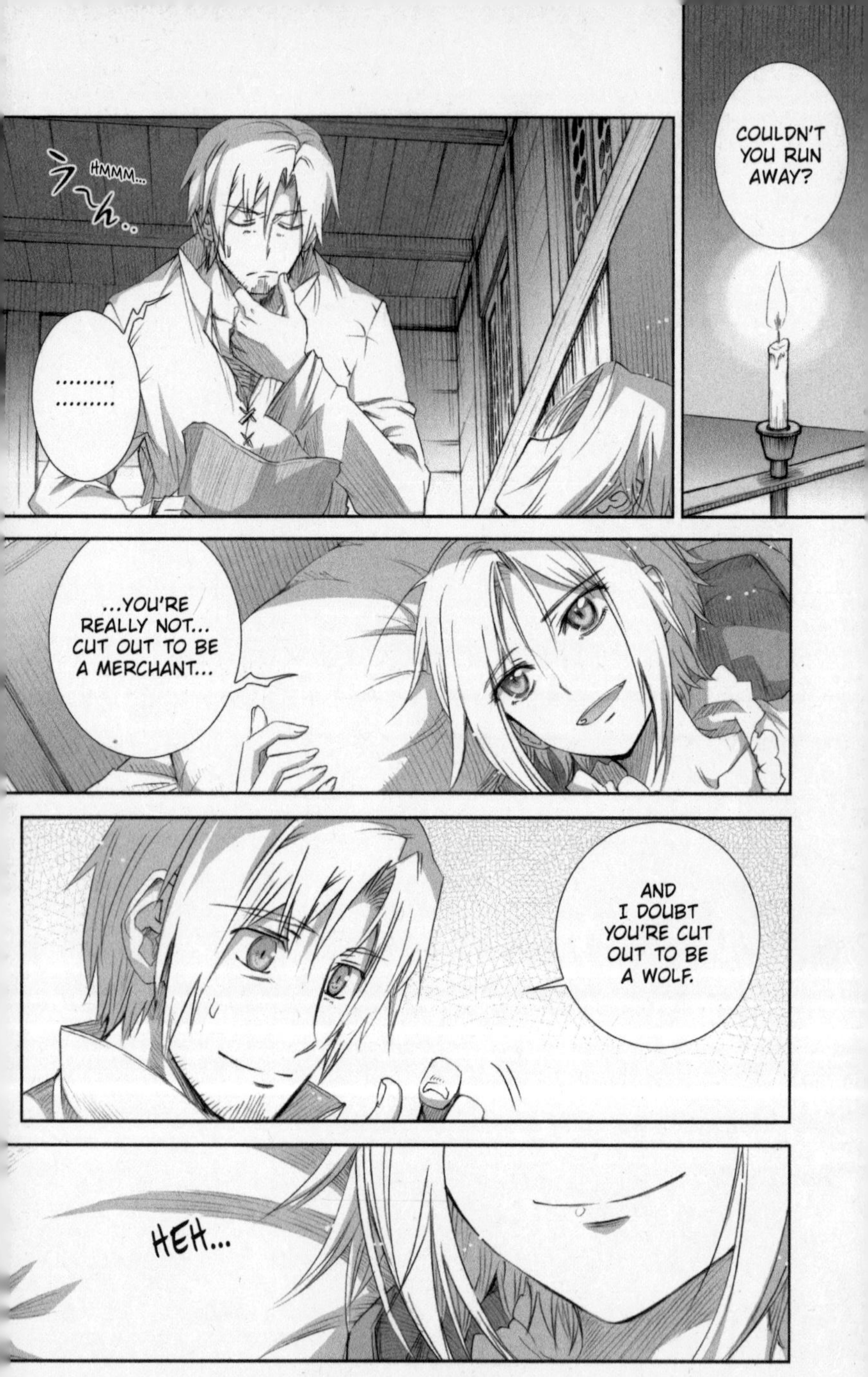
COULDN'T YOU RUN AWAY?
う～ん..
HMMM...
....
....
...YOU'RE REALLY NOT... CUT OUT TO BE A MERCHANT...
AND I DOUBT YOU'RE CUT OUT TO BE A WOLF.
HEH...

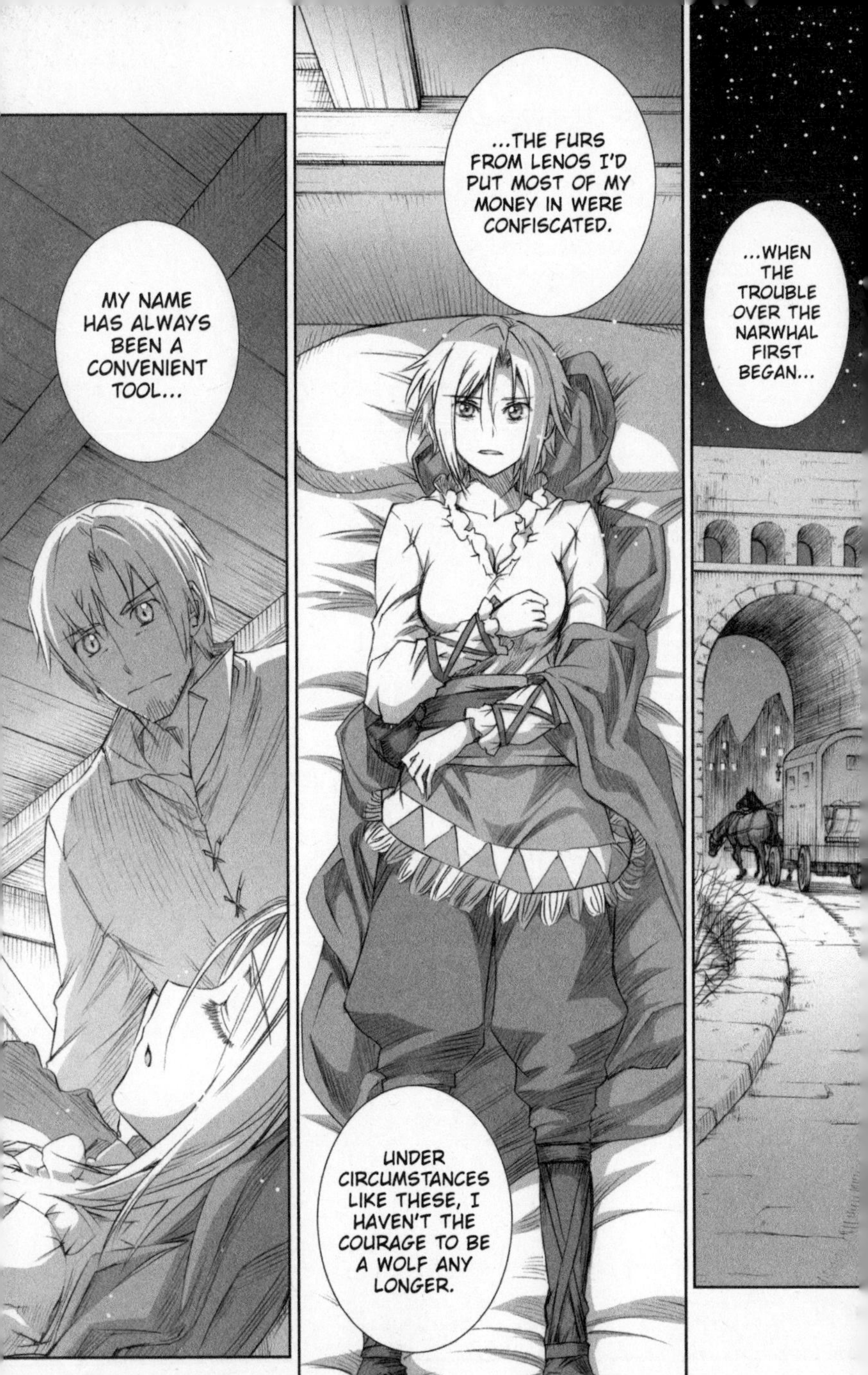
...WHEN THE TROUBLE OVER THE NARWHAL FIRST BEGAN...
...THE FURS FROM LENOS I'D PUT MOST OF MY MONEY IN WERE CONFISCATED.
UNDER CIRCUMSTANCES LIKE THESE, I HAVEN'T THE COURAGE TO BE A WOLF ANY LONGER.
MY NAME HAS ALWAYS BEEN A CONVENIENT TOOL...

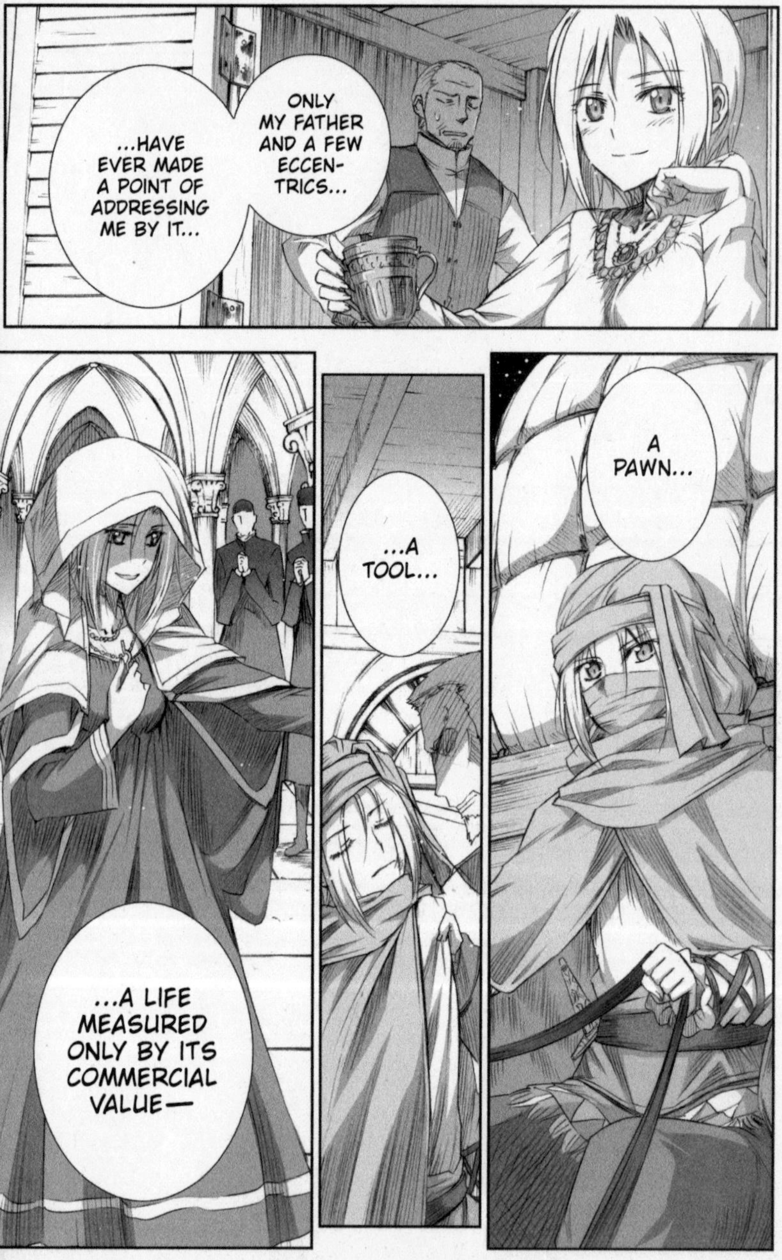
ONLY MY FATHER AND A FEW ECCEN-TRICS...
...HAVE EVER MADE A POINT OF ADDRESSING ME BY IT...
A PAWN...
...A TOOL...
...A LIFE MEASURED ONLY BY ITS COMMERCIAL VALUE—

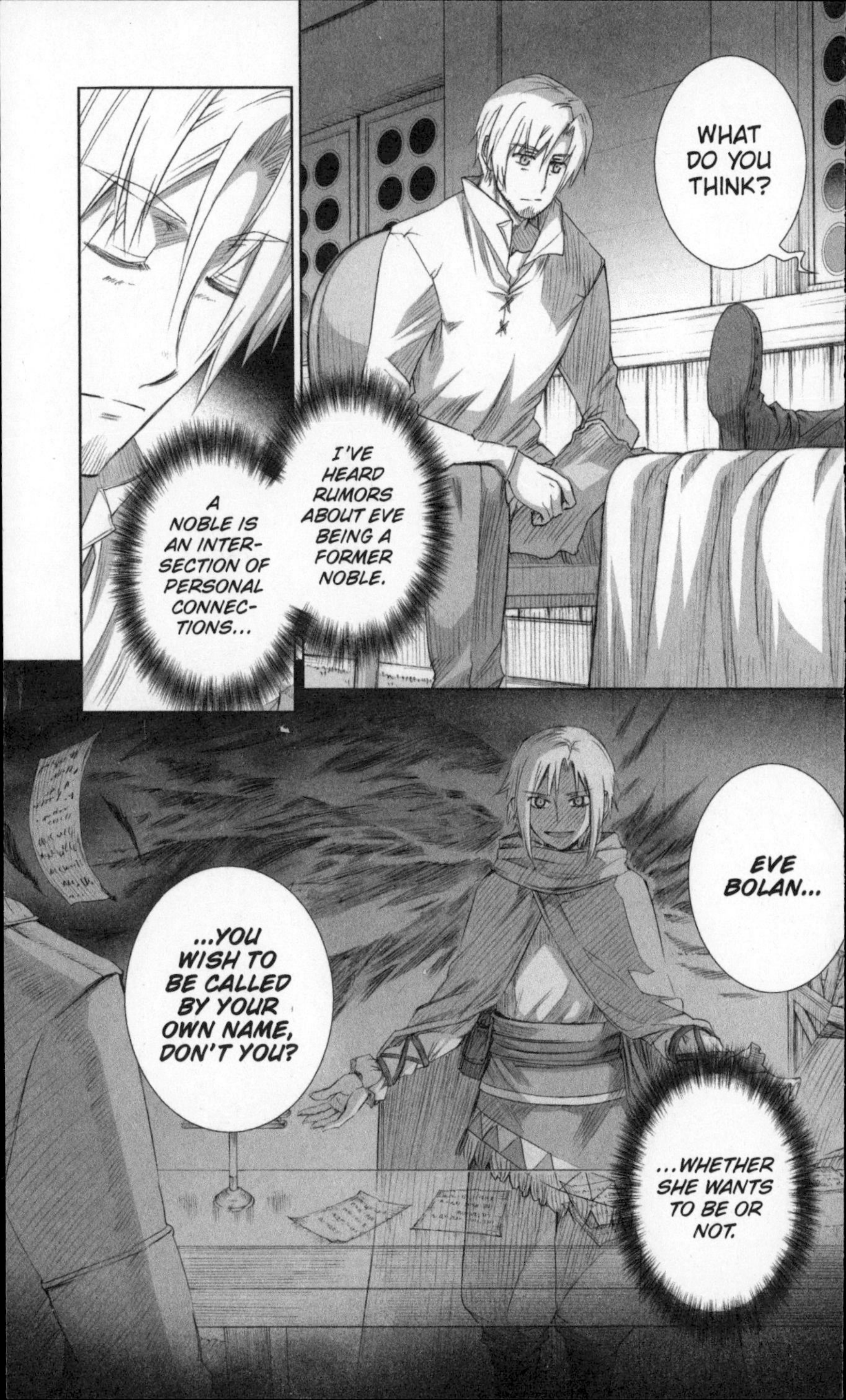
WHAT DO YOU THINK?
I'VE HEARD RUMORS ABOUT EVE BEING A FORMER NOBLE.
A NOBLE IS AN INTER-SECTION OF PERSONAL CONNEC-TIONS...
EVE BOLAN...
...YOU WISH TO BE CALLED BY YOUR OWN NAME, DON'T YOU?
...WHETHER SHE WANTS TO BE OR NOT.

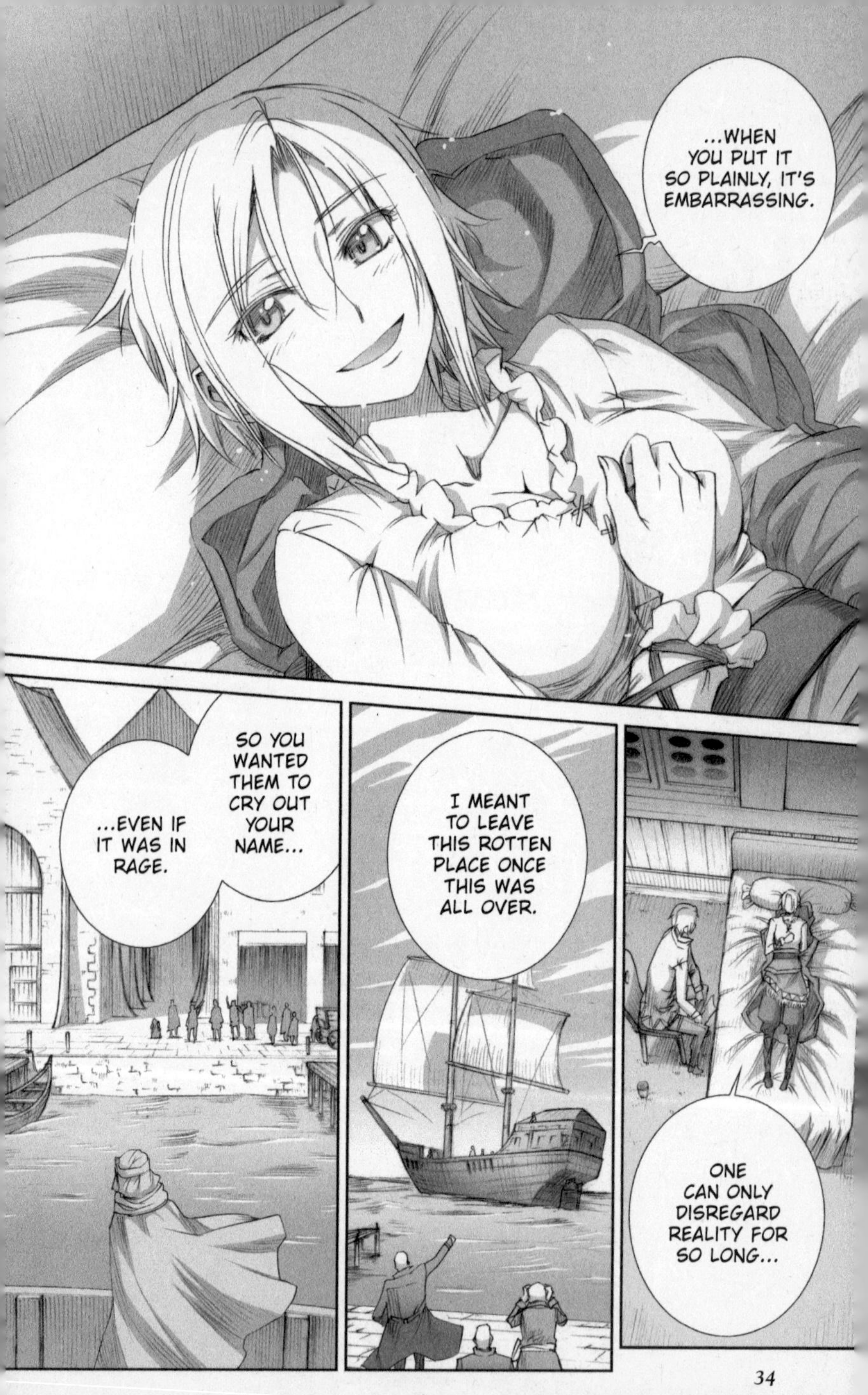
...WHEN YOU PUT IT SO PLAINLY, IT'S EMBARRASSING.
ONE CAN ONLY DISREGARD REALITY FOR SO LONG...
I MEANT TO LEAVE THIS ROTTEN PLACE ONCE THIS WAS ALL OVER.
SO YOU WANTED THEM TO CRY OUT YOUR NAME...
...EVEN IF IT WAS IN RAGE.

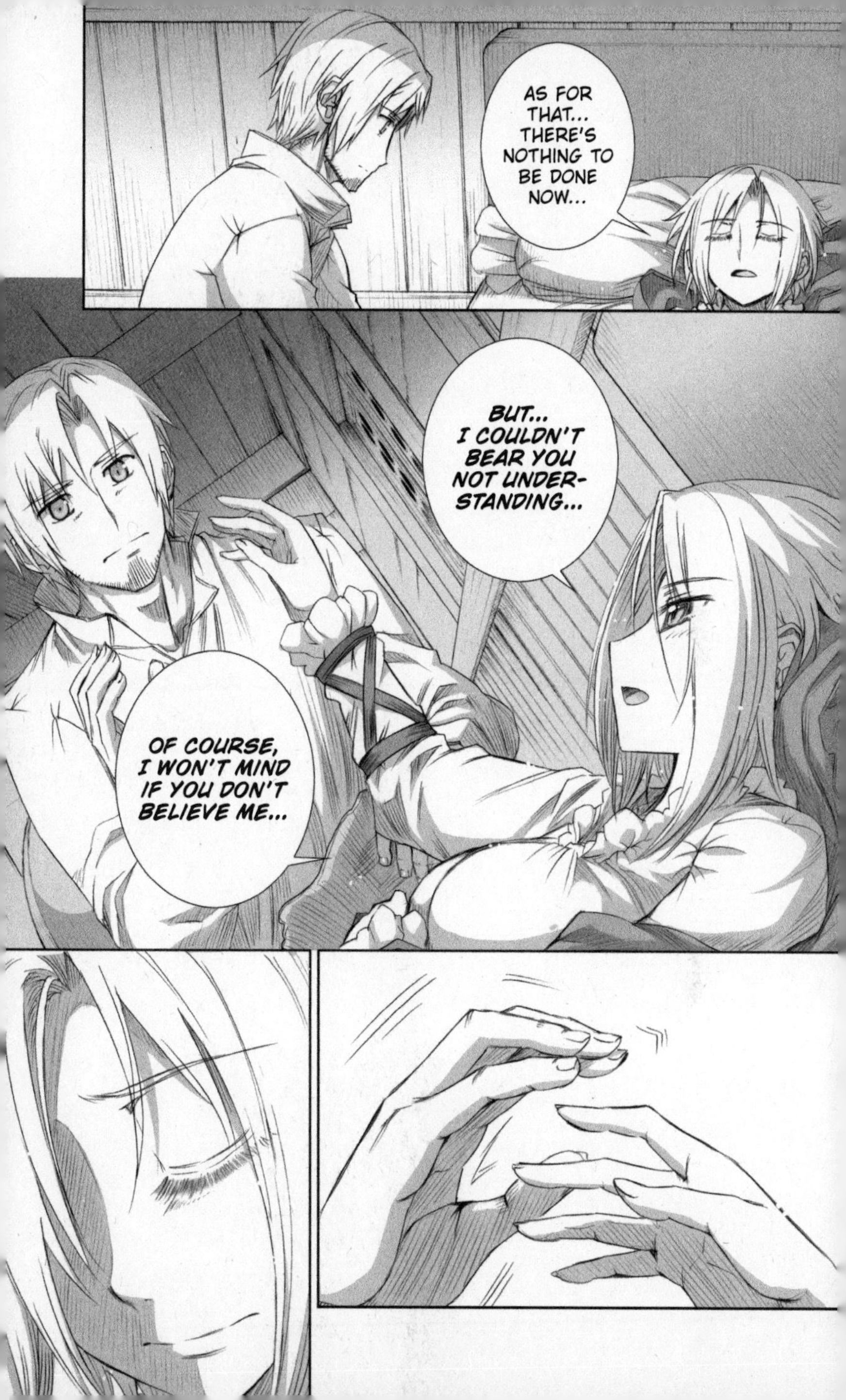
AS FOR THAT... THERE'S NOTHING TO BE DONE NOW...
BUT... I COULDN'T BEAR YOU NOT UNDER-STANDING...
OF COURSE, I WON'T MIND IF YOU DON'T BELIEVE ME...

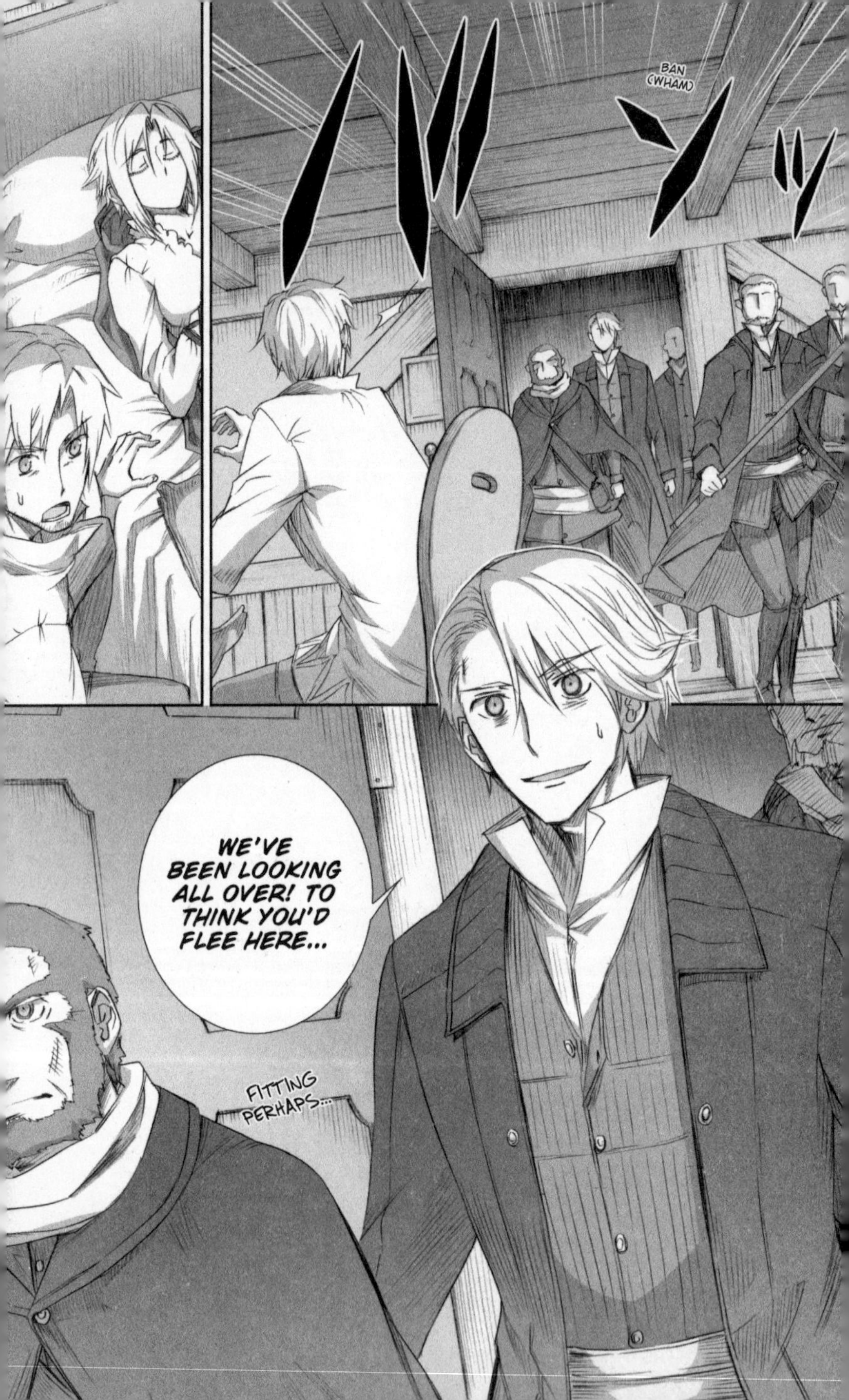
BAN
(WHAM)
WE'VE BEEN LOOKING ALL OVER! TO THINK YOU'D FLEE HERE...
FITTING PERHAPS...

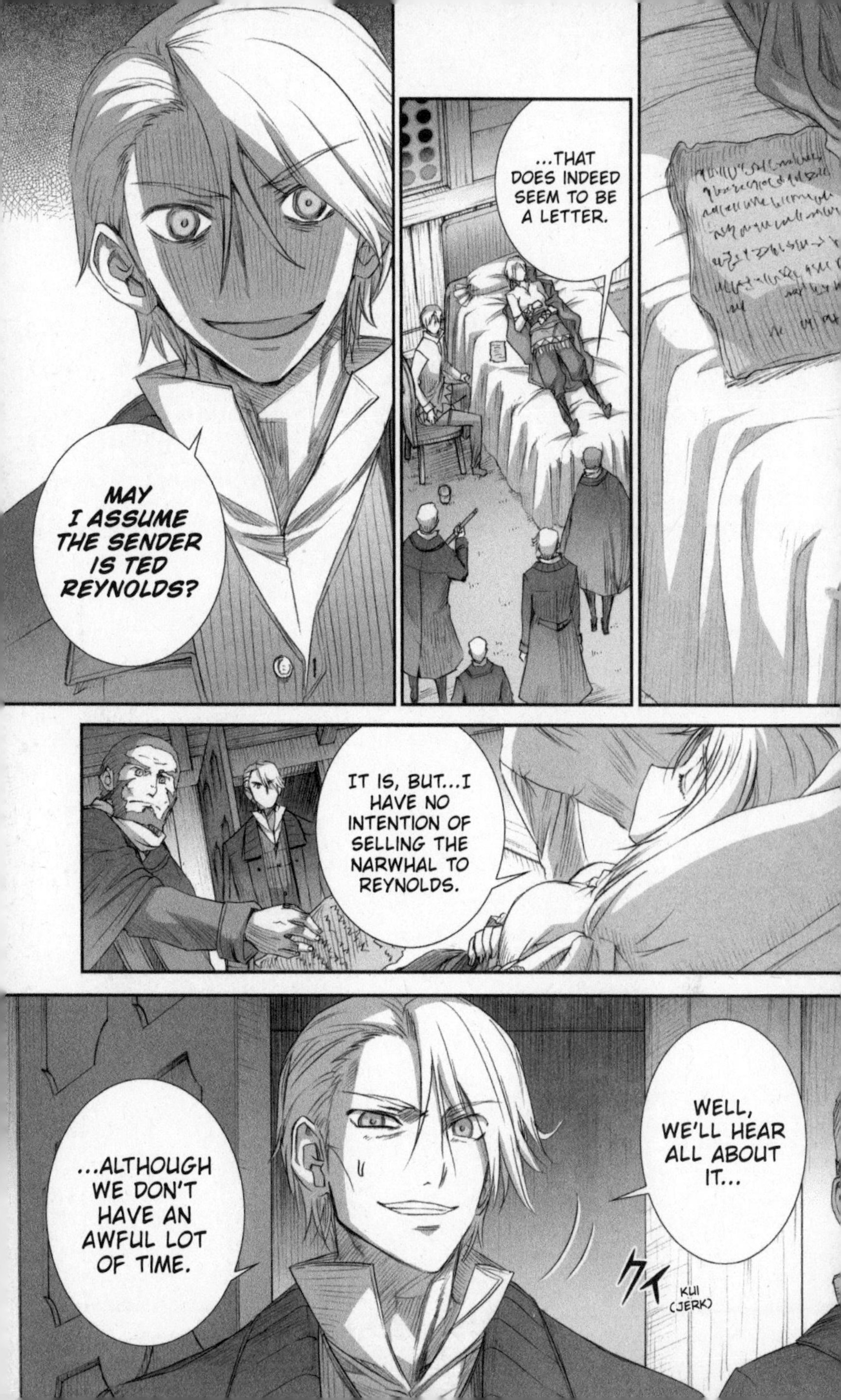
...THAT DOES INDEED SEEM TO BE A LETTER.
MAY I ASSUME THE SENDER IS TED REYNOLDS?
IT IS, BUT...I HAVE NO INTENTION OF SELLING THE NARWHAL TO REYNOLDS.
WELL, WE'LL HEAR ALL ABOUT IT...
クイ
KUI (JERK)
...ALTHOUGH WE DON'T HAVE AN AWFUL LOT OF TIME.

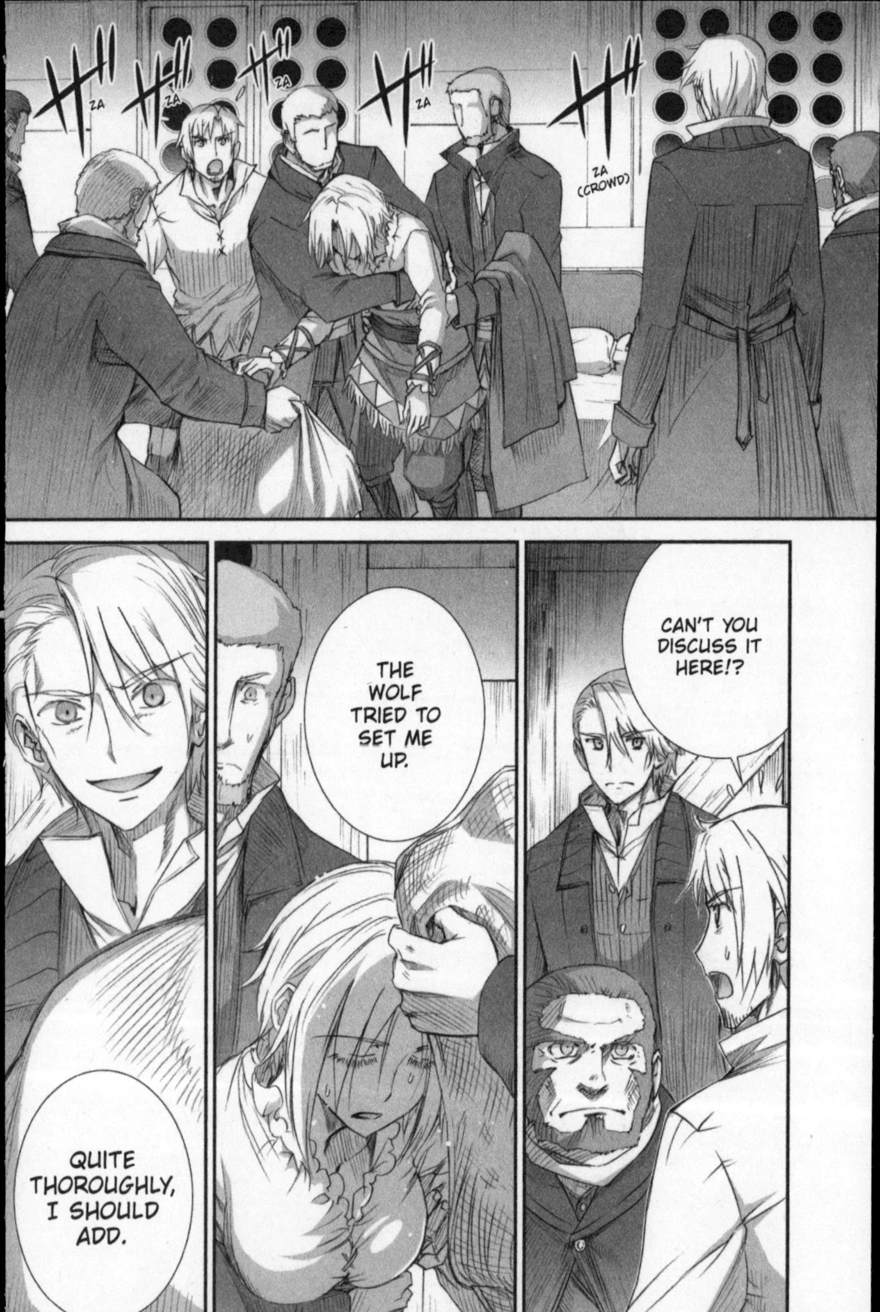
ZA (CROWD)
ZA
ZA
ZA
ZA
CAN'T YOU DISCUSS IT HERE!?
THE WOLF TRIED TO SET ME UP.
QUITE THOROUGHLY, I SHOULD ADD.

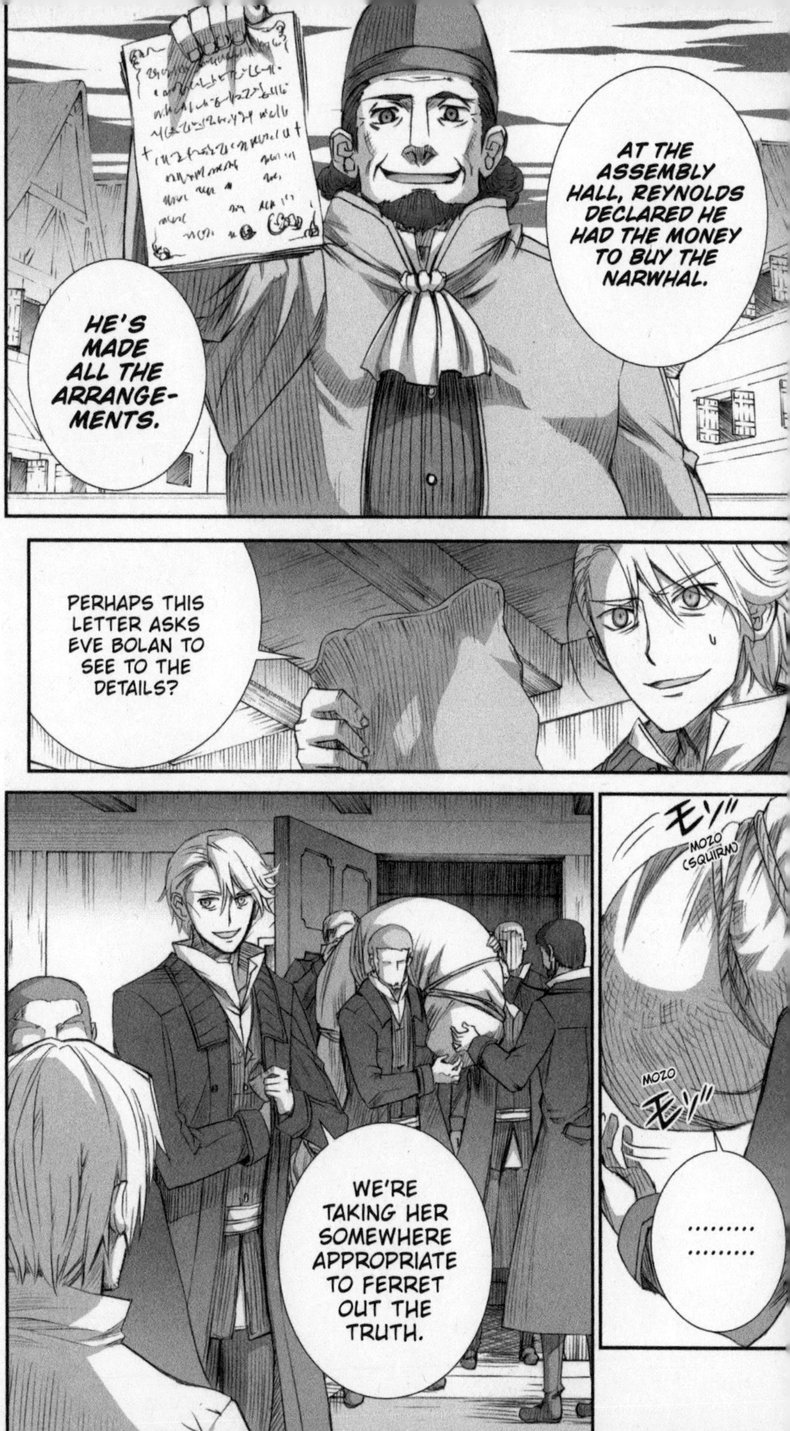
AT THE ASSEMBLY HALL, REYNOLDS DECLARED HE HAD THE MONEY TO BUY THE NARWHAL.
HE'S MADE ALL THE ARRANGE-MENTS.
PERHAPS THIS LETTER ASKS EVE BOLAN TO SEE TO THE DETAILS?
モゾ
MOZO (SQUIRM)
MOZO
モゾ
....
....
WE'RE TAKING HER SOMEWHERE APPROPRIATE TO FERRET OUT THE TRUTH.

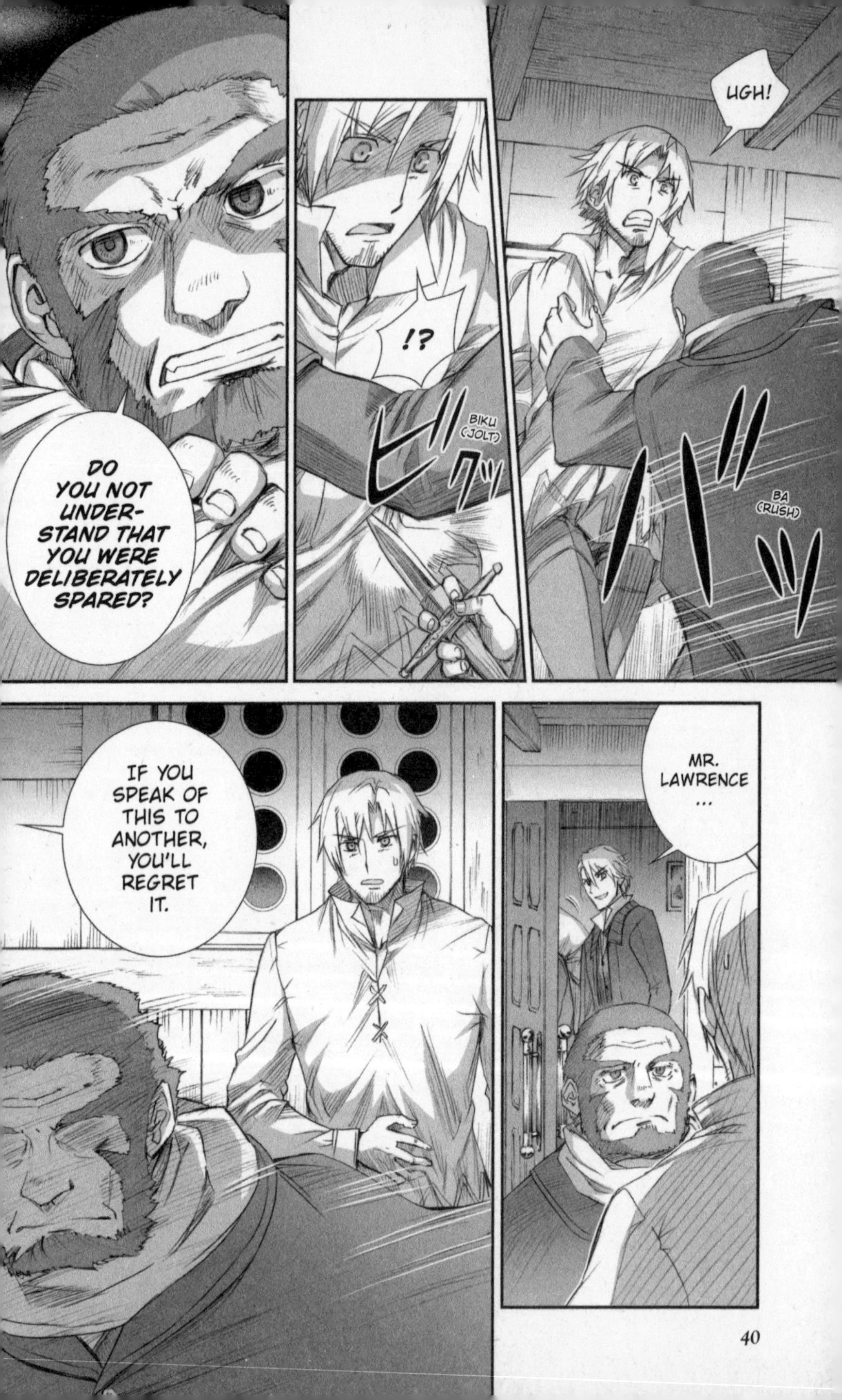
UGH!
BA (RUSH)
!?
BIKU (JOLT)
DO YOU NOT UNDER-STAND THAT YOU WERE DELIBERATELY SPARED?
MR. LAWRENCE ...
IF YOU SPEAK OF THIS TO ANOTHER, YOU'LL REGRET IT.

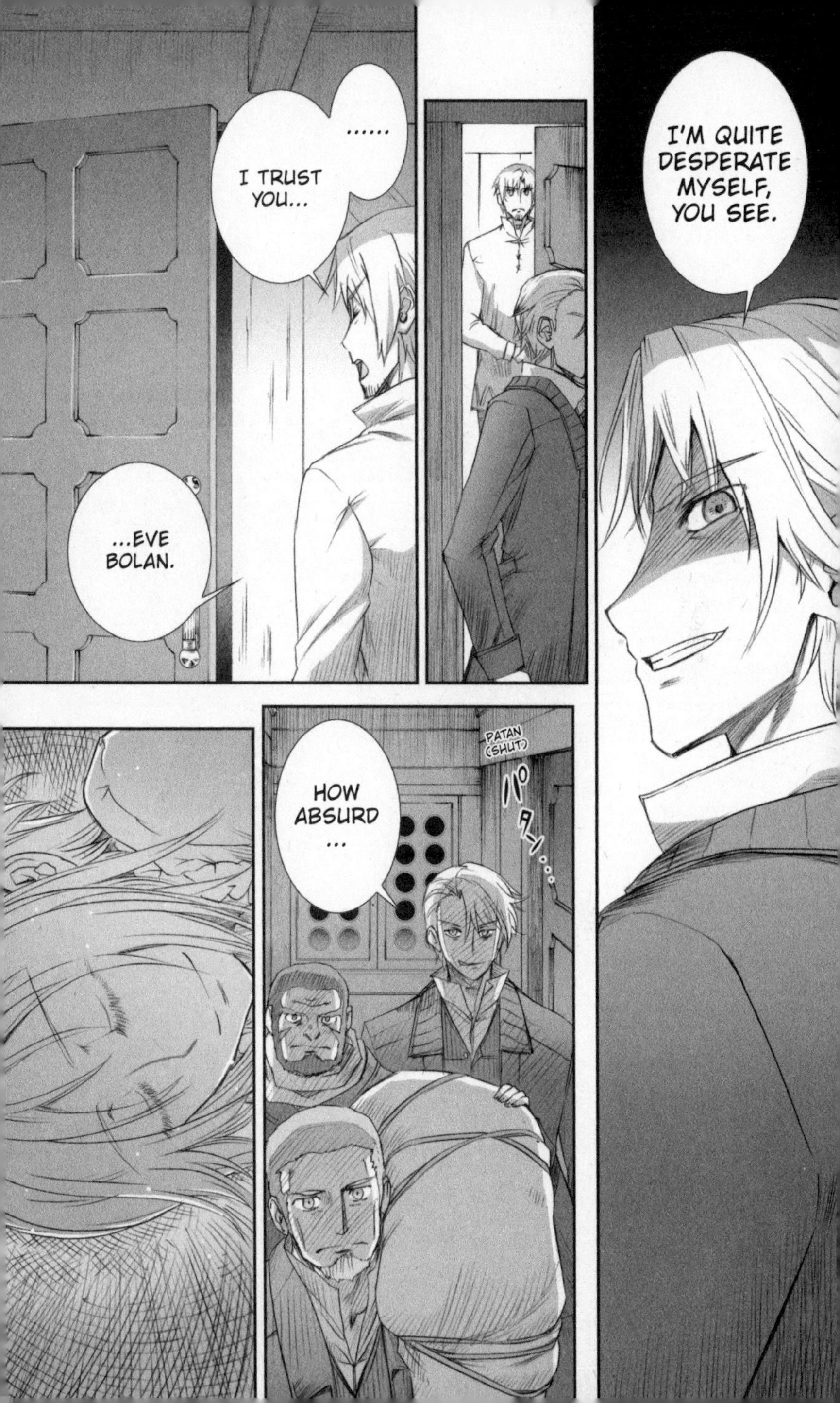
I'M QUITE DESPERATE MYSELF, YOU SEE.
......
I TRUST YOU...
...EVE BOLAN.
HOW ABSURD ...
PATAN (SHUT)

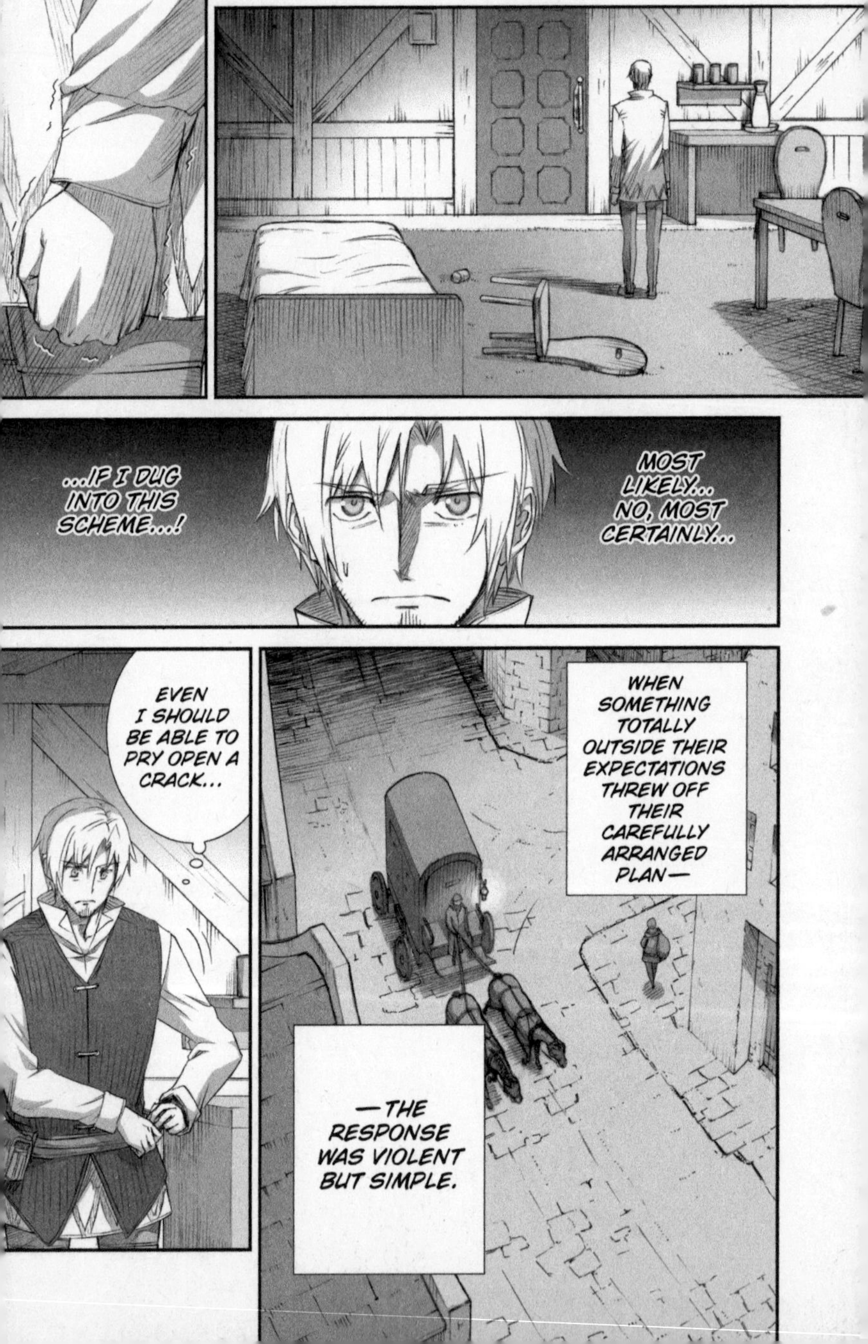
MOST LIKELY... NO, MOST CERTAINLY...
...IF I DUG INTO THIS SCHEME...!
WHEN SOMETHING TOTALLY OUTSIDE THEIR EXPECTATIONS THREW OFF THEIR CAREFULLY ARRANGED PLAN—
—THE RESPONSE WAS VIOLENT BUT SIMPLE.
EVEN I SHOULD BE ABLE TO PRY OPEN A CRACK...

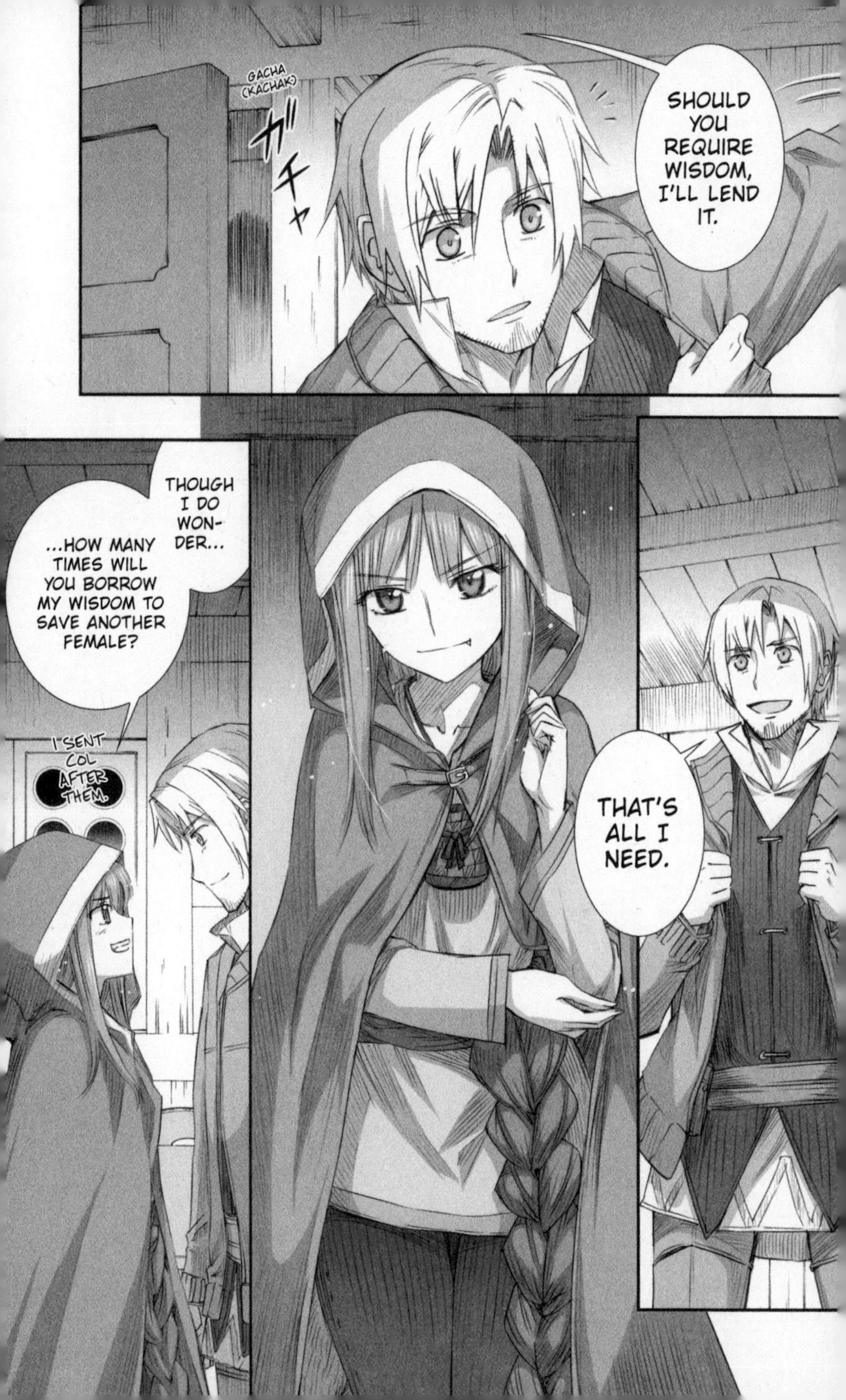
SHOULD YOU REQUIRE WISDOM, I'LL LEND IT.
GACHA (KACHAK)
ガチャ
THAT'S ALL I NEED.
THOUGH I DO WON-DER...
...HOW MANY TIMES WILL YOU BORROW MY WISDOM TO SAVE ANOTHER FEMALE?
I SENT COL AFTER THEM.

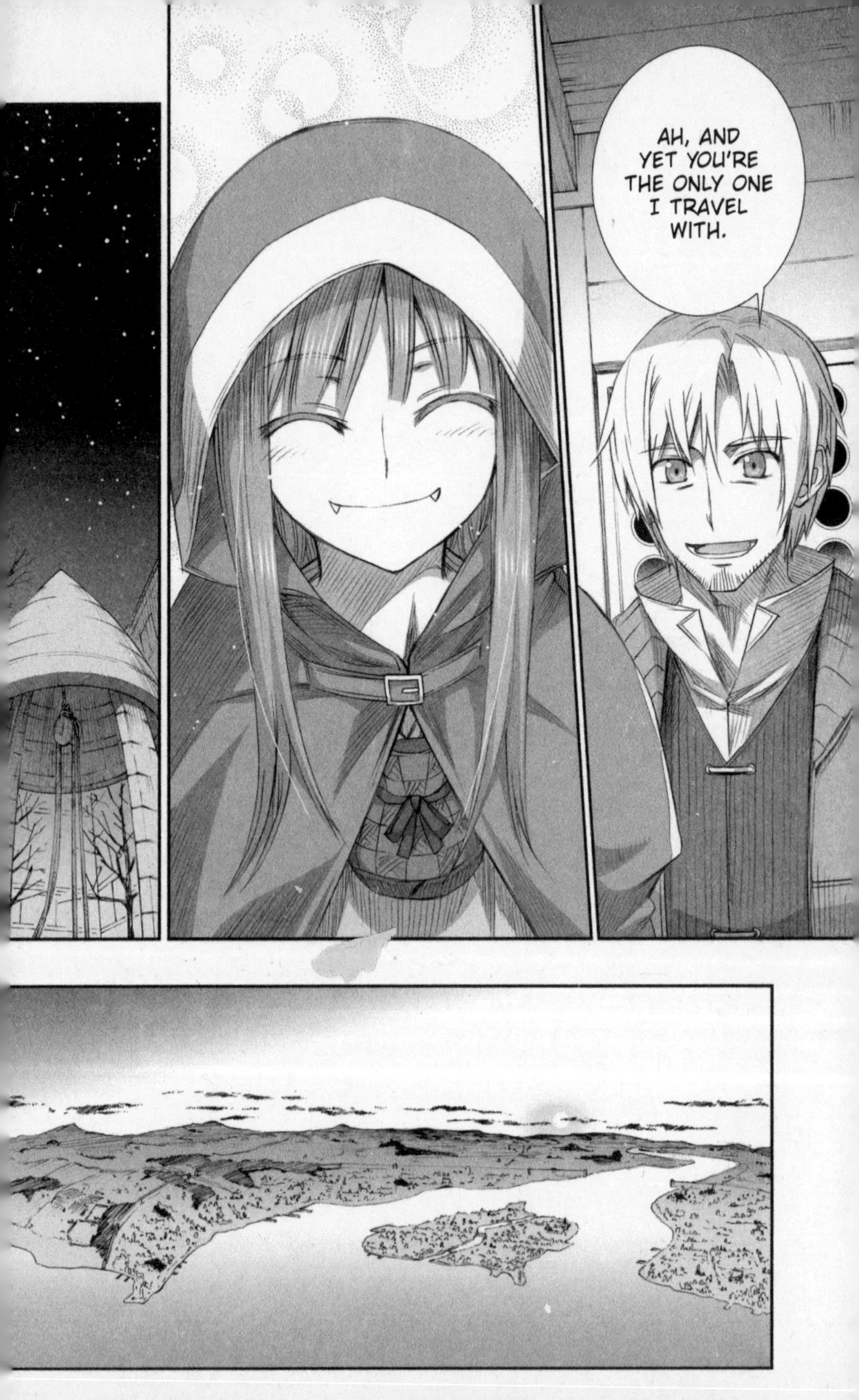
AH, AND YET YOU'RE THE ONLY ONE I TRAVEL WITH.

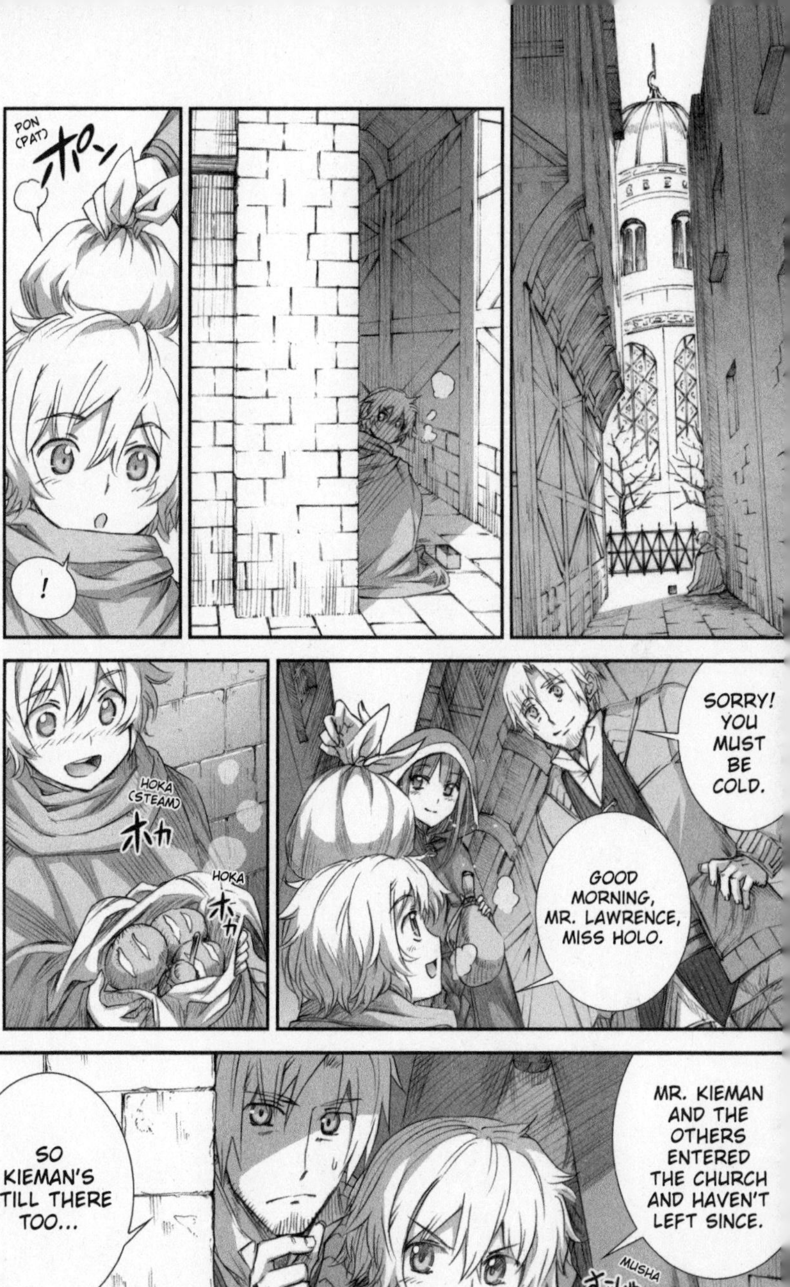
PON (PAT)
ポーン
!
SORRY! YOU MUST BE COLD.
GOOD MORNING, MR. LAWRENCE, MISS HOLO.
HOKA (STEAM)
ホカ
HOKA
ホカ
MR. KIEMAN AND THE OTHERS ENTERED THE CHURCH AND HAVEN'T LEFT SINCE.
MUSHA
むしゃ
MUSHA (KRONSH)
むしゃ
SO KIEMAN'S STILL THERE TOO...

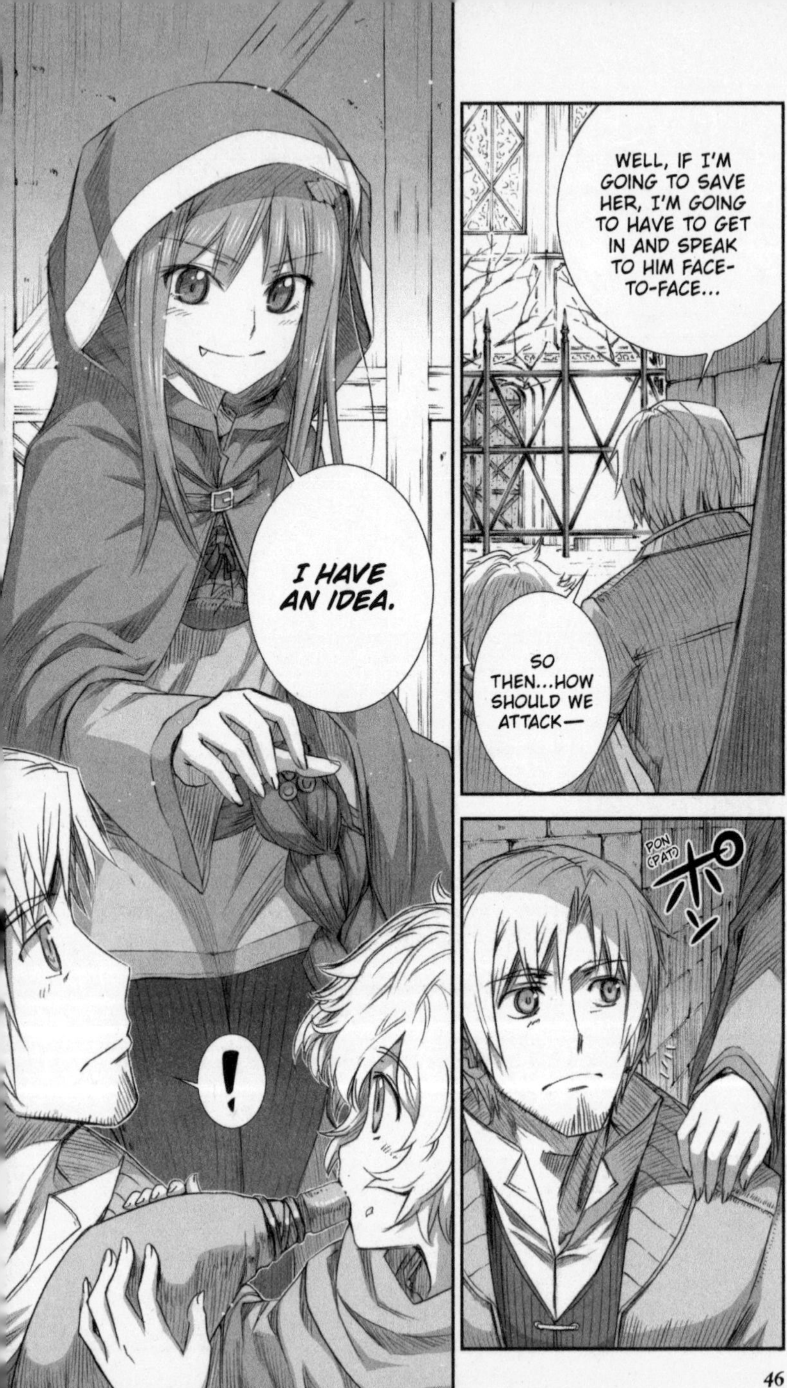
WELL, IF I'M GOING TO SAVE HER, I'M GOING TO HAVE TO GET IN AND SPEAK TO HIM FACE-TO-FACE...
SO THEN...HOW SHOULD WE ATTACK—
PON (PAT)
I HAVE AN IDEA.
!

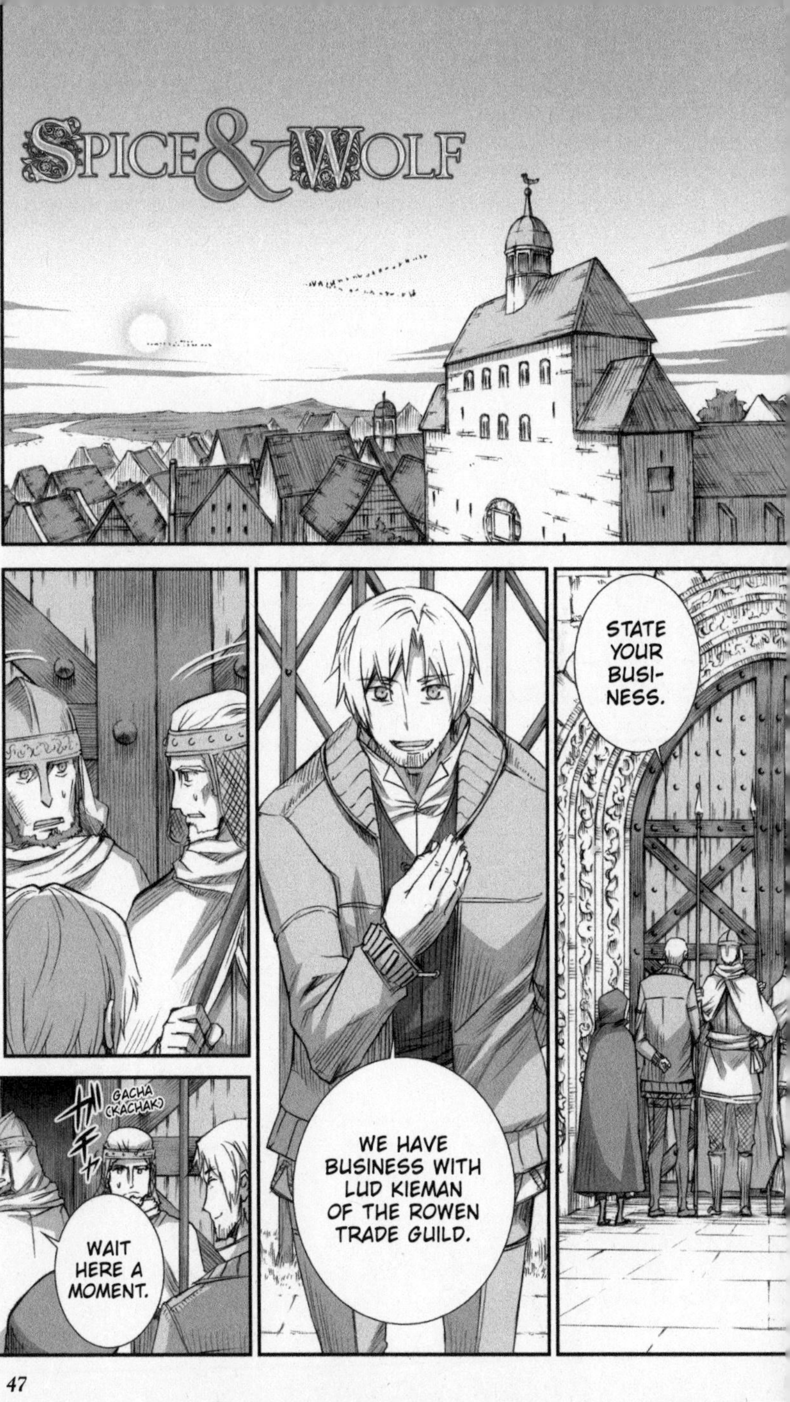
SPICE & WOLF
STATE YOUR BUSI- NESS.
WE HAVE BUSINESS WITH LUD KIEMAN OF THE ROWEN TRADE GUILD.
ガチャ
GACHA (KACHAK)
WAIT HERE A MOMENT.

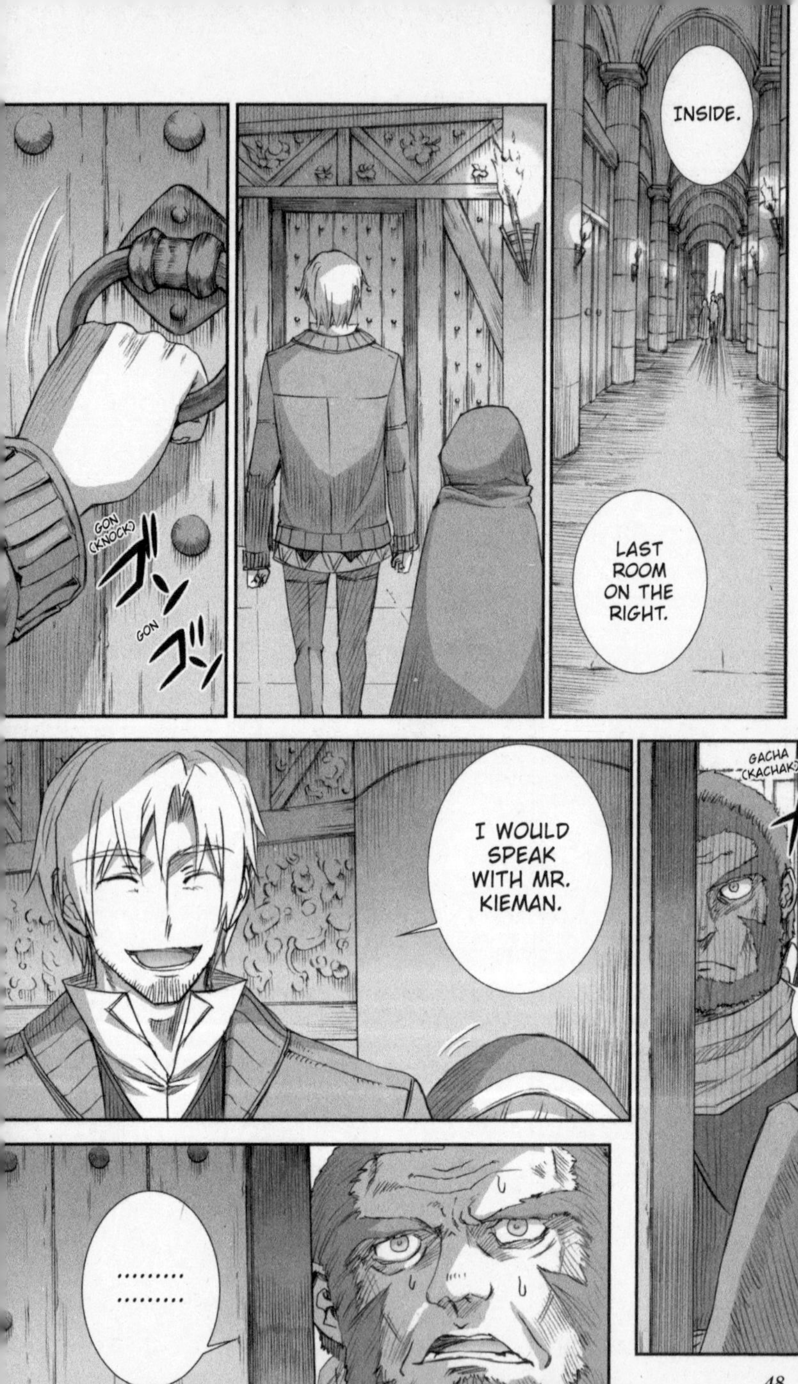
INSIDE.
LAST ROOM ON THE RIGHT.
GON (KNOCK)
ゴン
GON
ゴン
GACHA (KACHAK)
ガチャ
!
I WOULD SPEAK WITH MR. KIEMAN.
....

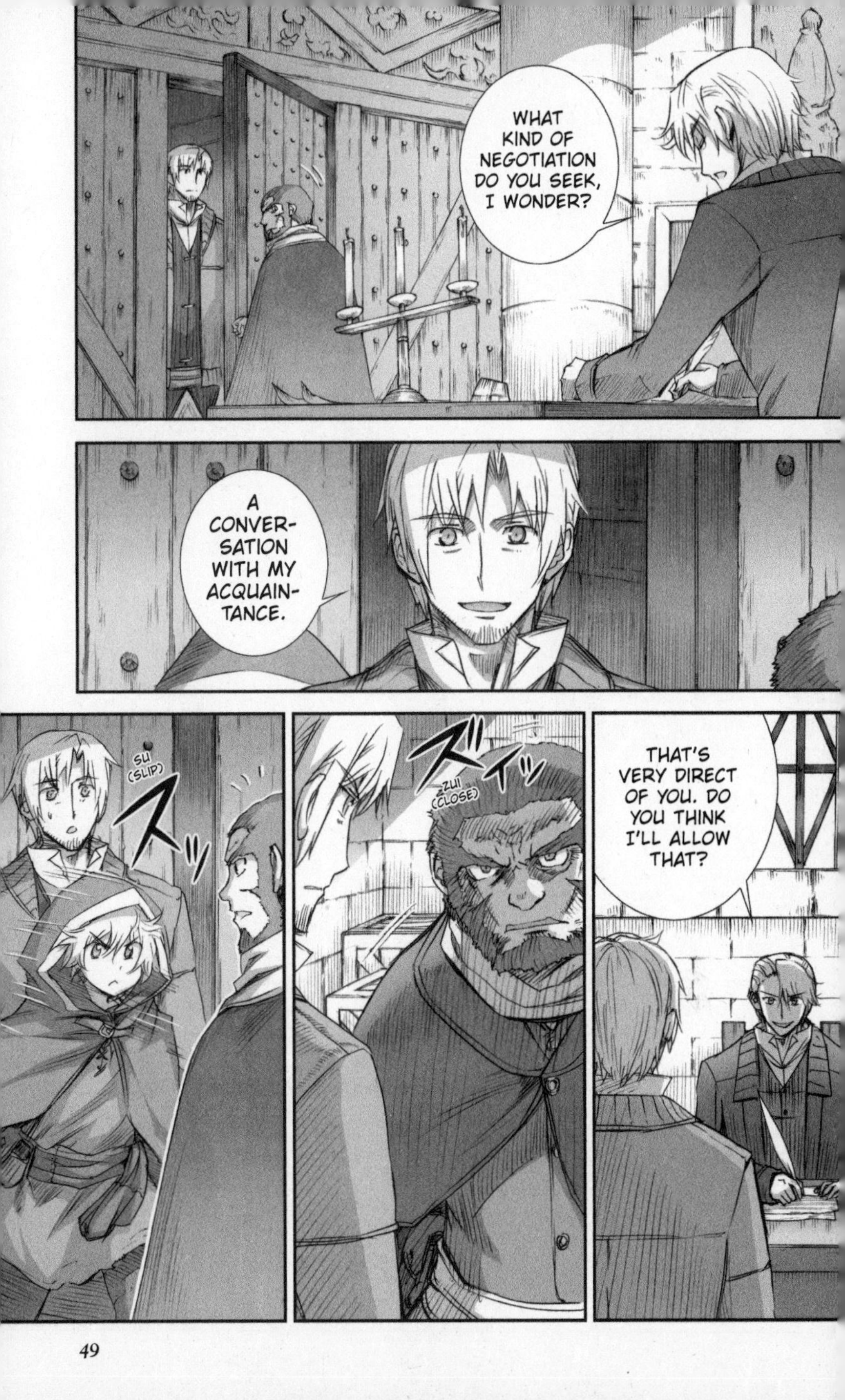
WHAT KIND OF NEGOTIATION DO YOU SEEK, I WONDER?
A CONVERSATION WITH MY ACQUAINTANCE.
THAT'S VERY DIRECT OF YOU. DO YOU THINK I'LL ALLOW THAT?
ズイッ
ZUI (CLOSE)
スッ
SU (SLIP)

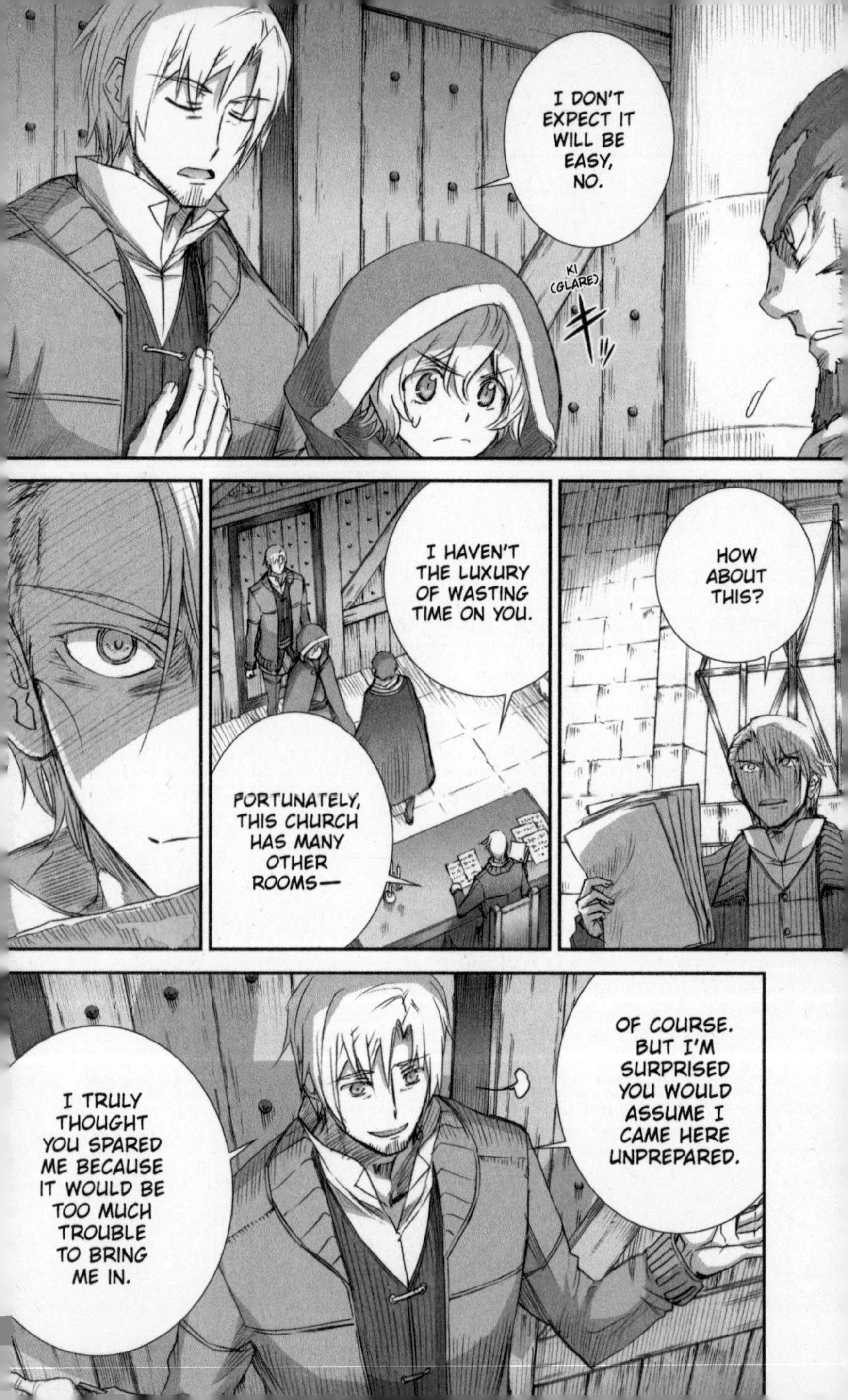
I DON'T EXPECT IT WILL BE EASY, NO.
KI (GLARE)
HOW ABOUT THIS?
I HAVEN'T THE LUXURY OF WASTING TIME ON YOU.
FORTUNATELY, THIS CHURCH HAS MANY OTHER ROOMS—
OF COURSE. BUT I'M SURPRISED YOU WOULD ASSUME I CAME HERE UNPREPARED.
I TRULY THOUGHT YOU SPARED ME BECAUSE IT WOULD BE TOO MUCH TROUBLE TO BRING ME IN.

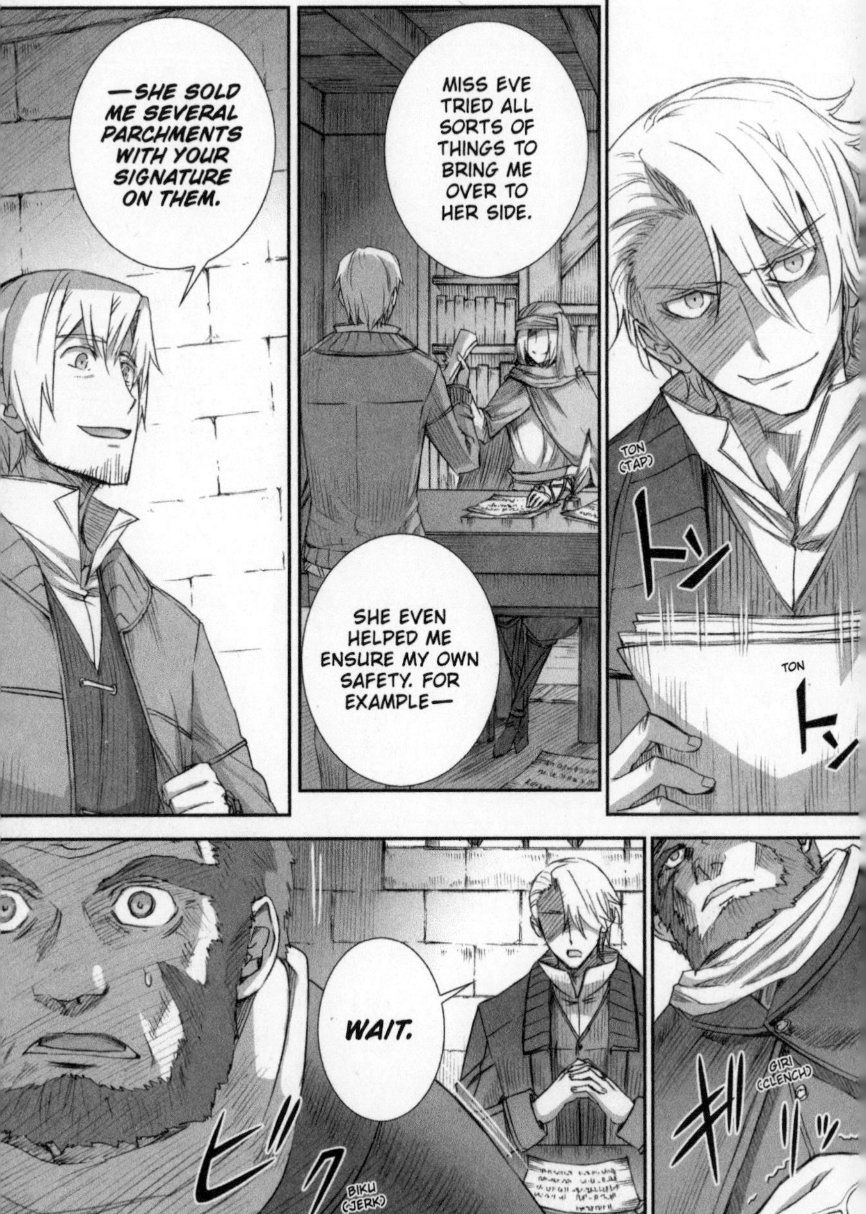
TON
(TAP)
トン
TON
トン
MISS EVE TRIED ALL SORTS OF THINGS TO BRING ME OVER TO HER SIDE.
SHE EVEN HELPED ME ENSURE MY OWN SAFETY. FOR EXAMPLE—
—SHE SOLD ME SEVERAL PARCHMENTS WITH YOUR SIGNATURE ON THEM.
GIRI
(CLENCH)
ギリッ
WAIT.
ビクッ
BIKU
(JERK)

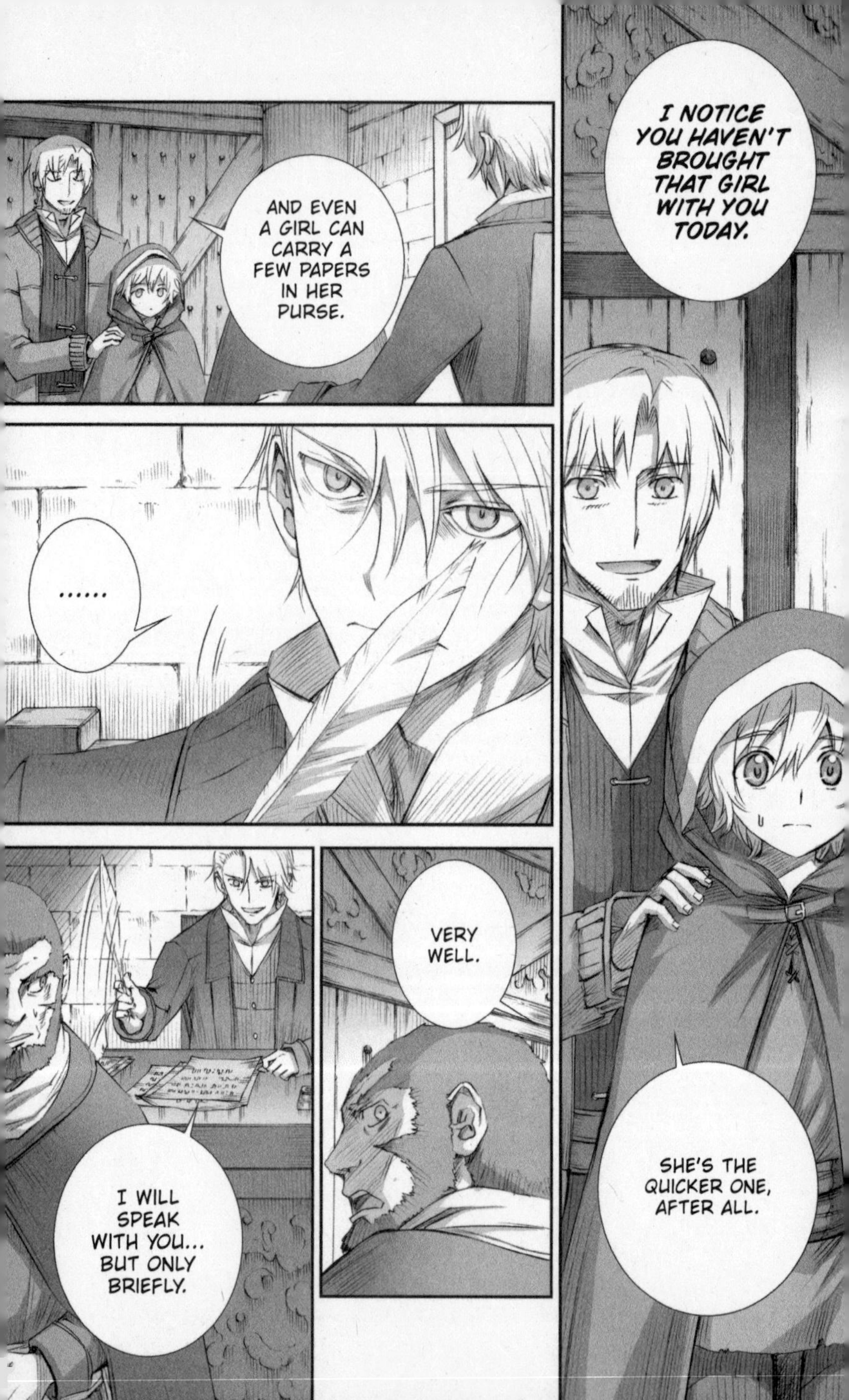
I NOTICE YOU HAVEN'T BROUGHT THAT GIRL WITH YOU TODAY.
SHE'S THE QUICKER ONE, AFTER ALL.
AND EVEN A GIRL CAN CARRY A FEW PAPERS IN HER PURSE.
......
VERY WELL.
I WILL SPEAK WITH YOU... BUT ONLY BRIEFLY.

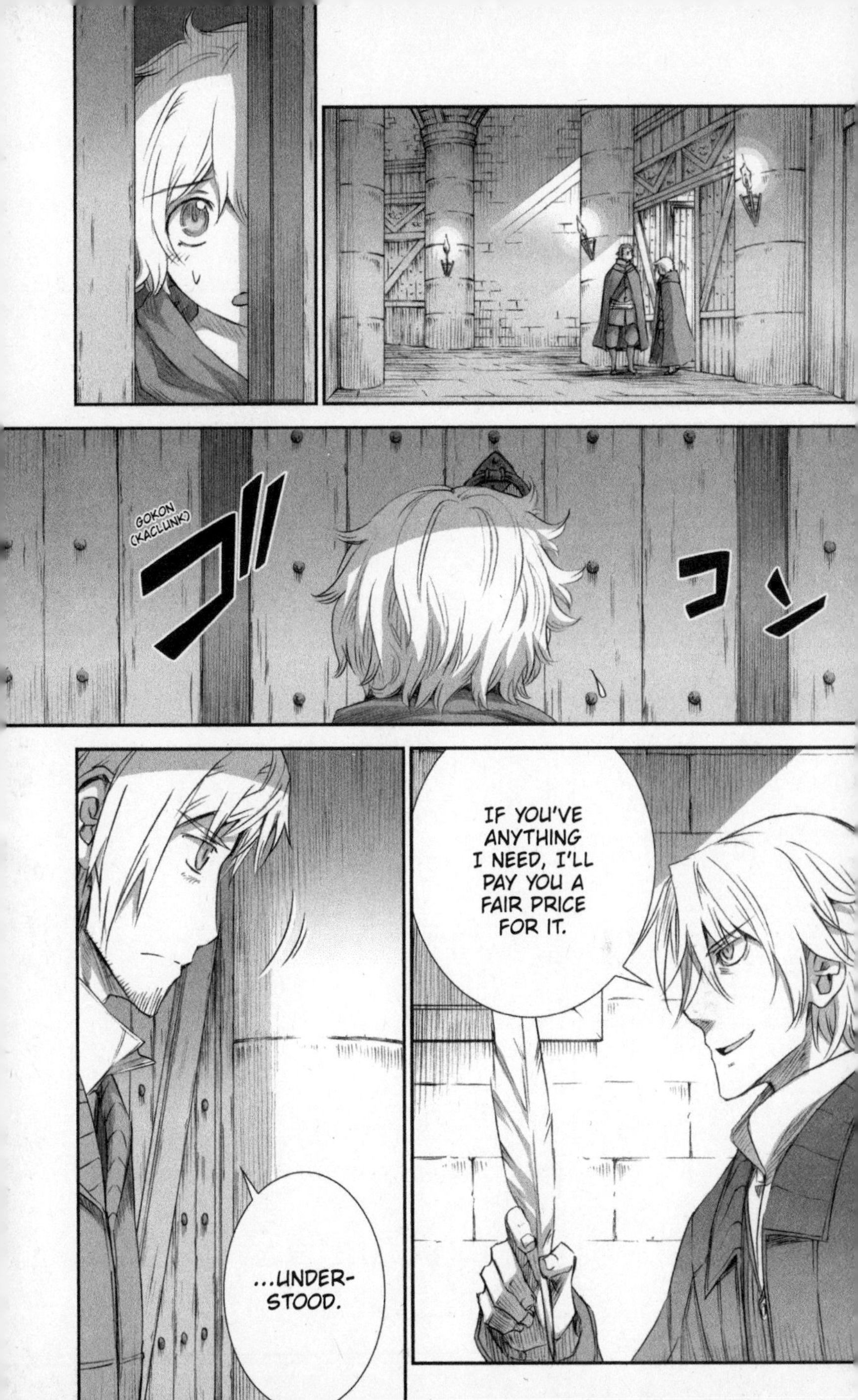
GOKON (KACLUNK)
IF YOU'VE ANYTHING I NEED, I'LL PAY YOU A FAIR PRICE FOR IT.
...UNDER-STOOD.

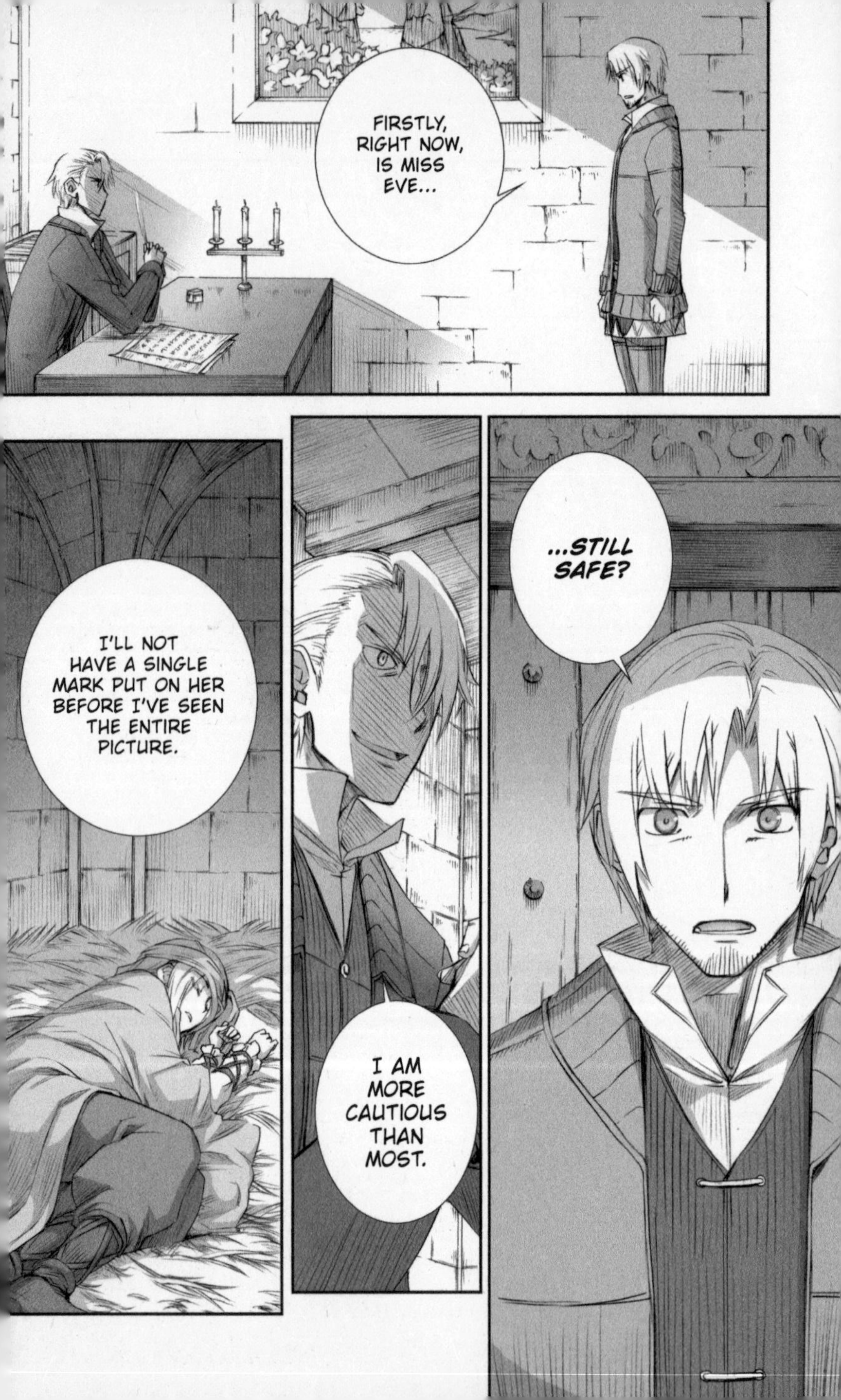
FIRSTLY, RIGHT NOW, IS MISS EVE...
...STILL SAFE?
I AM MORE CAUTIOUS THAN MOST.
I'LL NOT HAVE A SINGLE MARK PUT ON HER BEFORE I'VE SEEN THE ENTIRE PICTURE.

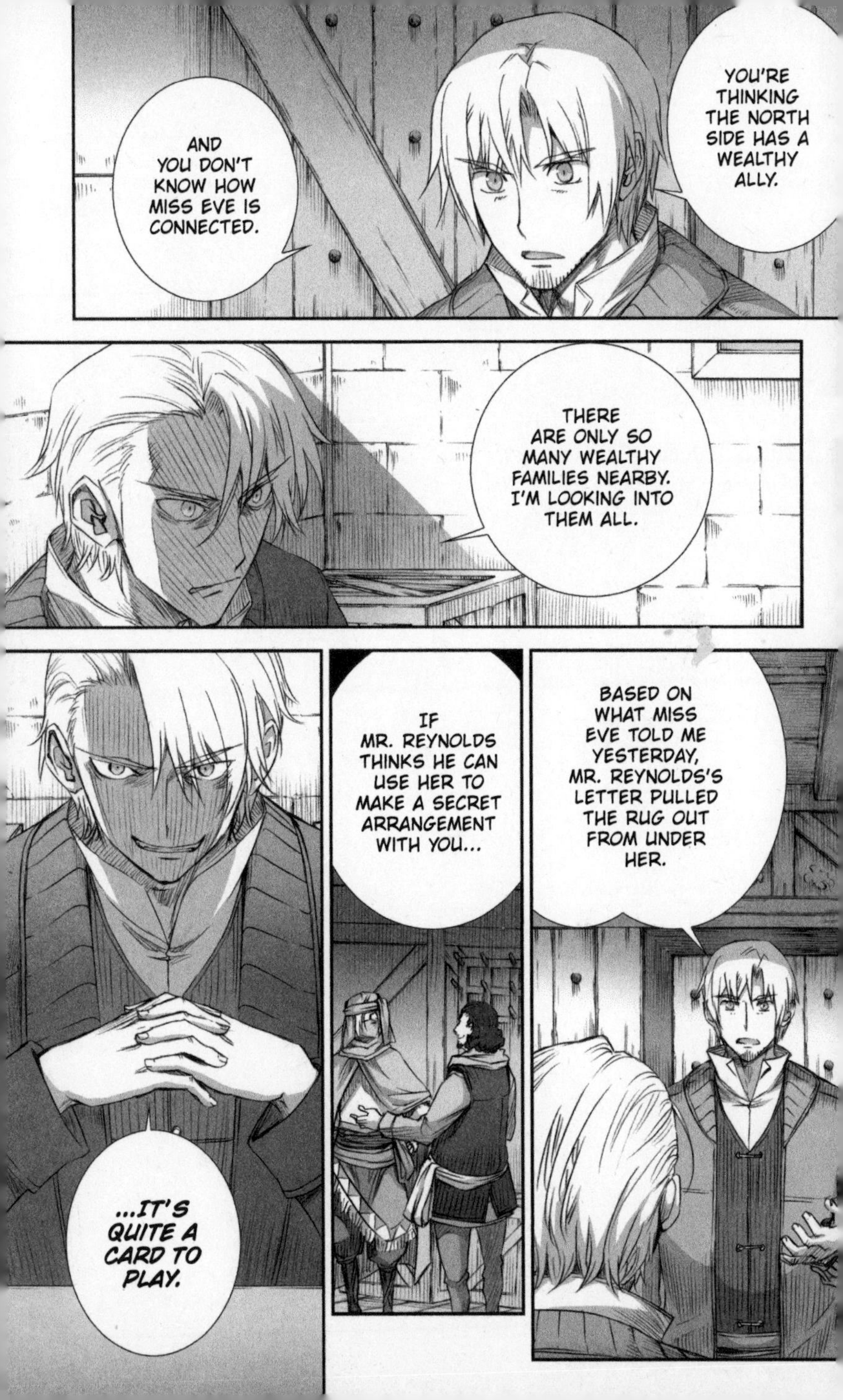
YOU'RE THINKING THE NORTH SIDE HAS A WEALTHY ALLY.
AND YOU DON'T KNOW HOW MISS EVE IS CONNECTED.
THERE ARE ONLY SO MANY WEALTHY FAMILIES NEARBY. I'M LOOKING INTO THEM ALL.
BASED ON WHAT MISS EVE TOLD ME YESTERDAY, MR. REYNOLDS'S LETTER PULLED THE RUG OUT FROM UNDER HER.
IF MR. REYNOLDS THINKS HE CAN USE HER TO MAKE A SECRET ARRANGEMENT WITH YOU...
...IT'S QUITE A CARD TO PLAY.

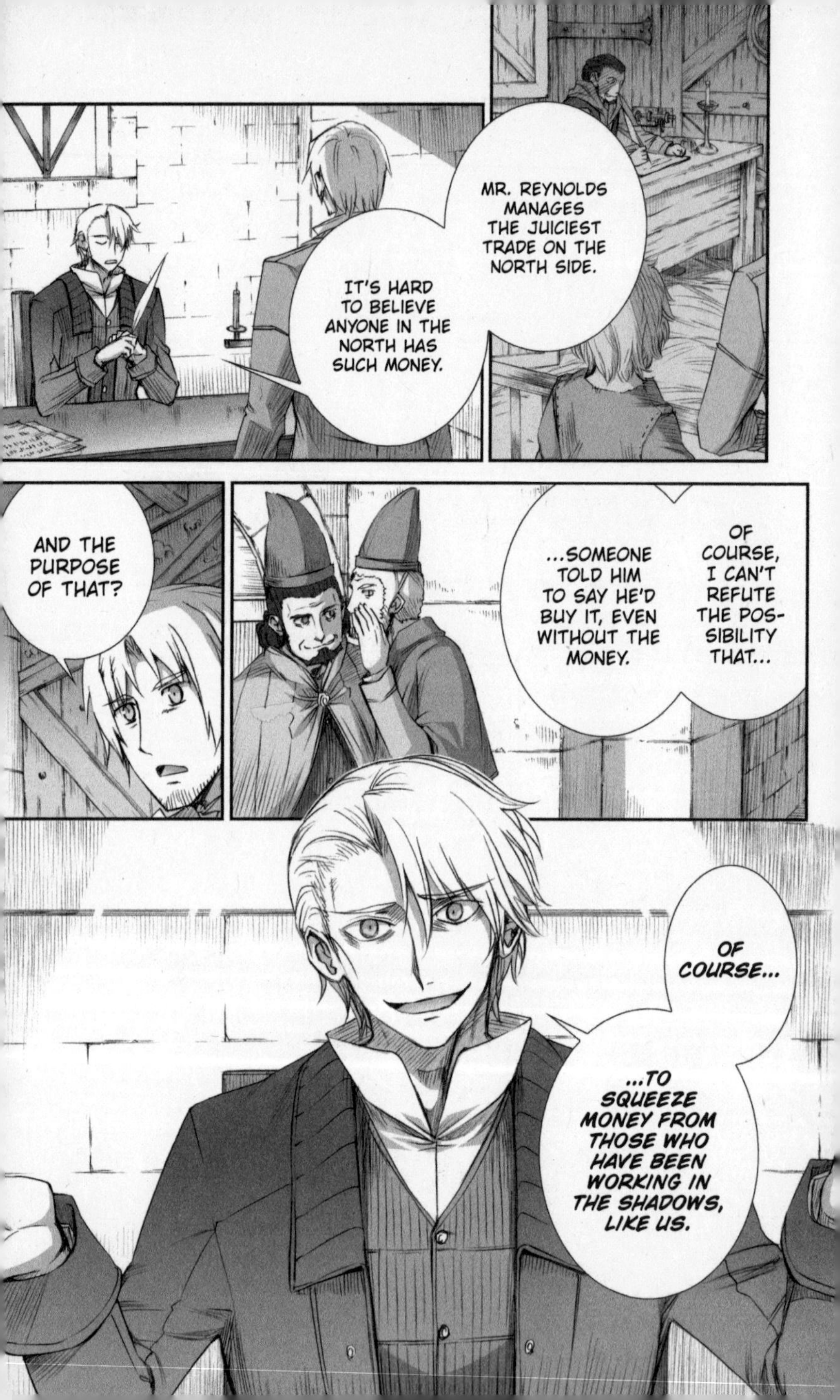
MR. REYNOLDS MANAGES THE JUICIEST TRADE ON THE NORTH SIDE.
IT'S HARD TO BELIEVE ANYONE IN THE NORTH HAS SUCH MONEY.
OF COURSE, I CAN'T REFUTE THE POSSIBILITY THAT...
...SOMEONE TOLD HIM TO SAY HE'D BUY IT, EVEN WITHOUT THE MONEY.
AND THE PURPOSE OF THAT?
OF COURSE...
...TO SQUEEZE MONEY FROM THOSE WHO HAVE BEEN WORKING IN THE SHADOWS, LIKE US.

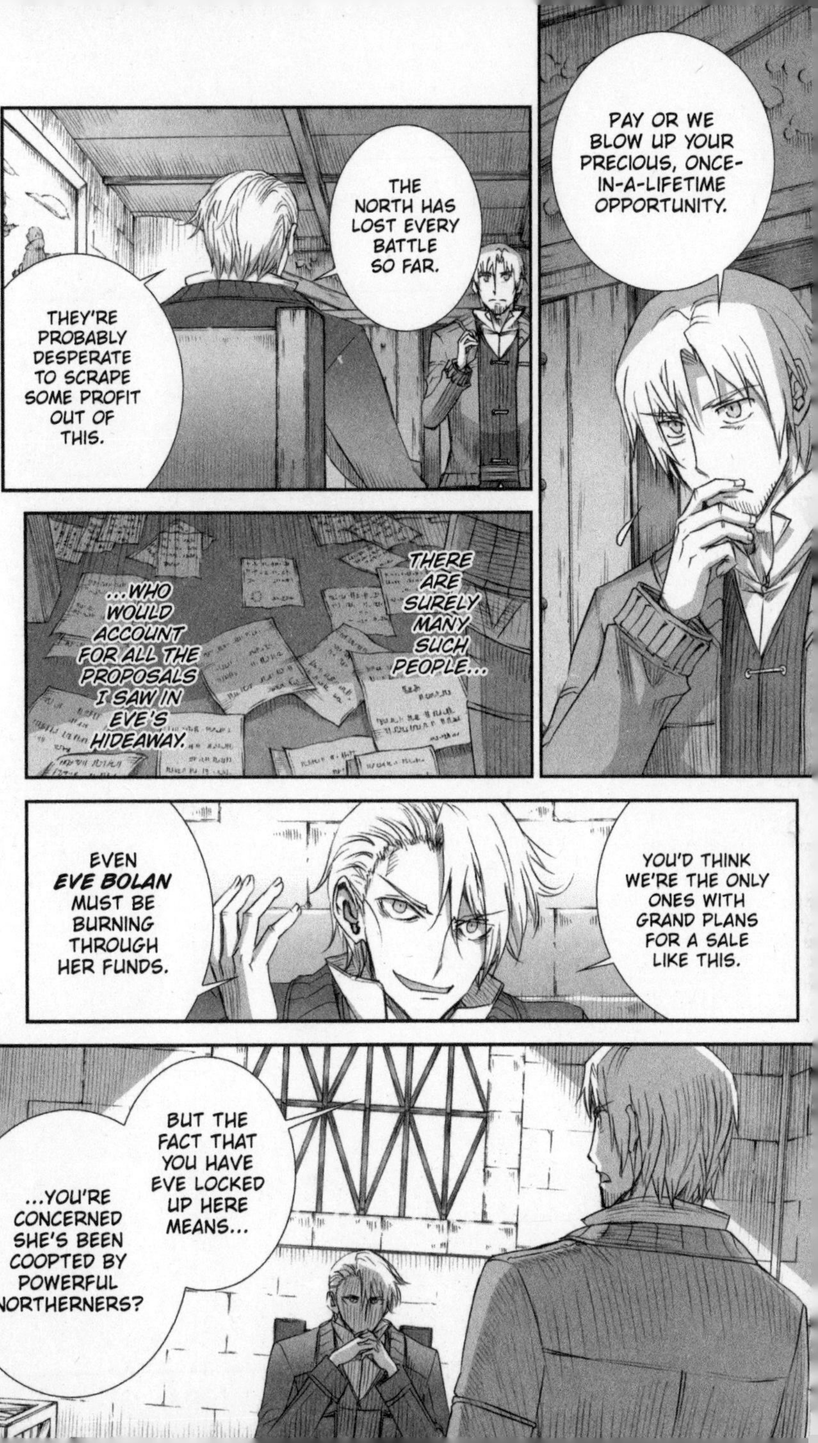
PAY OR WE BLOW UP YOUR PRECIOUS, ONCE-IN-A-LIFETIME OPPORTUNITY.
THE NORTH HAS LOST EVERY BATTLE SO FAR.
THEY'RE PROBABLY DESPERATE TO SCRAPE SOME PROFIT OUT OF THIS.
THERE ARE SURELY MANY SUCH PEOPLE...
...WHO WOULD ACCOUNT FOR ALL THE PROPOSALS I SAW IN EVE'S HIDEAWAY.
YOU'D THINK WE'RE THE ONLY ONES WITH GRAND PLANS FOR A SALE LIKE THIS.
EVEN EVE BOLAN MUST BE BURNING THROUGH HER FUNDS.
BUT THE FACT THAT YOU HAVE EVE LOCKED UP HERE MEANS...
...YOU'RE CONCERNED SHE'S BEEN COOPTED BY POWERFUL NORTHERNERS?

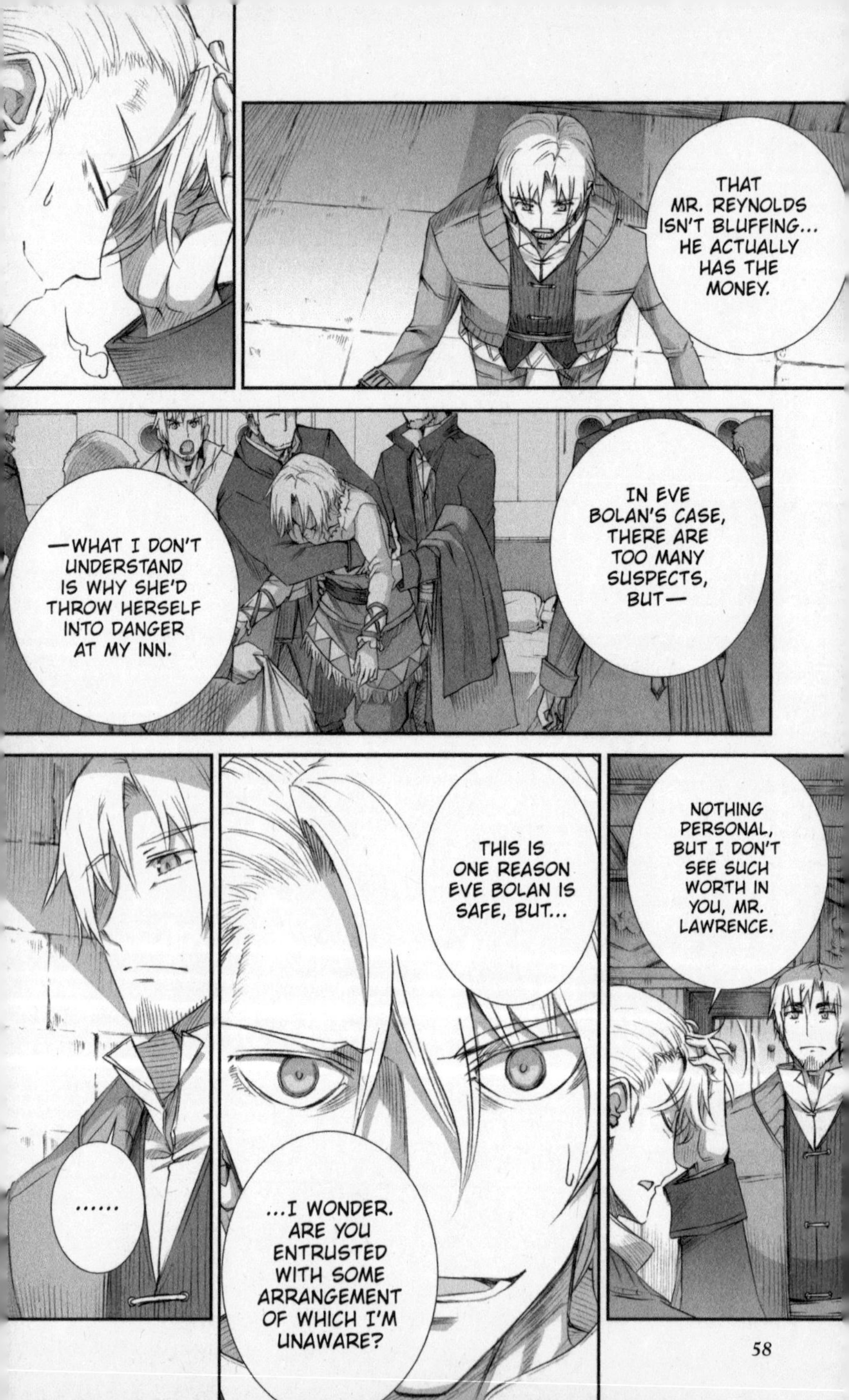
THAT MR. REYNOLDS ISN'T BLUFFING... HE ACTUALLY HAS THE MONEY.
IN EVE BOLAN'S CASE, THERE ARE TOO MANY SUSPECTS, BUT—
—WHAT I DON'T UNDERSTAND IS WHY SHE'D THROW HERSELF INTO DANGER AT MY INN.
NOTHING PERSONAL, BUT I DON'T SEE SUCH WORTH IN YOU, MR. LAWRENCE.
THIS IS ONE REASON EVE BOLAN IS SAFE, BUT...
...I WONDER. ARE YOU ENTRUSTED WITH SOME ARRANGEMENT OF WHICH I'M UNAWARE?
......

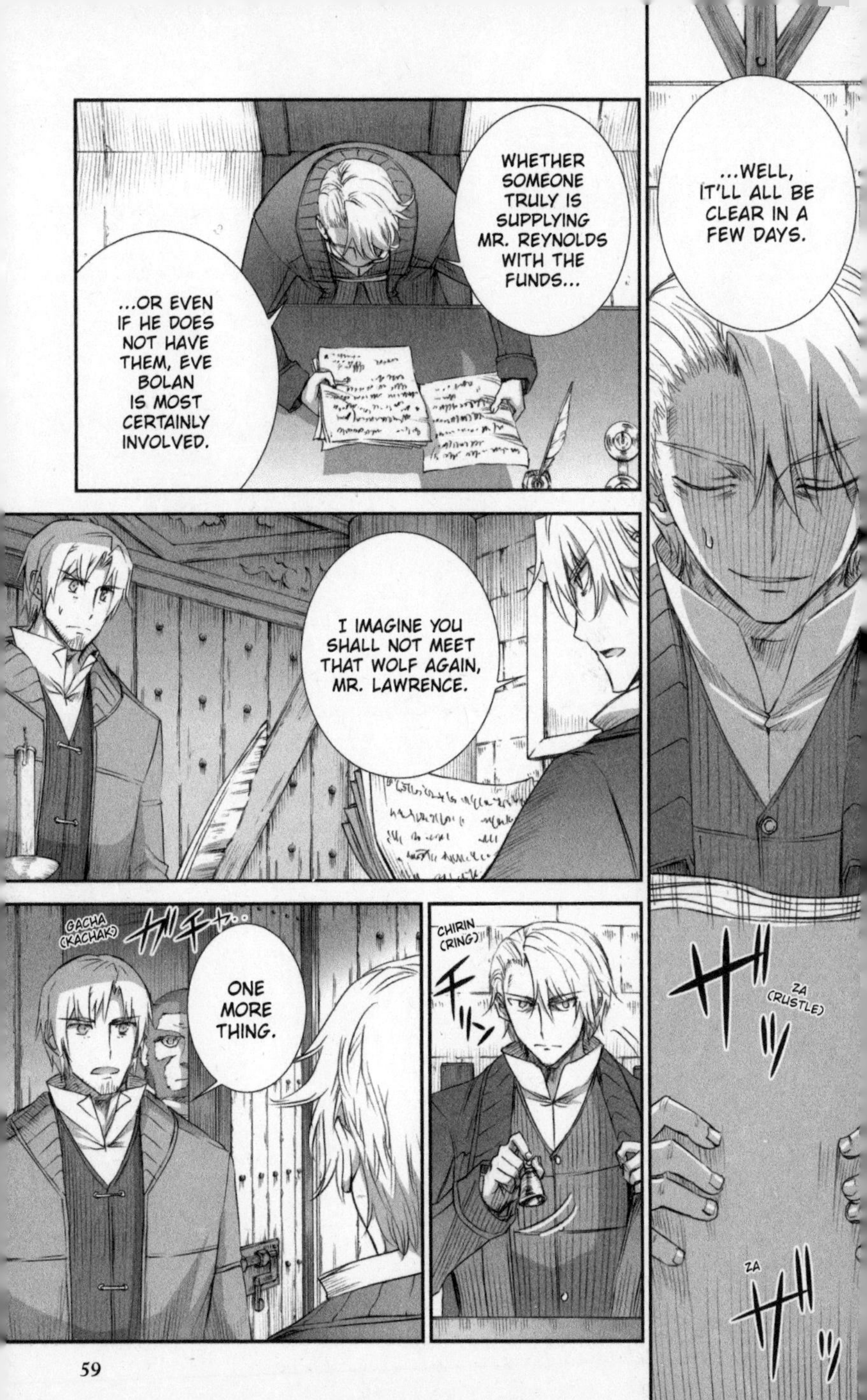
...WELL, IT'LL ALL BE CLEAR IN A FEW DAYS.
ZA (RUSTLE)
ZA
WHETHER SOMEONE TRULY IS SUPPLYING MR. REYNOLDS WITH THE FUNDS...
...OR EVEN IF HE DOES NOT HAVE THEM, EVE BOLAN IS MOST CERTAINLY INVOLVED.
I IMAGINE YOU SHALL NOT MEET THAT WOLF AGAIN, MR. LAWRENCE.
CHIRIN (RING)
GACHA (KACHAK)
ONE MORE THING.

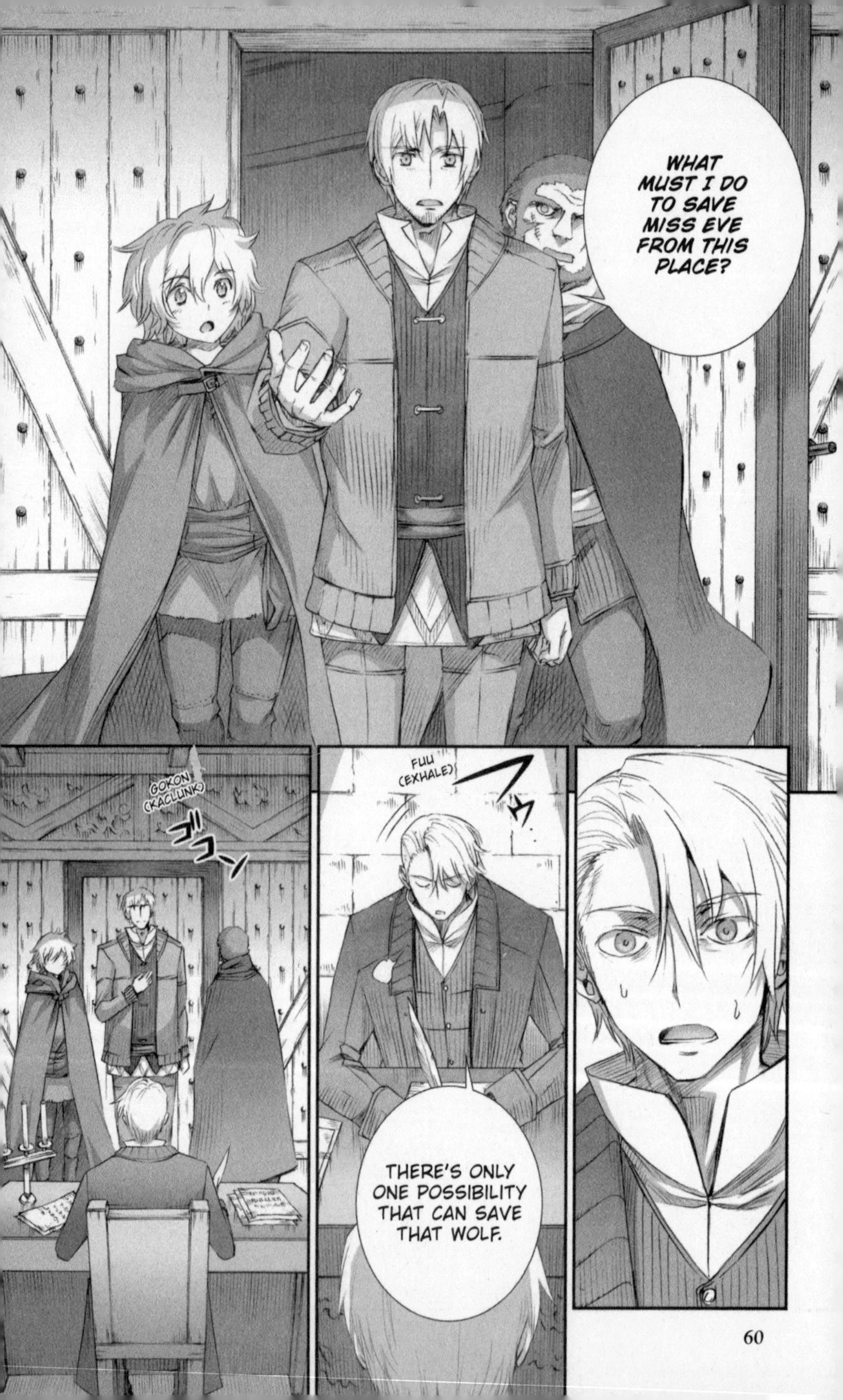
WHAT MUST I DO TO SAVE MISS EVE FROM THIS PLACE?
FUU (EXHALE)
THERE'S ONLY ONE POSSIBILITY THAT CAN SAVE THAT WOLF.
GOKON (KACLUNK)

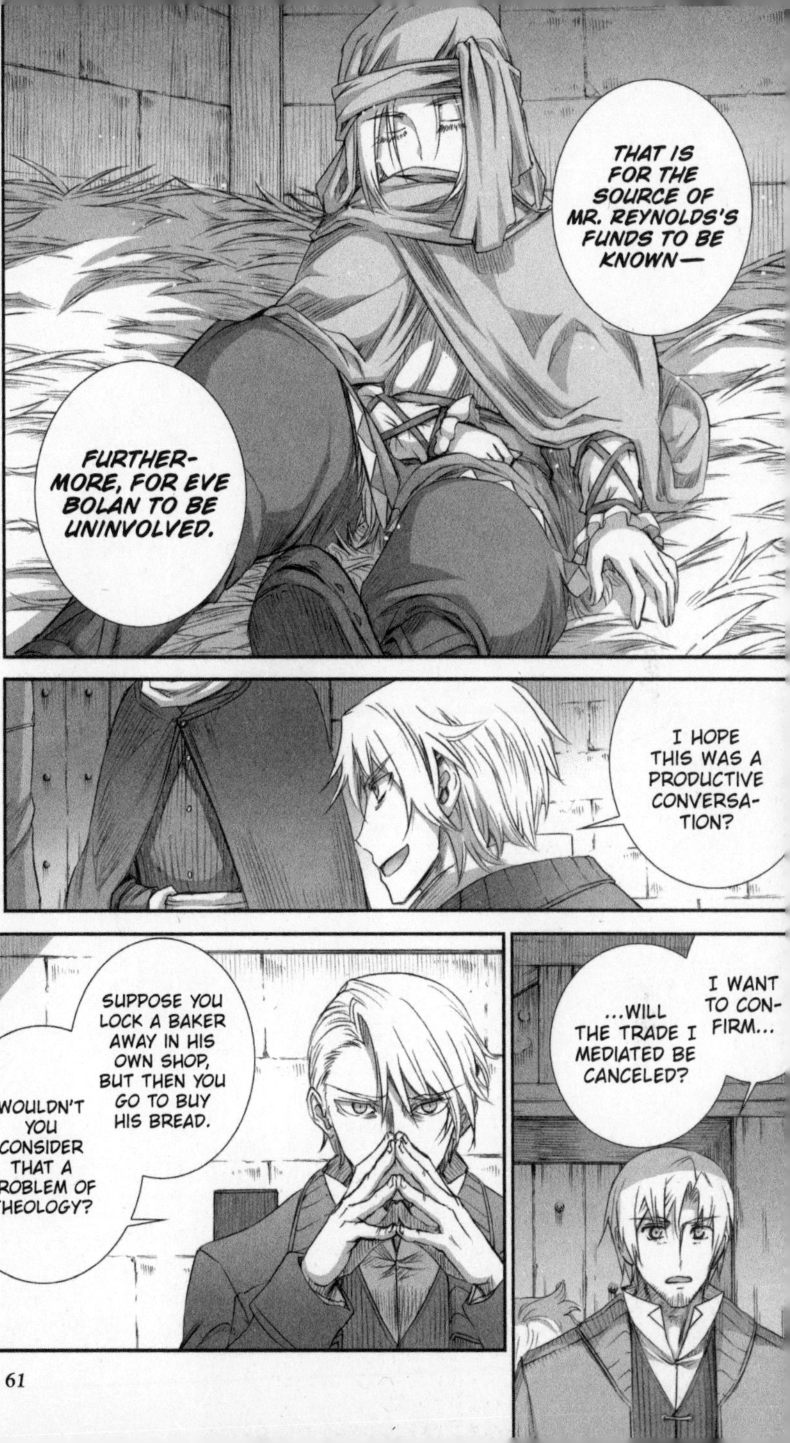
THAT IS FOR THE SOURCE OF MR. REYNOLDS'S FUNDS TO BE KNOWN—
FURTHER-MORE, FOR EVE BOLAN TO BE UNINVOLVED.
I HOPE THIS WAS A PRODUCTIVE CONVERSA-TION?
I WANT TO CON-FIRM...
...WILL THE TRADE I MEDIATED BE CANCELED?
SUPPOSE YOU LOCK A BAKER AWAY IN HIS OWN SHOP, BUT THEN YOU GO TO BUY HIS BREAD.
WOULDN'T YOU CONSIDER THAT A PROBLEM OF THEOLOGY?

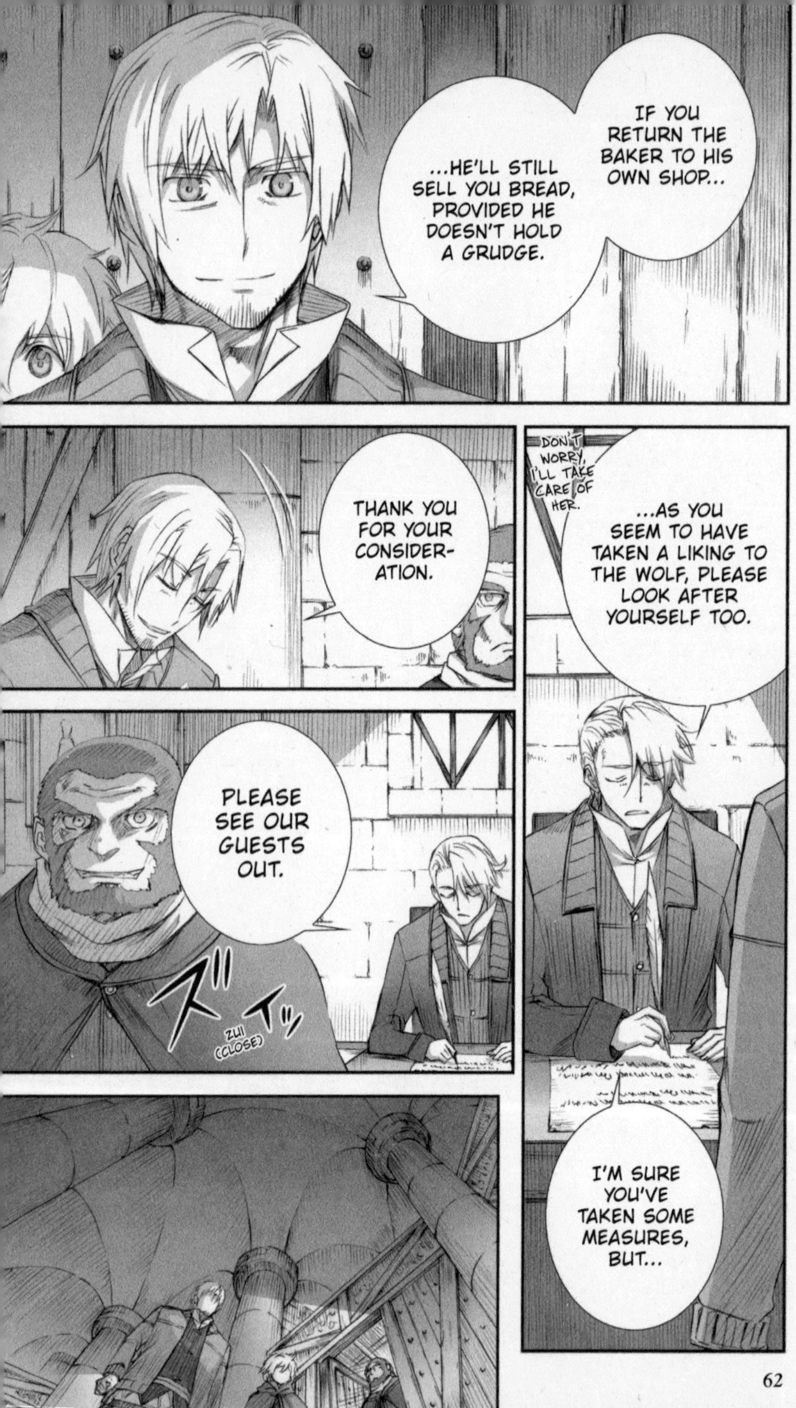
IF YOU RETURN THE BAKER TO HIS OWN SHOP...
...HE'LL STILL SELL YOU BREAD, PROVIDED HE DOESN'T HOLD A GRUDGE.
DON'T WORRY, I'LL TAKE CARE OF HER.
...AS YOU SEEM TO HAVE TAKEN A LIKING TO THE WOLF, PLEASE LOOK AFTER YOURSELF TOO.
I'M SURE YOU'VE TAKEN SOME MEASURES, BUT...
THANK YOU FOR YOUR CONSIDER-ATION.
PLEASE SEE OUR GUESTS OUT.
ズイッ
ZUI (CLOSE)

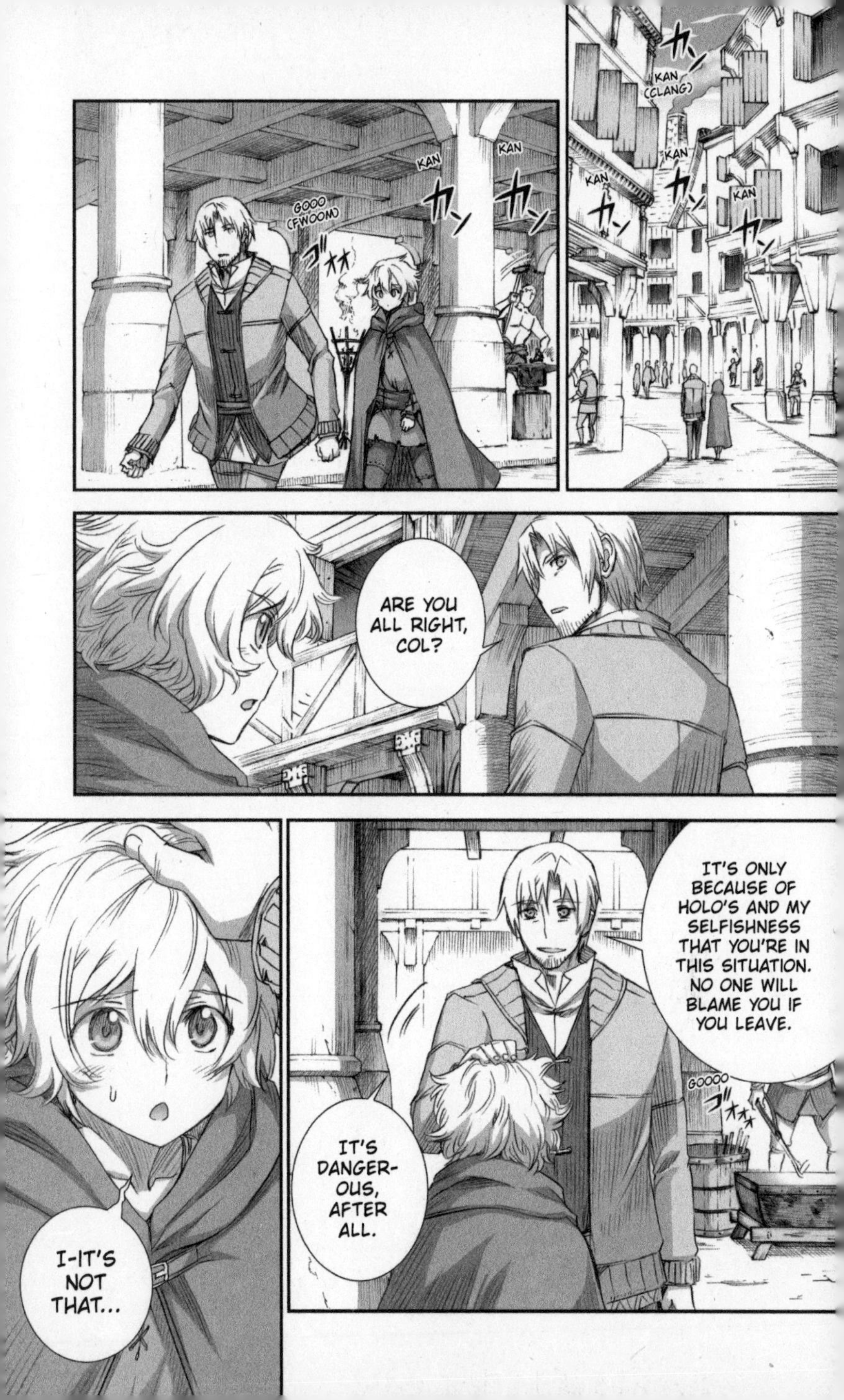

KAN (CLANG)
KAN
KAN
KAN
KAN
KAN
GOOO (FWOOM)
ARE YOU ALL RIGHT, COL?
IT'S ONLY BECAUSE OF HOLO'S AND MY SELFISHNESS THAT YOU'RE IN THIS SITUATION. NO ONE WILL BLAME YOU IF YOU LEAVE.
GOOOO
IT'S DANGER-OUS, AFTER ALL.
I-IT'S NOT THAT...

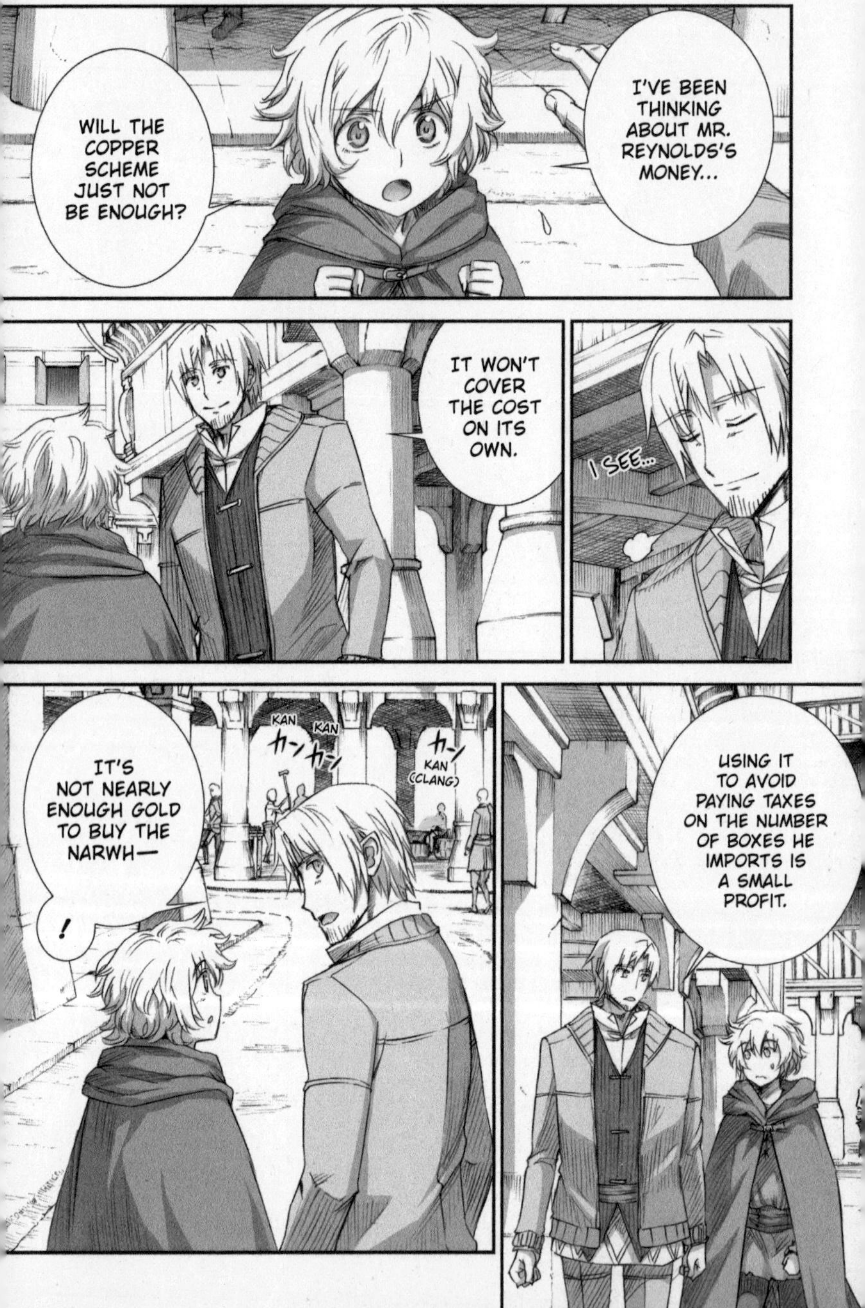
I'VE BEEN THINKING ABOUT MR. REYNOLDS'S MONEY...
WILL THE COPPER SCHEME JUST NOT BE ENOUGH?
I SEE...
IT WON'T COVER THE COST ON ITS OWN.
USING IT TO AVOID PAYING TAXES ON THE NUMBER OF BOXES HE IMPORTS IS A SMALL PROFIT.
カーン KAN (CLANG)
カーン KAN
カーン KAN
IT'S NOT NEARLY ENOUGH GOLD TO BUY THE NARWH—
!

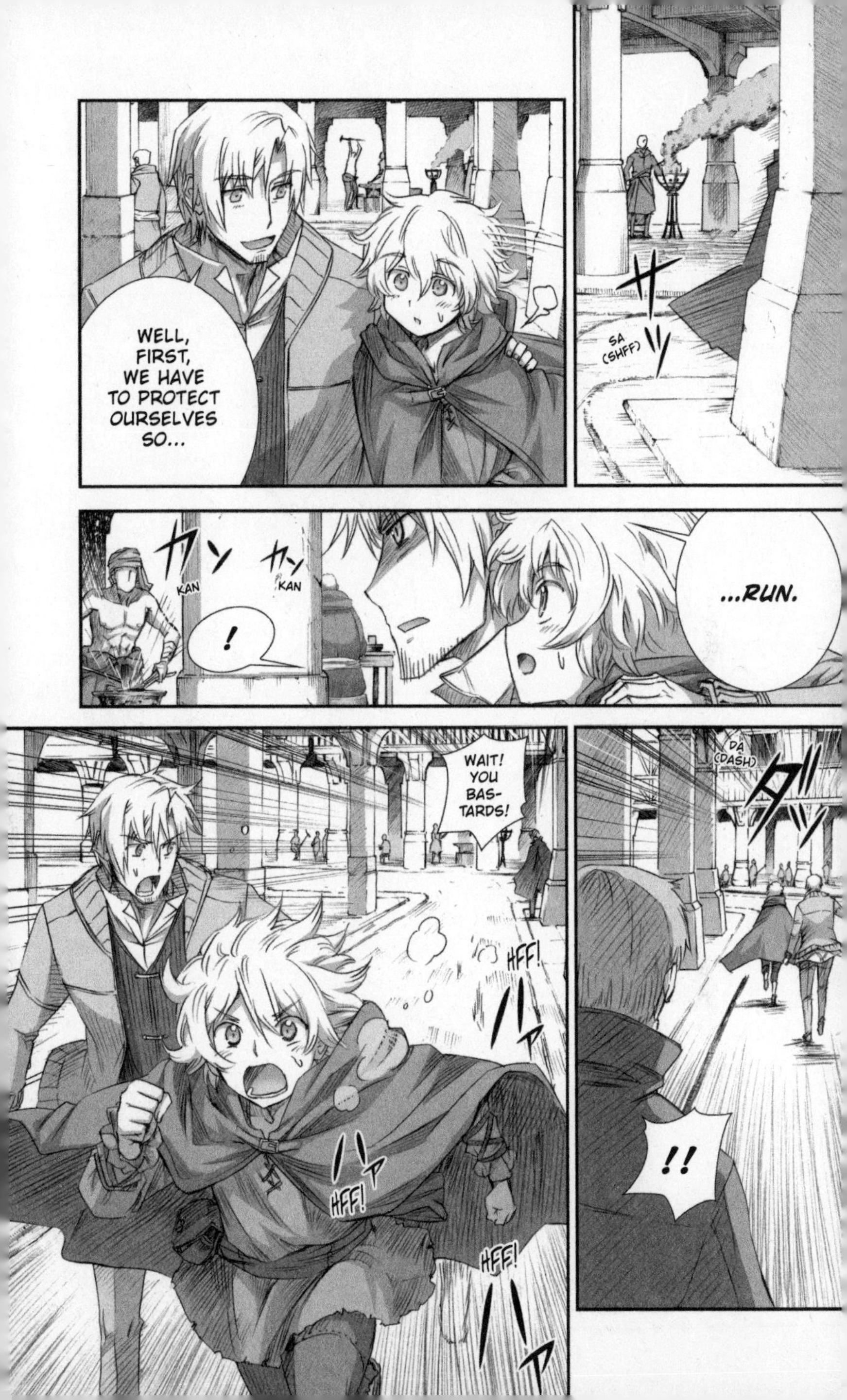
SA (SHFF)
WELL, FIRST, WE HAVE TO PROTECT OURSELVES SO...
...RUN.
!
KAN
KAN
DA (DASH)
!!
WAIT! YOU BASTARDS!
HFF!
HFF!
HFF!

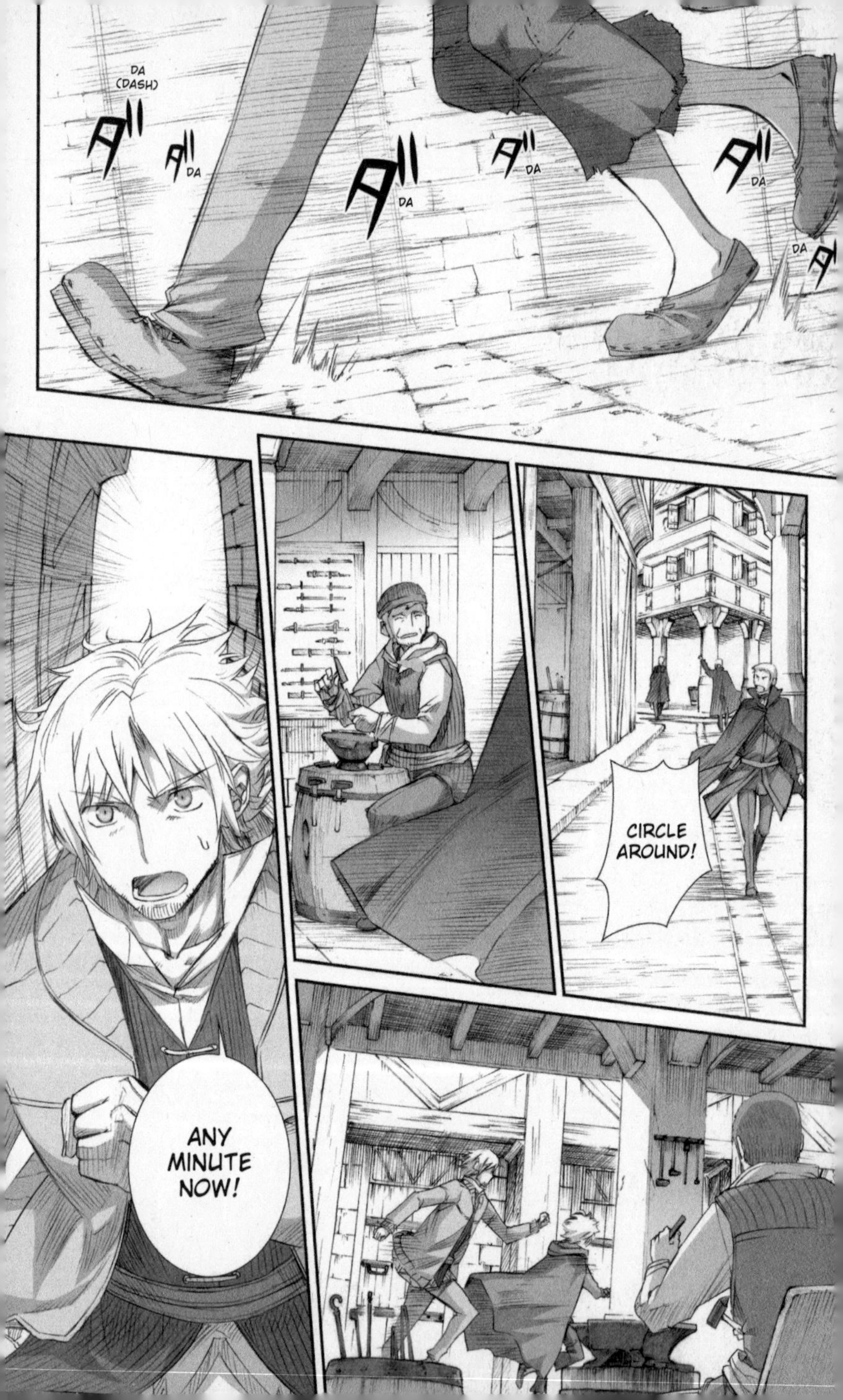
DA
DA
DA
DA
DA
DA (DASH)
CIRCLE AROUND!
ANY MINUTE NOW!

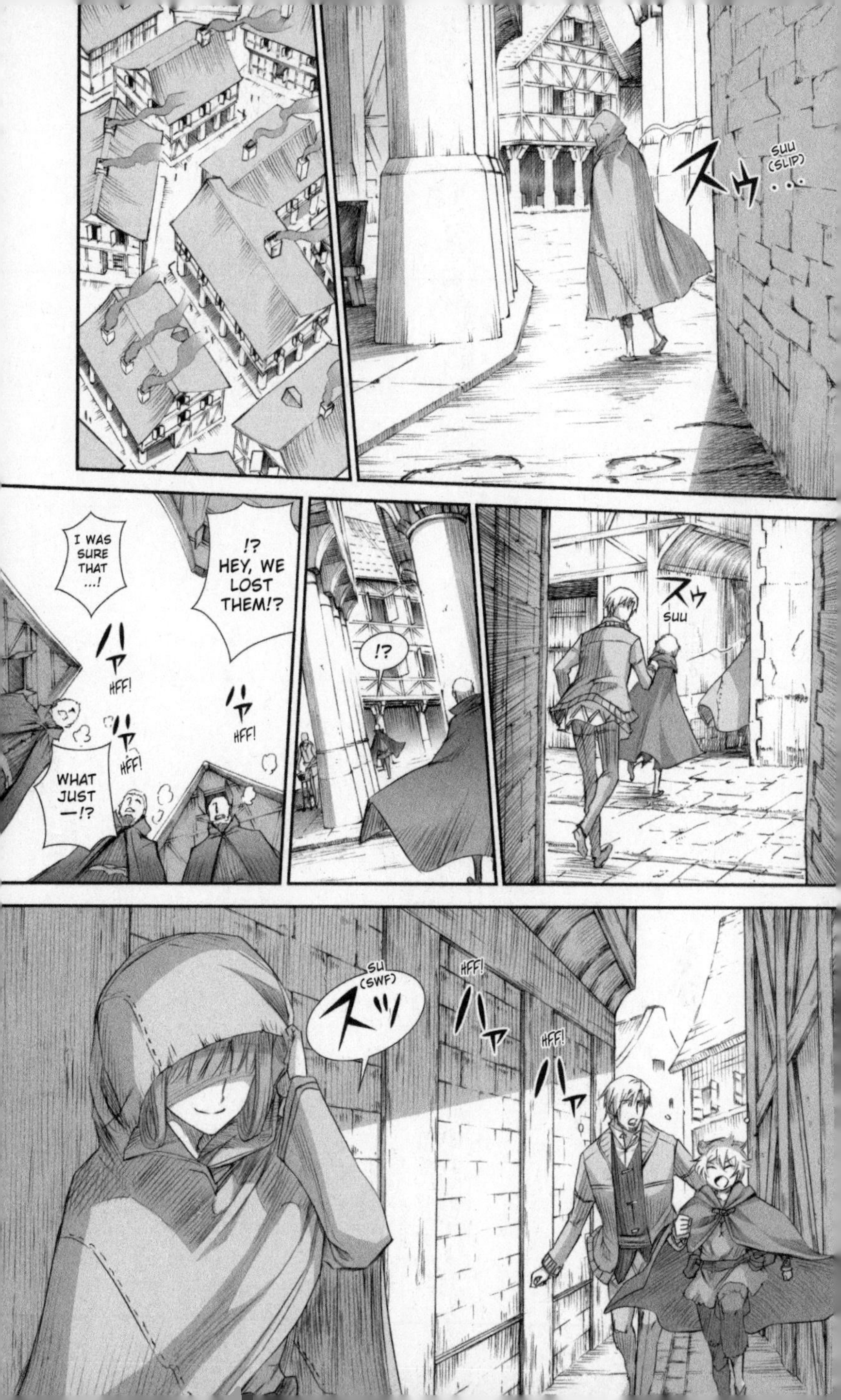

スゥ
SUU (SLIP)...
スゥ
SUU
!?
!? HEY, WE LOST THEM!?
I WAS SURE THAT ...!
ハァ
HFF!
ハァ
HFF!
ハァ
HFF!
WHAT JUST—!?
ハァ
HFF!
ハァ
HFF!
ズッ
SU (SWF)

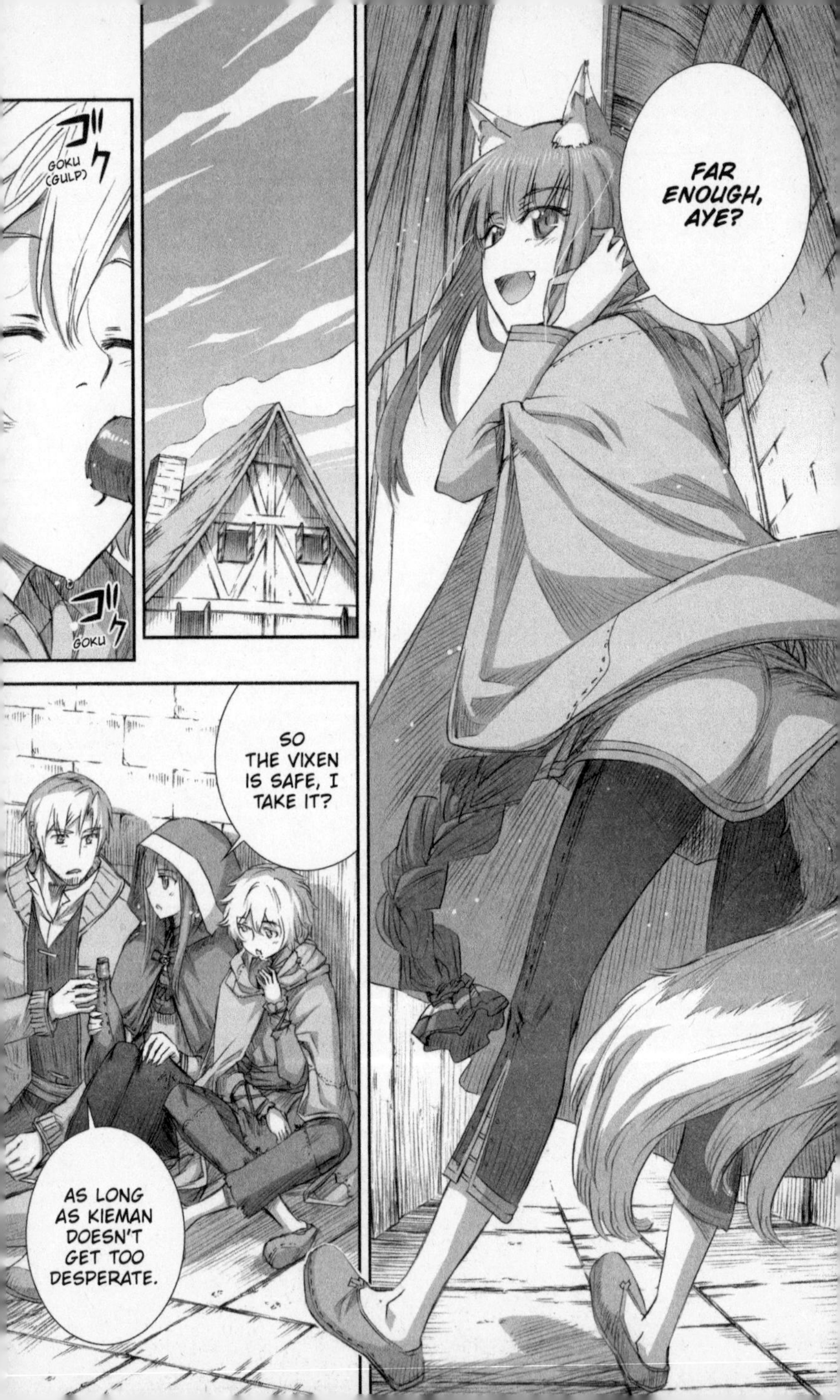
FAR ENOUGH, AYE?
ゴク
GOKU (GULP)
ゴク
GOKU
SO THE VIXEN IS SAFE, I TAKE IT?
AS LONG AS KIEMAN DOESN'T GET TOO DESPERATE.

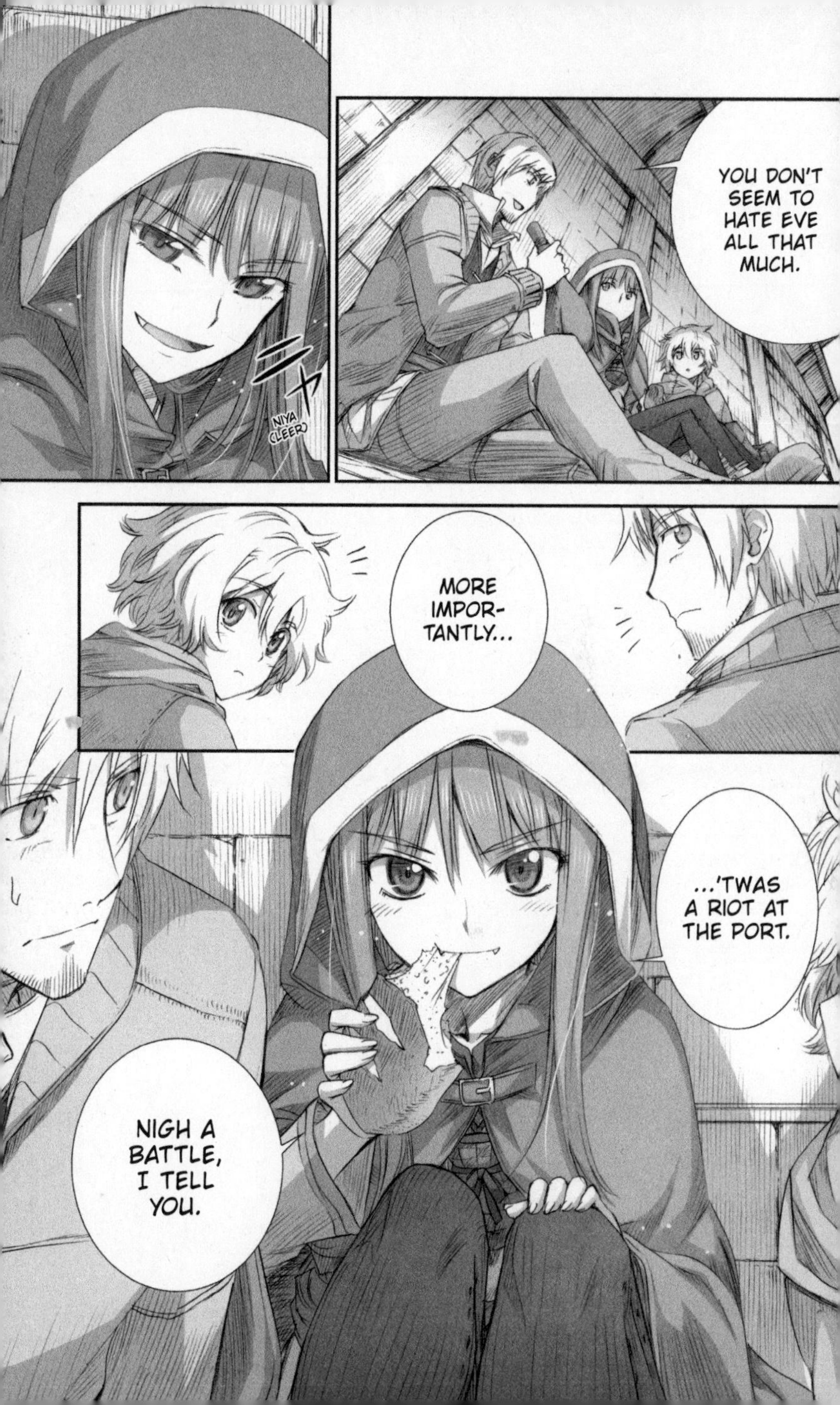
YOU DON'T SEEM TO HATE EVE ALL THAT MUCH.
NIYA (LEER)
MORE IMPORTANTLY...
...'TWAS A RIOT AT THE PORT.
NIGH A BATTLE, I TELL YOU.

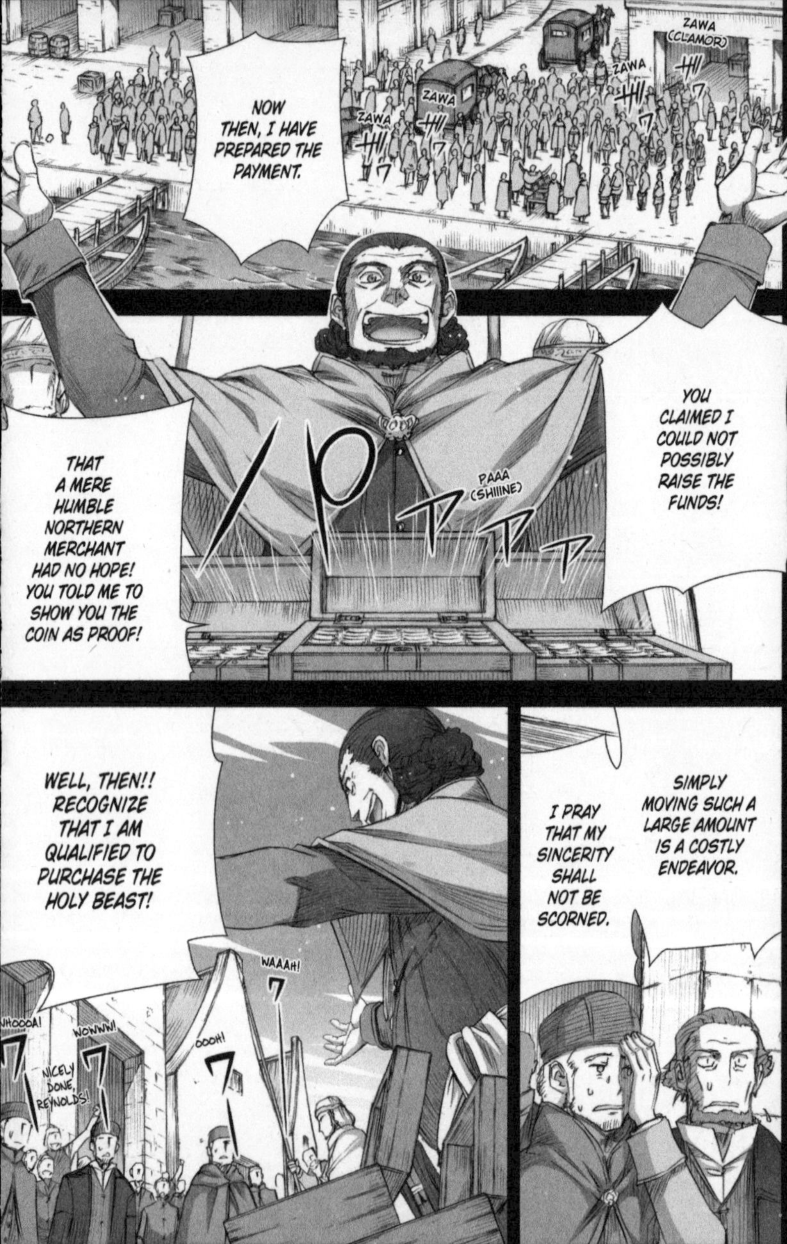
ZAWA (CLAMOR)
ZAWA
ZAWA
ZAWA
NOW THEN, I HAVE PREPARED THE PAYMENT.
YOU CLAIMED I COULD NOT POSSIBLY RAISE THE FUNDS!
PAAA (SHIIINE)
THAT A MERE HUMBLE NORTHERN MERCHANT HAD NO HOPE! YOU TOLD ME TO SHOW YOU THE COIN AS PROOF!
SIMPLY MOVING SUCH A LARGE AMOUNT IS A COSTLY ENDEAVOR.
I PRAY THAT MY SINCERITY SHALL NOT BE SCORNED.
WELL, THEN!! RECOGNIZE THAT I AM QUALIFIED TO PURCHASE THE HOLY BEAST!
WAAAH!
OOOH!
WOWWW!
NICELY DONE, REYNOLDS!
HOOOA!

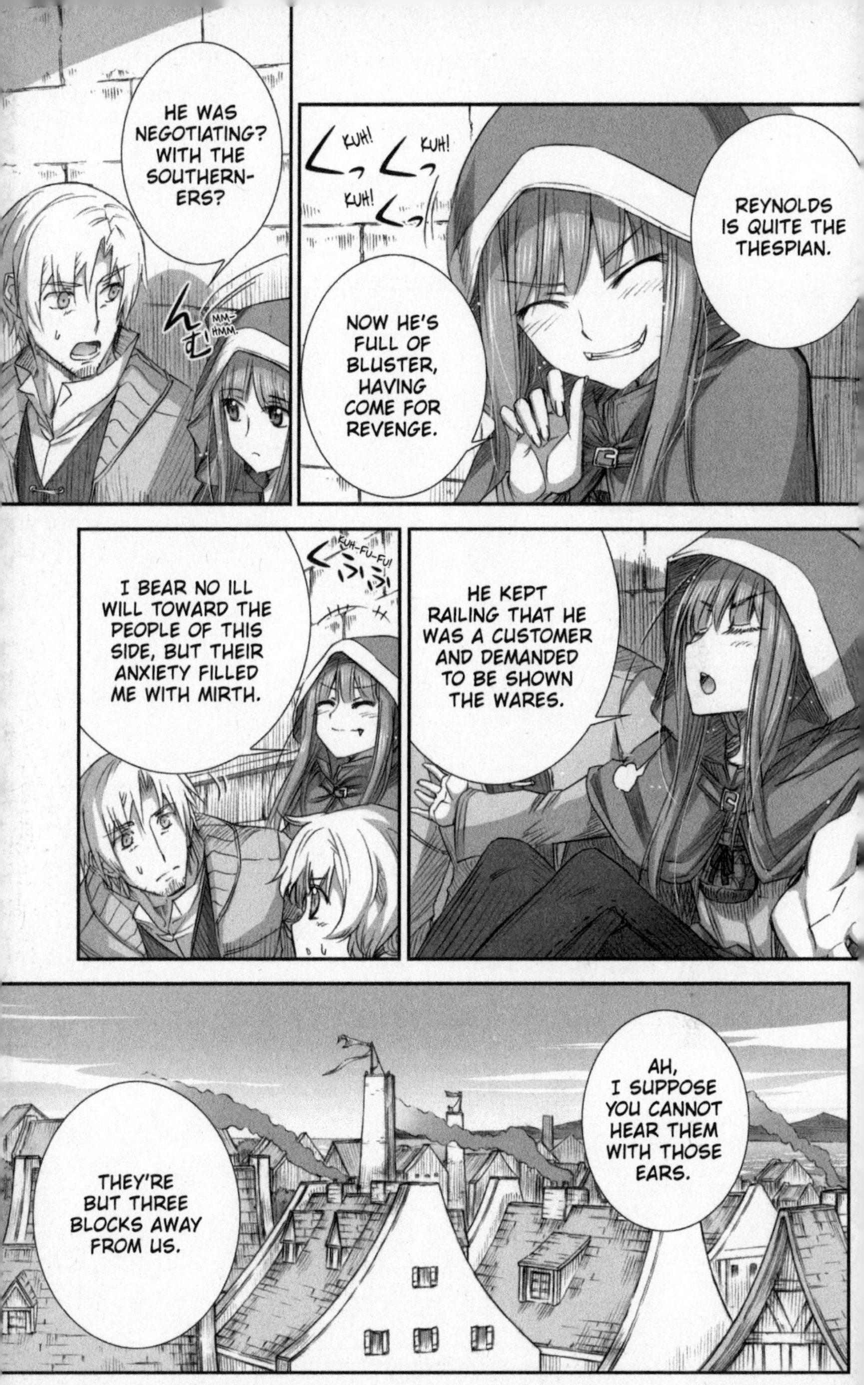
REYNOLDS IS QUITE THE THESPIAN.
KUH! KUH! KUH!
NOW HE'S FULL OF BLUSTER, HAVING COME FOR REVENGE.
HE WAS NEGOTIATING? WITH THE SOUTHERNERS?
MM-HMM.
HE KEPT RAILING THAT HE WAS A CUSTOMER AND DEMANDED TO BE SHOWN THE WARES.
KUH-FU-FU!
I BEAR NO ILL WILL TOWARD THE PEOPLE OF THIS SIDE, BUT THEIR ANXIETY FILLED ME WITH MIRTH.
AH, I SUPPOSE YOU CANNOT HEAR THEM WITH THOSE EARS.
THEY'RE BUT THREE BLOCKS AWAY FROM US.

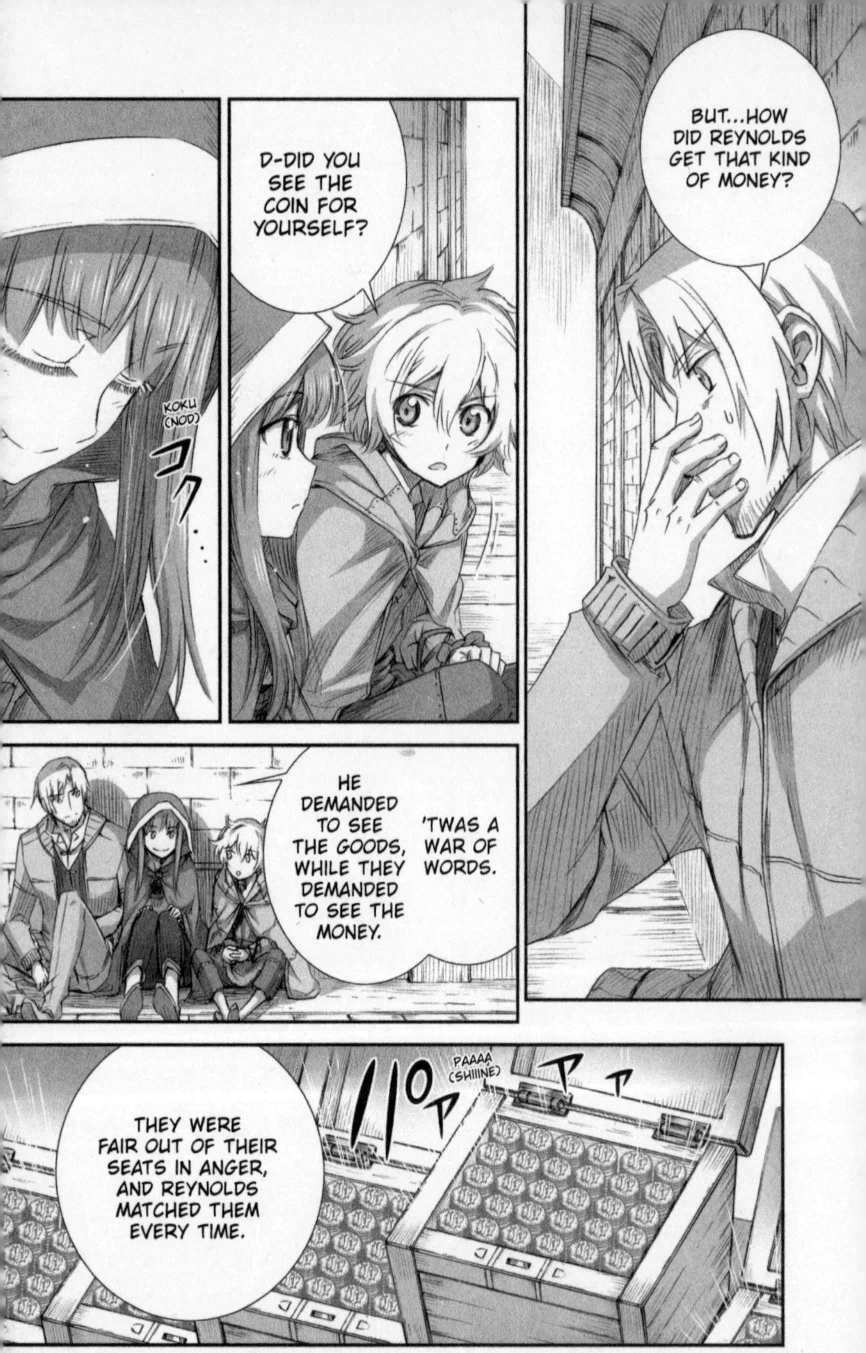

BUT...HOW DID REYNOLDS GET THAT KIND OF MONEY?
D-DID YOU SEE THE COIN FOR YOURSELF?
KOKU (NOD)
'TWAS A WAR OF WORDS.
HE DEMANDED TO SEE THE GOODS, WHILE THEY DEMANDED TO SEE THE MONEY.
PAAAA (SHIIINE)
THEY WERE FAIR OUT OF THEIR SEATS IN ANGER, AND REYNOLDS MATCHED THEM EVERY TIME.

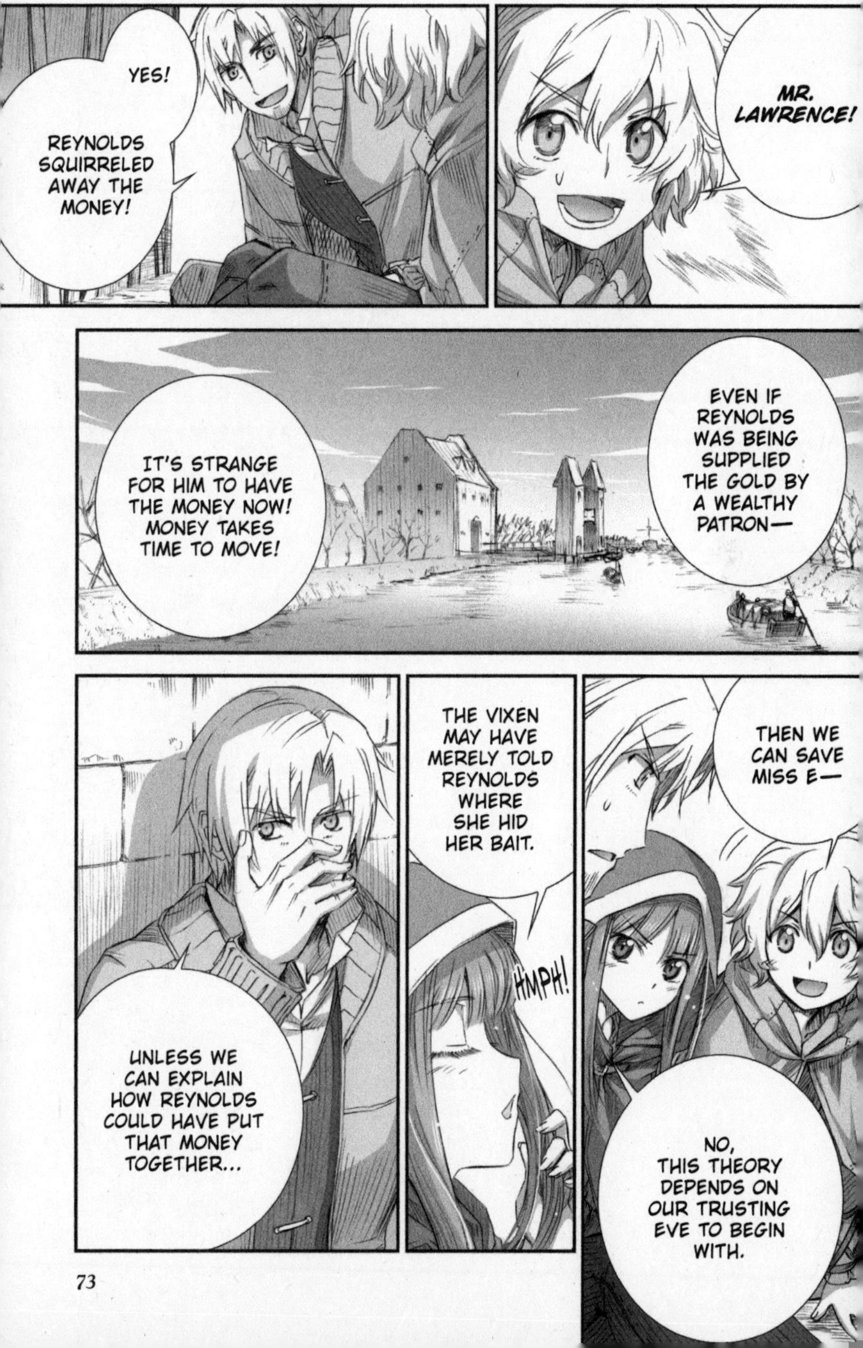
MR. LAWRENCE!
YES!
REYNOLDS SQUIRRELED AWAY THE MONEY!
EVEN IF REYNOLDS WAS BEING SUPPLIED THE GOLD BY A WEALTHY PATRON—
IT'S STRANGE FOR HIM TO HAVE THE MONEY NOW! MONEY TAKES TIME TO MOVE!
THEN WE CAN SAVE MISS E—
NO, THIS THEORY DEPENDS ON OUR TRUSTING EVE TO BEGIN WITH.
THE VIXEN MAY HAVE MERELY TOLD REYNOLDS WHERE SHE HID HER BAIT.
HMPH!
UNLESS WE CAN EXPLAIN HOW REYNOLDS COULD HAVE PUT THAT MONEY TOGETHER...

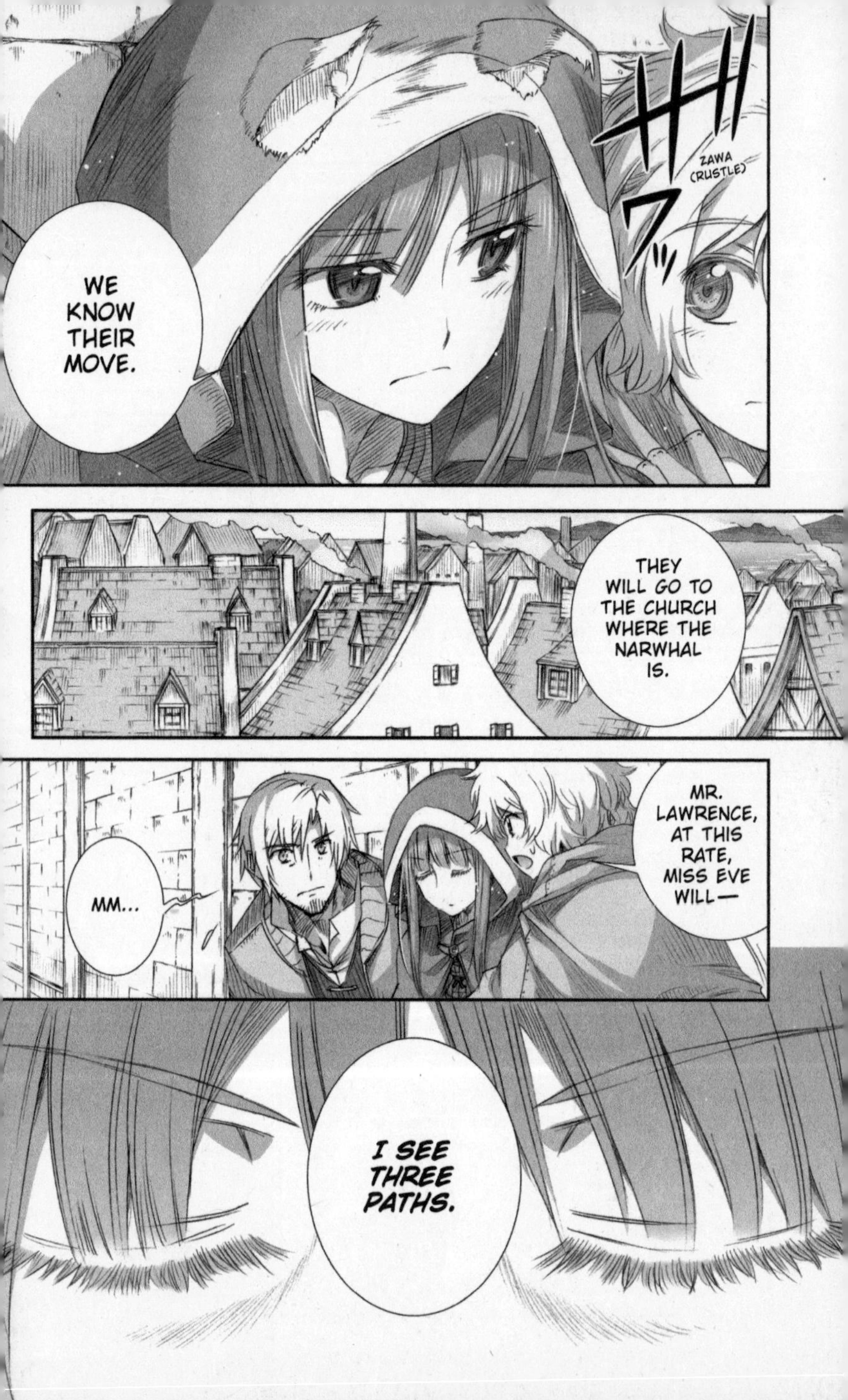
ZAWA (RUSTLE)
WE KNOW THEIR MOVE.
THEY WILL GO TO THE CHURCH WHERE THE NARWHAL IS.
MR. LAWRENCE, AT THIS RATE, MISS EVE WILL—
MM...
I SEE THREE PATHS.

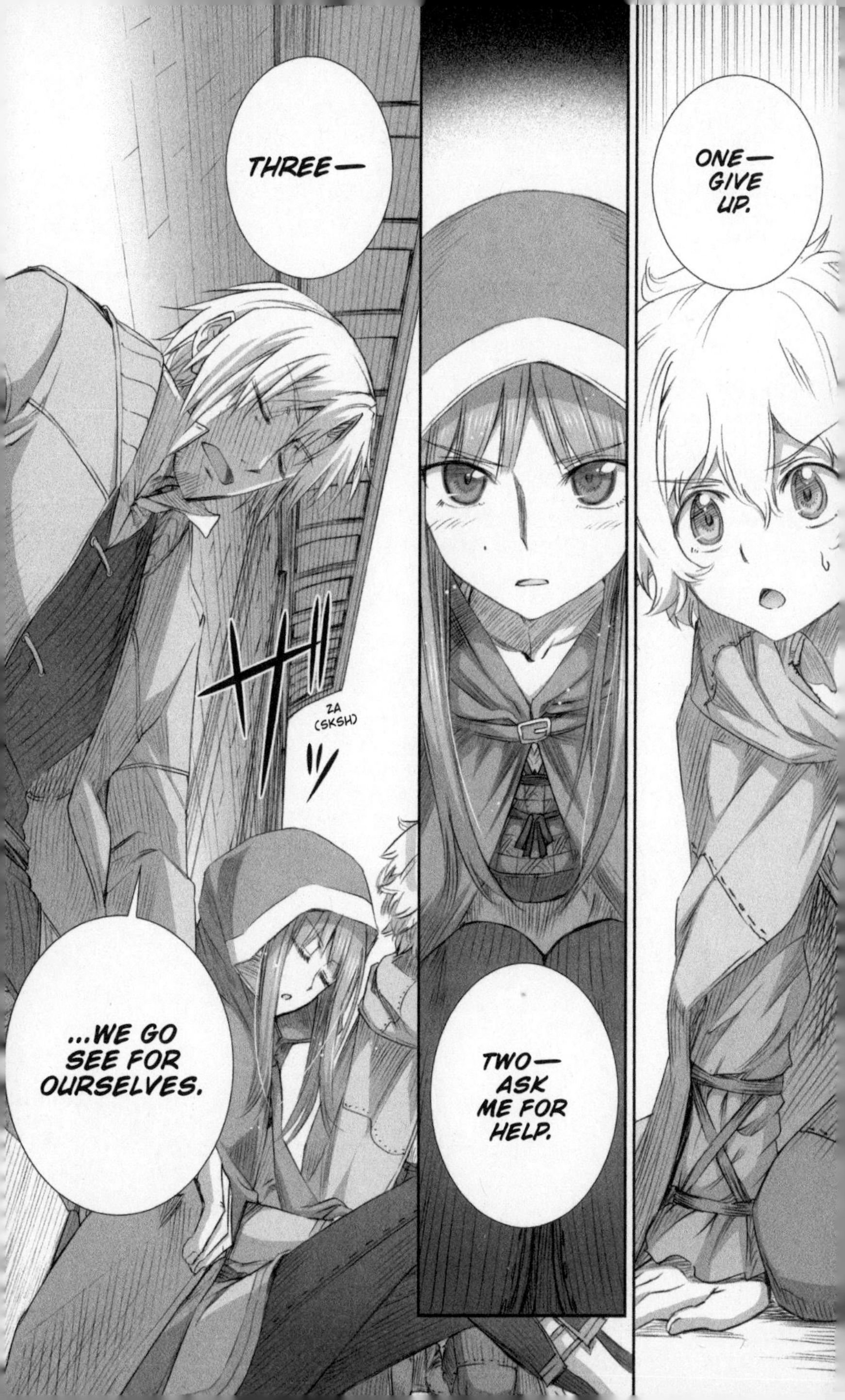
ONE— GIVE UP.
TWO— ASK ME FOR HELP.
THREE—
ZA (SKSH)
...WE GO SEE FOR OURSELVES.

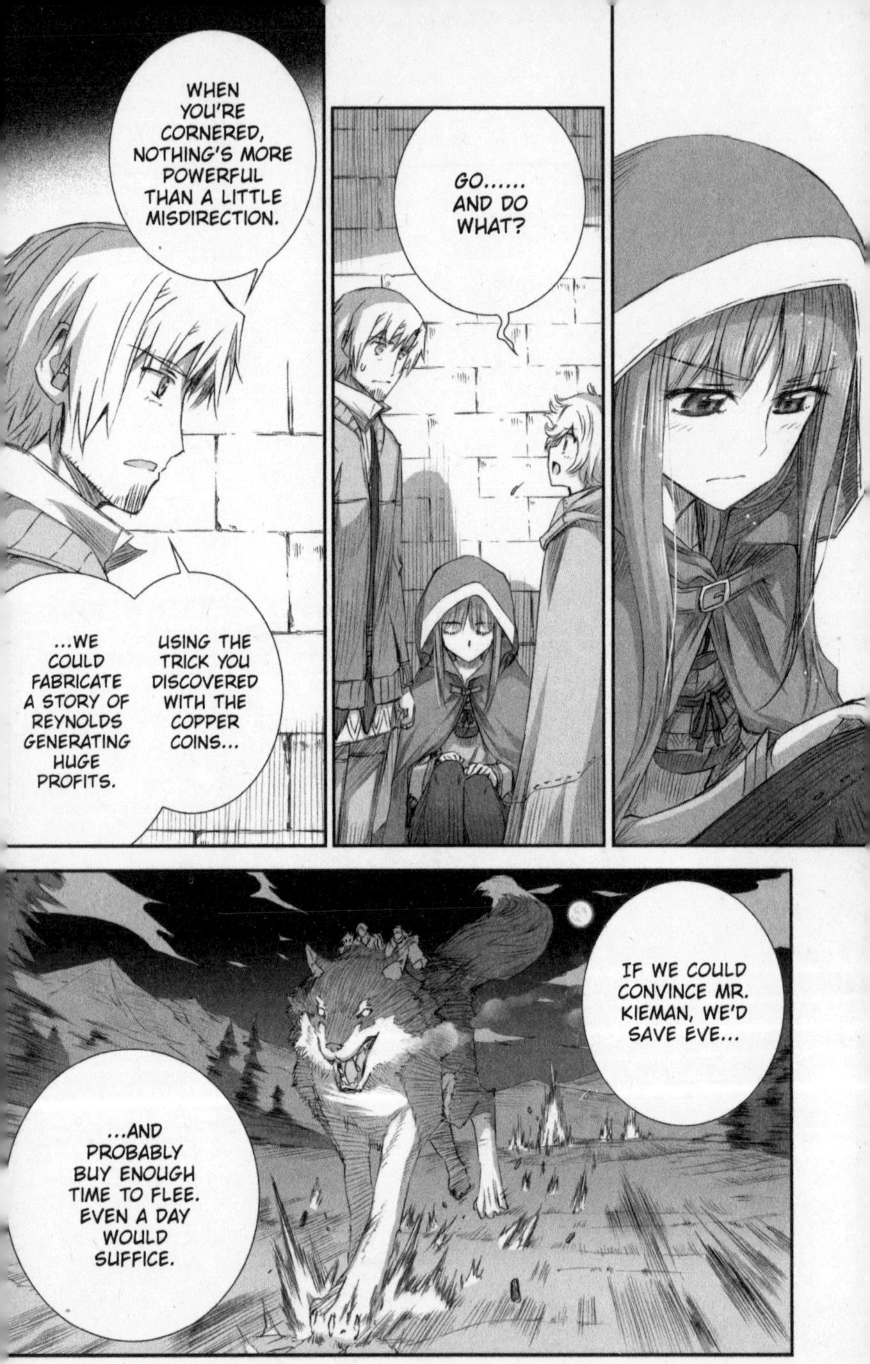
GO...... AND DO WHAT?
WHEN YOU'RE CORNERED, NOTHING'S MORE POWERFUL THAN A LITTLE MISDIRECTION.
USING THE TRICK YOU DISCOVERED WITH THE COPPER COINS...
...WE COULD FABRICATE A STORY OF REYNOLDS GENERATING HUGE PROFITS.
IF WE COULD CONVINCE MR. KIEMAN, WE'D SAVE EVE...
...AND PROBABLY BUY ENOUGH TIME TO FLEE. EVEN A DAY WOULD SUFFICE.

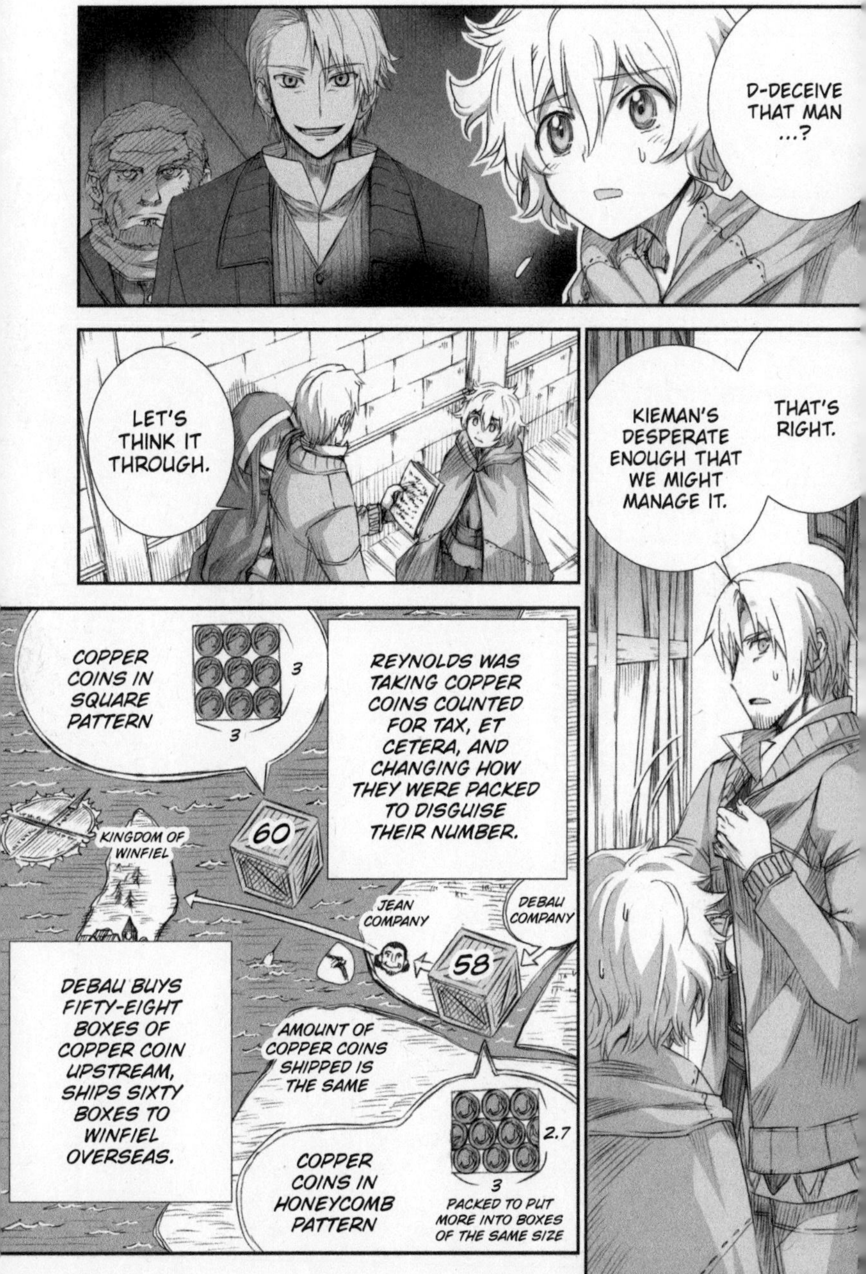
D-DECEIVE THAT MAN ...?
THAT'S RIGHT.
KIEMAN'S DESPERATE ENOUGH THAT WE MIGHT MANAGE IT.
LET'S THINK IT THROUGH.
REYNOLDS WAS TAKING COPPER COINS COUNTED FOR TAX, ET CETERA, AND CHANGING HOW THEY WERE PACKED TO DISGUISE THEIR NUMBER.
COPPER COINS IN SQUARE PATTERN
3
3
60
KINGDOM OF WINFIEL
DEBAU COMPANY
58
JEAN COMPANY
AMOUNT OF COPPER COINS SHIPPED IS THE SAME
2.7
3
PACKED TO PUT MORE INTO BOXES OF THE SAME SIZE
COPPER COINS IN HONEYCOMB PATTERN
DEBAU BUYS FIFTY-EIGHT BOXES OF COPPER COIN UPSTREAM, SHIPS SIXTY BOXES TO WINFIEL OVERSEAS.

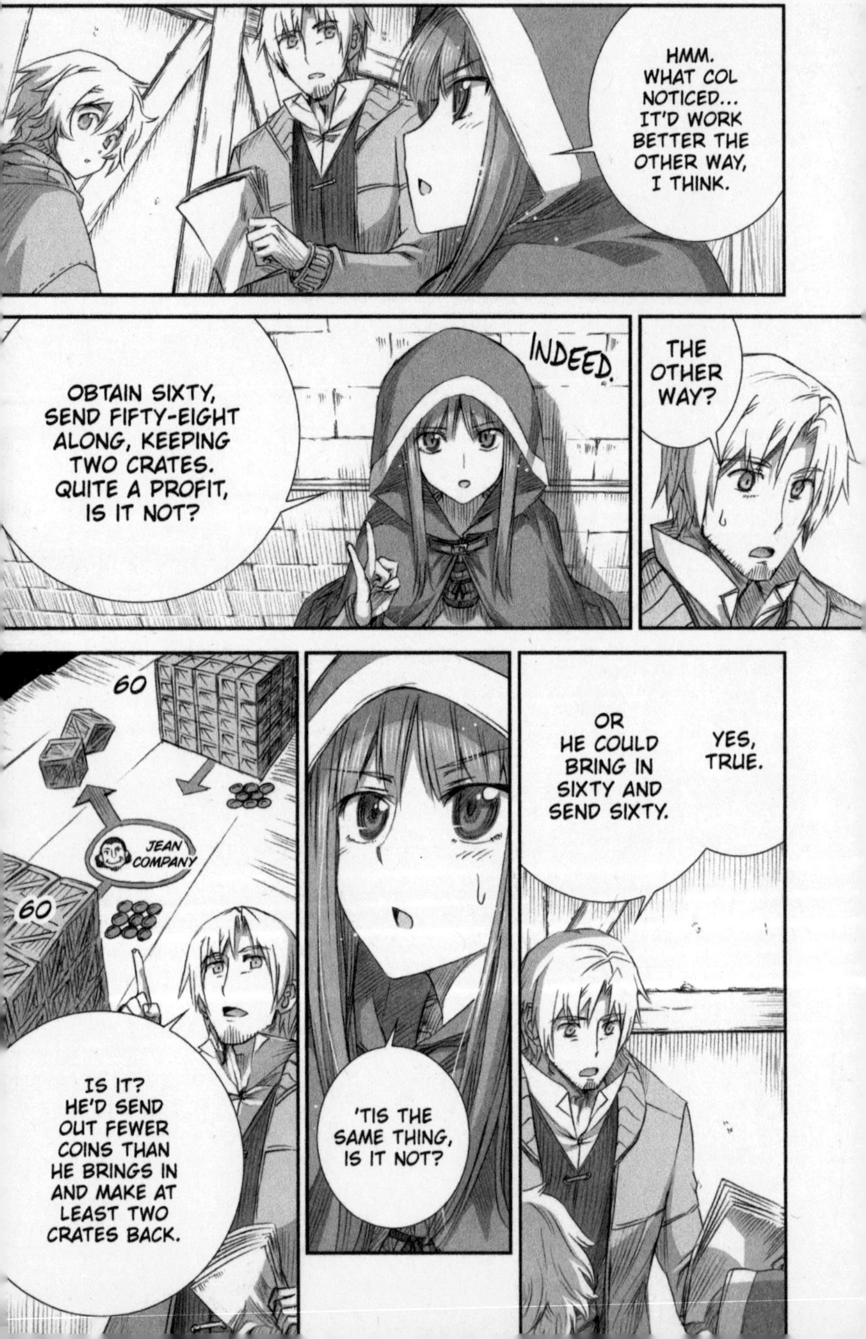
HMM. WHAT COL NOTICED... IT'D WORK BETTER THE OTHER WAY, I THINK.
THE OTHER WAY?
INDEED.
OBTAIN SIXTY, SEND FIFTY-EIGHT ALONG, KEEPING TWO CRATES. QUITE A PROFIT, IS IT NOT?
YES, TRUE.
OR HE COULD BRING IN SIXTY AND SEND SIXTY.
'TIS THE SAME THING, IS IT NOT?
60
JEAN COMPANY
60
IS IT? HE'D SEND OUT FEWER COINS THAN HE BRINGS IN AND MAKE AT LEAST TWO CRATES BACK.

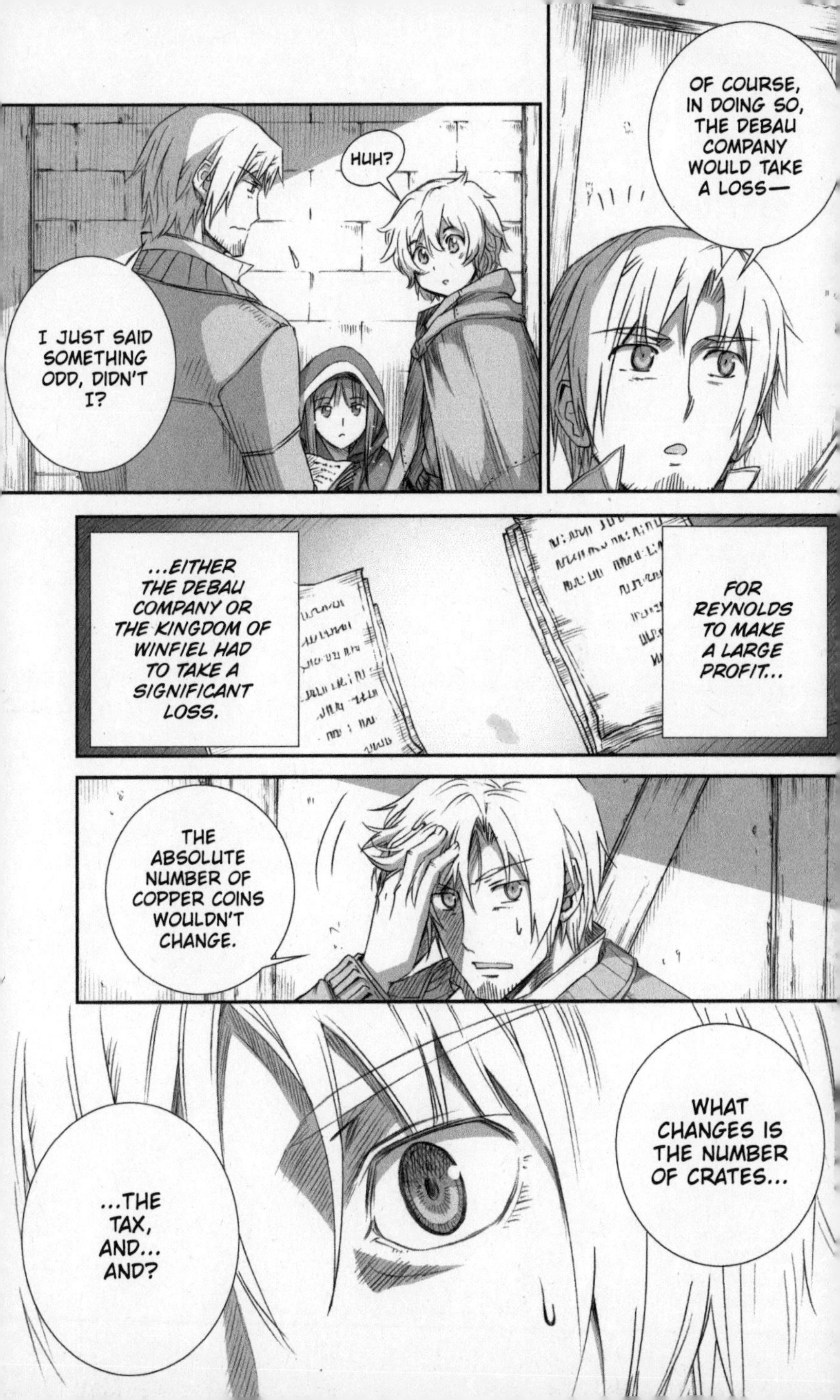
OF COURSE, IN DOING SO, THE DEBAU COMPANY WOULD TAKE A LOSS—
HUH?
I JUST SAID SOMETHING ODD, DIDN'T I?
FOR REYNOLDS TO MAKE A LARGE PROFIT...
...EITHER THE DEBAU COMPANY OR THE KINGDOM OF WINFIEL HAD TO TAKE A SIGNIFICANT LOSS.
THE ABSOLUTE NUMBER OF COPPER COINS WOULDN'T CHANGE.
WHAT CHANGES IS THE NUMBER OF CRATES...
...THE TAX, AND... AND?

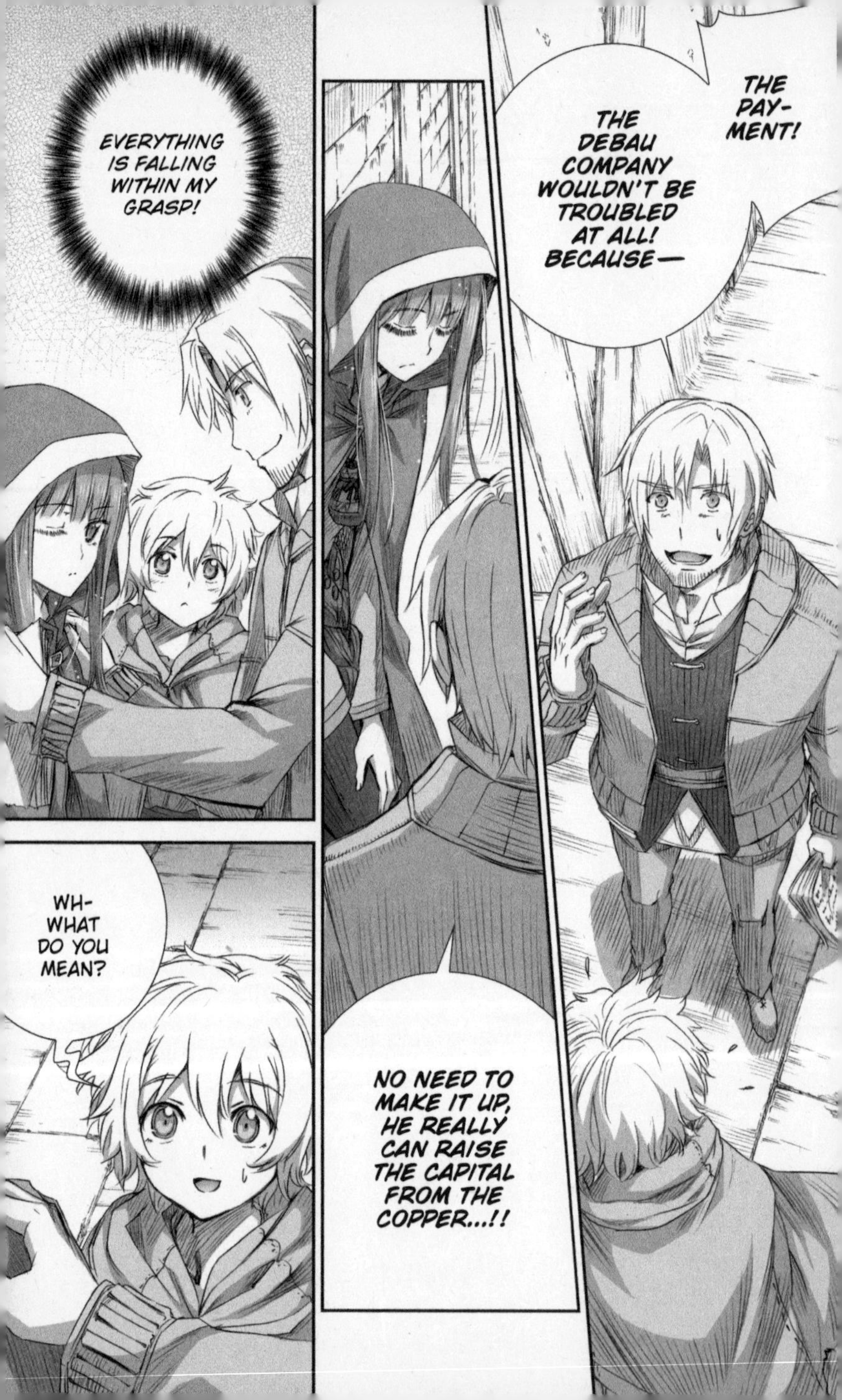
THE PAY-MENT!
THE DEBAU COMPANY WOULDN'T BE TROUBLED AT ALL! BECAUSE—
NO NEED TO MAKE IT UP, HE REALLY CAN RAISE THE CAPITAL FROM THE COPPER...!!
EVERYTHING IS FALLING WITHIN MY GRASP!
WH-WHAT DO YOU MEAN?

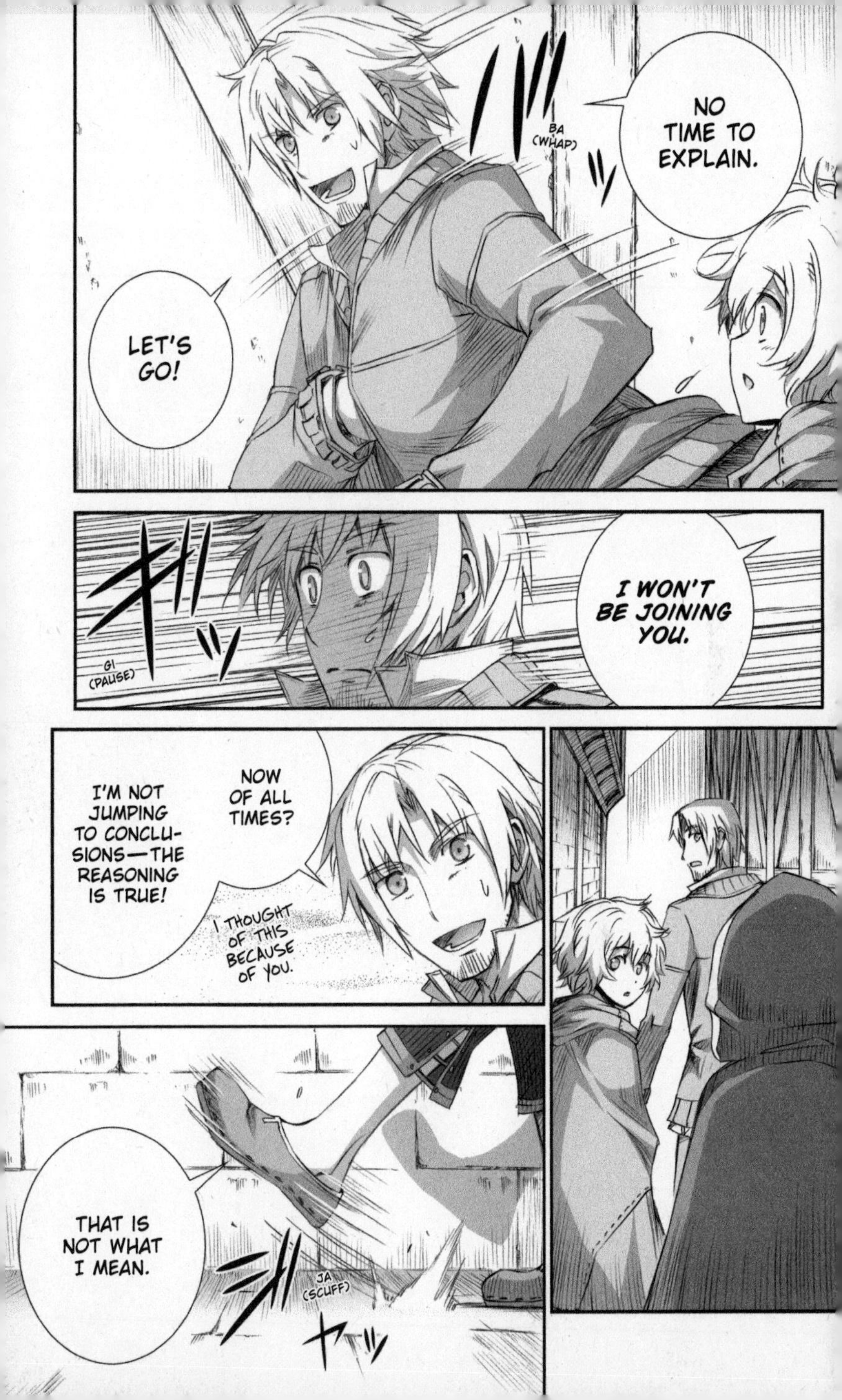
NO TIME TO EXPLAIN.
BA (WHAP)
LET'S GO!
I WON'T BE JOINING YOU.
GI (PAUSE)
NOW OF ALL TIMES?
I'M NOT JUMPING TO CONCLUSIONS—THE REASONING IS TRUE!
I THOUGHT OF THIS BECAUSE OF YOU.
THAT IS NOT WHAT I MEAN.
JA (SCUFF)

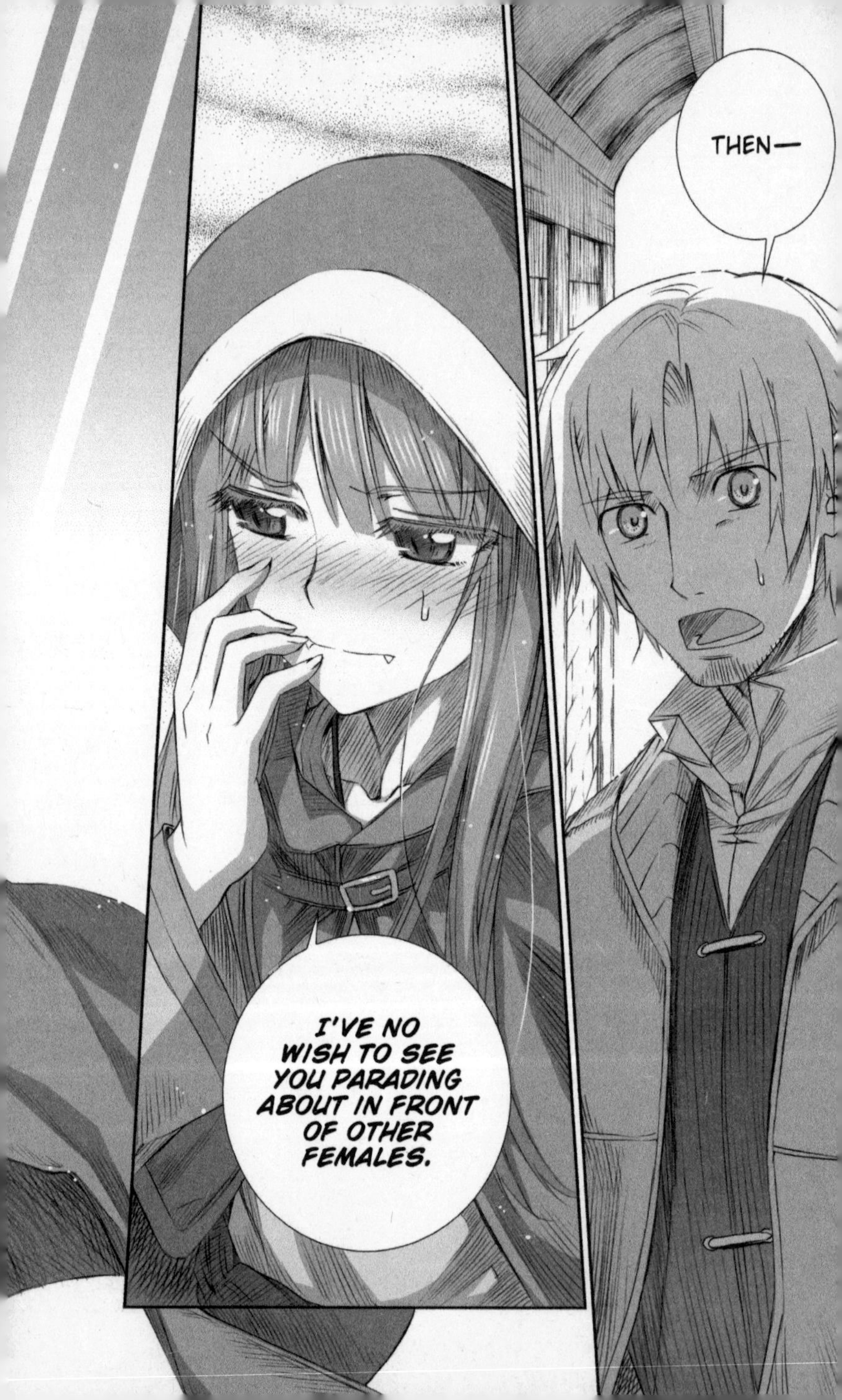
THEN—
I'VE NO WISH TO SEE YOU PARADING ABOUT IN FRONT OF OTHER FEMALES.

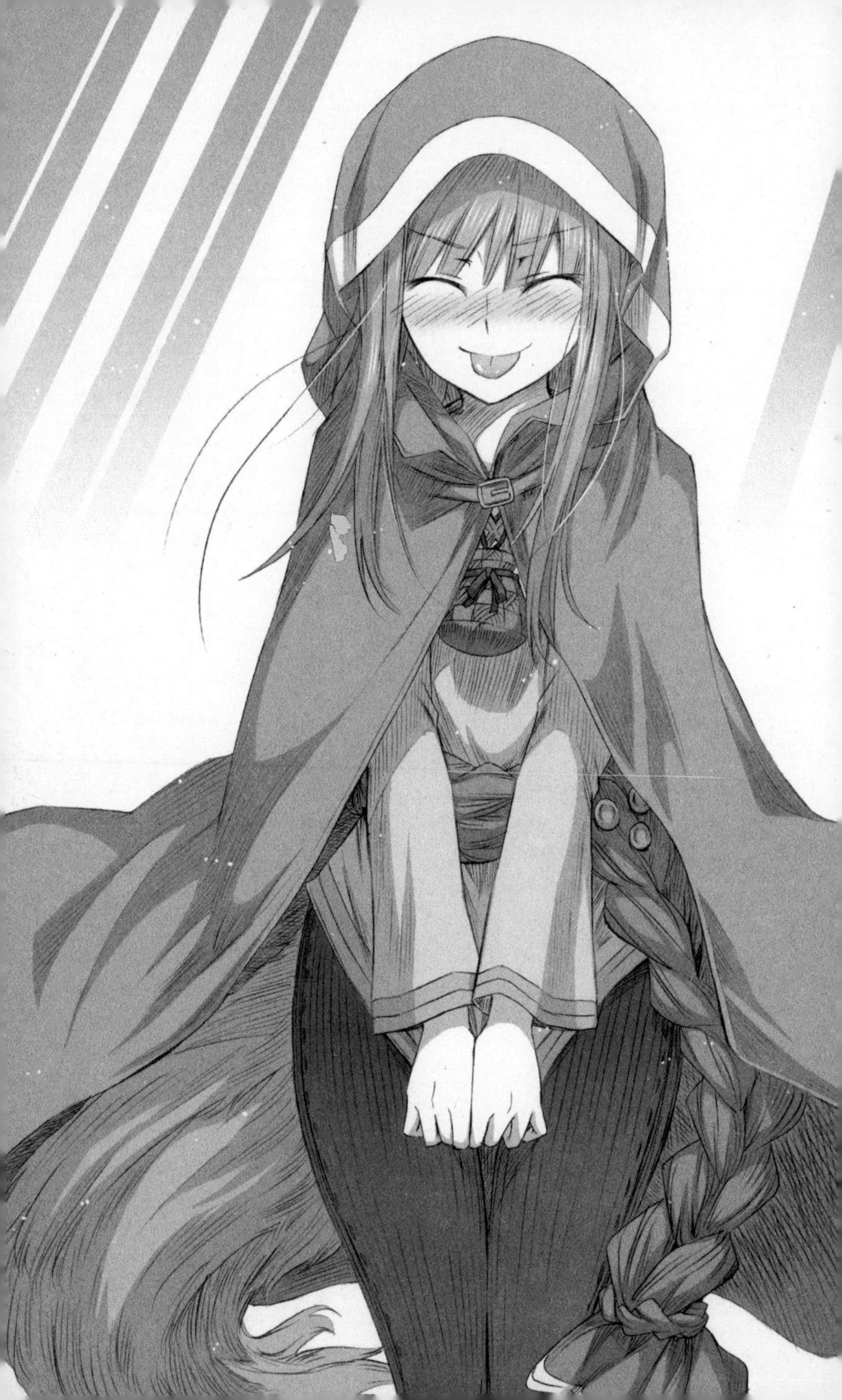

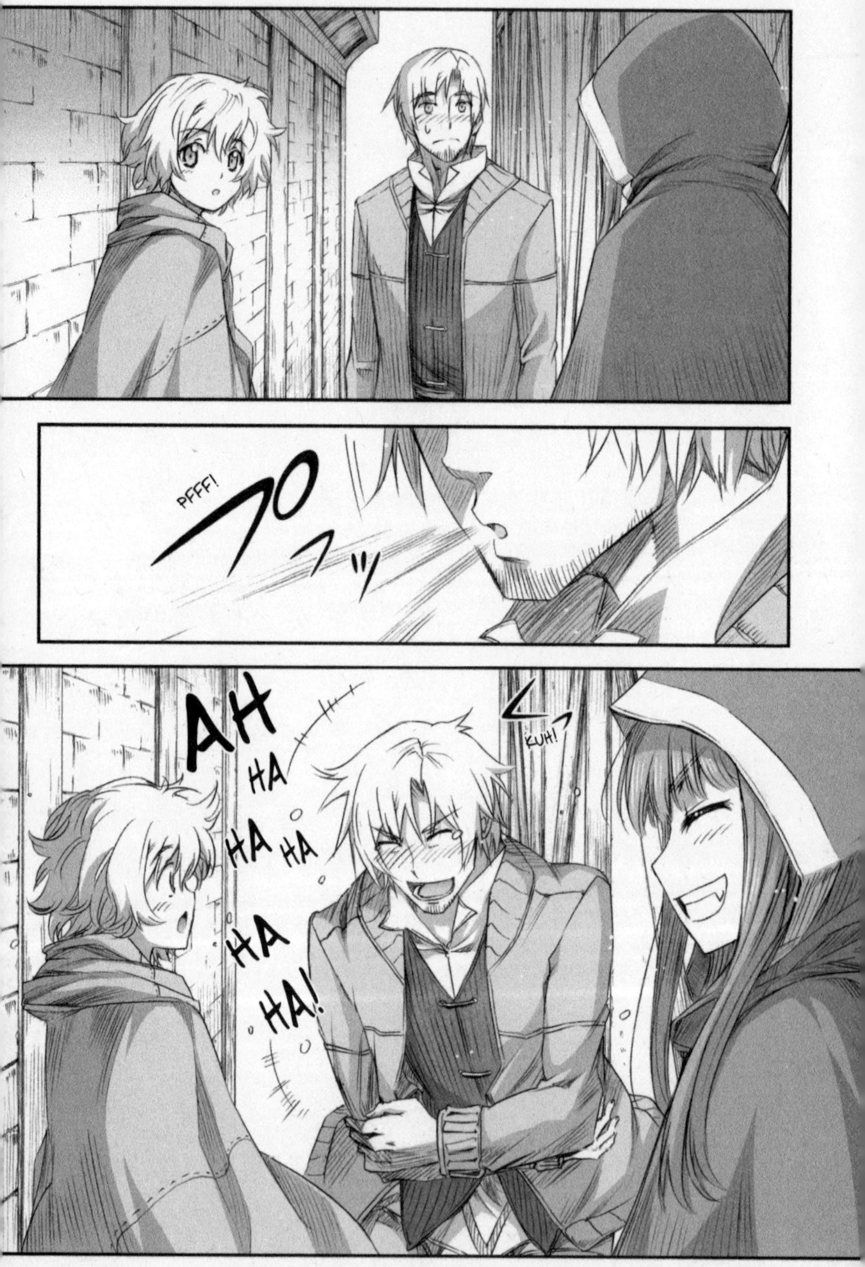
PFFF!
プッ
AH HA HA HA HA HA HA!
KUH!
くっ

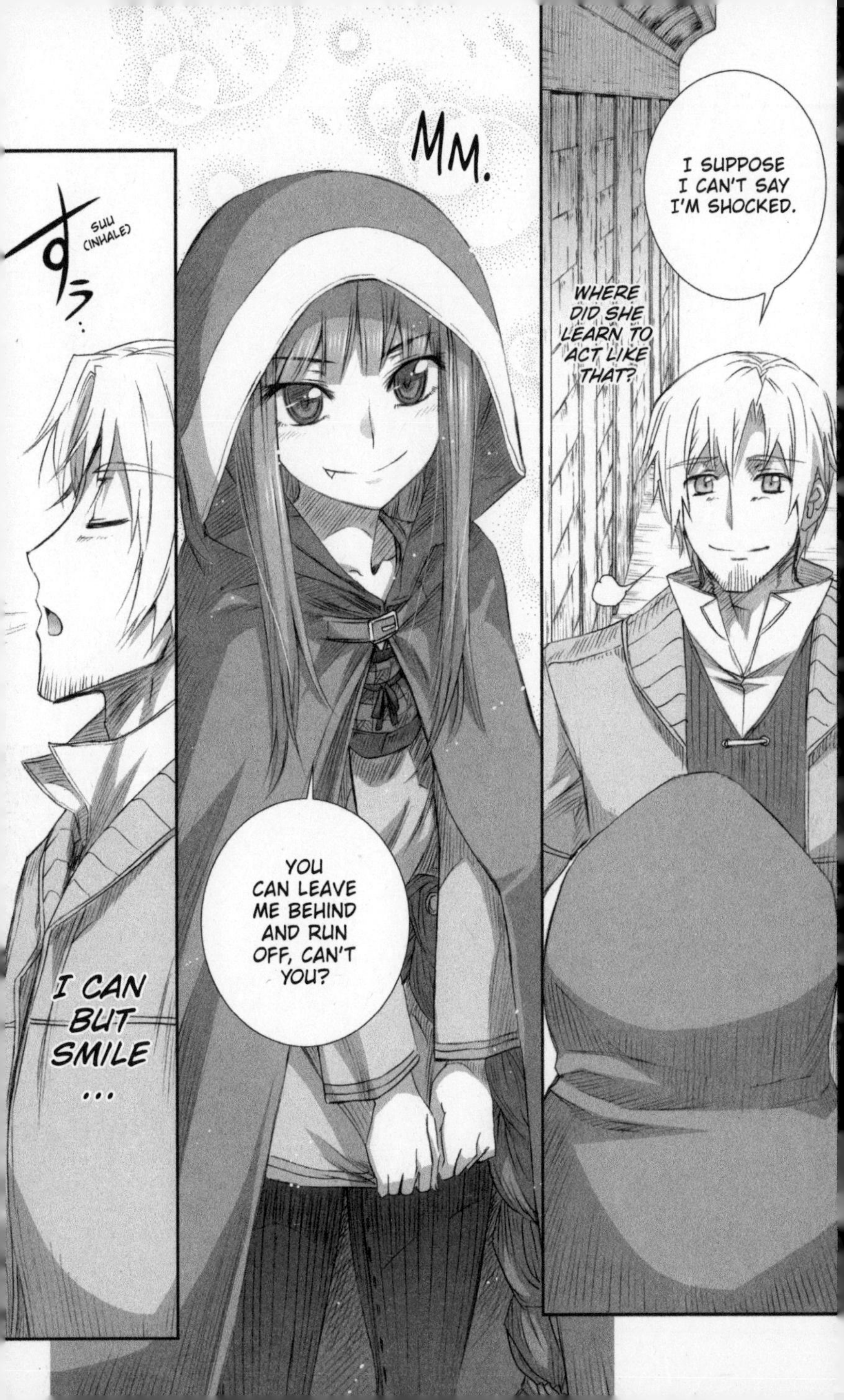
I SUPPOSE I CAN'T SAY I'M SHOCKED.
WHERE DID SHE LEARN TO ACT LIKE THAT?
MM.
YOU CAN LEAVE ME BEHIND AND RUN OFF, CAN'T YOU?
すぅ
SUU (INHALE)
I CAN BUT SMILE...

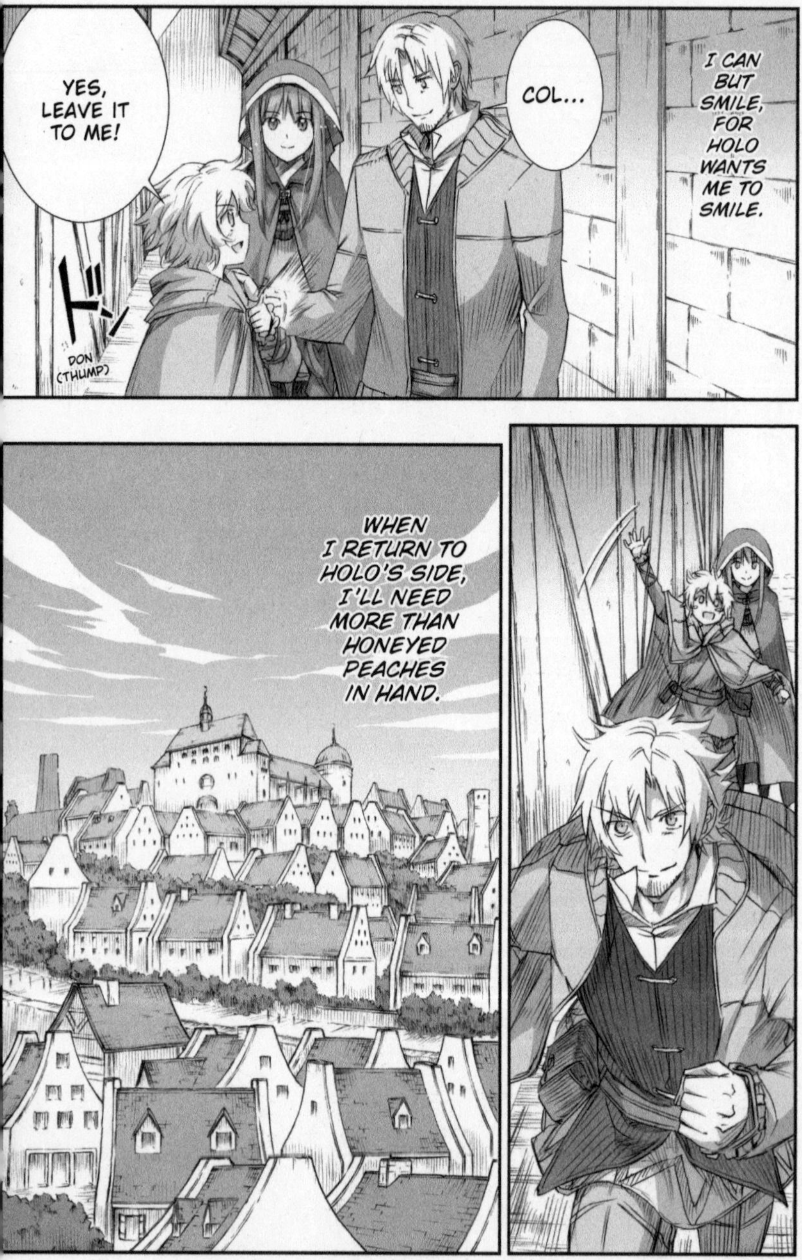
I CAN BUT SMILE, FOR HOLO WANTS ME TO SMILE.
COL...
YES, LEAVE IT TO ME!
ドン
DON (THUMP)
WHEN I RETURN TO HOLO'S SIDE, I'LL NEED MORE THAN HONEYED PEACHES IN HAND.

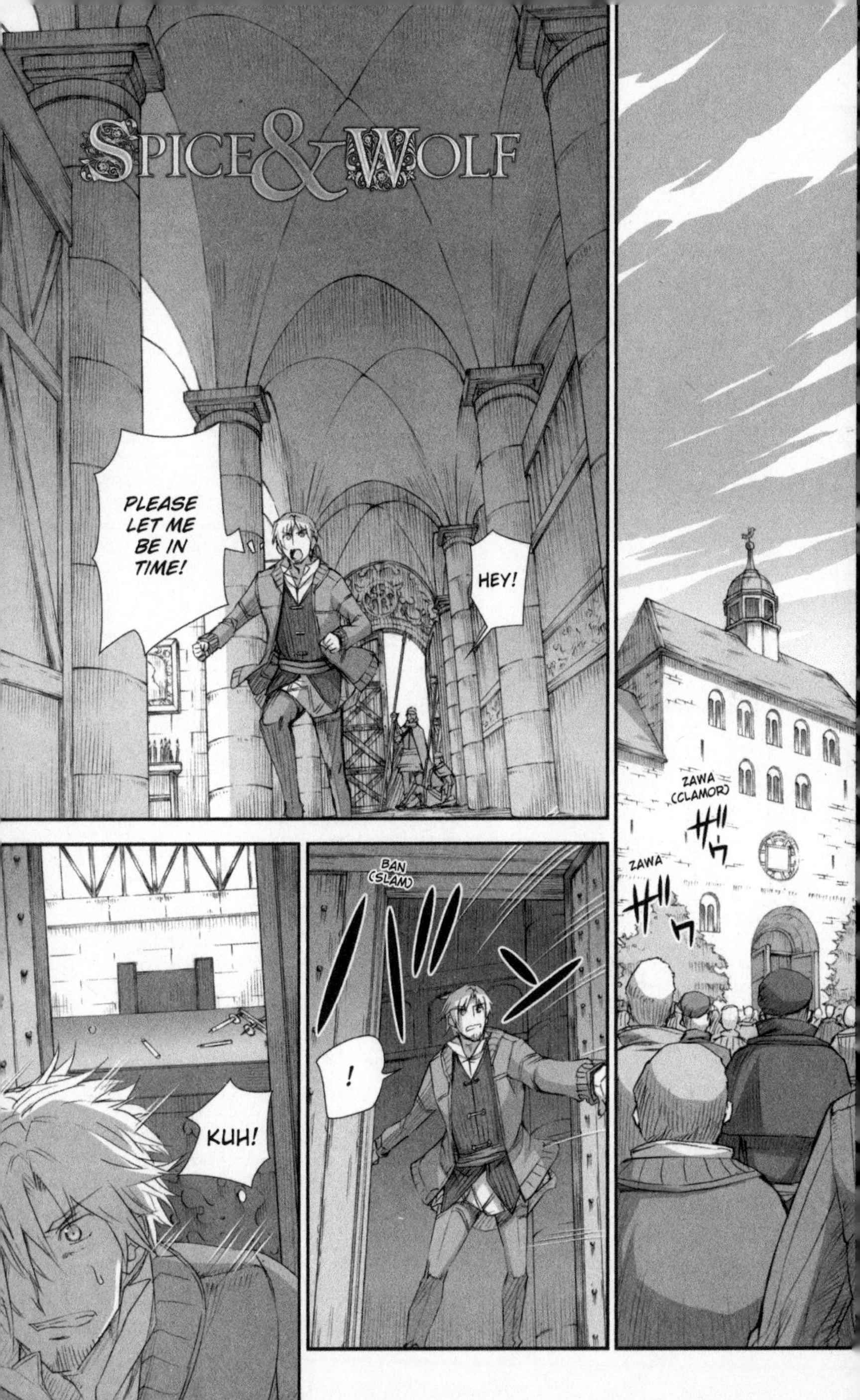
ZAWA (CLAMOR)
ZAWA
SPICE & WOLF
PLEASE LET ME BE IN TIME!
HEY!
BAN (SLAM)
!
KUH!

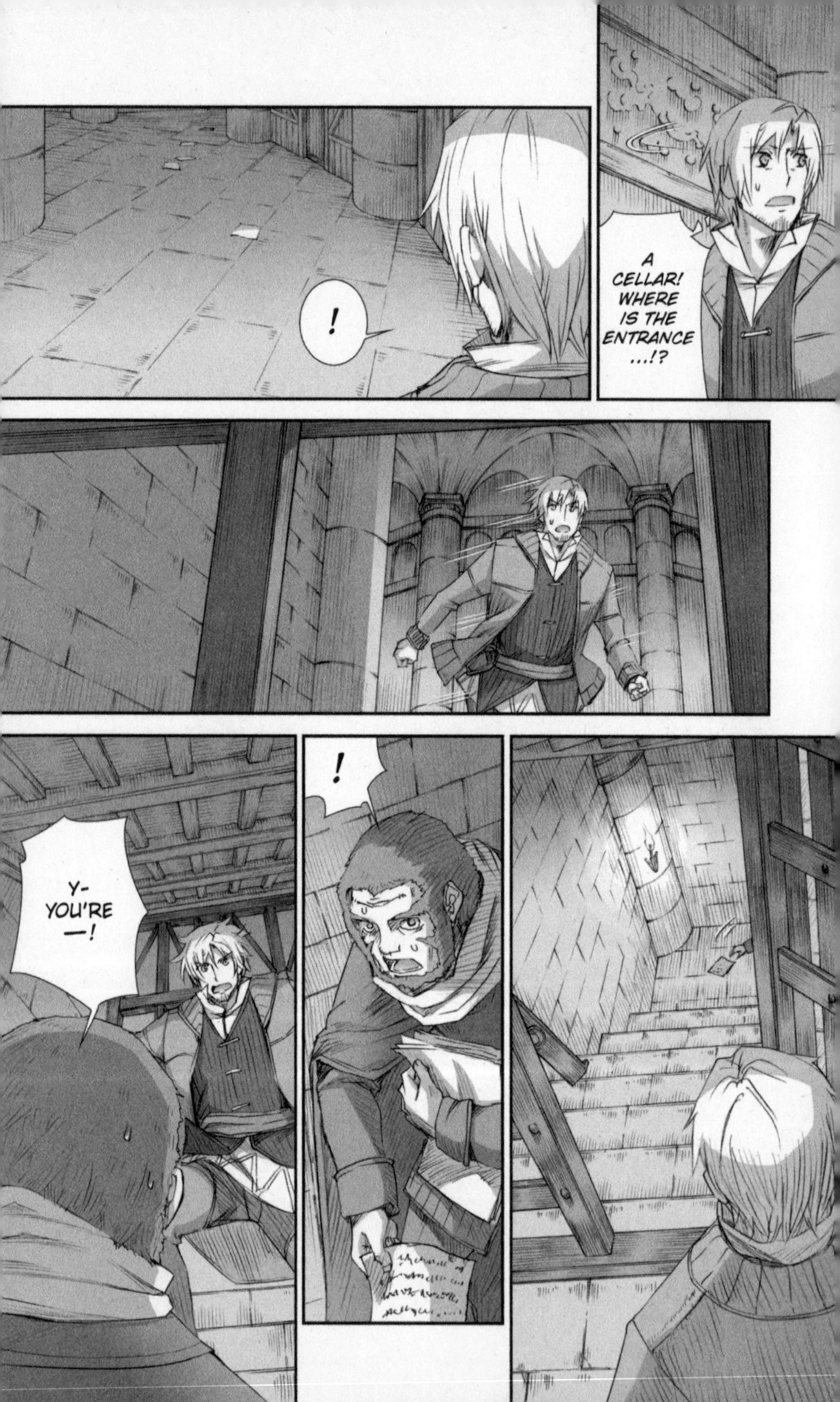
A CELLAR! WHERE IS THE ENTRANCE ...!?
!
!
Y- YOU'RE —!

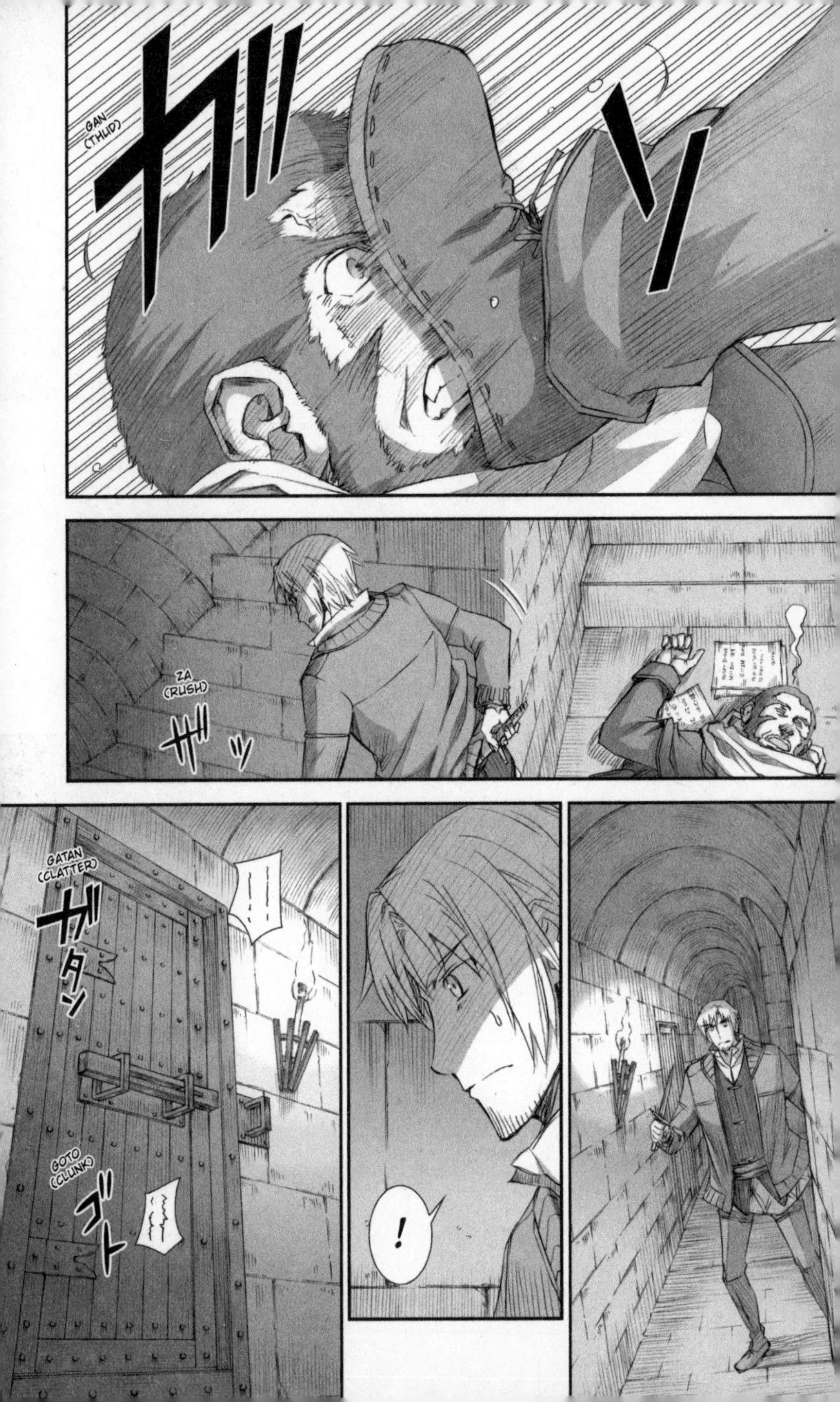
ガン
GAN (THUD)
ザッ
ZA (RUSH)
!
!!
GATAN (CLATTER)
ガタン
GOTO (CLUNK)
ゴト

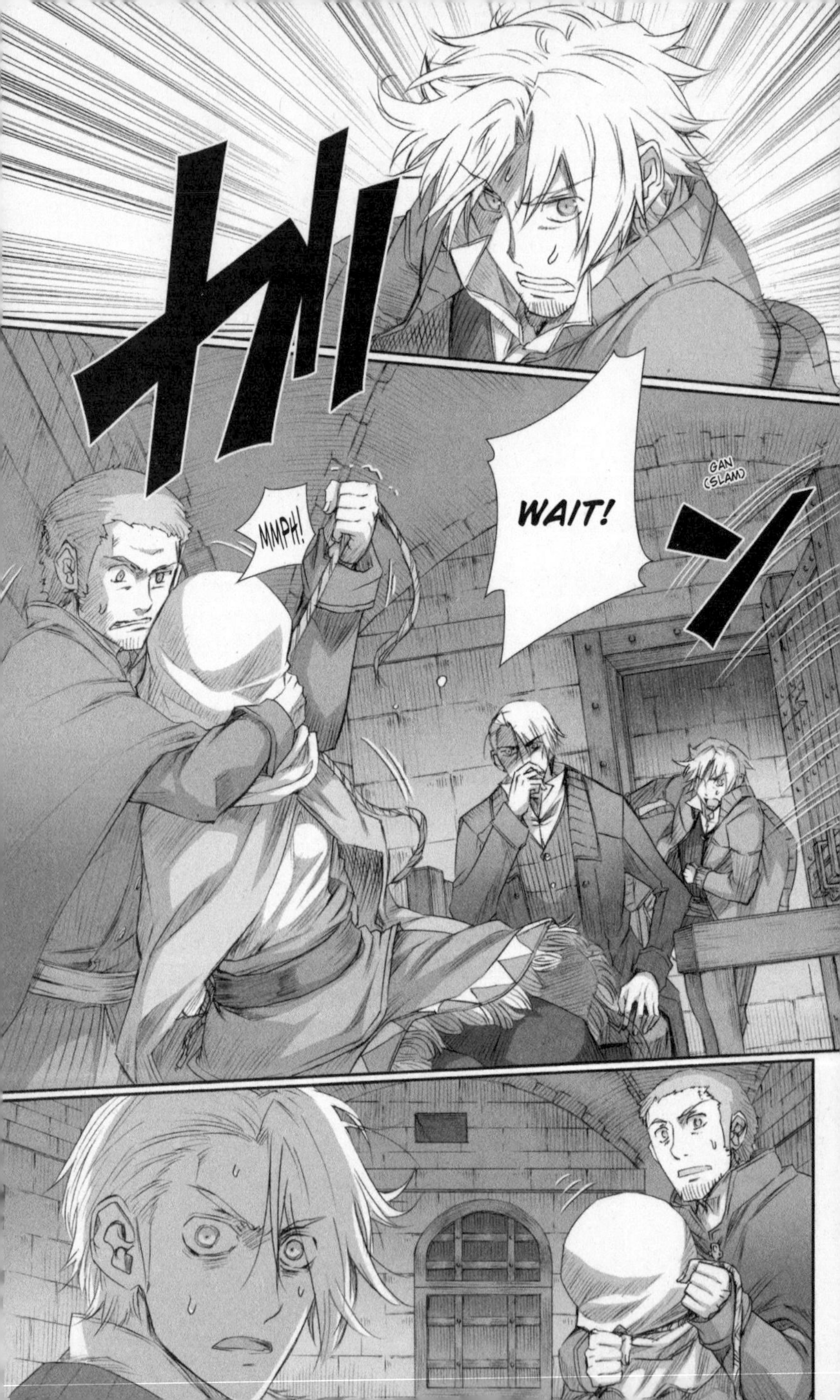
GAN (SLAM)
WAIT!
MMPH!

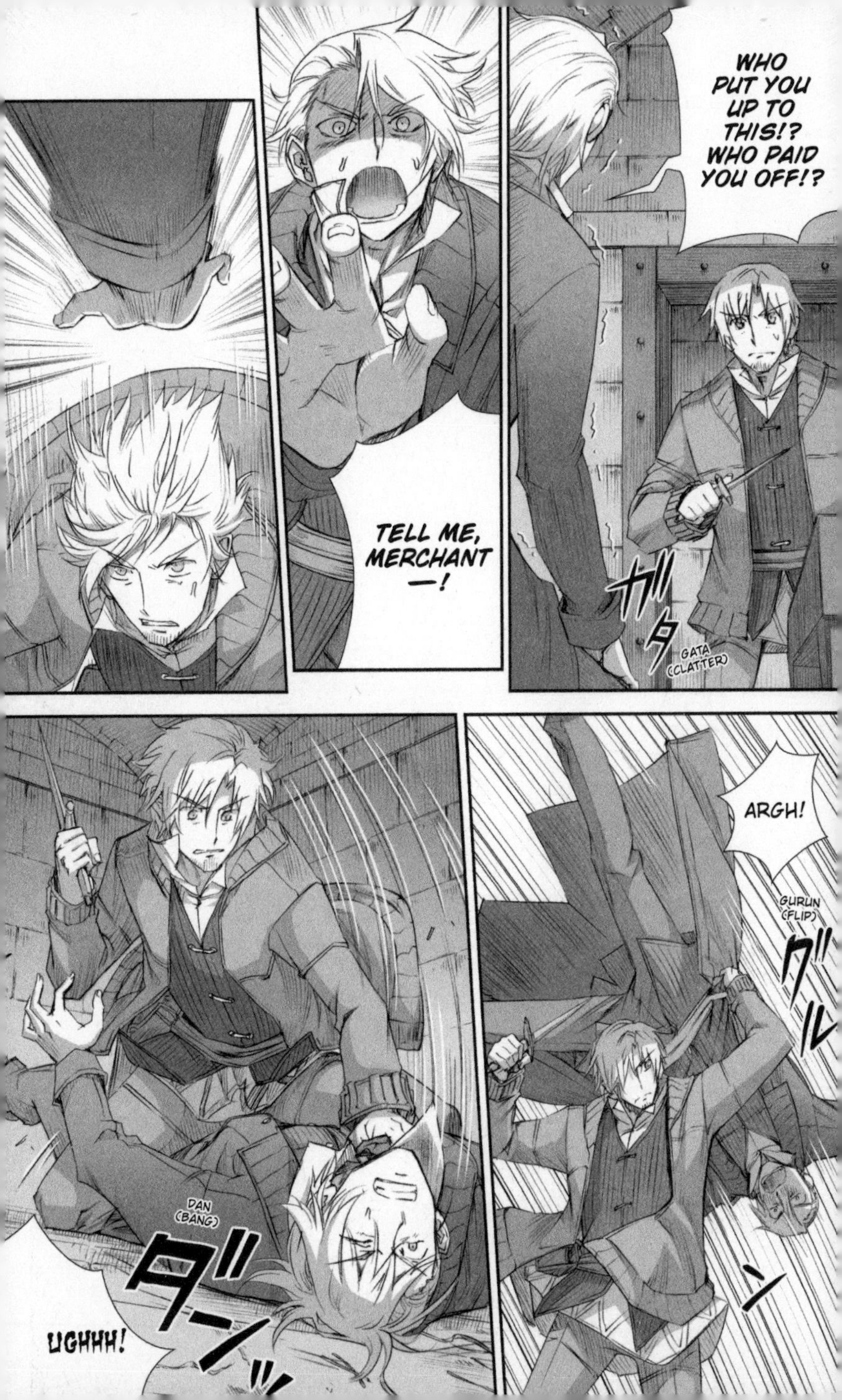
WHO PUT YOU UP TO THIS!? WHO PAID YOU OFF!?
GATA (CLATTER)
TELL ME, MERCHANT —!
ARGH!
GURUN (FLIP)
DAN (BANG)
UGHHH!

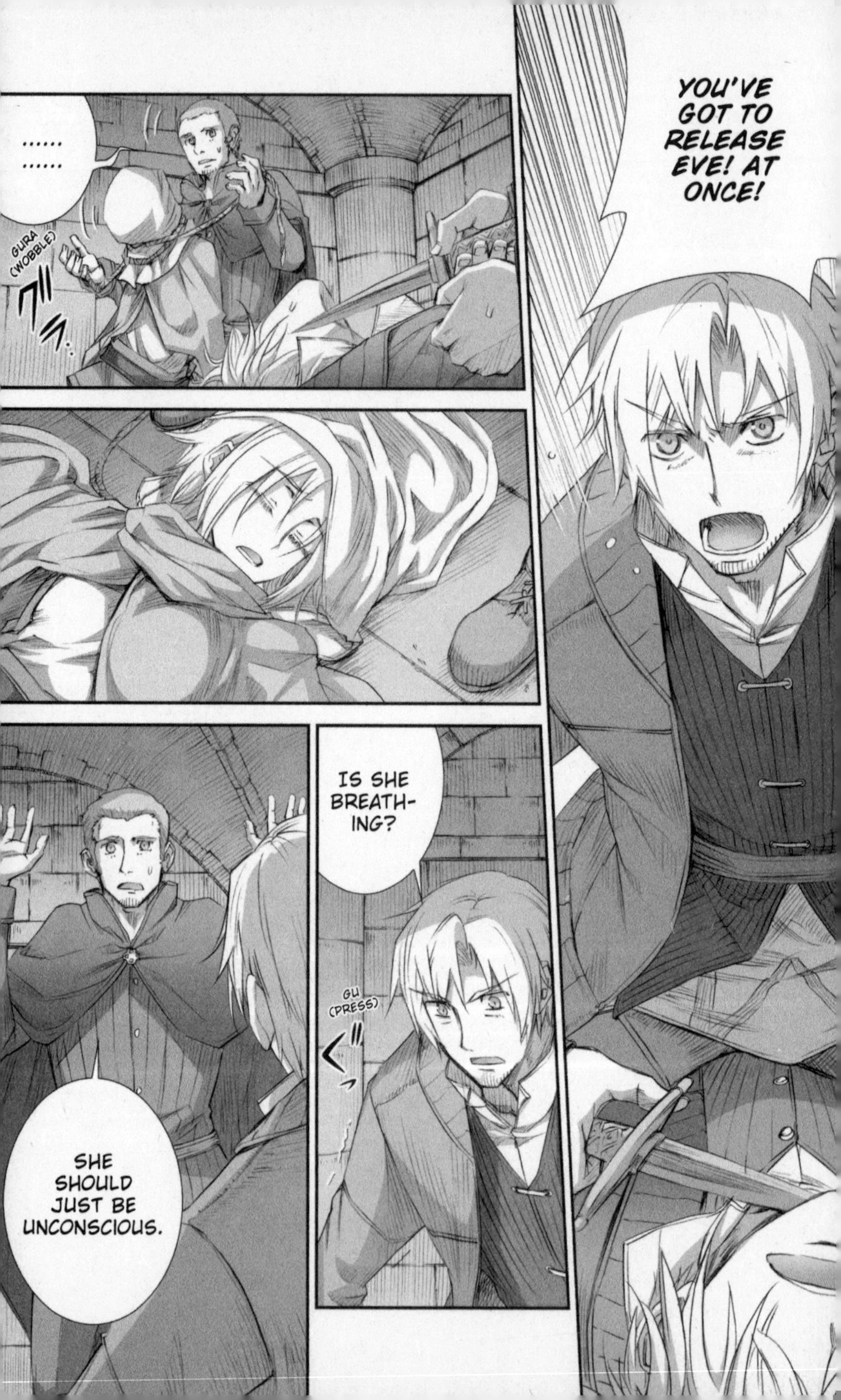
YOU'VE GOT TO RELEASE EVE! AT ONCE!
......
......
GURA (WOBBLE)
IS SHE BREATH-ING?
GU (PRESS)
SHE SHOULD JUST BE UNCONSCIOUS.

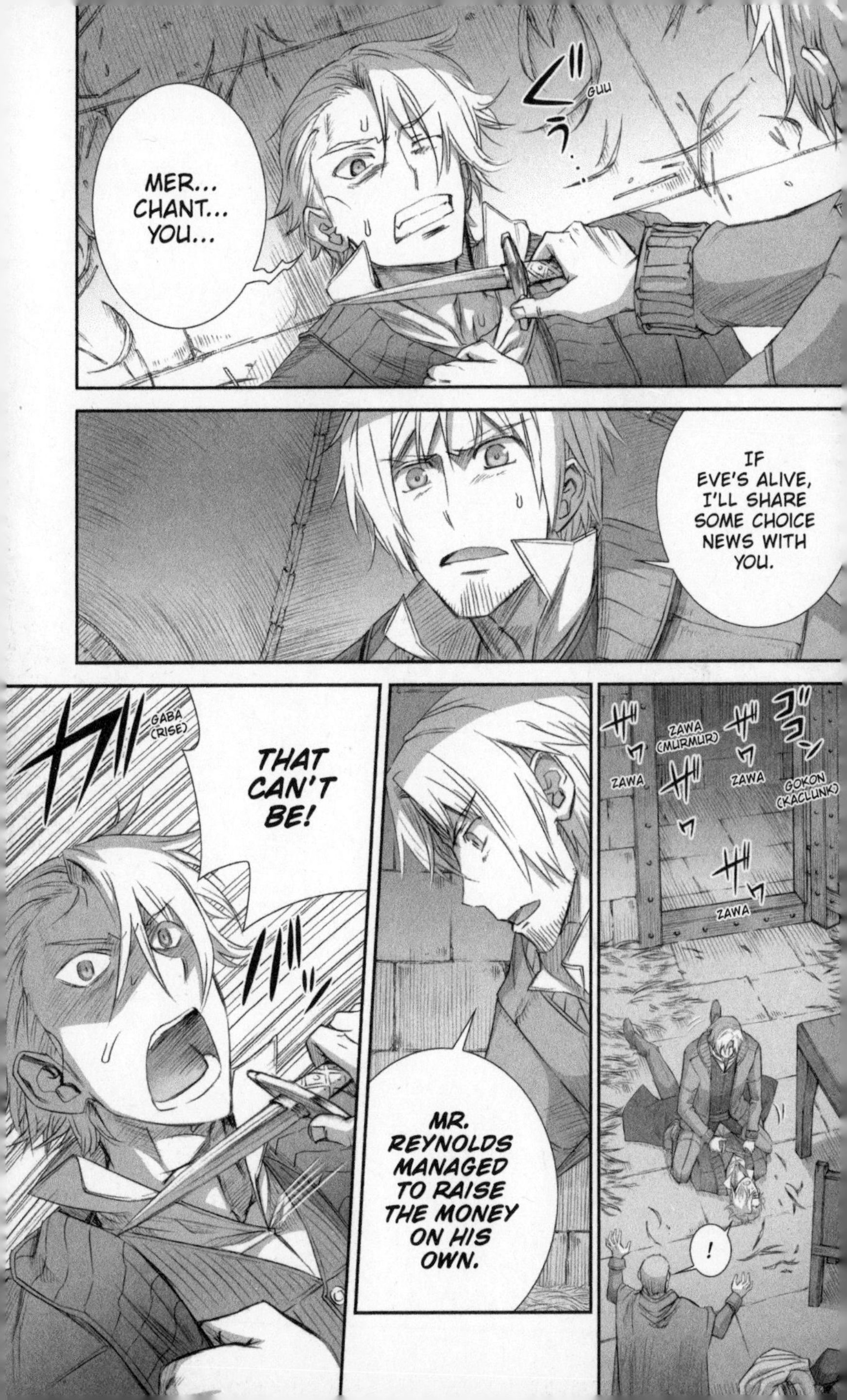

GUU
MER... CHANT... YOU...
IF EVE'S ALIVE, I'LL SHARE SOME CHOICE NEWS WITH YOU.
ZAWA (MURMUR)
ZAWA
ZAWA
ZAWA
GOKON (KACLUNK)
!
MR. REYNOLDS MANAGED TO RAISE THE MONEY ON HIS OWN.
GABA (RISE)
THAT CAN'T BE!

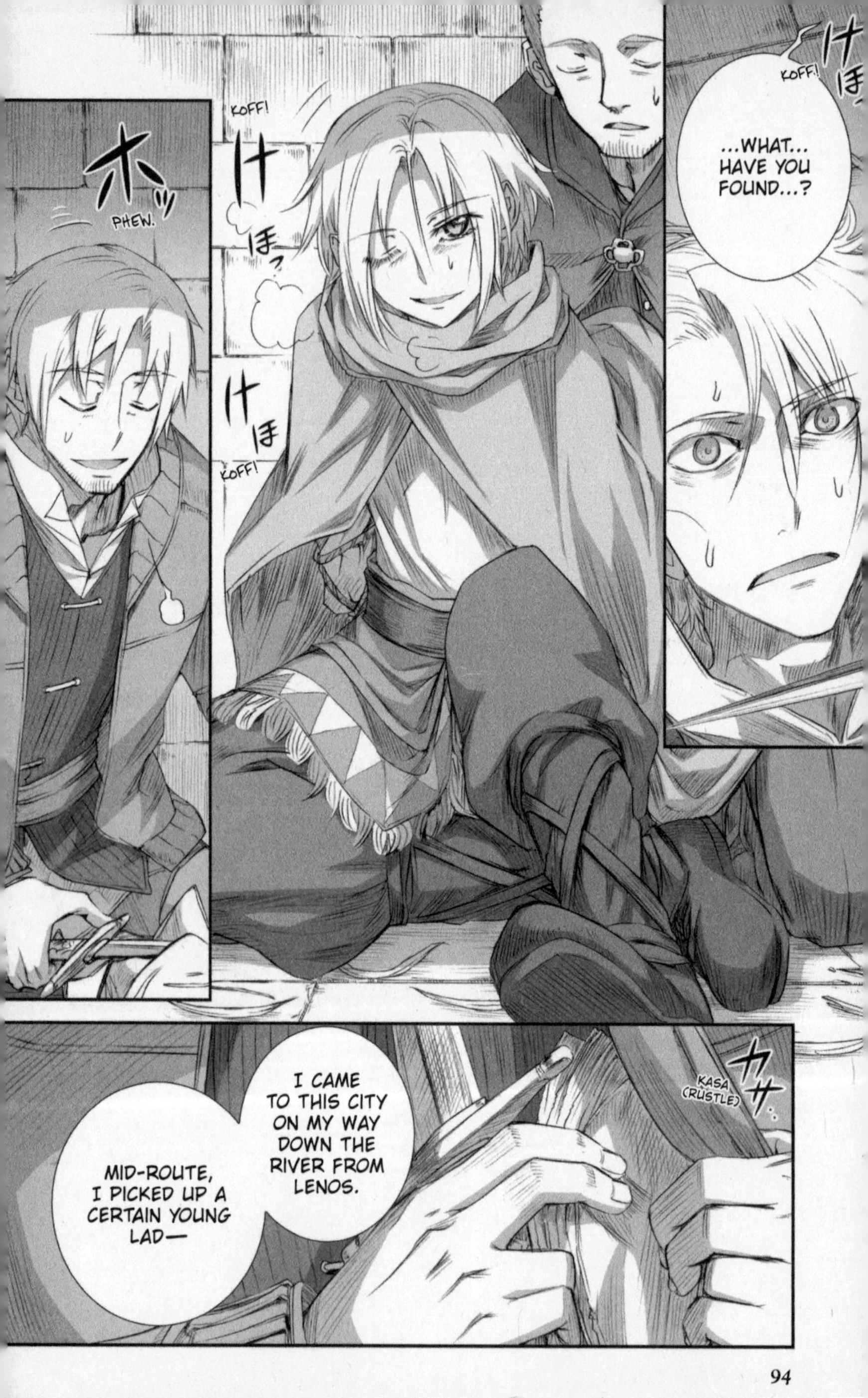
けほ
KOFF!
...WHAT... HAVE YOU FOUND...?
KOFF!
けほっ
けほ
KOFF!
ホッ
PHEW.
カサ
KASA (RUSTLE)
I CAME TO THIS CITY ON MY WAY DOWN THE RIVER FROM LENOS.
MID-ROUTE, I PICKED UP A CERTAIN YOUNG LAD—

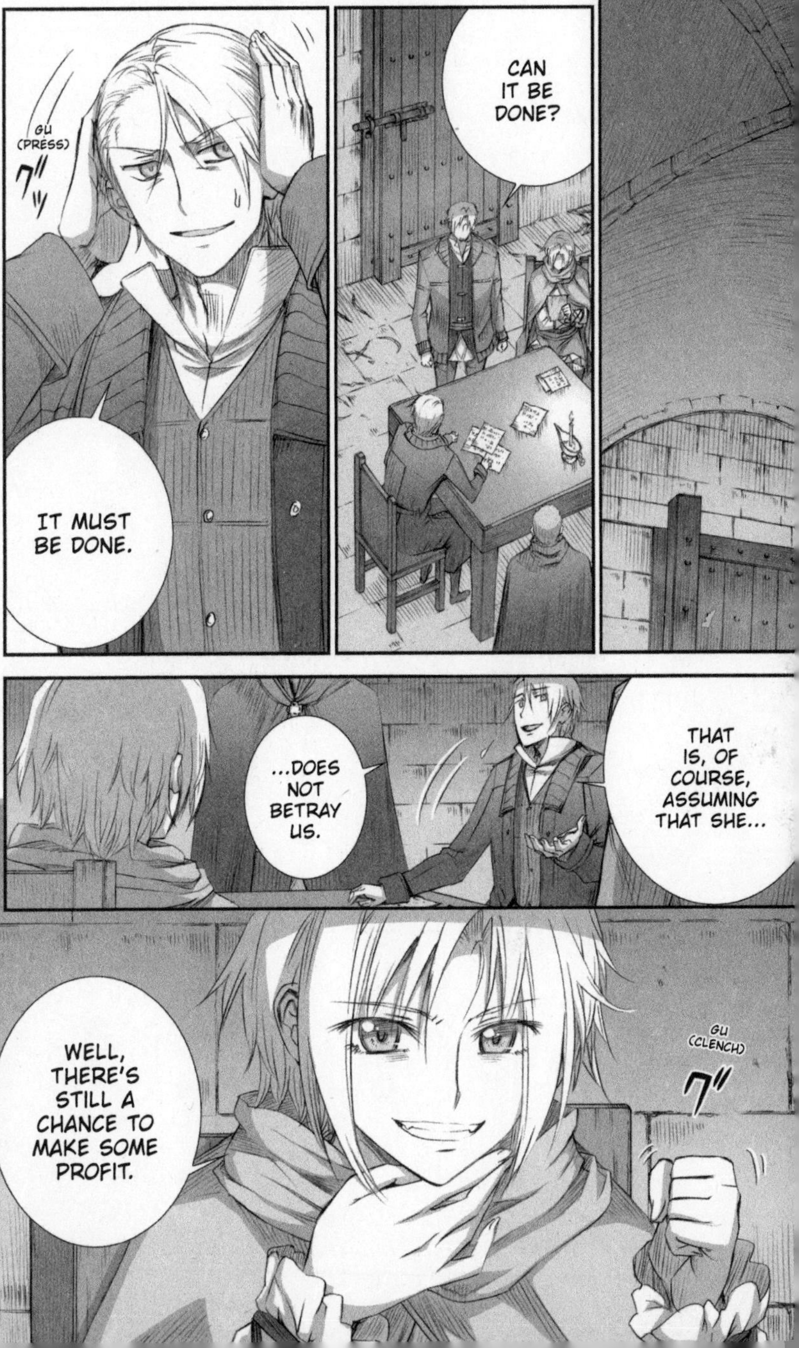
CAN IT BE DONE?
GU (PRESS)
IT MUST BE DONE.
THAT IS, OF COURSE, ASSUMING THAT SHE...
...DOES NOT BETRAY US.
GU (CLENCH)
WELL, THERE'S STILL A CHANCE TO MAKE SOME PROFIT.

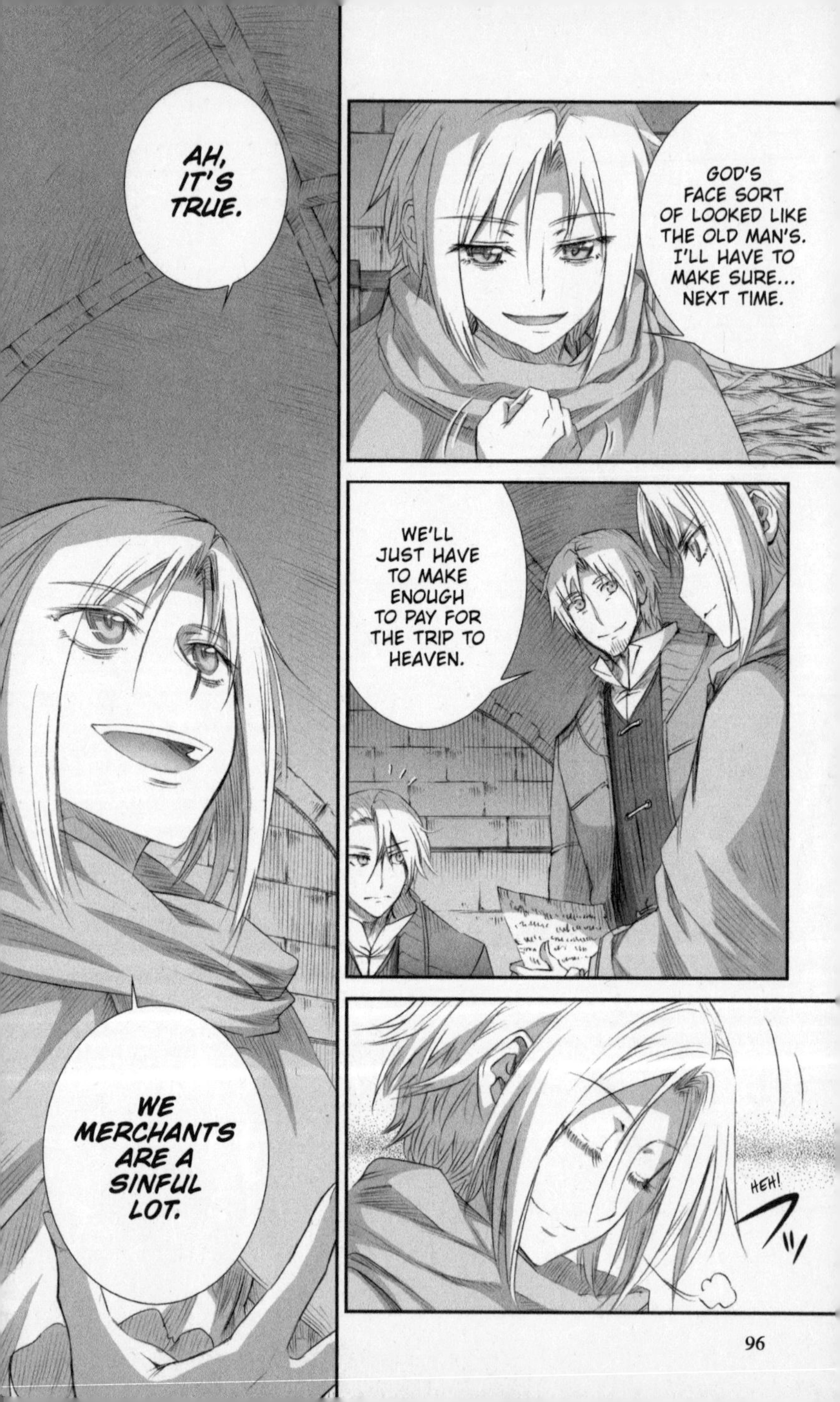
GOD'S FACE SORT OF LOOKED LIKE THE OLD MAN'S. I'LL HAVE TO MAKE SURE... NEXT TIME.
WE'LL JUST HAVE TO MAKE ENOUGH TO PAY FOR THE TRIP TO HEAVEN.
HEH!
AH, IT'S TRUE.
WE MERCHANTS ARE A SINFUL LOT.

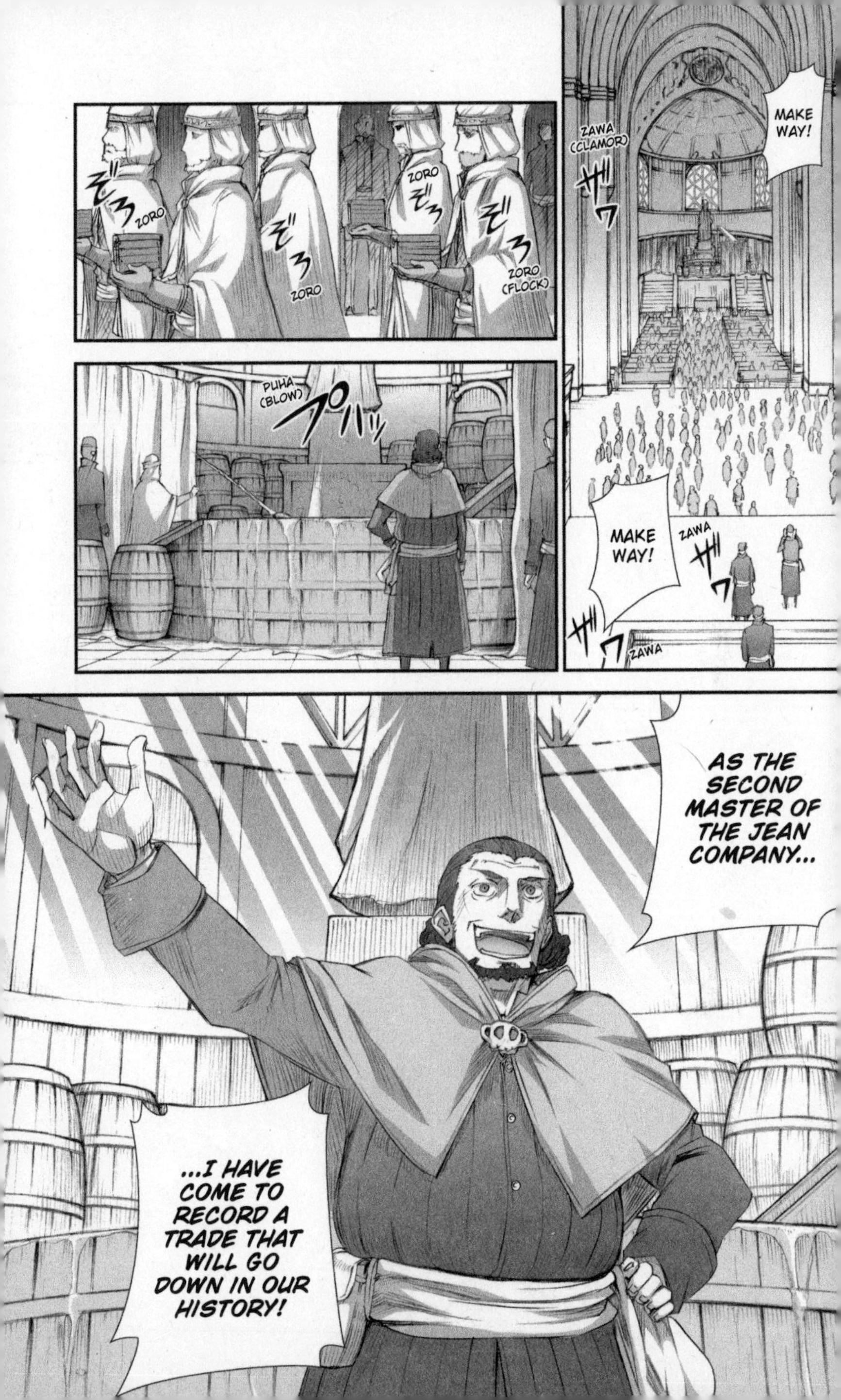
MAKE WAY!
ZAWA (CLAMOR)
MAKE WAY!
ZAWA
ZAWA
ZORO (FLOCK)
ZORO
ZORO
ZORO
PUHA (BLOW)
AS THE SECOND MASTER OF THE JEAN COMPANY...
...I HAVE COME TO RECORD A TRADE THAT WILL GO DOWN IN OUR HISTORY!

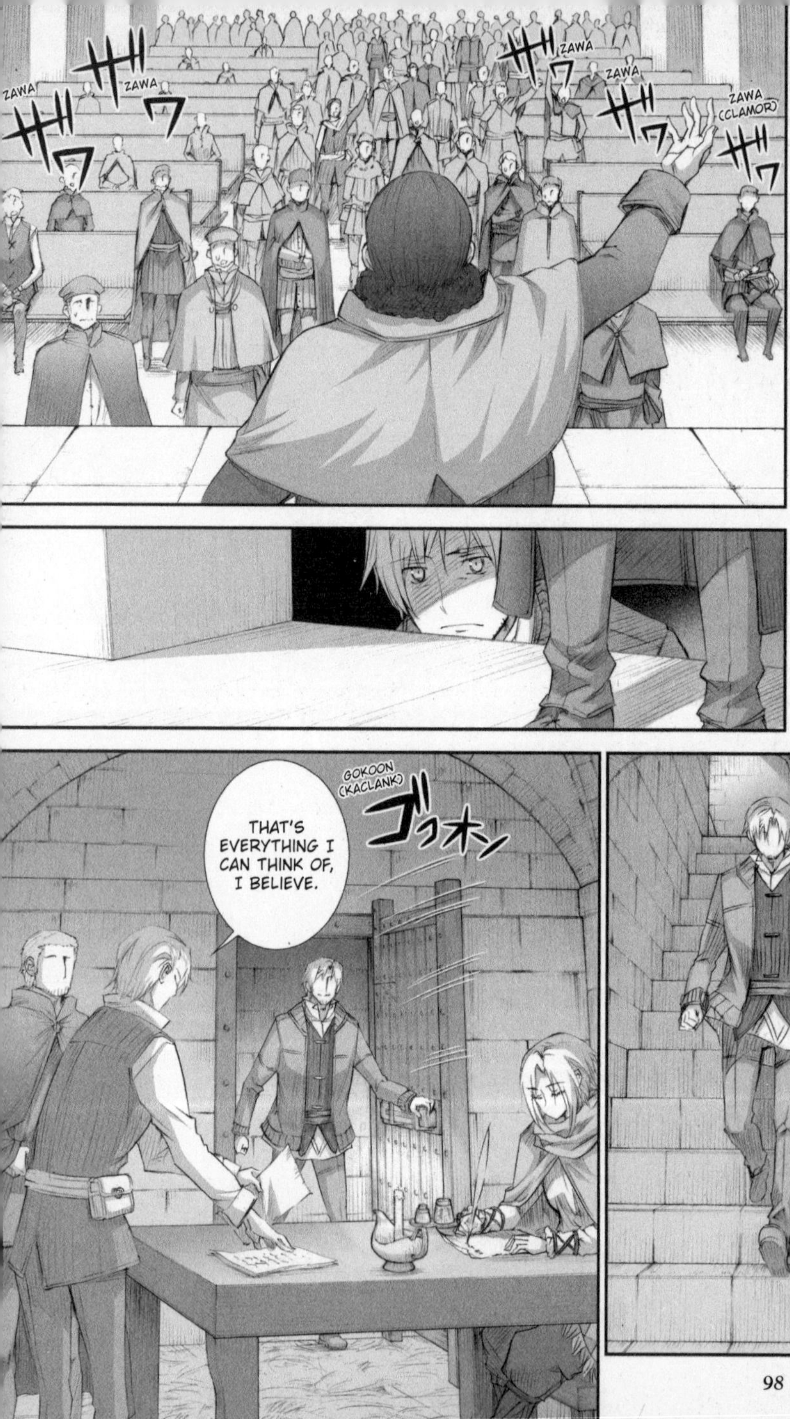
ザワ
ZAWA (CLAMOR)
ザワ
ZAWA
ザワ
ZAWA
ザワ
ZAWA
ザワ
ZAWA
THAT'S EVERYTHING I CAN THINK OF, I BELIEVE.
ゴッオン
GOKOON (KACLANK)

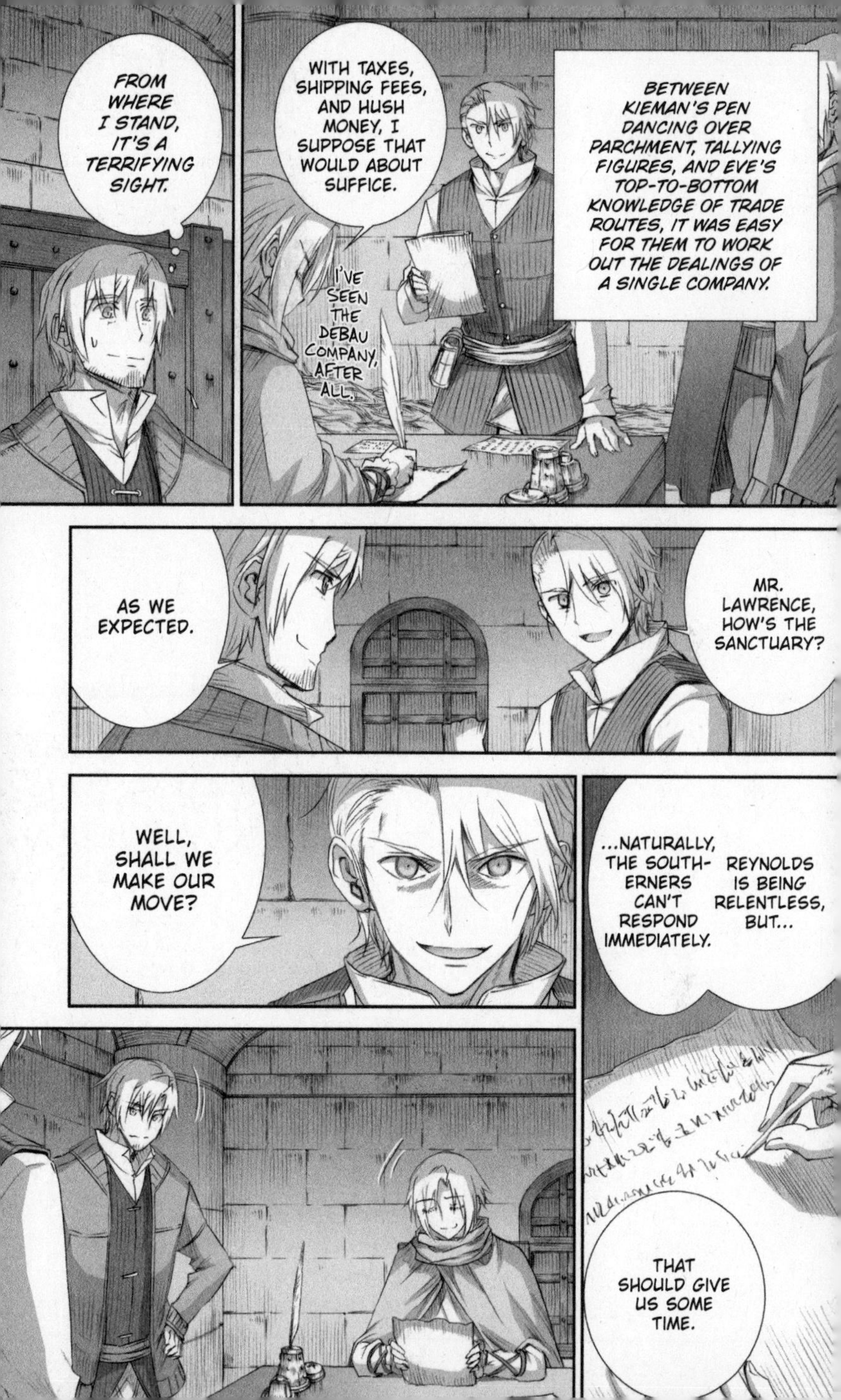
BETWEEN KIEMAN'S PEN DANCING OVER PARCHMENT, TALLYING FIGURES, AND EVE'S TOP-TO-BOTTOM KNOWLEDGE OF TRADE ROUTES, IT WAS EASY FOR THEM TO WORK OUT THE DEALINGS OF A SINGLE COMPANY.
WITH TAXES, SHIPPING FEES, AND HUSH MONEY, I SUPPOSE THAT WOULD ABOUT SUFFICE.
I'VE SEEN THE DEBAU COMPANY, AFTER ALL.
FROM WHERE I STAND, IT'S A TERRIFYING SIGHT.
MR. LAWRENCE, HOW'S THE SANCTUARY?
AS WE EXPECTED.
REYNOLDS IS BEING RELENTLESS, BUT...
...NATURALLY, THE SOUTHERNERS CAN'T RESPOND IMMEDIATELY.
THAT SHOULD GIVE US SOME TIME.
WELL, SHALL WE MAKE OUR MOVE?

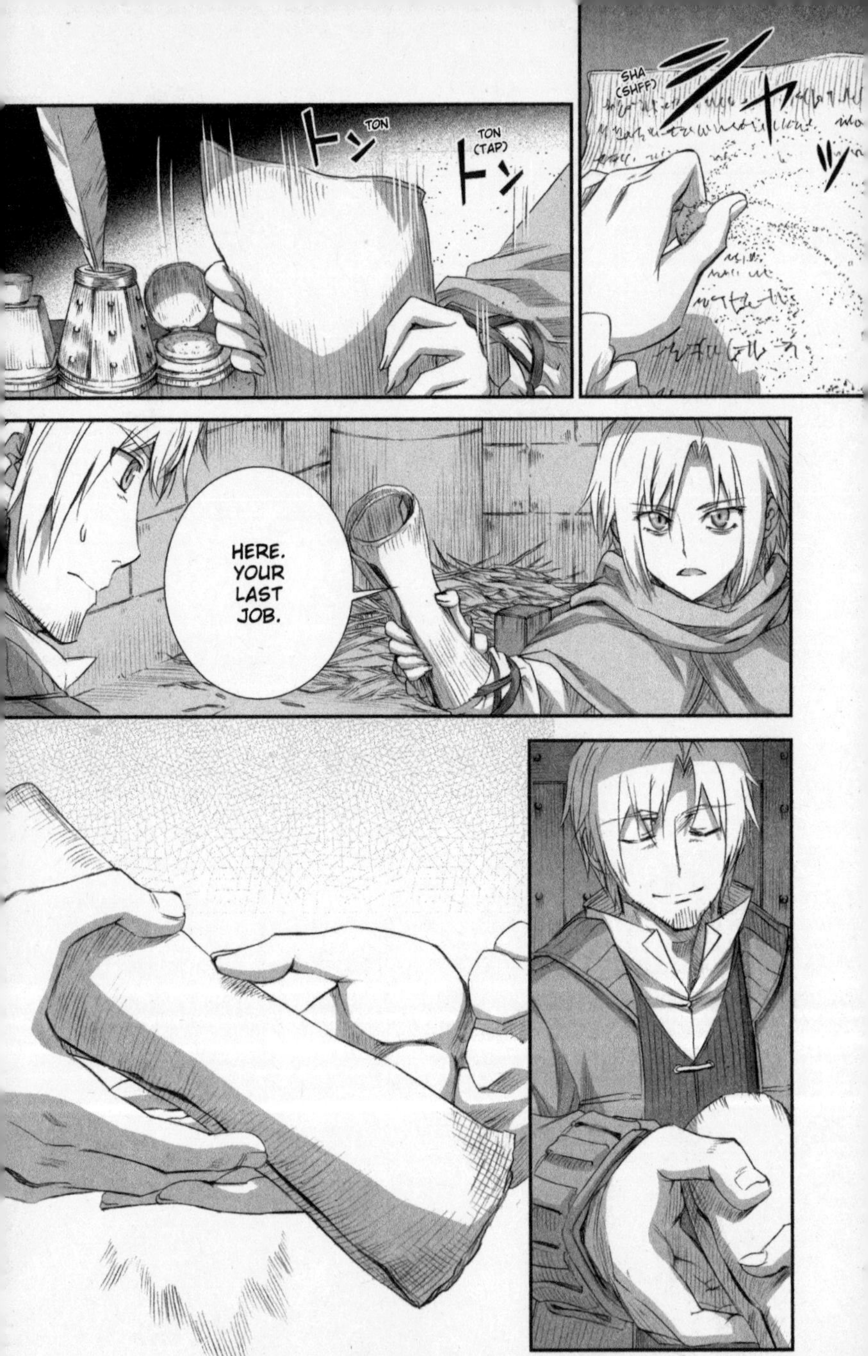

シャッ
SHA (SHFF)
トン
TON
トン
TON (TAP)
HERE. YOUR LAST JOB.

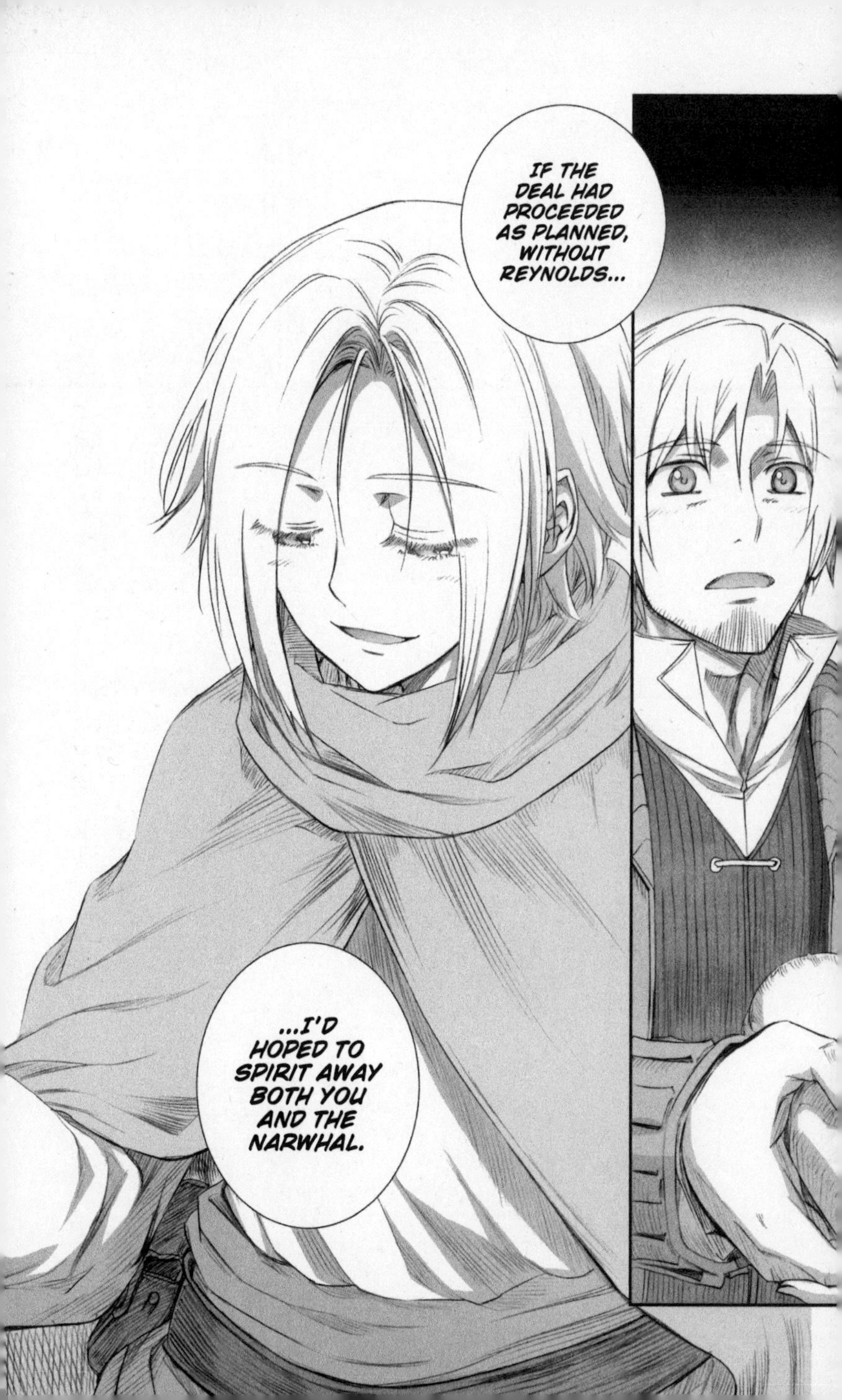
IF THE DEAL HAD PROCEEDED AS PLANNED, WITHOUT REYNOLDS...
...I'D HOPED TO SPIRIT AWAY BOTH YOU AND THE NARWHAL.

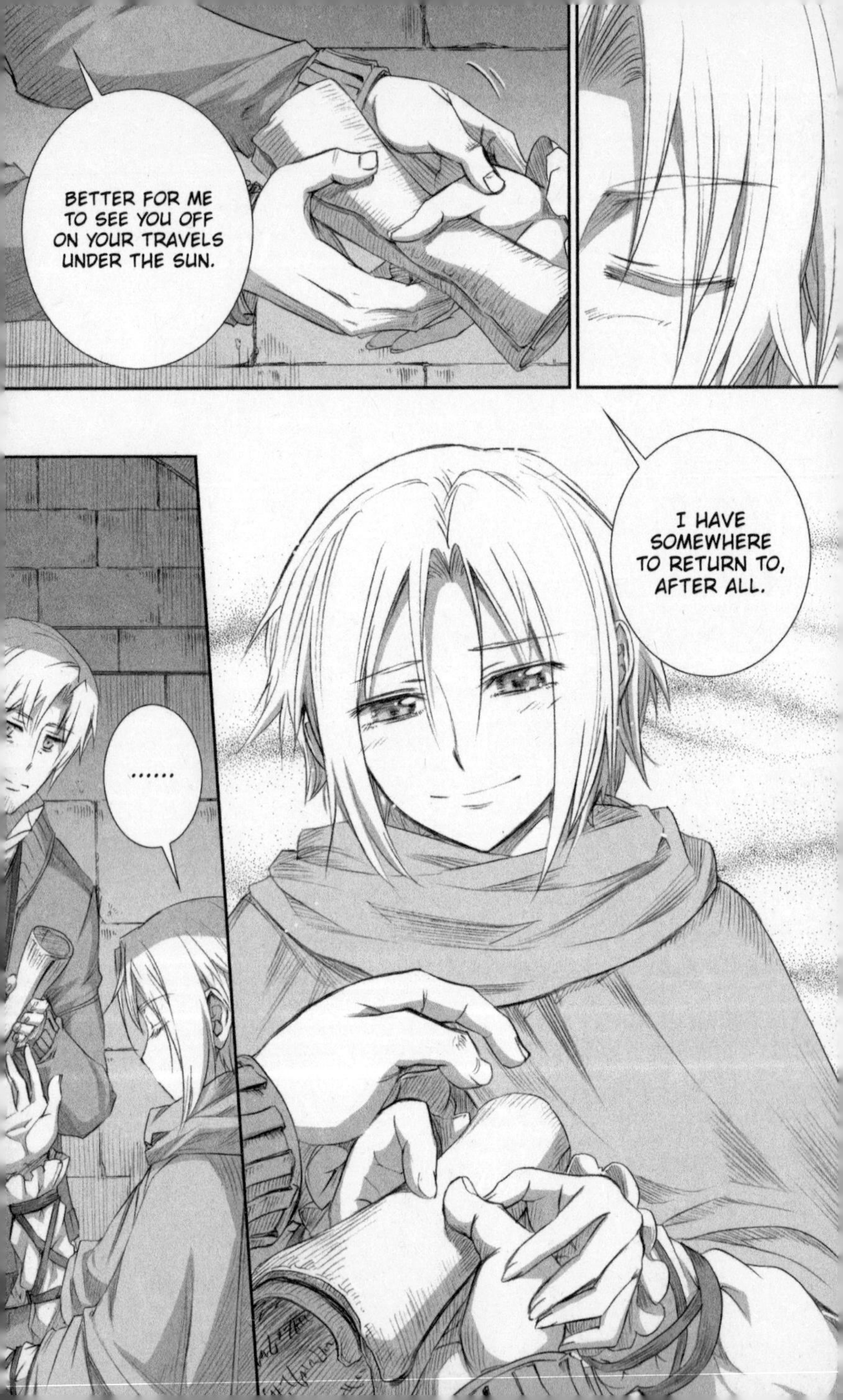
BETTER FOR ME TO SEE YOU OFF ON YOUR TRAVELS UNDER THE SUN.
I HAVE SOMEWHERE TO RETURN TO, AFTER ALL.
......

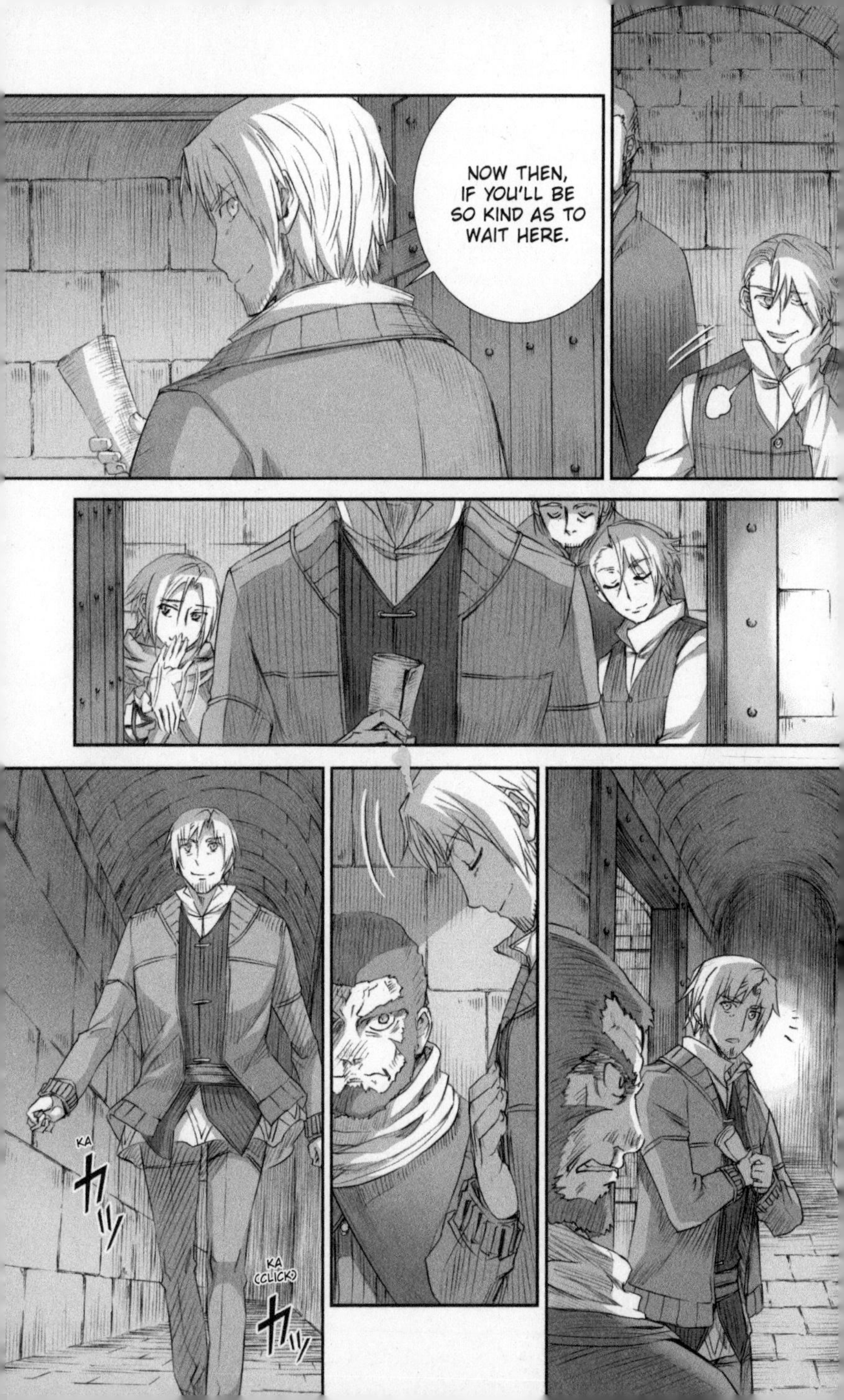
NOW THEN, IF YOU'LL BE SO KIND AS TO WAIT HERE.
KA
カッ
KA (CLICK)
カッ

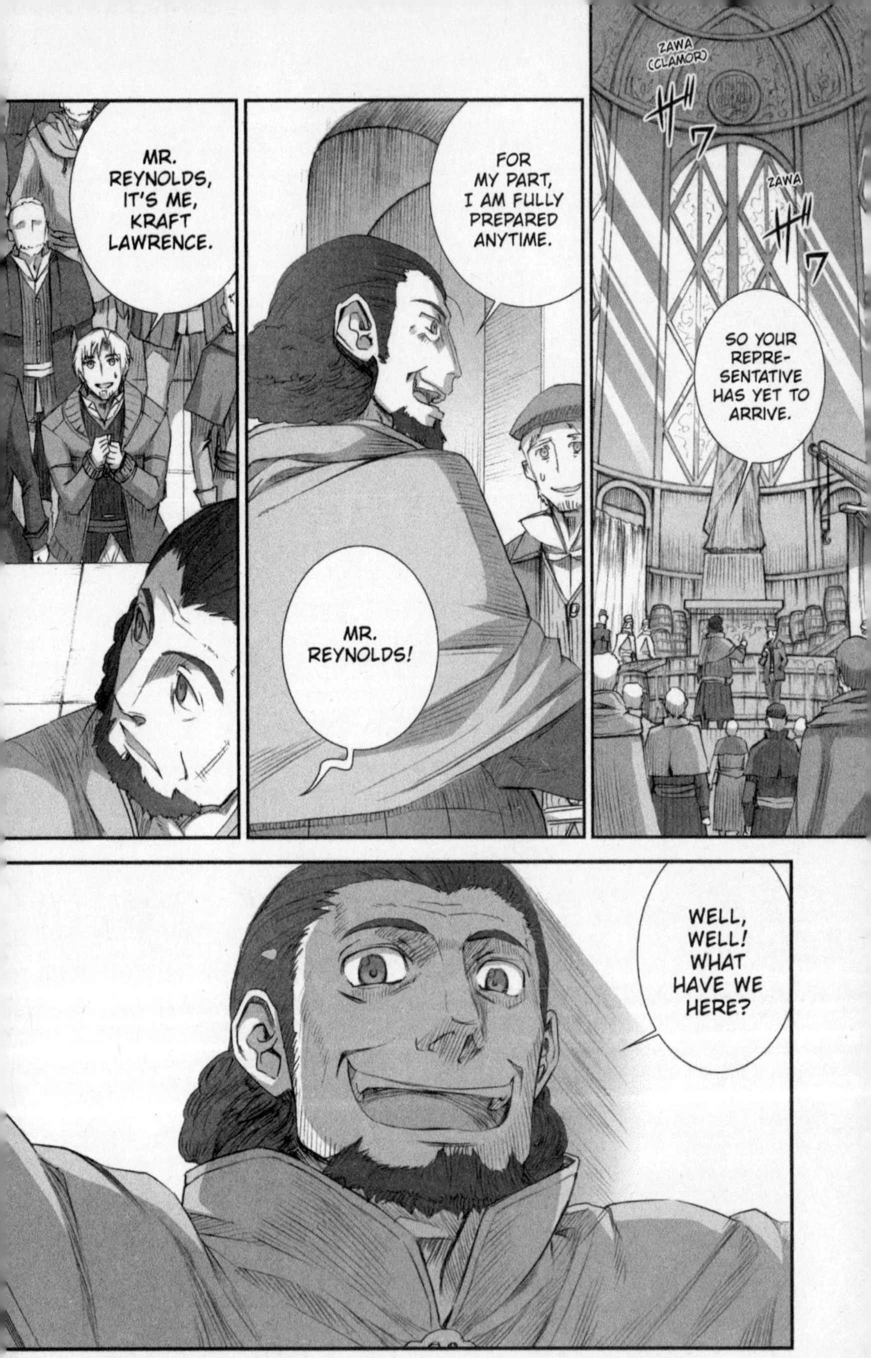
ZAWA (CLAMOR)
ZAWA
SO YOUR REPRESENTATIVE HAS YET TO ARRIVE.
FOR MY PART, I AM FULLY PREPARED ANYTIME.
MR. REYNOLDS!
MR. REYNOLDS, IT'S ME, KRAFT LAWRENCE.
WELL, WELL! WHAT HAVE WE HERE?

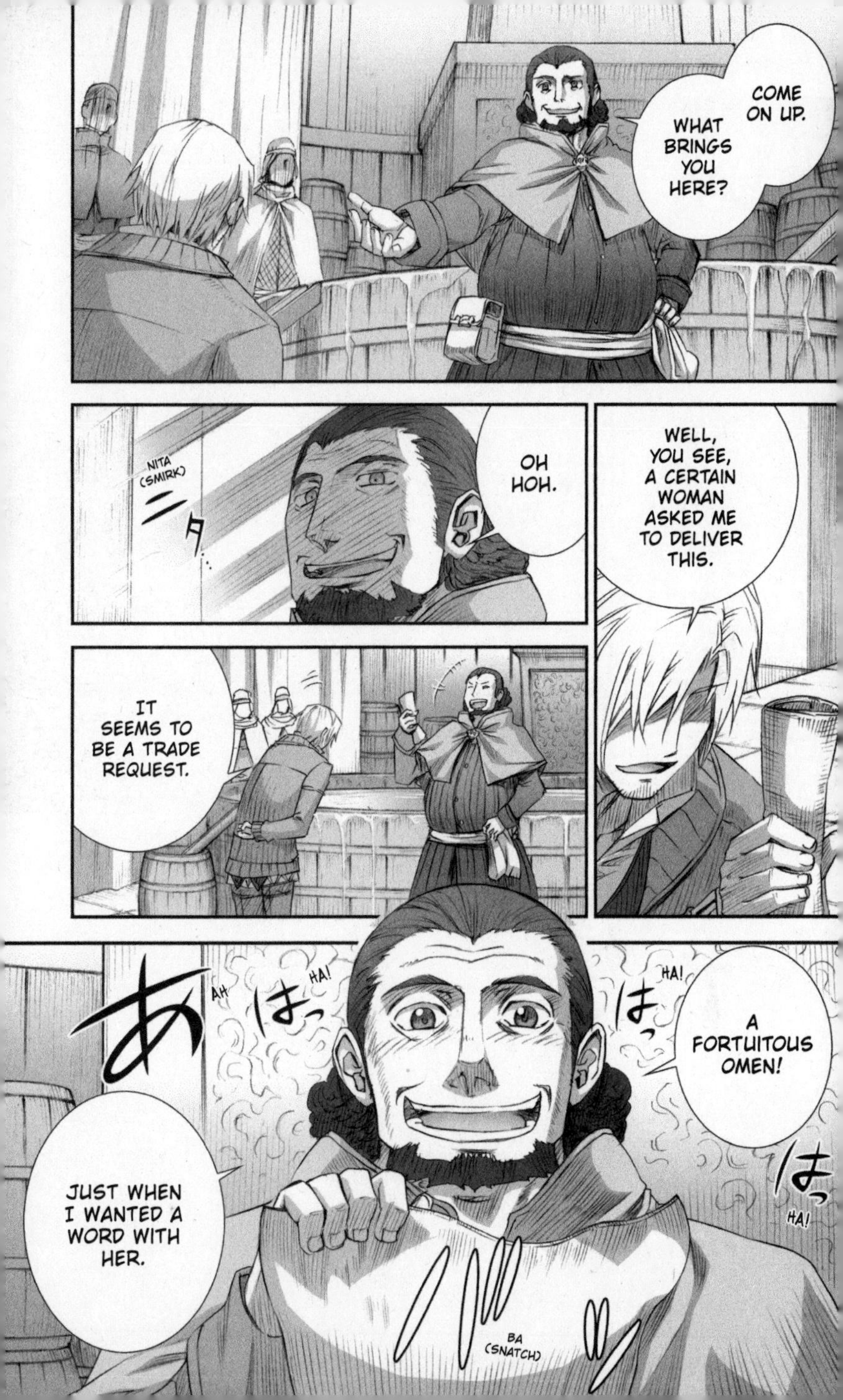
COME ON UP.
WHAT BRINGS YOU HERE?
WELL, YOU SEE, A CERTAIN WOMAN ASKED ME TO DELIVER THIS.
OH HOH.
ニタ
NITA (SMIRK)
IT SEEMS TO BE A TRADE REQUEST.
はっ
HA!
A FORTUITOUS OMEN!
はっ
HA!
あはっ
AH HA!
JUST WHEN I WANTED A WORD WITH HER.
BA (SNATCH)

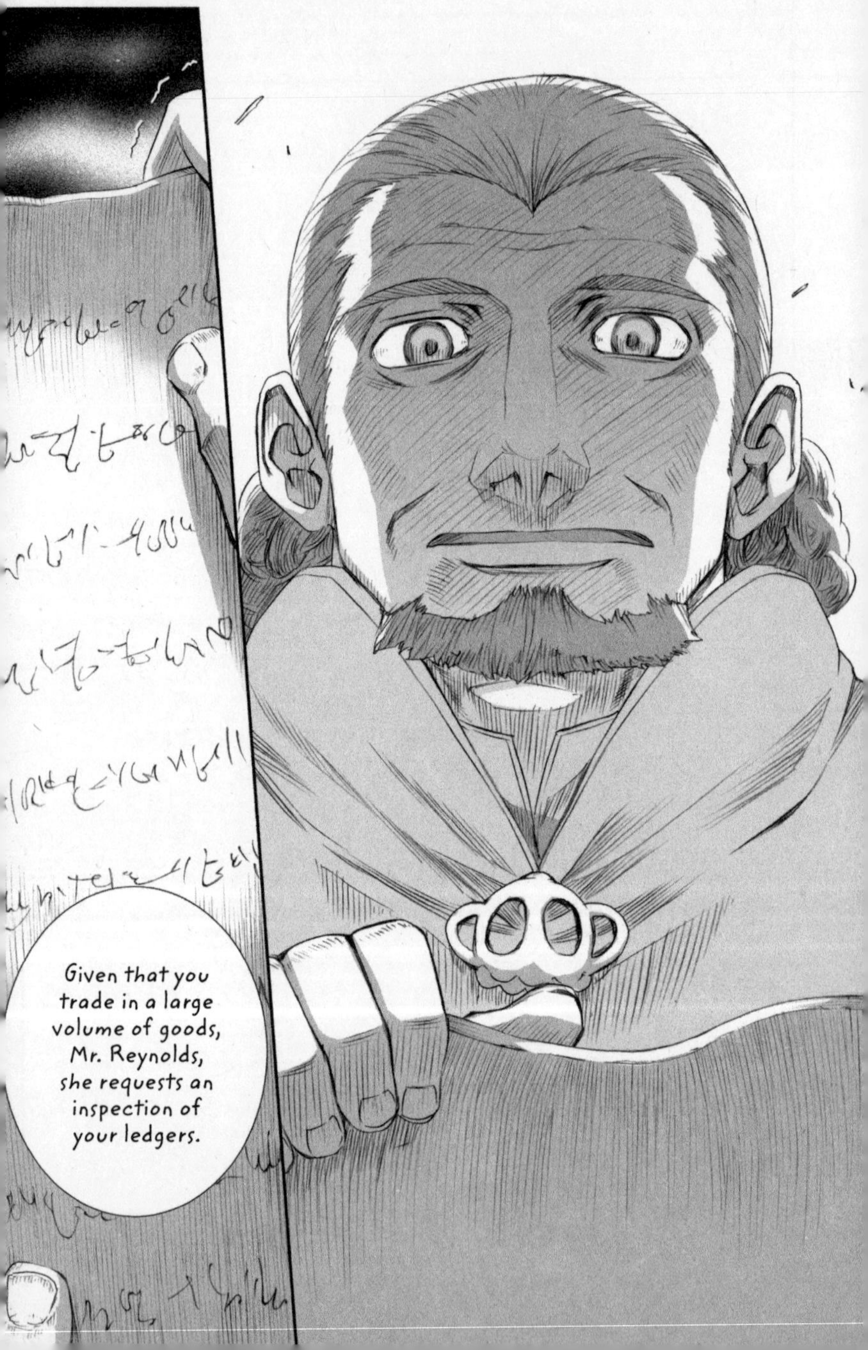
Given that you trade in a large volume of goods, Mr. Reynolds, she requests an inspection of your ledgers.

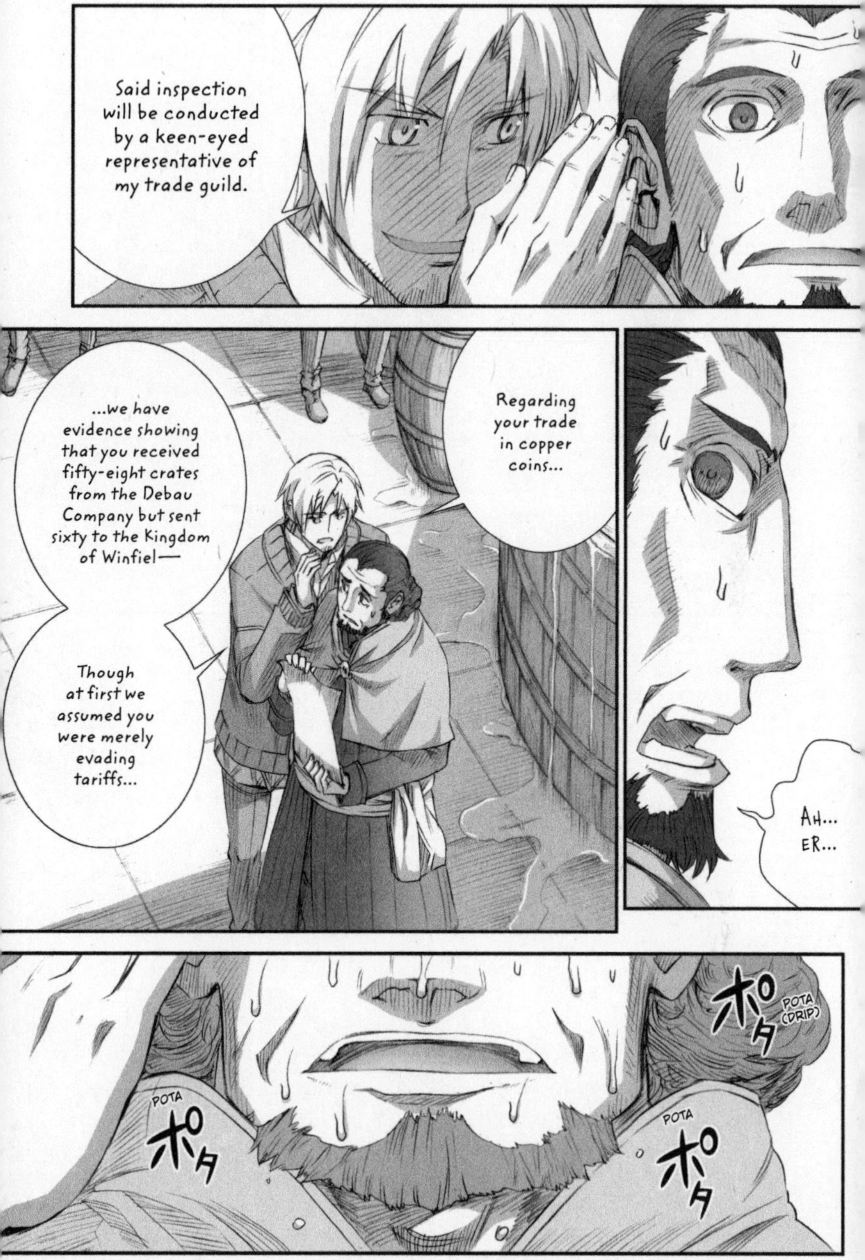
Said inspection will be conducted by a keen-eyed representative of my trade guild.
Ah... Er...
Regarding your trade in copper coins...
...we have evidence showing that you received fifty-eight crates from the Debau Company but sent sixty to the Kingdom of Winfiel—
Though at first we assumed you were merely evading tariffs...
ポタ
POTA (DRIP)
ポタ
POTA
ポタ
POTA

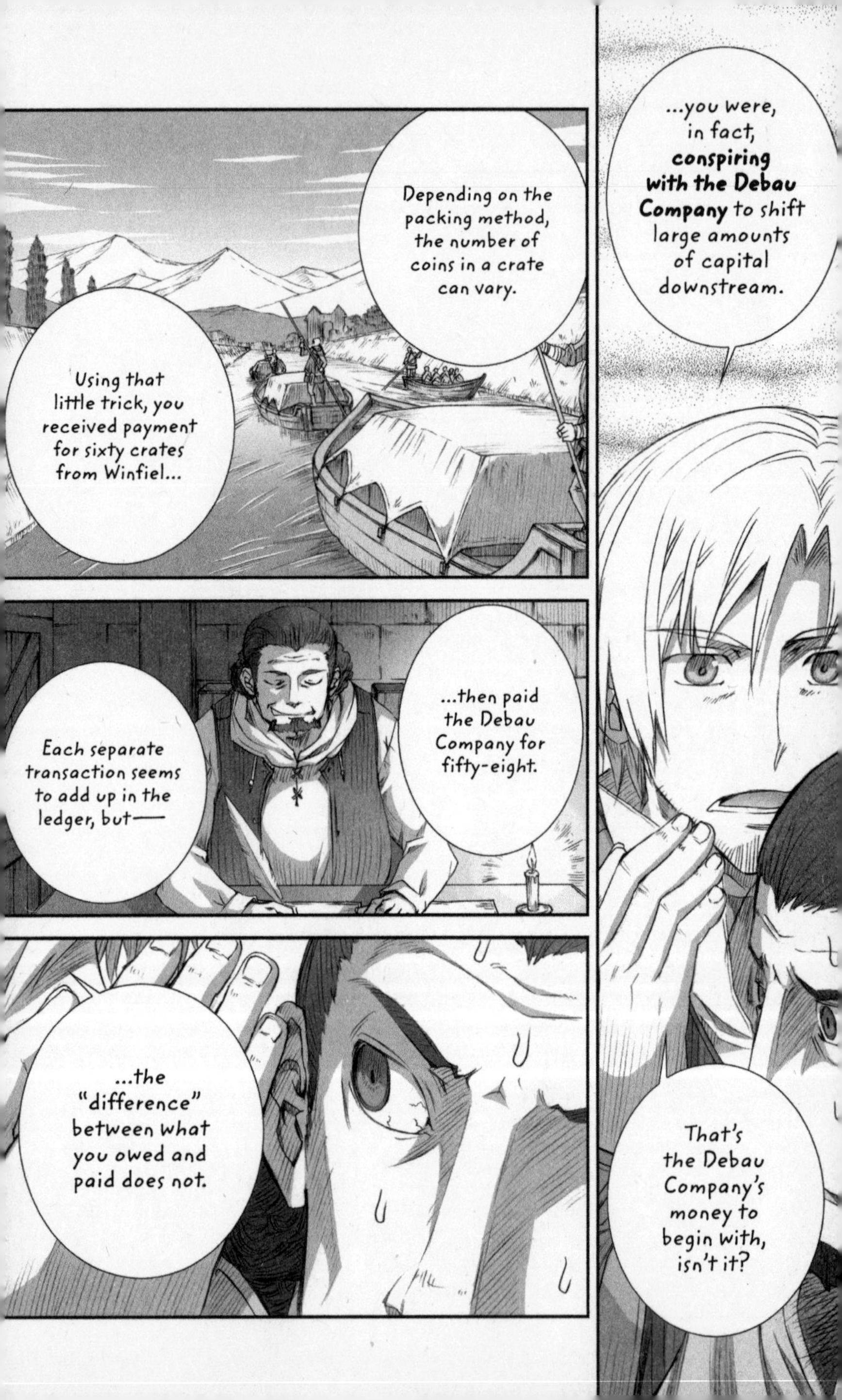
...you were, in fact, conspiring with the Debau Company to shift large amounts of capital downstream.
That's the Debau Company's money to begin with, isn't it?
Depending on the packing method, the number of coins in a crate can vary.
Using that little trick, you received payment for sixty crates from Winfiel...
...then paid the Debau Company for fifty-eight.
Each separate transaction seems to add up in the ledger, but—
...the "difference" between what you owed and paid does not.

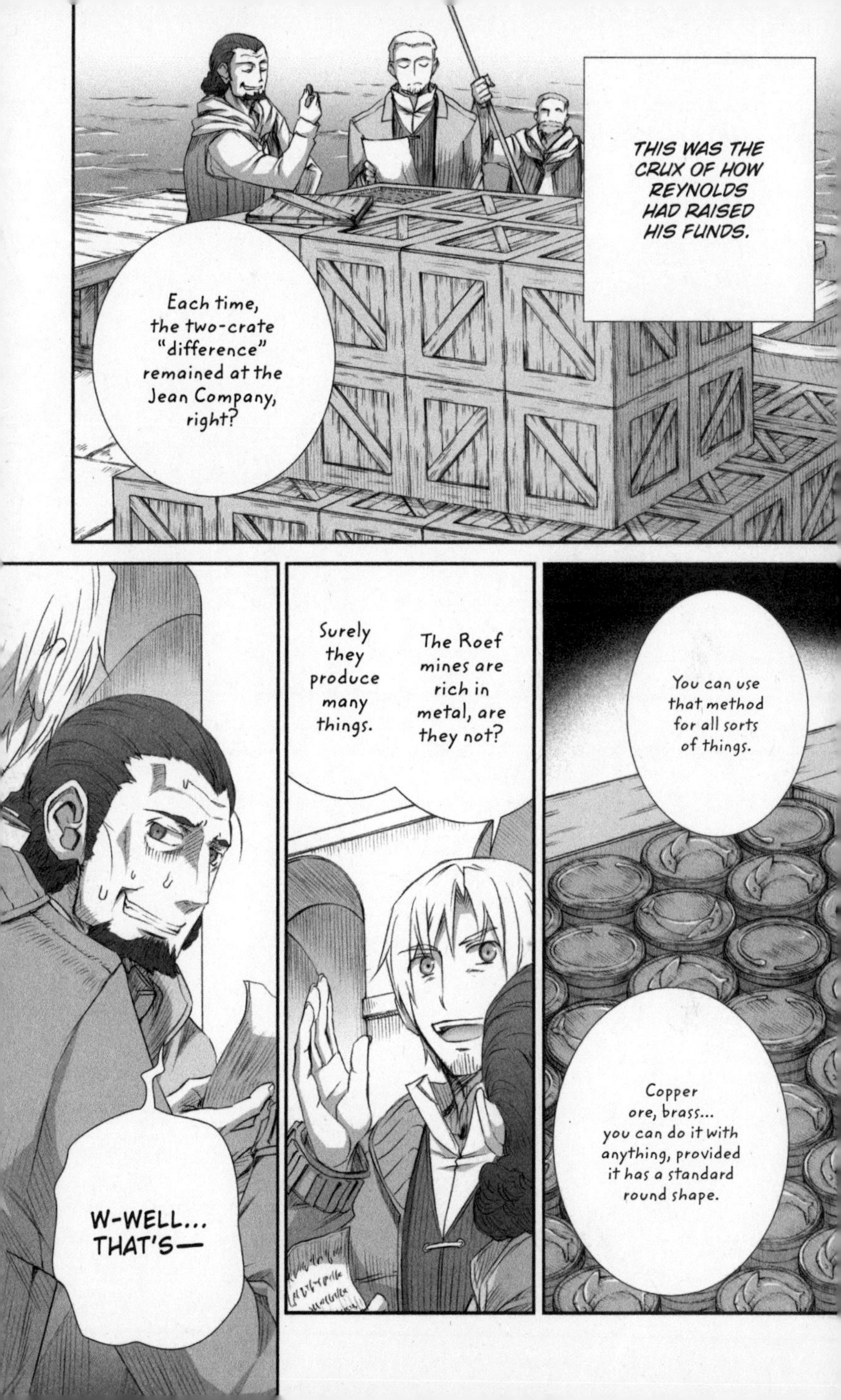
THIS WAS THE CRUX OF HOW REYNOLDS HAD RAISED HIS FUNDS.
Each time, the two-crate "difference" remained at the Jean Company, right?
You can use that method for all sorts of things.
Copper ore, brass... you can do it with anything, provided it has a standard round shape.
The Roef mines are rich in metal, are they not?
Surely they produce many things.
W-WELL... THAT'S—

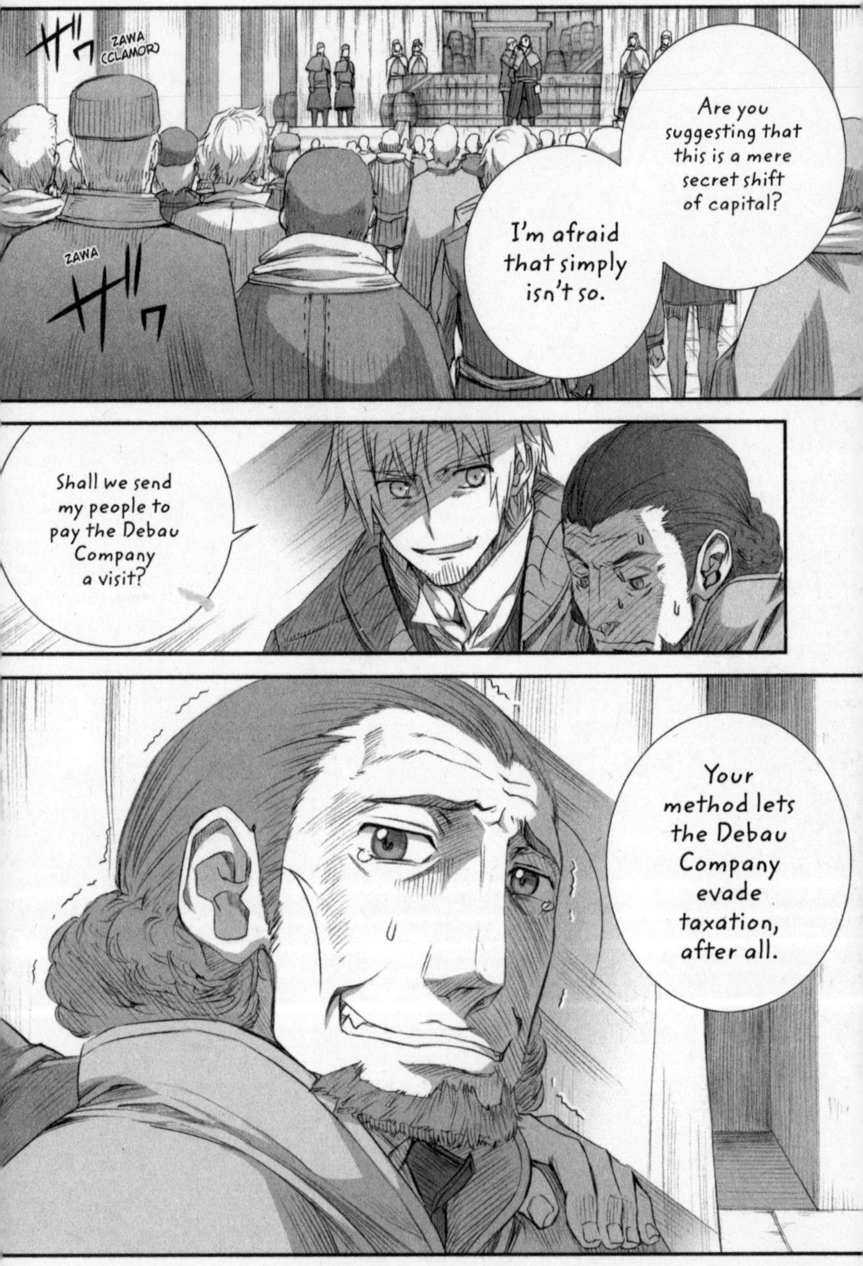
Are you suggesting that this is a mere secret shift of capital?
I'm afraid that simply isn't so.
ZAWA (CLAMOR)
ZAWA
Shall we send my people to pay the Debau Company a visit?
Your method lets the Debau Company evade taxation, after all.

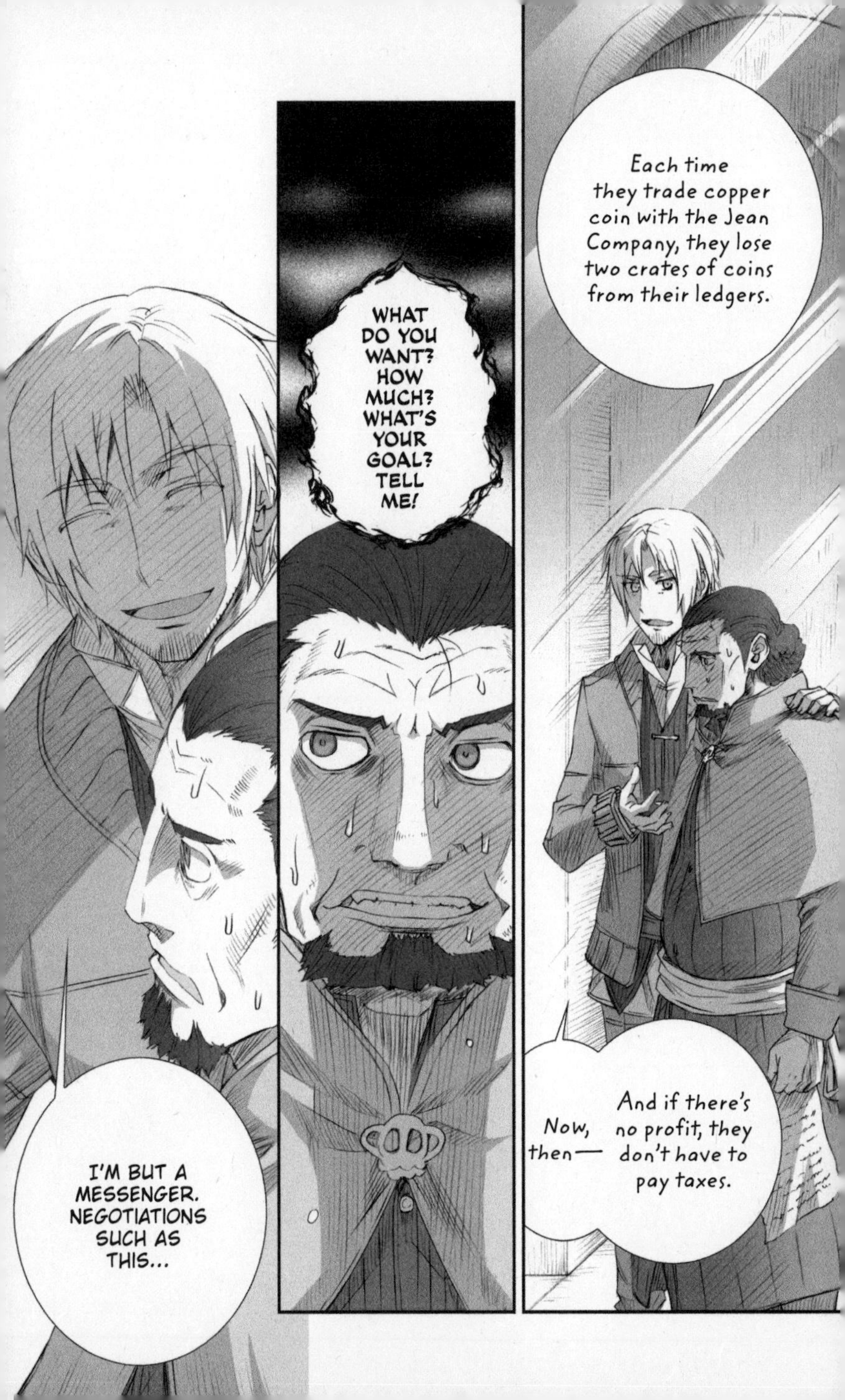
Each time they trade copper coin with the Jean Company, they lose two crates of coins from their ledgers.
And if there's no profit, they don't have to pay taxes.
Now, then—
WHAT DO YOU WANT? HOW MUCH? WHAT'S YOUR GOAL? TELL ME!
I'M BUT A MESSENGER. NEGOTIATIONS SUCH AS THIS...

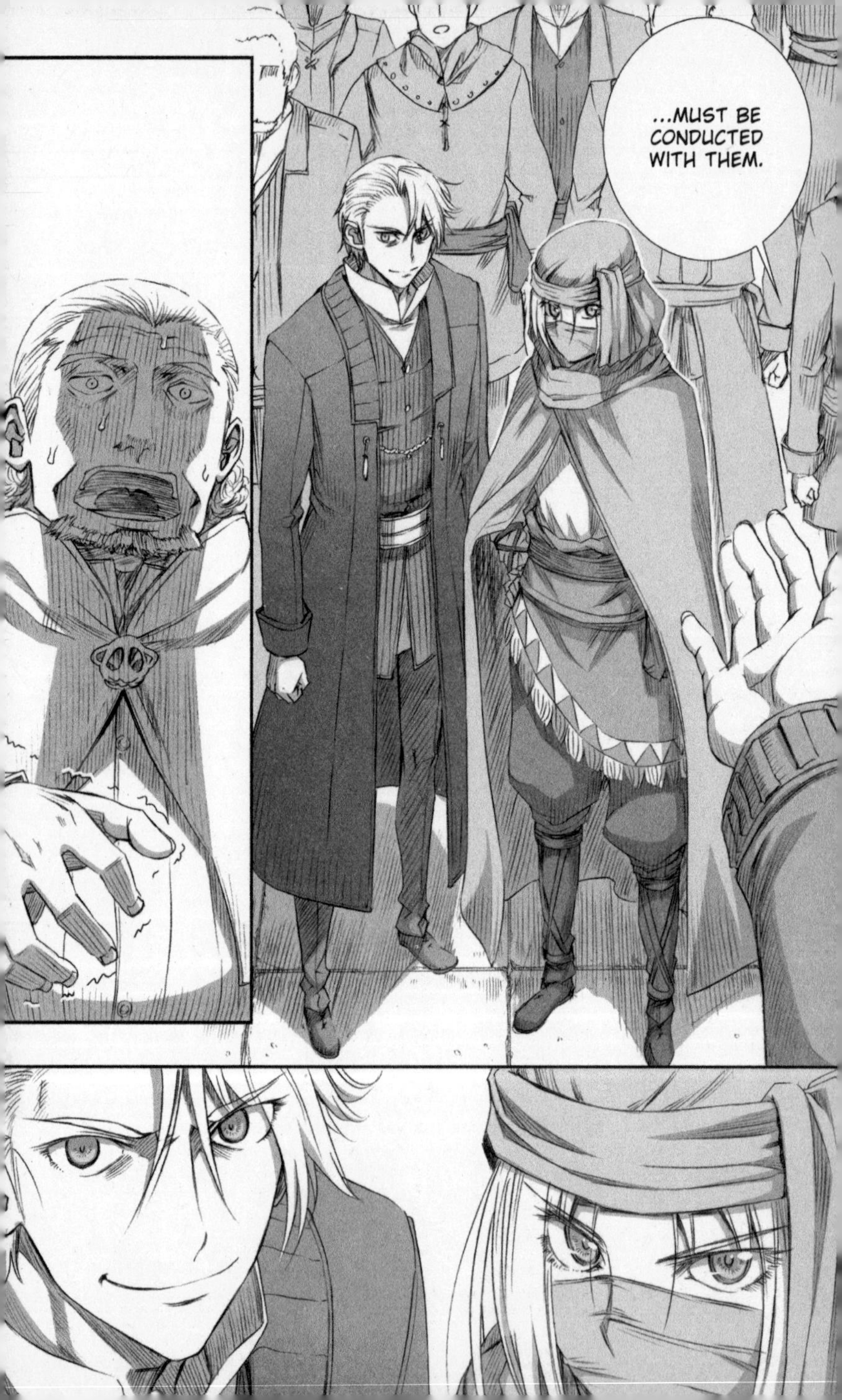
...MUST BE CONDUCTED WITH THEM.

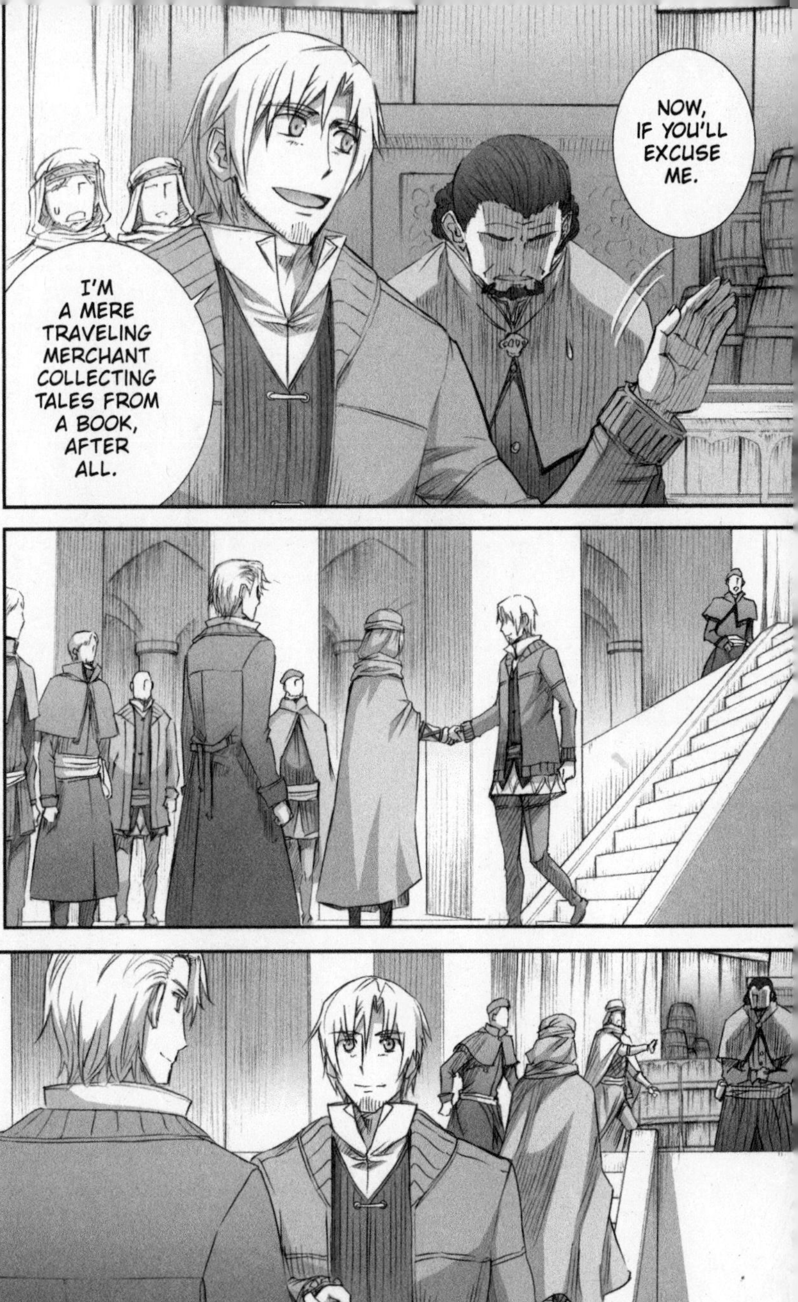
NOW, IF YOU'LL EXCUSE ME.
I'M A MERE TRAVELING MERCHANT COLLECTING TALES FROM A BOOK, AFTER ALL.

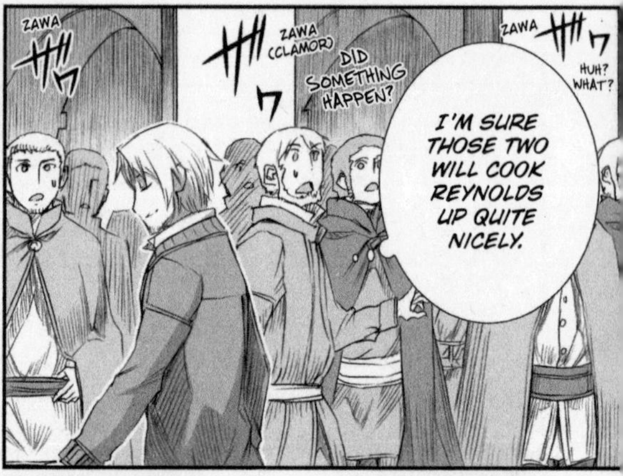
ZAWA
HUH? WHAT?
I'M SURE THOSE TWO WILL COOK REYNOLDS UP QUITE NICELY.
ZAWA (CLAMOR)
DID SOMETHING HAPPEN?
ZAWA

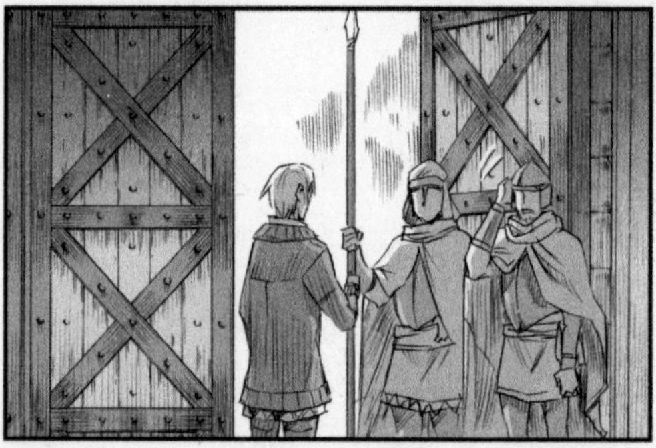

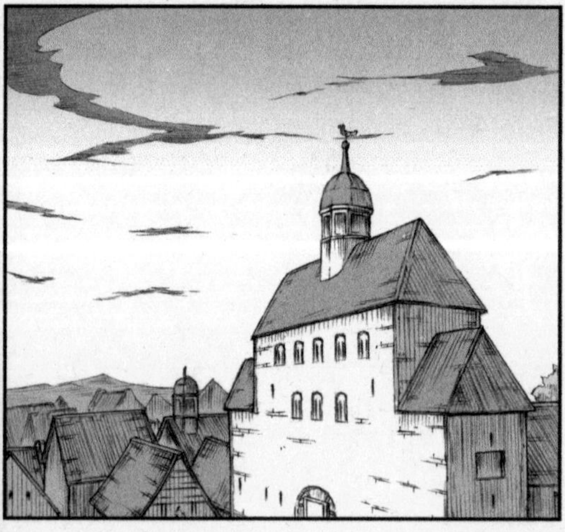

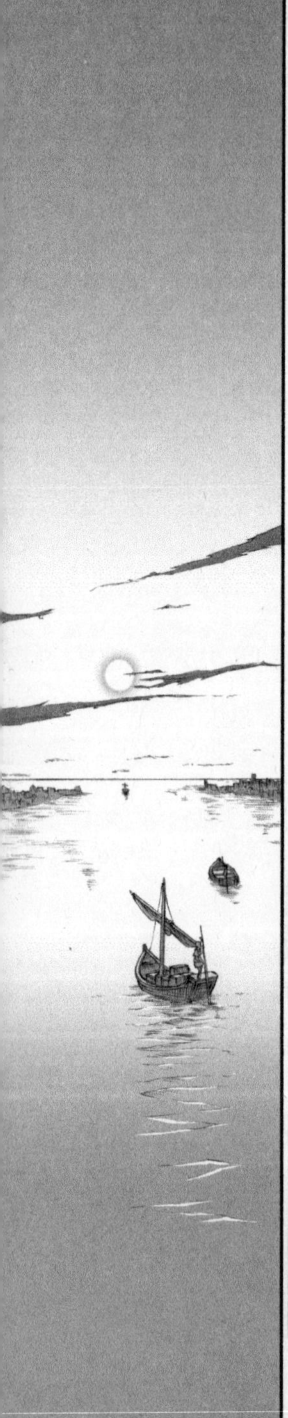

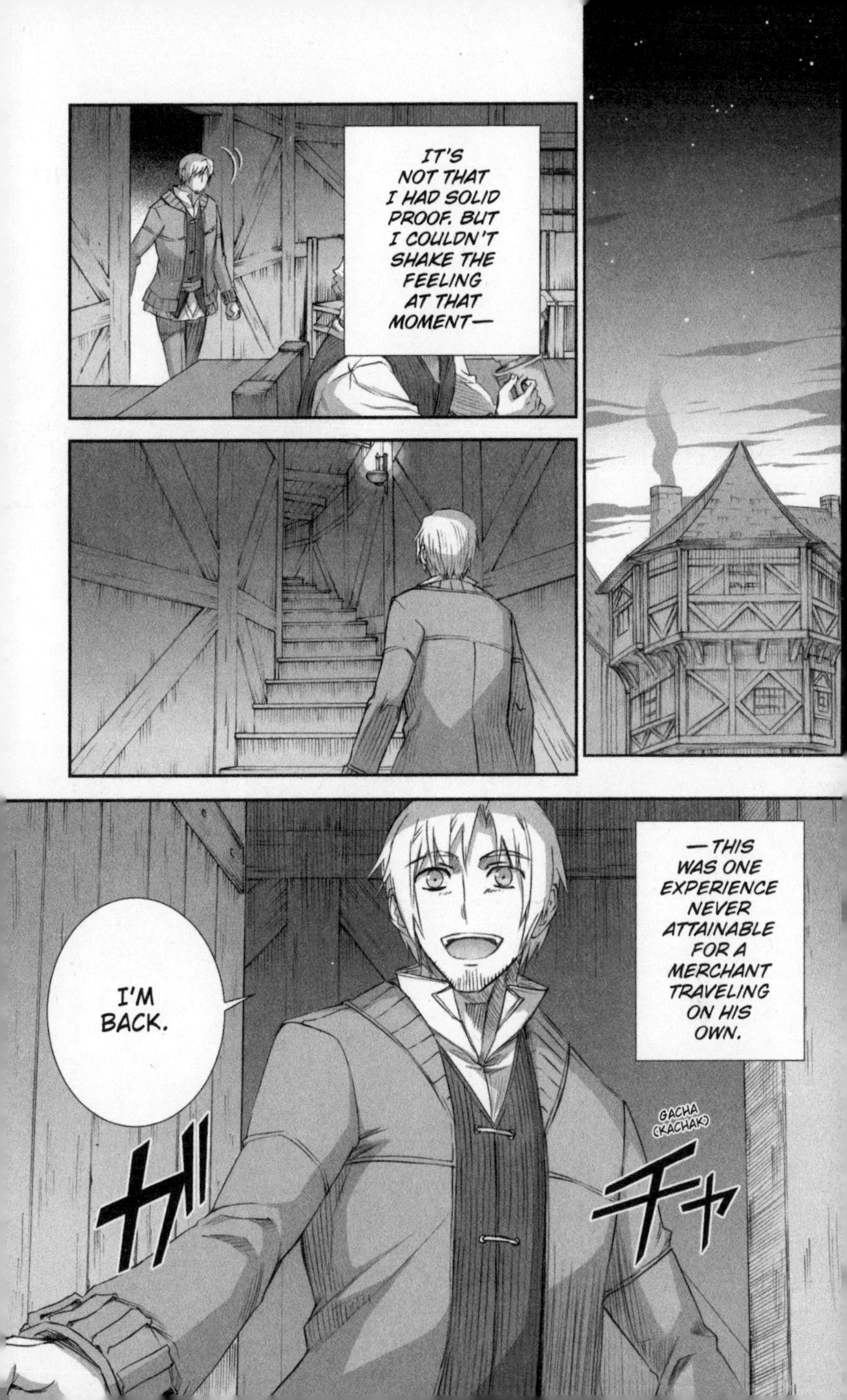
IT'S NOT THAT I HAD SOLID PROOF. BUT I COULDN'T SHAKE THE FEELING AT THAT MOMENT—
—THIS WAS ONE EXPERIENCE NEVER ATTAINABLE FOR A MERCHANT TRAVELING ON HIS OWN.
I'M BACK.
GACHA (KACHAK)

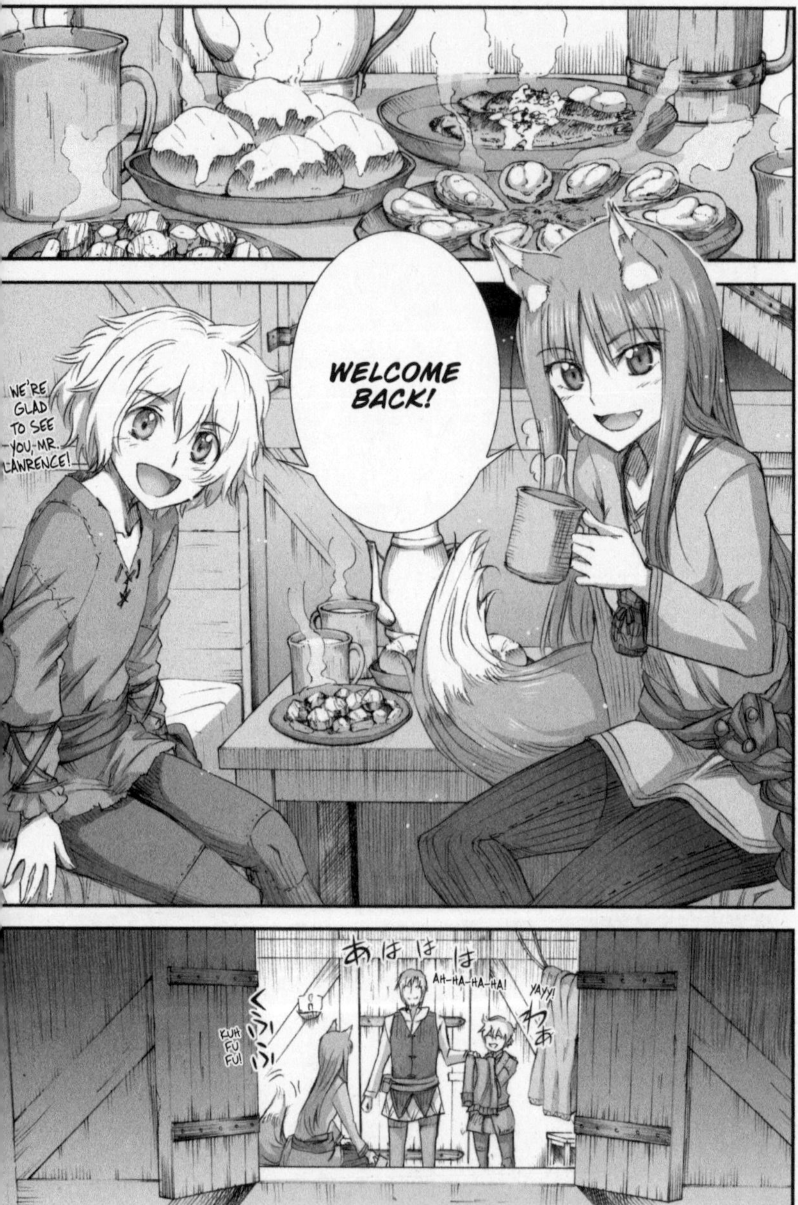
WELCOME BACK!
WE'RE GLAD TO SEE YOU, MR. LAWRENCE!
わあ
YAYY!
あははは
AH-HA-HA-HA!
くふふ
KUH FU FU!

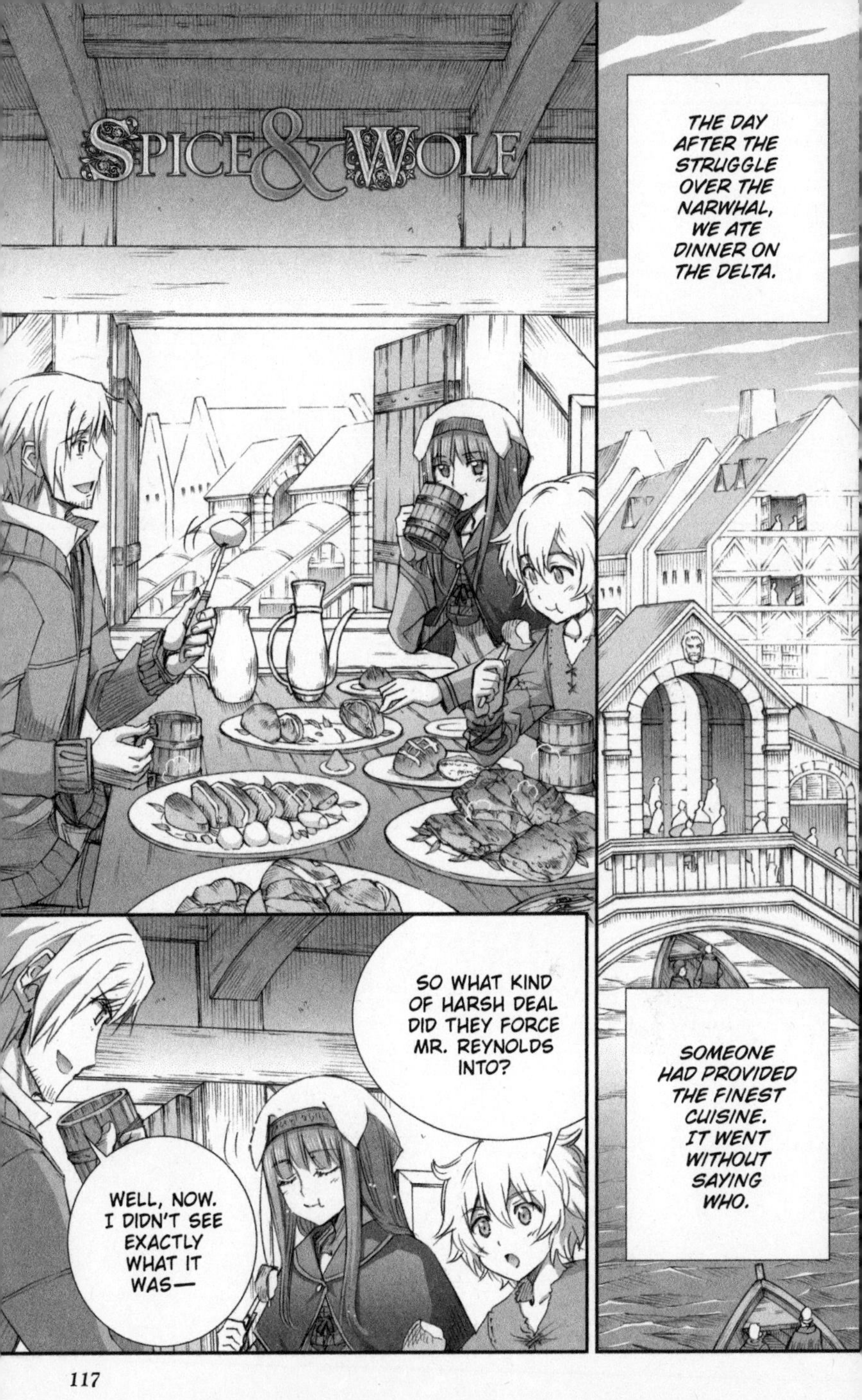
THE DAY AFTER THE STRUGGLE OVER THE NARWHAL, WE ATE DINNER ON THE DELTA.
SOMEONE HAD PROVIDED THE FINEST CUISINE. IT WENT WITHOUT SAYING WHO.
SPICE & WOLF
SO WHAT KIND OF HARSH DEAL DID THEY FORCE MR. REYNOLDS INTO?
WELL, NOW. I DIDN'T SEE EXACTLY WHAT IT WAS—

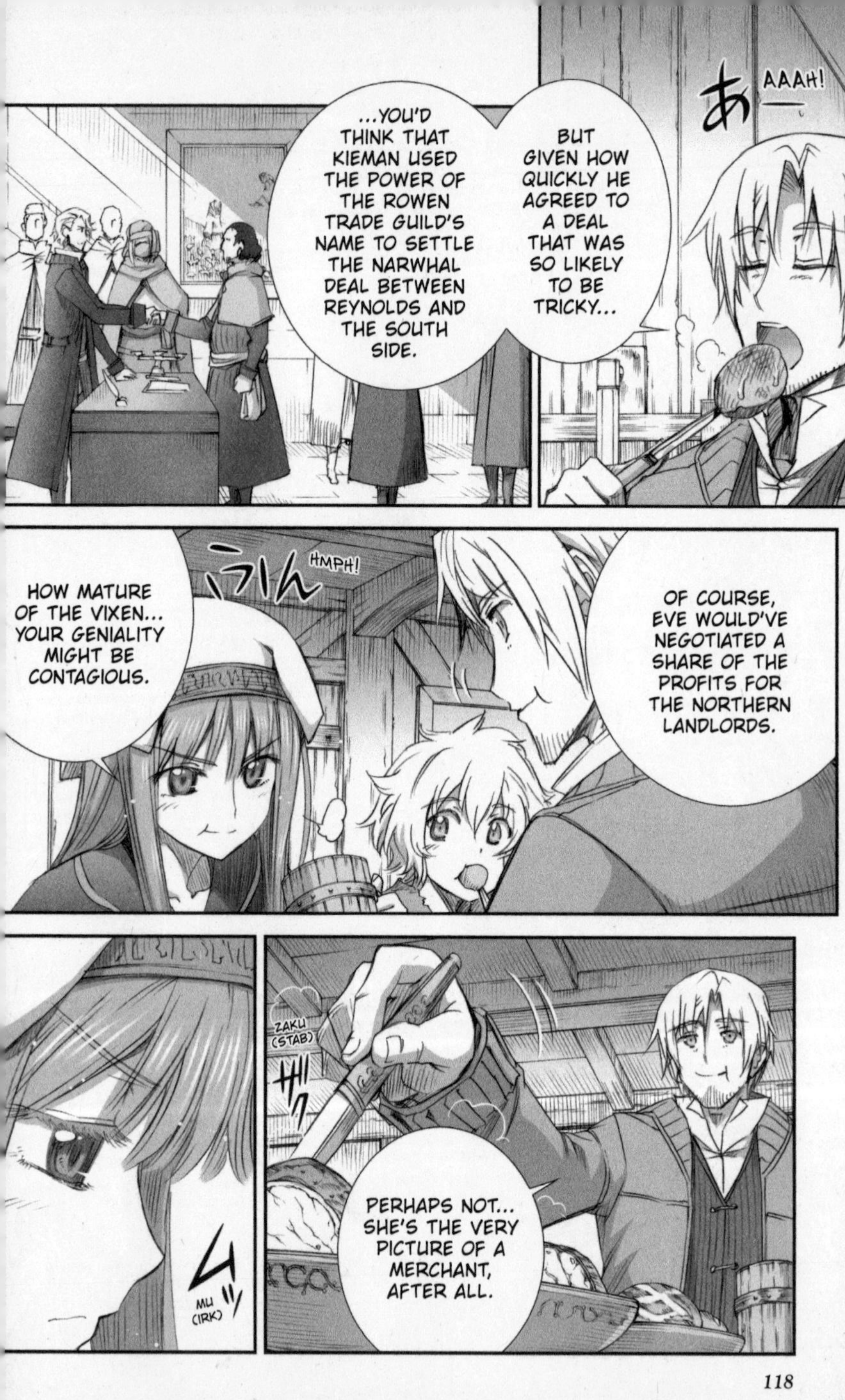
あー
AAAH!
...YOU'D THINK THAT KIEMAN USED THE POWER OF THE ROWEN TRADE GUILD'S NAME TO SETTLE THE NARWHAL DEAL BETWEEN REYNOLDS AND THE SOUTH SIDE.
BUT GIVEN HOW QUICKLY HE AGREED TO A DEAL THAT WAS SO LIKELY TO BE TRICKY...
OF COURSE, EVE WOULD'VE NEGOTIATED A SHARE OF THE PROFITS FOR THE NORTHERN LANDLORDS.
ふん
HMPH!
HOW MATURE OF THE VIXEN... YOUR GENIALITY MIGHT BE CONTAGIOUS.
ザク
ZAKU (STAB)
PERHAPS NOT... SHE'S THE VERY PICTURE OF A MERCHANT, AFTER ALL.
ムッ
MU (IRK)

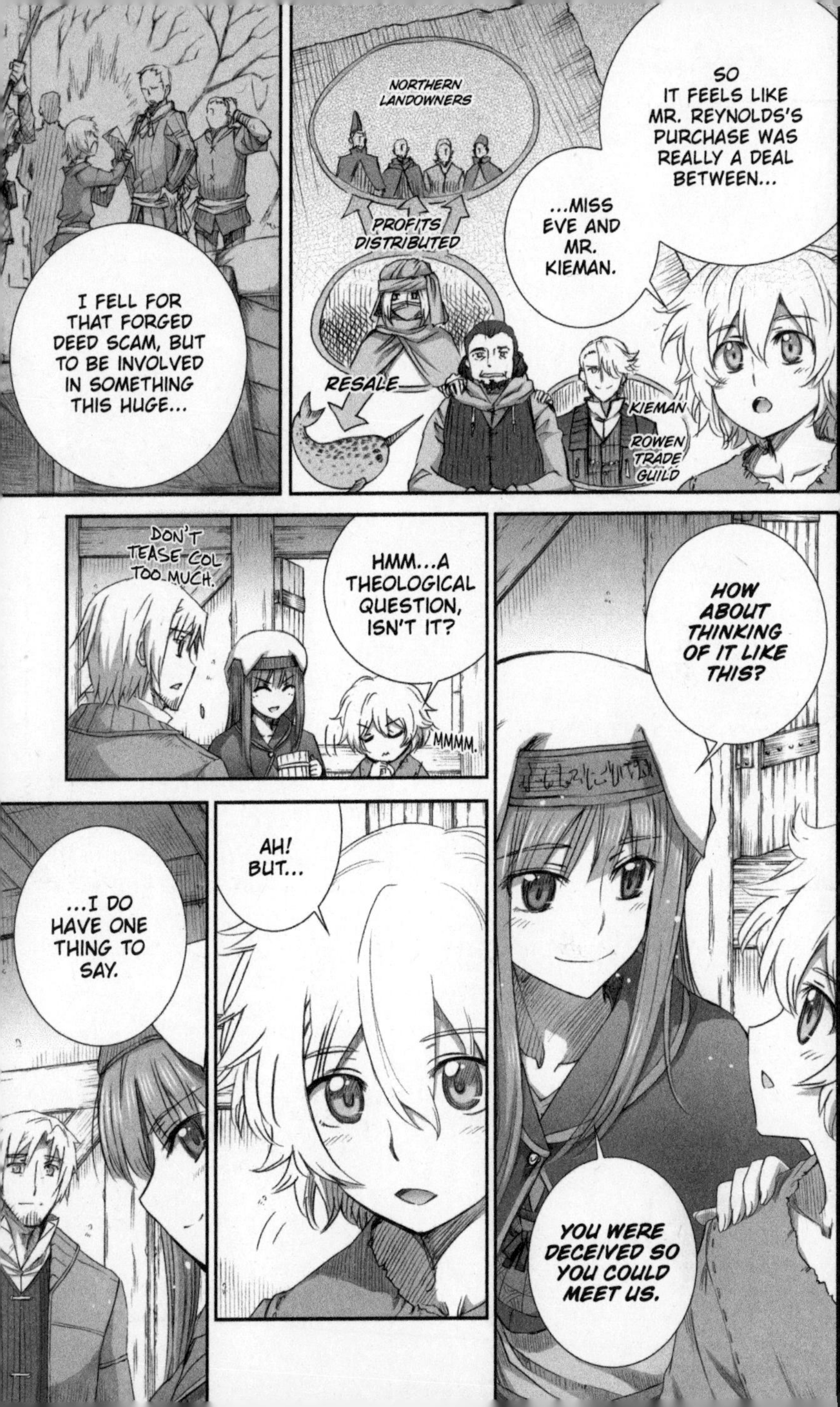
I FELL FOR THAT FORGED DEED SCAM, BUT TO BE INVOLVED IN SOMETHING THIS HUGE...
NORTHERN LANDOWNERS
PROFITS DISTRIBUTED
RESALE
KIEMAN
ROWEN TRADE GUILD
SO IT FEELS LIKE MR. REYNOLDS'S PURCHASE WAS REALLY A DEAL BETWEEN...
...MISS EVE AND MR. KIEMAN.
MMMM.
HMM...A THEOLOGICAL QUESTION, ISN'T IT?
DON'T TEASE COL TOO MUCH.
HOW ABOUT THINKING OF IT LIKE THIS?
YOU WERE DECEIVED SO YOU COULD MEET US.
AH! BUT...
...I DO HAVE ONE THING TO SAY.

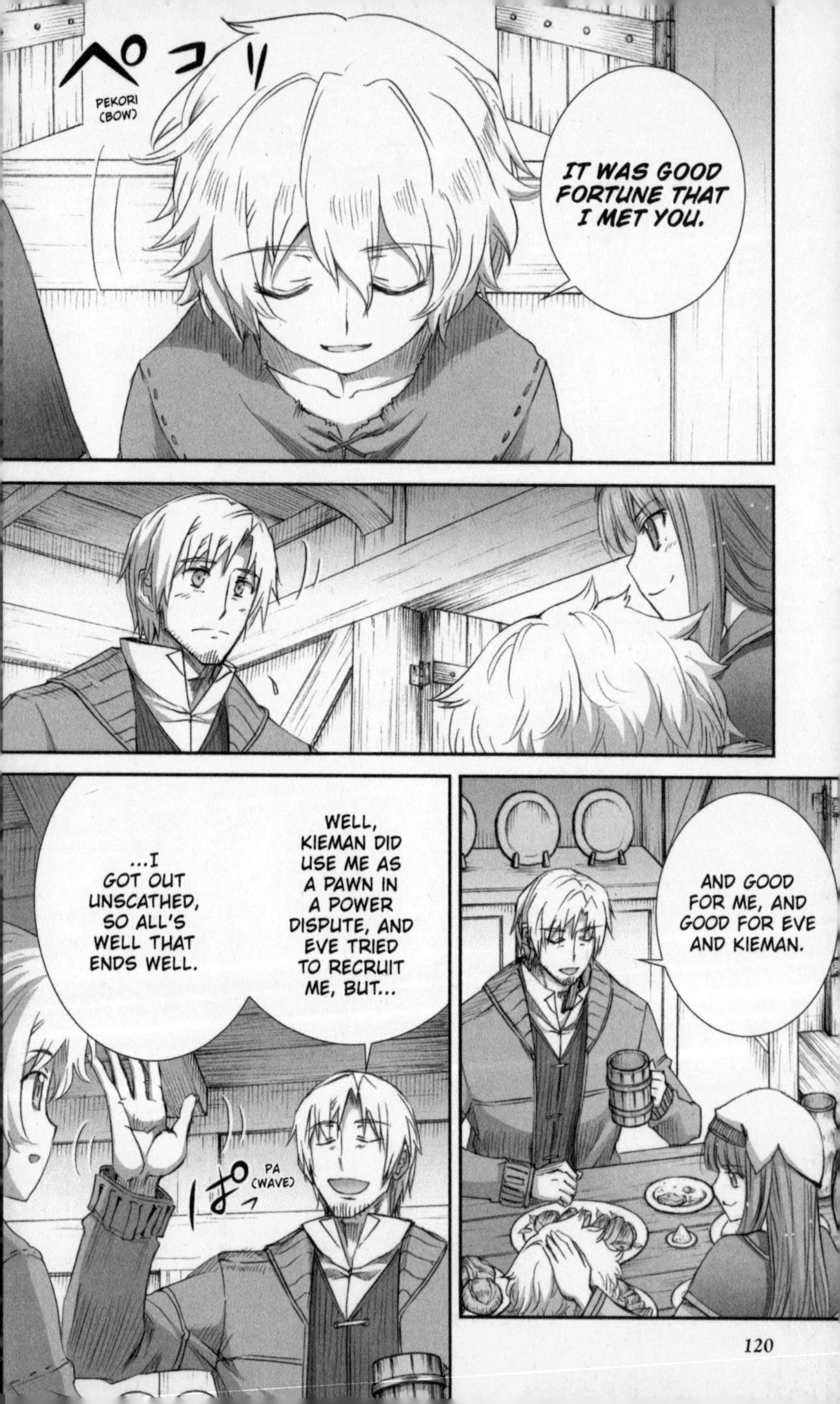
ペコリ
PEKORI (BOW)
IT WAS GOOD FORTUNE THAT I MET YOU.
AND GOOD FOR ME, AND GOOD FOR EVE AND KIEMAN.
WELL, KIEMAN DID USE ME AS A PAWN IN A POWER DISPUTE, AND EVE TRIED TO RECRUIT ME, BUT...
...I GOT OUT UNSCATHED, SO ALL'S WELL THAT ENDS WELL.
ぱっ
PA (WAVE)

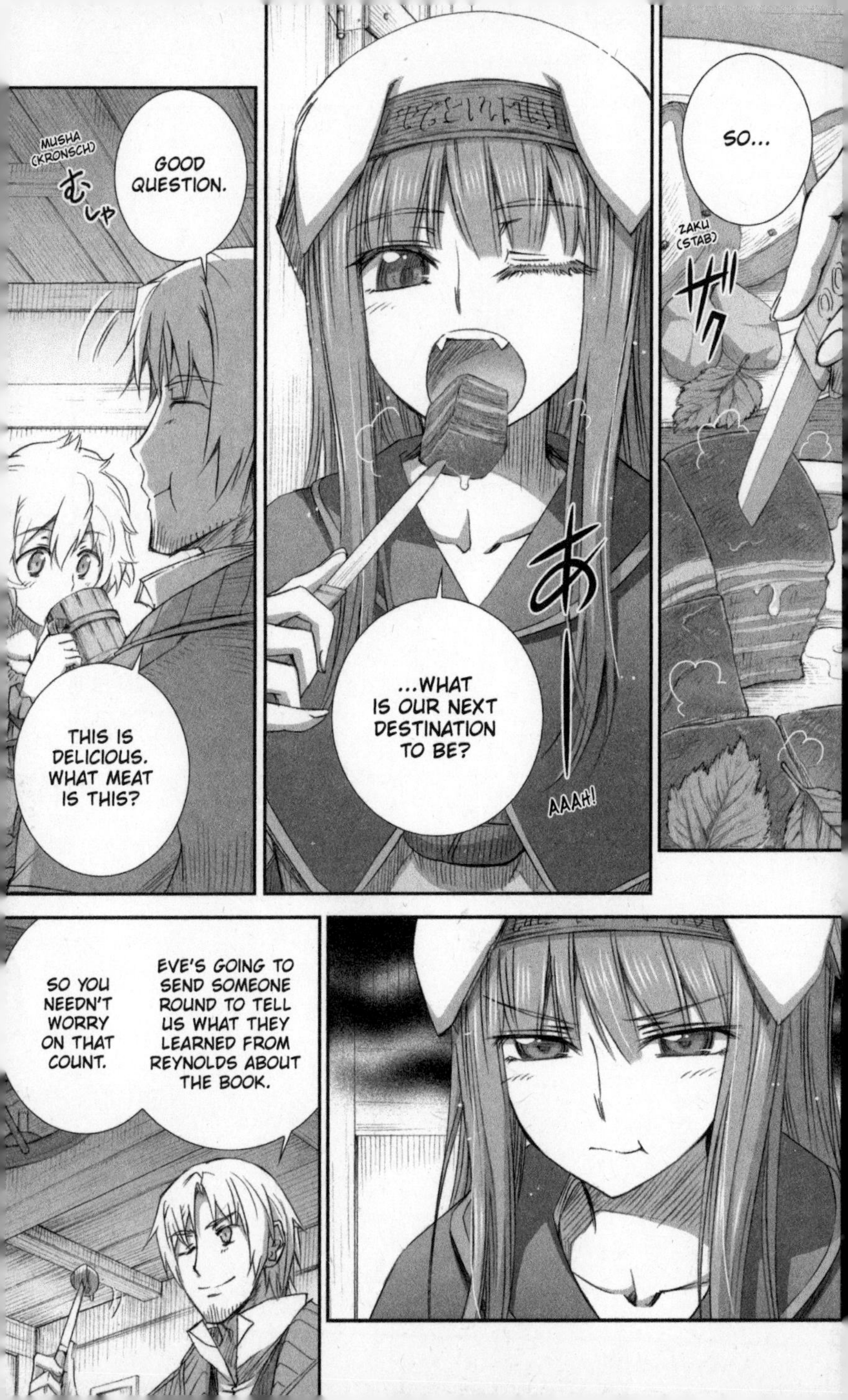
SO...
ZAKU (STAB)
ザク
...WHAT IS OUR NEXT DESTINATION TO BE?
あー
AAAH!
GOOD QUESTION.
MUSHA (KRONSCH)
むしゃ
THIS IS DELICIOUS. WHAT MEAT IS THIS?
EVE'S GOING TO SEND SOMEONE ROUND TO TELL US WHAT THEY LEARNED FROM REYNOLDS ABOUT THE BOOK.
SO YOU NEEDN'T WORRY ON THAT COUNT.

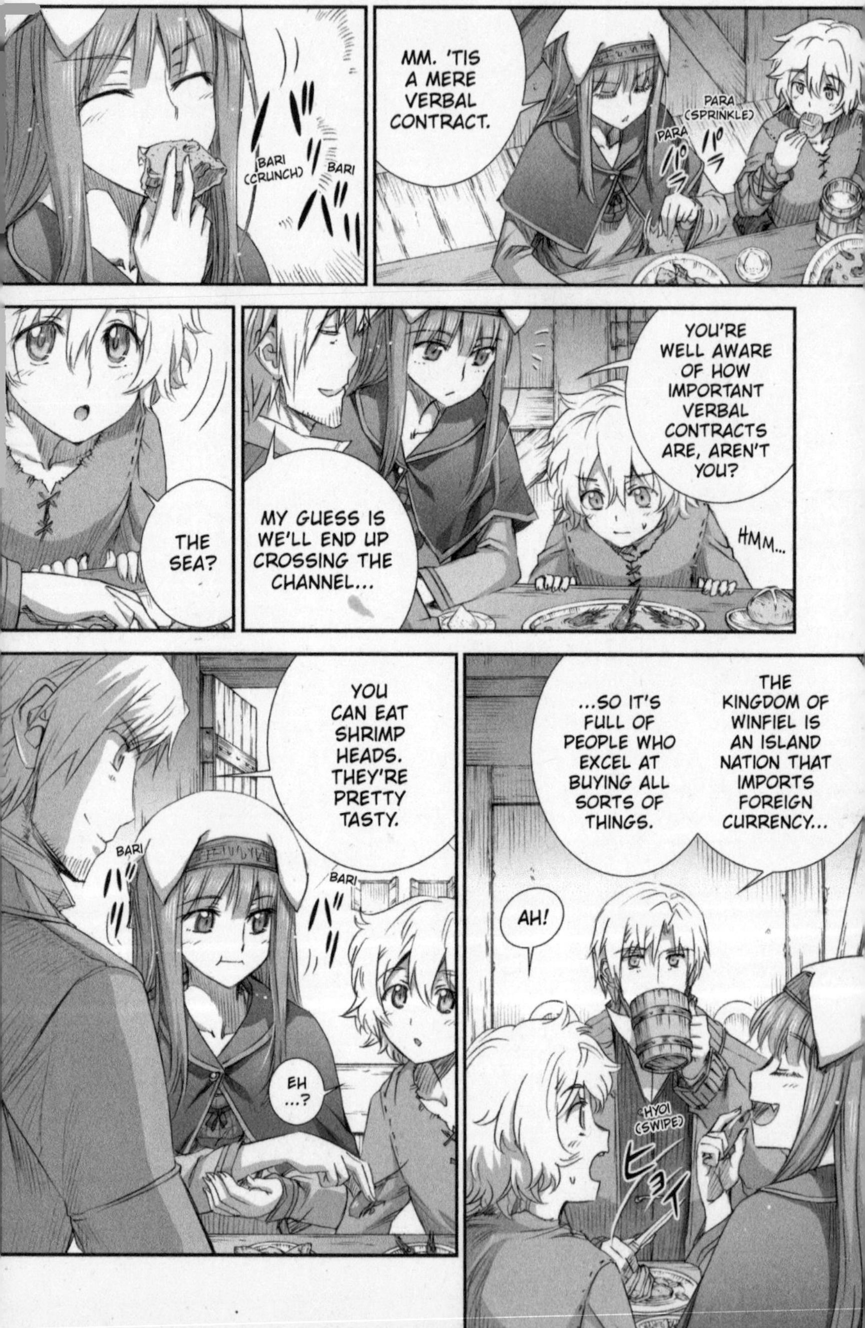
MM. 'TIS A MERE VERBAL CONTRACT.
PARA (SPRINKLE)
PARA
BARI (CRUNCH)
BARI
YOU'RE WELL AWARE OF HOW IMPORTANT VERBAL CONTRACTS ARE, AREN'T YOU?
HMM...
MY GUESS IS WE'LL END UP CROSSING THE CHANNEL...
THE SEA?
THE KINGDOM OF WINFIEL IS AN ISLAND NATION THAT IMPORTS FOREIGN CURRENCY...
...SO IT'S FULL OF PEOPLE WHO EXCEL AT BUYING ALL SORTS OF THINGS.
AH!
HYOI (SWIPE)
YOU CAN EAT SHRIMP HEADS. THEY'RE PRETTY TASTY.
BARI
BARI
EH ...?

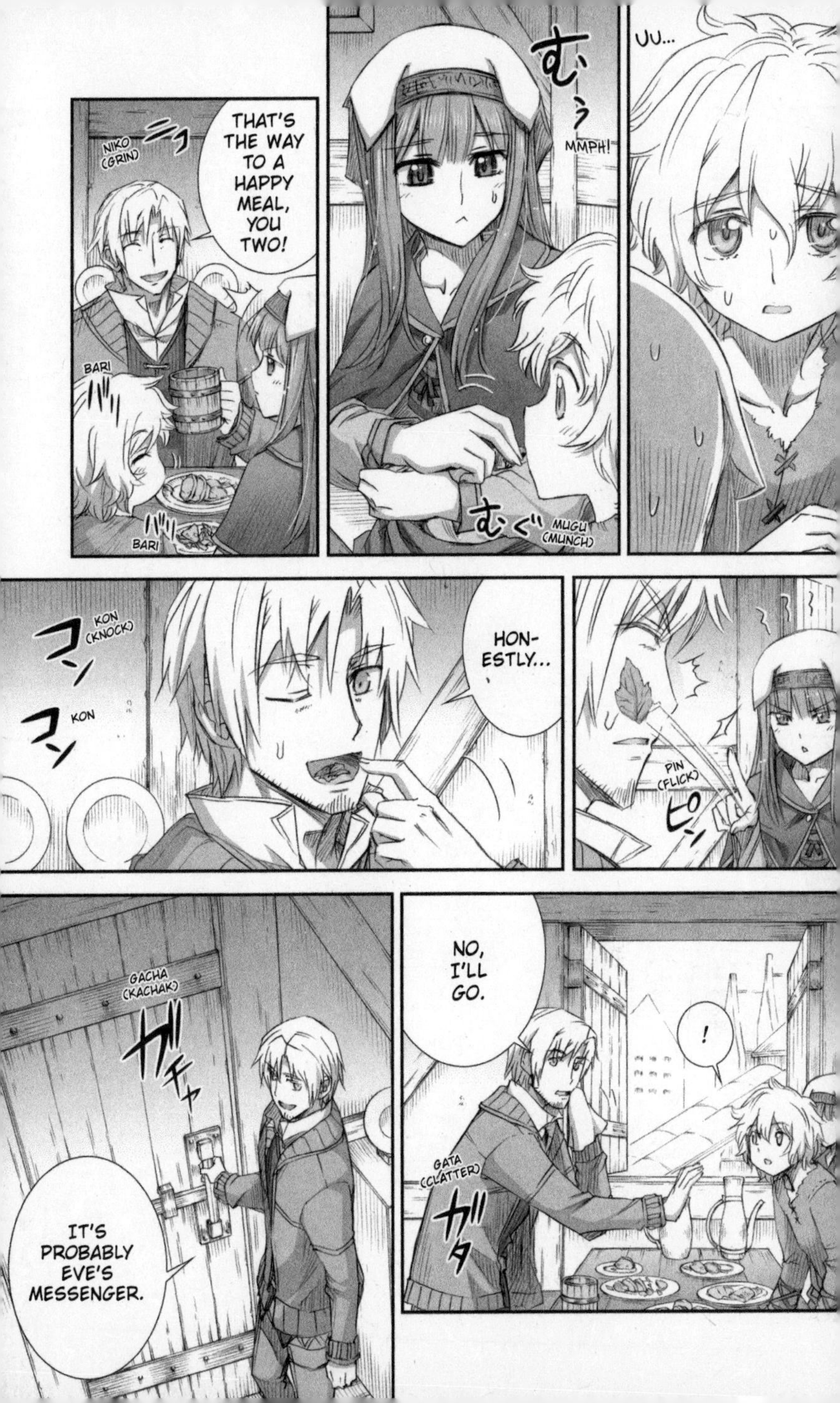
UU...
MMPH!
MUGU (MUNCH)
NIKO (GRIN)
THAT'S THE WAY TO A HAPPY MEAL, YOU TWO!
BARI
BARI
PIN (FLICK)
KON (KNOCK)
KON
HON-ESTLY...
NO, I'LL GO.
!
GATA (CLATTER)
GACHA (KACHAK)
IT'S PROBABLY EVE'S MESSENGER.

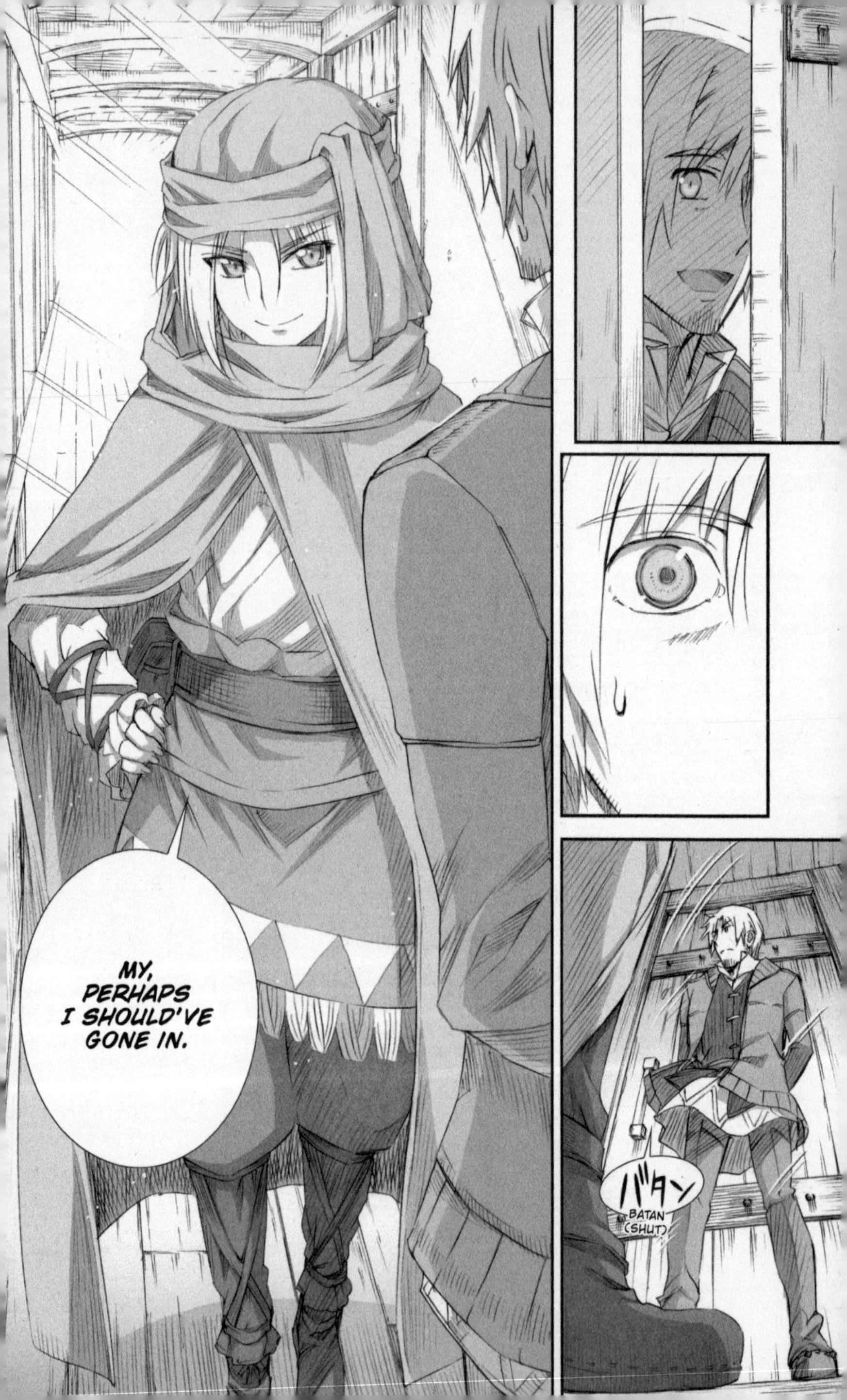
MY, PERHAPS I SHOULD'VE GONE IN.
バタン
BATAN (SHUT)

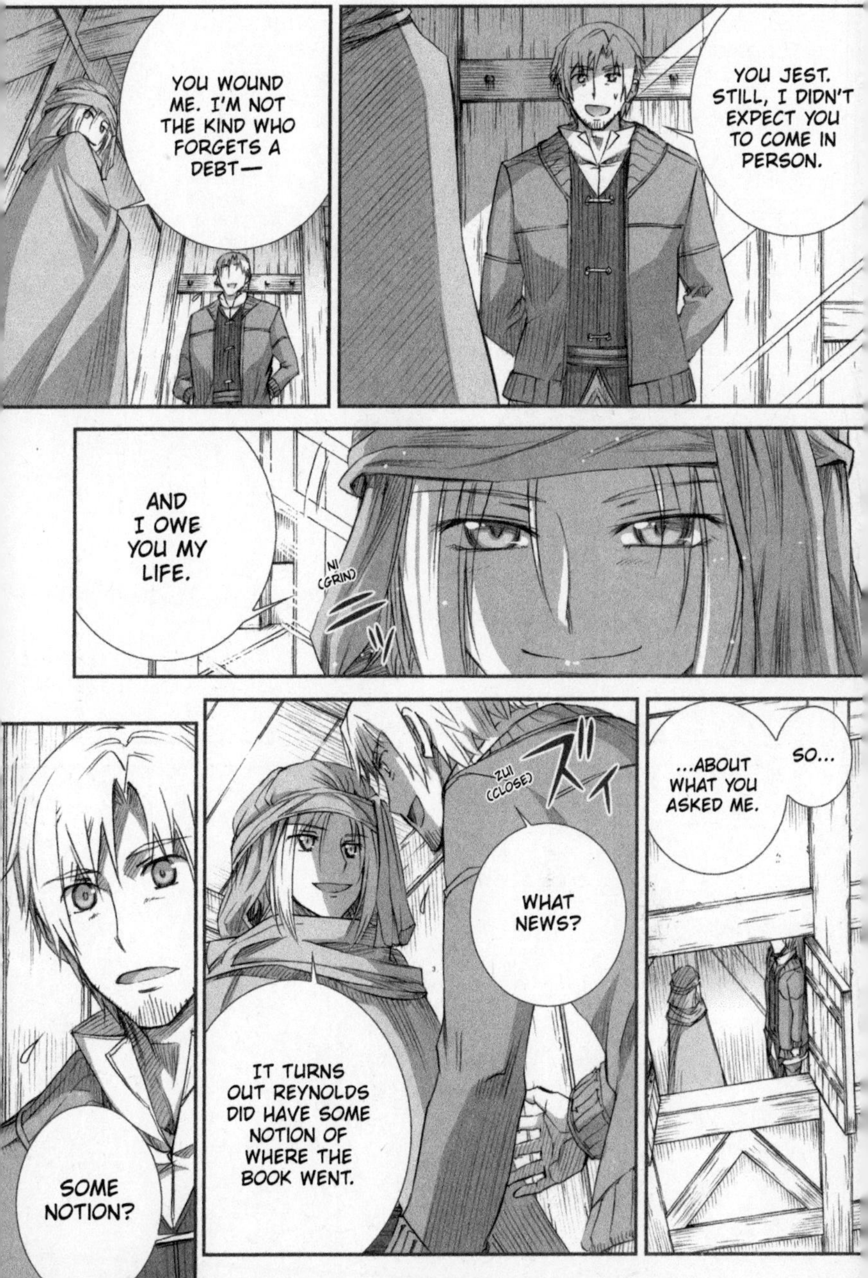
YOU JEST. STILL, I DIDN'T EXPECT YOU TO COME IN PERSON.
YOU WOUND ME. I'M NOT THE KIND WHO FORGETS A DEBT—
AND I OWE YOU MY LIFE.
NI (GRIN)
SO...
...ABOUT WHAT YOU ASKED ME.
ZUI (CLOSE)
WHAT NEWS?
IT TURNS OUT REYNOLDS DID HAVE SOME NOTION OF WHERE THE BOOK WENT.
SOME NOTION?

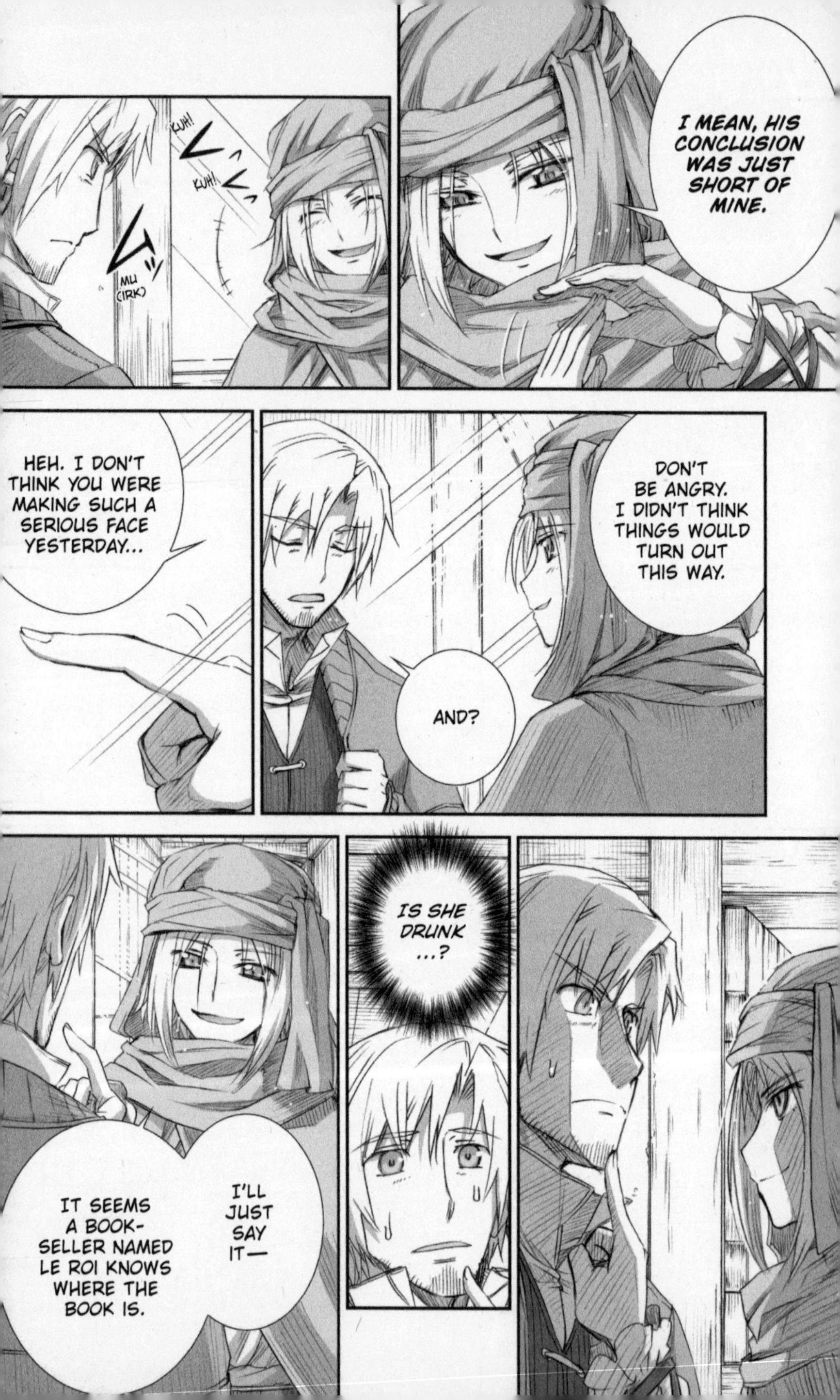
I MEAN, HIS CONCLUSION WAS JUST SHORT OF MINE.
KUH!
KUH!
MU (IRK)
DON'T BE ANGRY. I DIDN'T THINK THINGS WOULD TURN OUT THIS WAY.
AND?
HEH. I DON'T THINK YOU WERE MAKING SUCH A SERIOUS FACE YESTERDAY...
IS SHE DRUNK ...?
I'LL JUST SAY IT—
IT SEEMS A BOOK-SELLER NAMED LE ROI KNOWS WHERE THE BOOK IS.

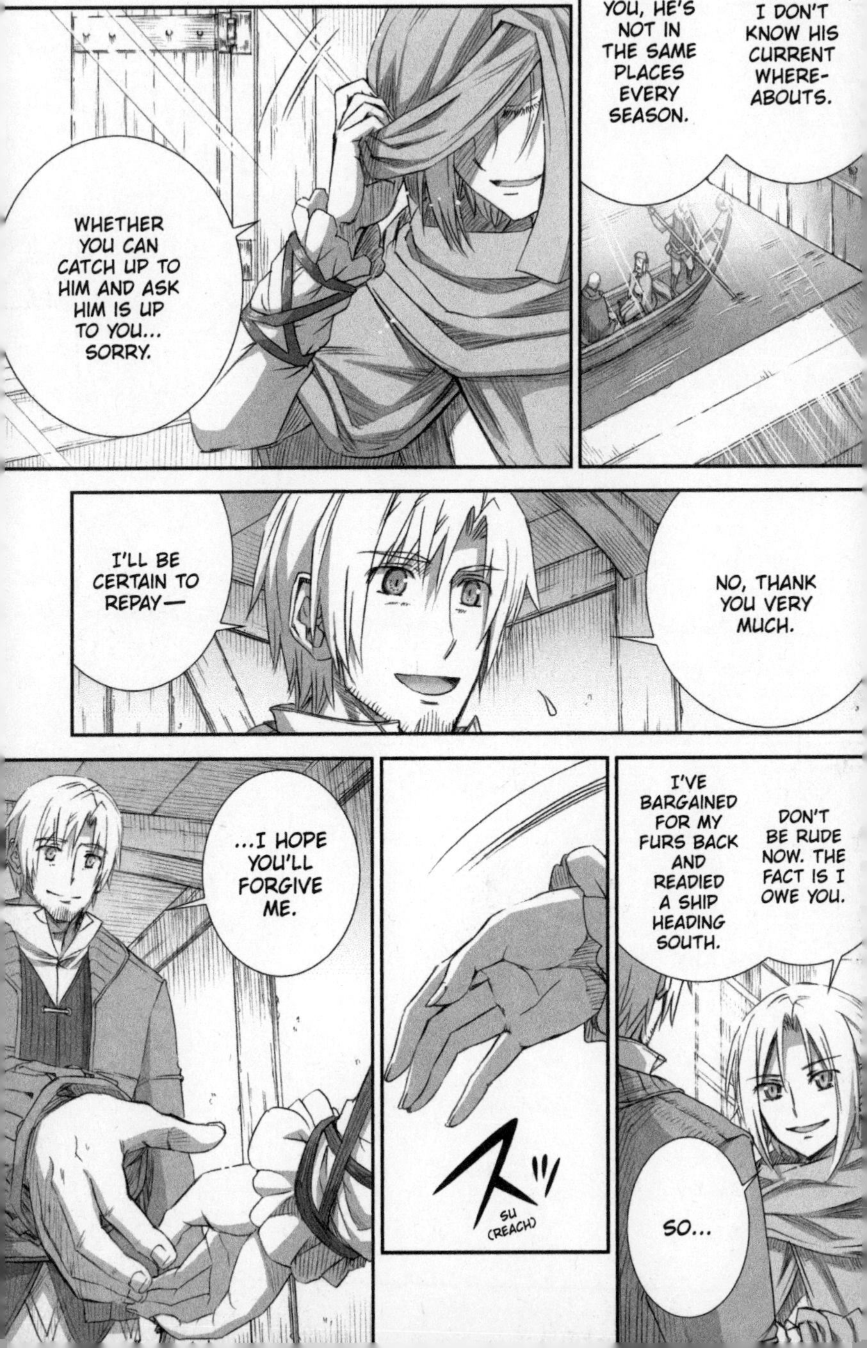
—HOWEVER, I DON'T KNOW HIS CURRENT WHEREABOUTS.
UNLIKE YOU, HE'S NOT IN THE SAME PLACES EVERY SEASON.
WHETHER YOU CAN CATCH UP TO HIM AND ASK HIM IS UP TO YOU... SORRY.
NO, THANK YOU VERY MUCH.
I'LL BE CERTAIN TO REPAY—
DON'T BE RUDE NOW. THE FACT IS I OWE YOU.
I'VE BARGAINED FOR MY FURS BACK AND READIED A SHIP HEADING SOUTH.
SO...
SU (REACH)
...I HOPE YOU'LL FORGIVE ME.

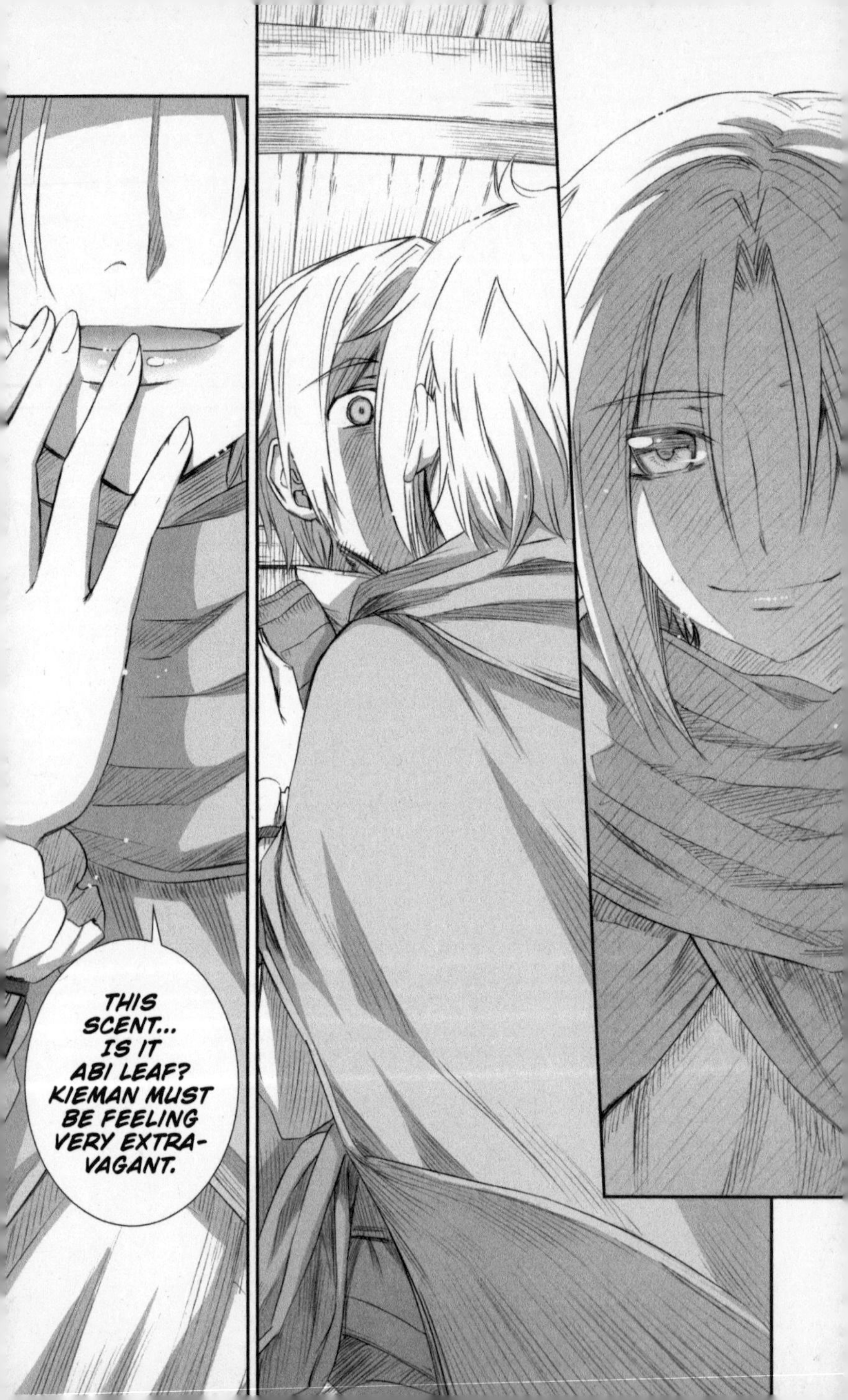
THIS SCENT... IS IT ABI LEAF? KIEMAN MUST BE FEELING VERY EXTRA-VAGANT.

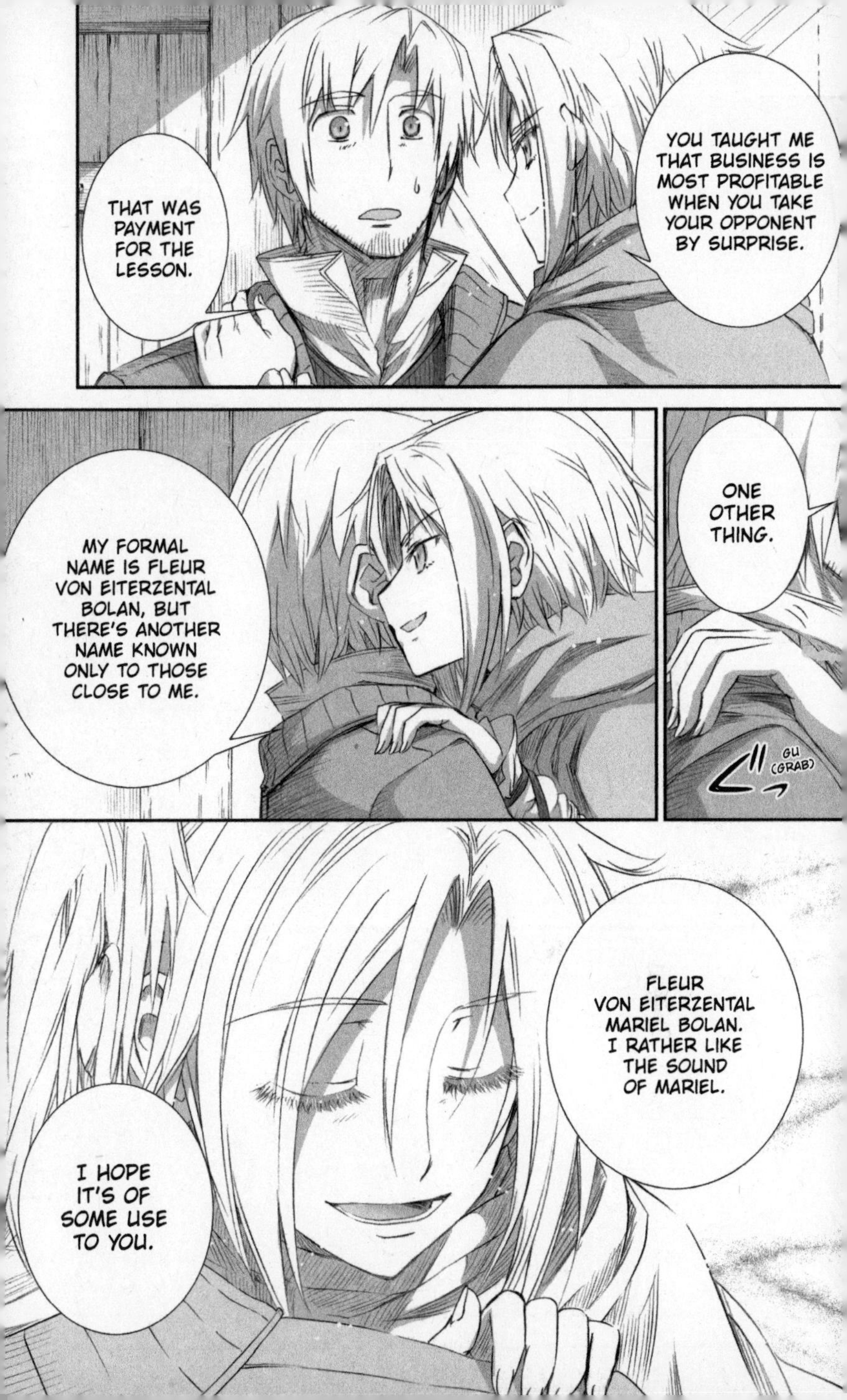
YOU TAUGHT ME THAT BUSINESS IS MOST PROFITABLE WHEN YOU TAKE YOUR OPPONENT BY SURPRISE.
THAT WAS PAYMENT FOR THE LESSON.
ONE OTHER THING.
GU (GRAB)
MY FORMAL NAME IS FLEUR VON EITERZENTAL BOLAN, BUT THERE'S ANOTHER NAME KNOWN ONLY TO THOSE CLOSE TO ME.
FLEUR VON EITERZENTAL MARIEL BOLAN. I RATHER LIKE THE SOUND OF MARIEL.
I HOPE IT'S OF SOME USE TO YOU.

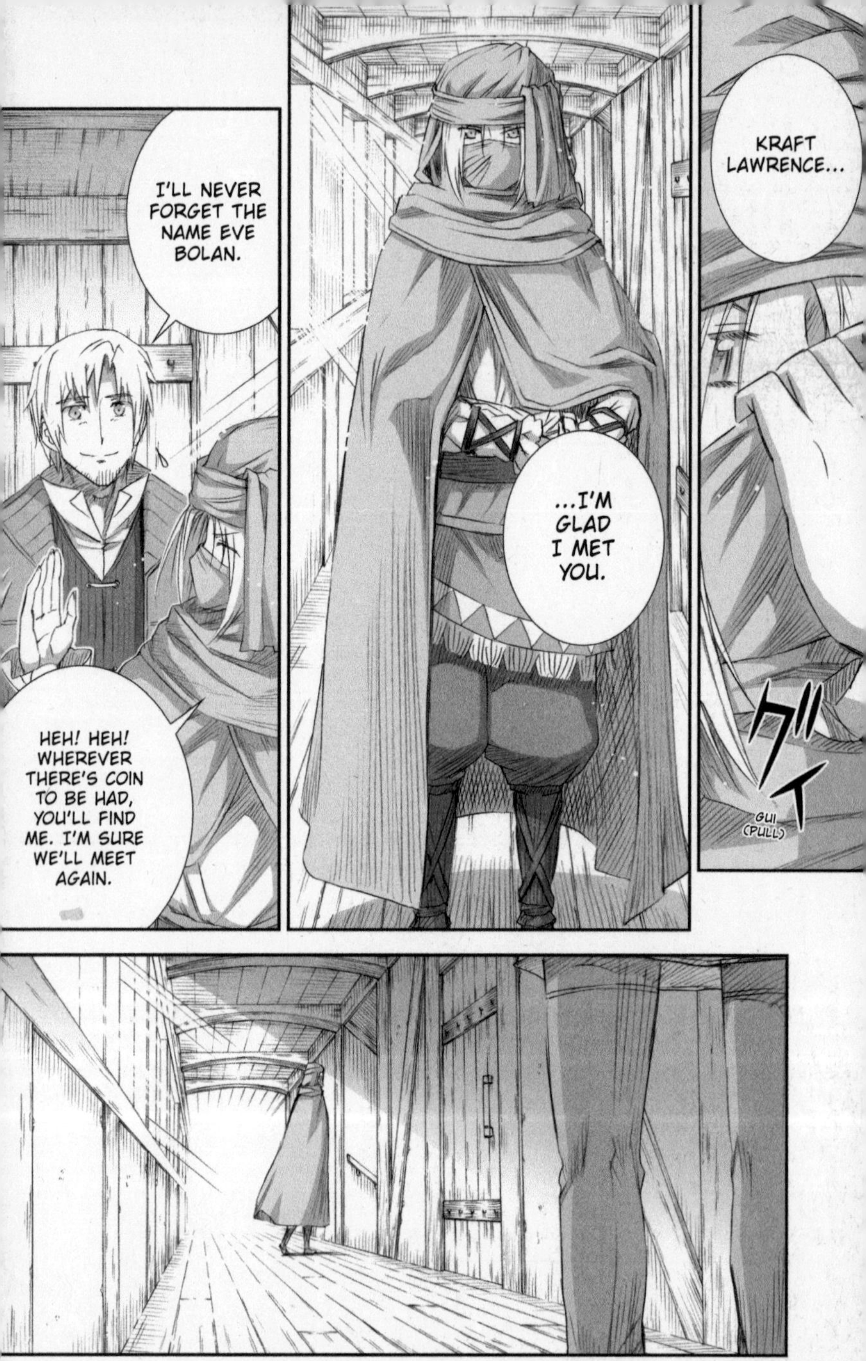
KRAFT LAWRENCE...
GUI (PULL)
...I'M GLAD I MET YOU.
I'LL NEVER FORGET THE NAME EVE BOLAN.
HEH! HEH! WHEREVER THERE'S COIN TO BE HAD, YOU'LL FIND ME. I'M SURE WE'LL MEET AGAIN.

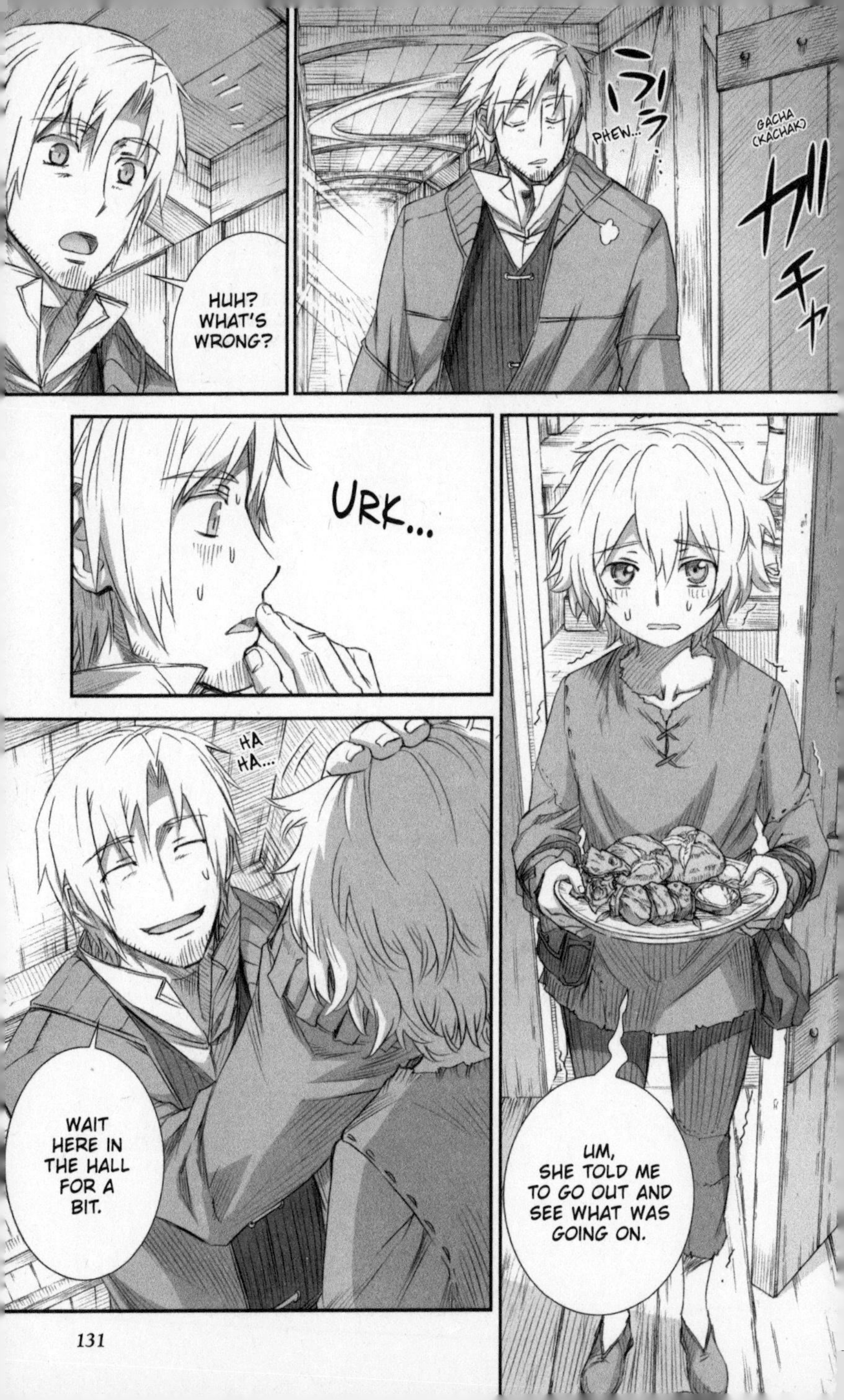
GACHA (KACHAK)
ガチャ
PHEW...
HUH? WHAT'S WRONG?
UM, SHE TOLD ME TO GO OUT AND SEE WHAT WAS GOING ON.
URK...
HA HA...
WAIT HERE IN THE HALL FOR A BIT.

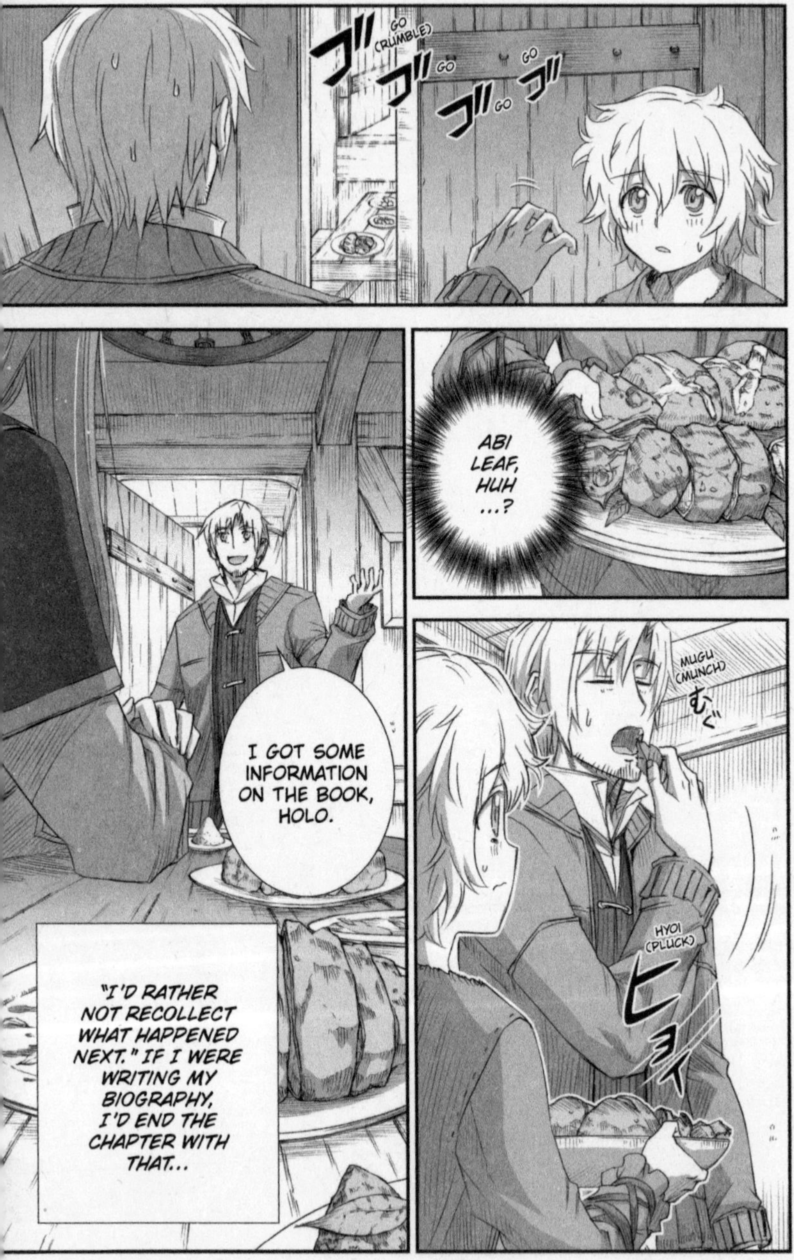
ゴ GO (RUMBLE)
ゴ GO
ゴ GO
ゴ GO
ABI LEAF, HUH ...?
むぐ MUGU (MUNCH)
ヒョイ HYOI (PLUCK)
I GOT SOME INFORMATION ON THE BOOK, HOLO.
"I'D RATHER NOT RECOLLECT WHAT HAPPENED NEXT." IF I WERE WRITING MY BIOGRAPHY, I'D END THE CHAPTER WITH THAT...

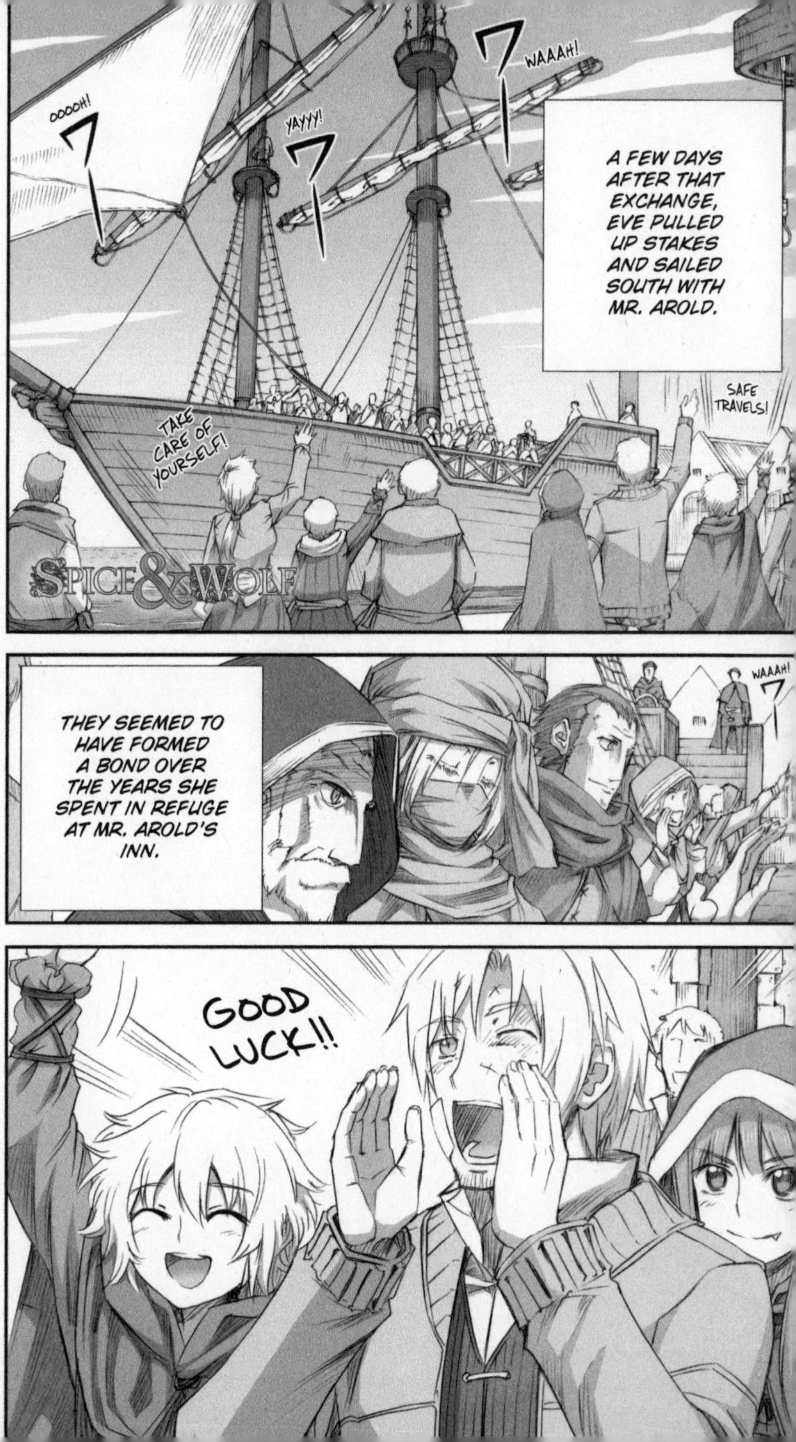
WAAAH!
A FEW DAYS AFTER THAT EXCHANGE, EVE PULLED UP STAKES AND SAILED SOUTH WITH MR. AROLD.
YAYYY!
OOOOH!
SAFE TRAVELS!
TAKE CARE OF YOURSELF!
SPICE & WOLF
WAAAH!
THEY SEEMED TO HAVE FORMED A BOND OVER THE YEARS SHE SPENT IN REFUGE AT MR. AROLD'S INN.
GOOD LUCK!!

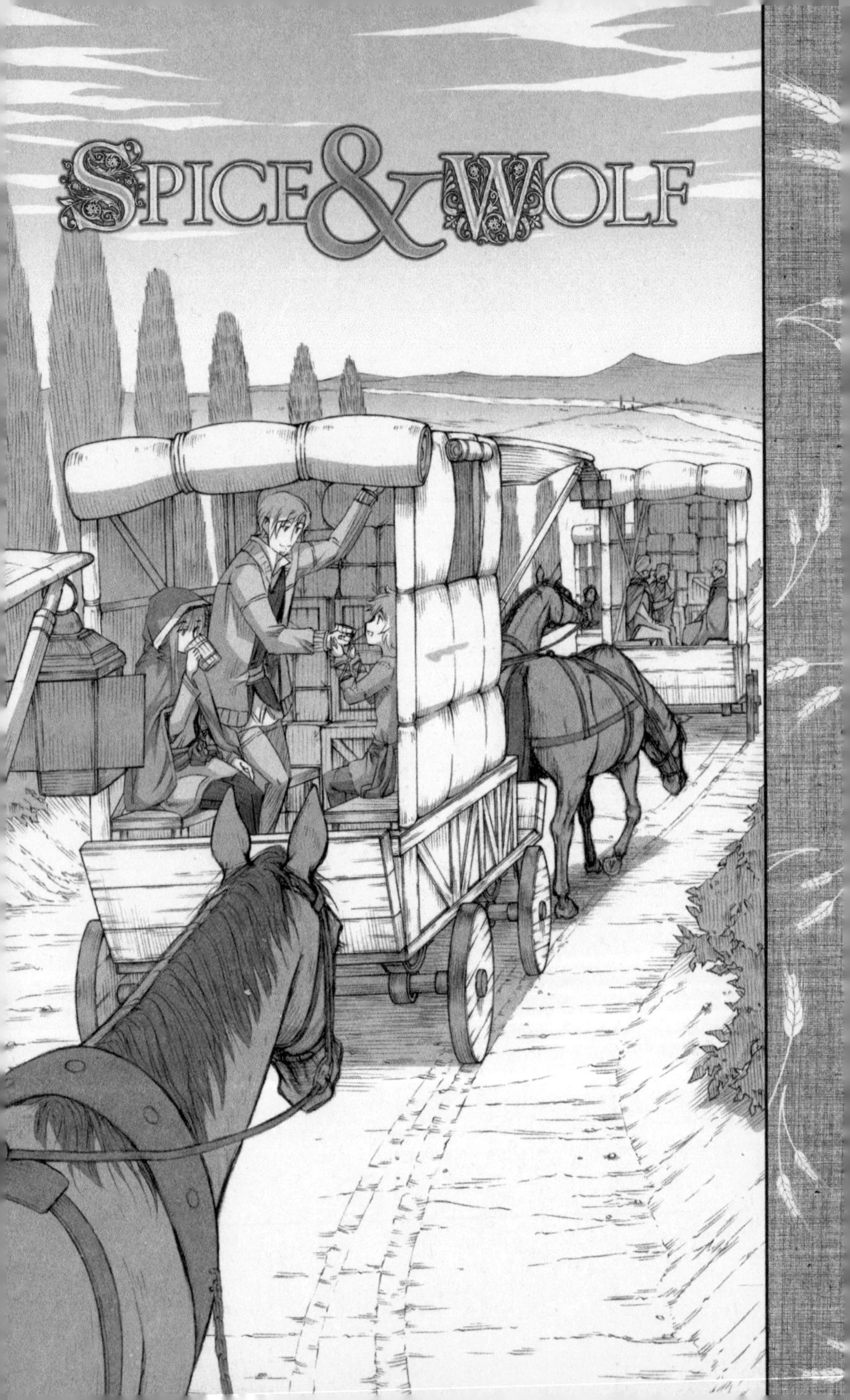
SPICE & WOLF

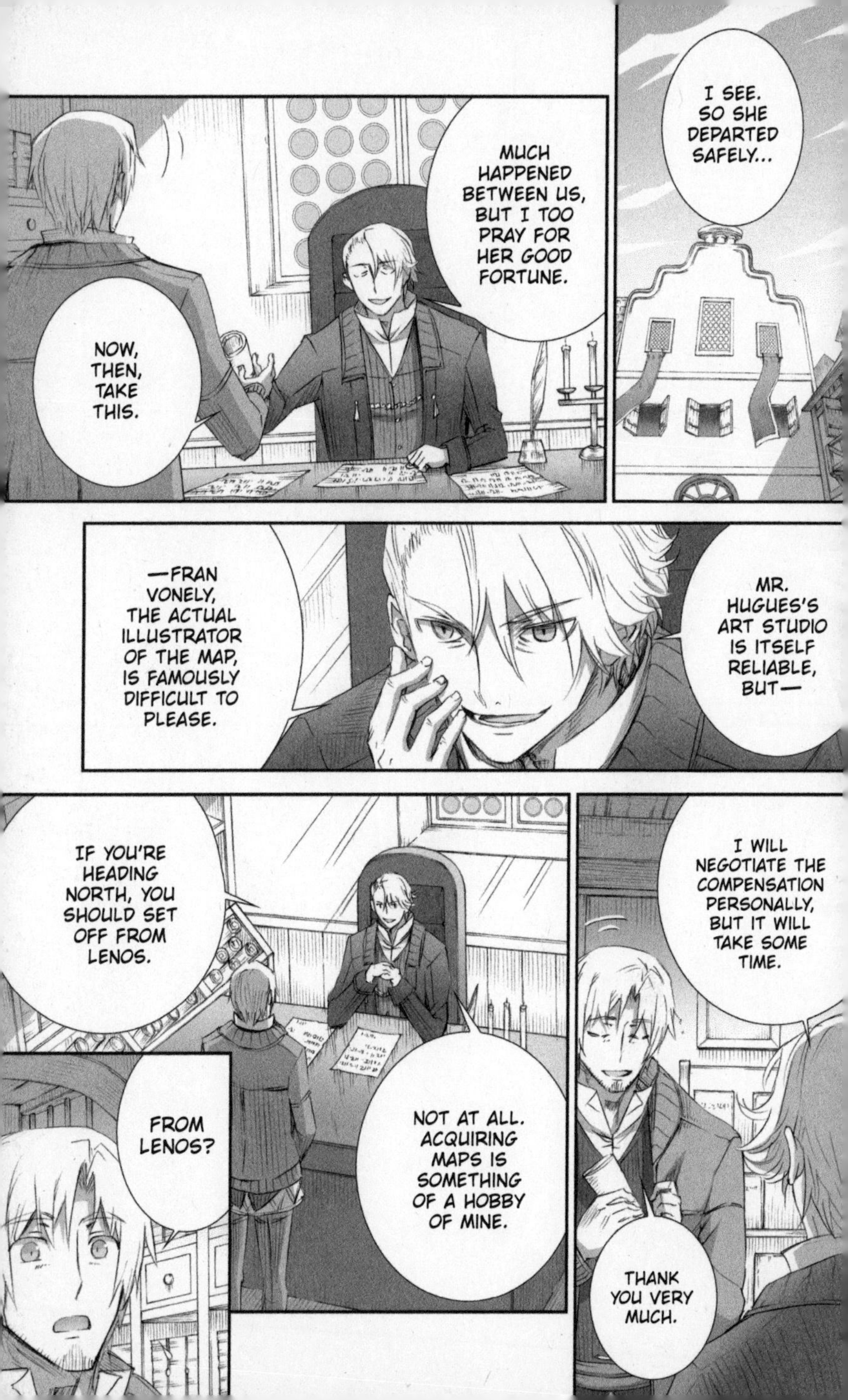
I SEE. SO SHE DEPARTED SAFELY...
MUCH HAPPENED BETWEEN US, BUT I TOO PRAY FOR HER GOOD FORTUNE.
NOW, THEN, TAKE THIS.
MR. HUGUES'S ART STUDIO IS ITSELF RELIABLE, BUT—
—FRAN VONELY, THE ACTUAL ILLUSTRATOR OF THE MAP, IS FAMOUSLY DIFFICULT TO PLEASE.
I WILL NEGOTIATE THE COMPENSATION PERSONALLY, BUT IT WILL TAKE SOME TIME.
THANK YOU VERY MUCH.
NOT AT ALL. ACQUIRING MAPS IS SOMETHING OF A HOBBY OF MINE.
IF YOU'RE HEADING NORTH, YOU SHOULD SET OFF FROM LENOS.
FROM LENOS?

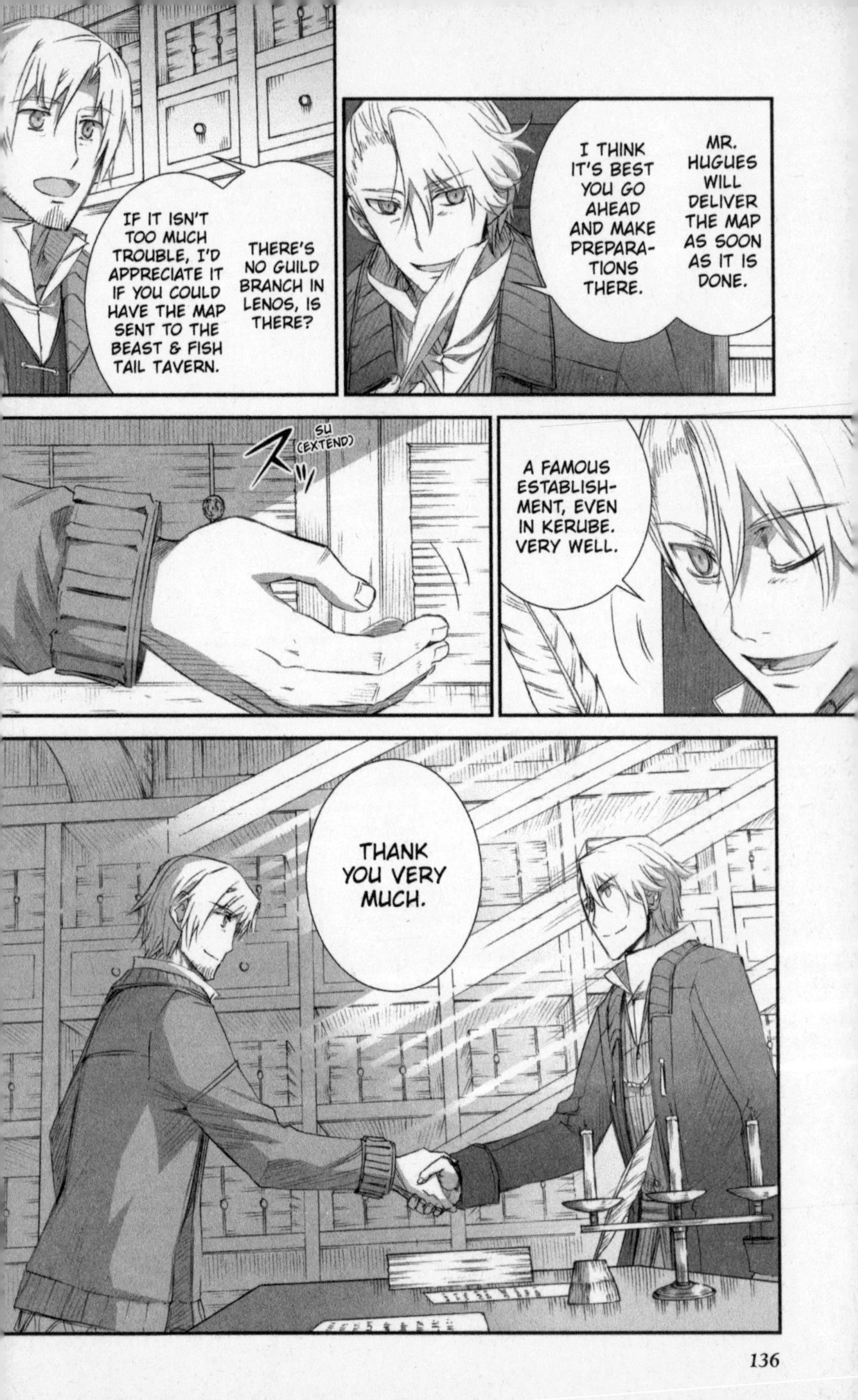
MR. HUGUES WILL DELIVER THE MAP AS SOON AS IT IS DONE.
I THINK IT'S BEST YOU GO AHEAD AND MAKE PREPARATIONS THERE.
THERE'S NO GUILD BRANCH IN LENOS, IS THERE?
IF IT ISN'T TOO MUCH TROUBLE, I'D APPRECIATE IT IF YOU COULD HAVE THE MAP SENT TO THE BEAST & FISH TAIL TAVERN.
A FAMOUS ESTABLISHMENT, EVEN IN KERUBE. VERY WELL.
SU (EXTEND)
THANK YOU VERY MUCH.

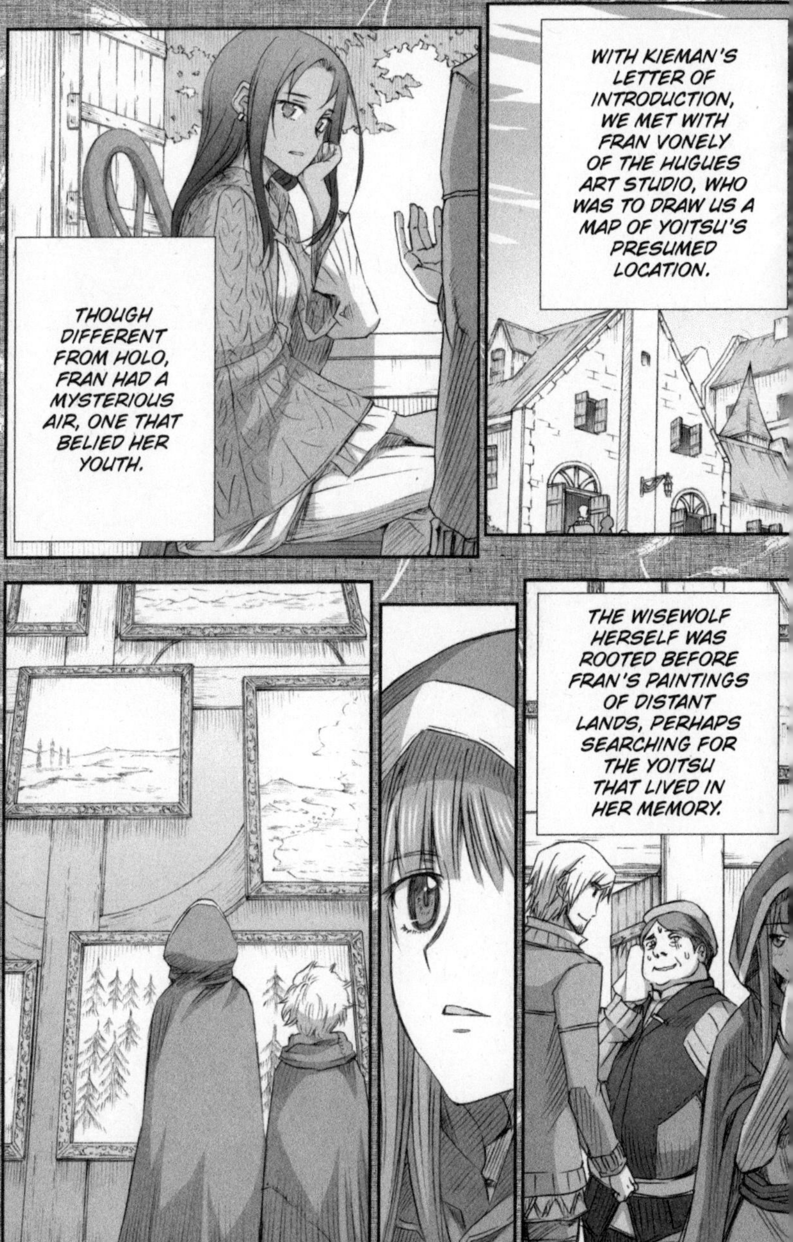
WITH KIEMAN'S LETTER OF INTRODUCTION, WE MET WITH FRAN VONELY OF THE HUGUES ART STUDIO, WHO WAS TO DRAW US A MAP OF YOITSU'S PRESUMED LOCATION.
THOUGH DIFFERENT FROM HOLO, FRAN HAD A MYSTERIOUS AIR, ONE THAT BELIED HER YOUTH.
THE WISEWOLF HERSELF WAS ROOTED BEFORE FRAN'S PAINTINGS OF DISTANT LANDS, PERHAPS SEARCHING FOR THE YOITSU THAT LIVED IN HER MEMORY.

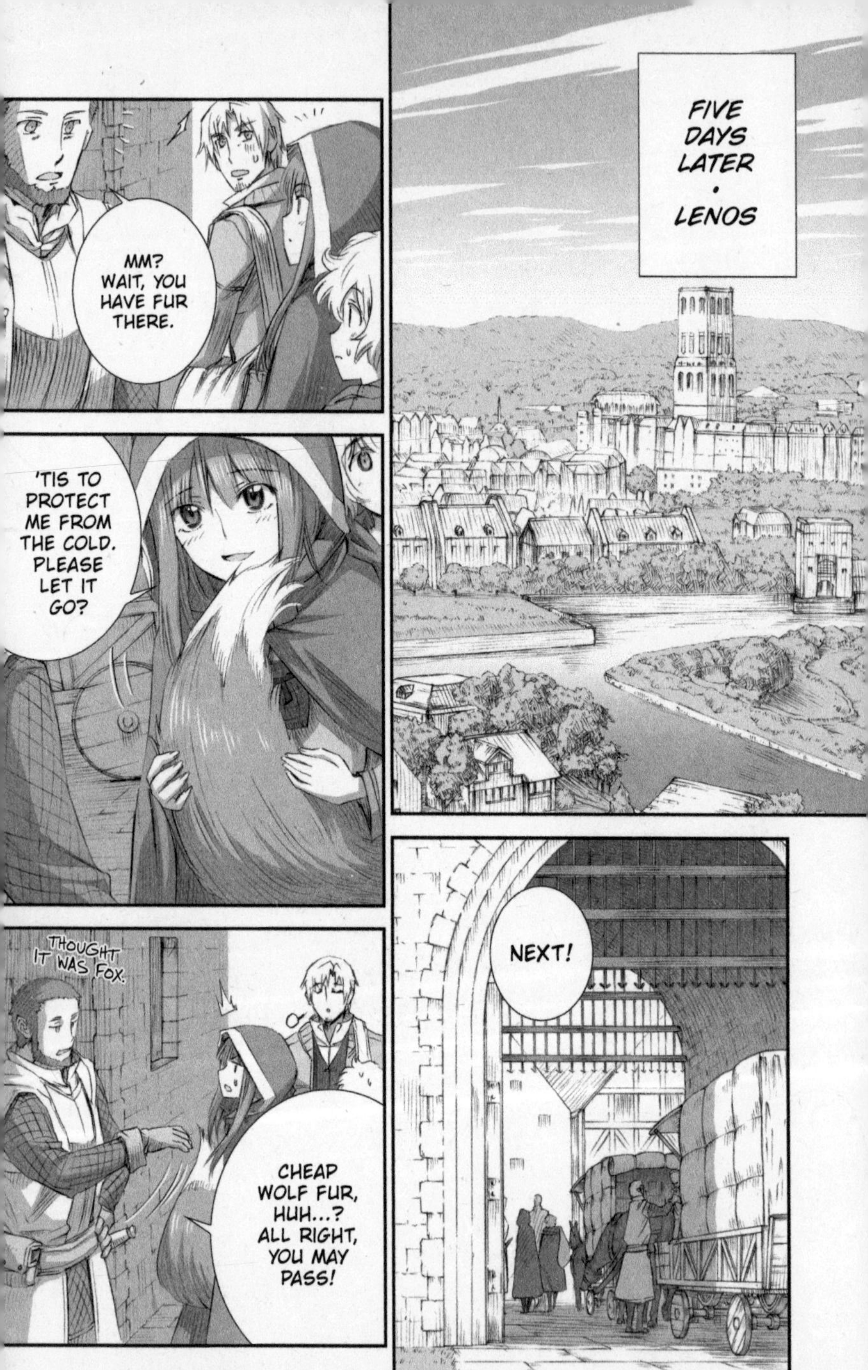
FIVE DAYS LATER • LENOS
NEXT!
MM? WAIT, YOU HAVE FUR THERE.
'TIS TO PROTECT ME FROM THE COLD. PLEASE LET IT GO?
CHEAP WOLF FUR, HUH...? ALL RIGHT, YOU MAY PASS!
THOUGHT IT WAS FOX.

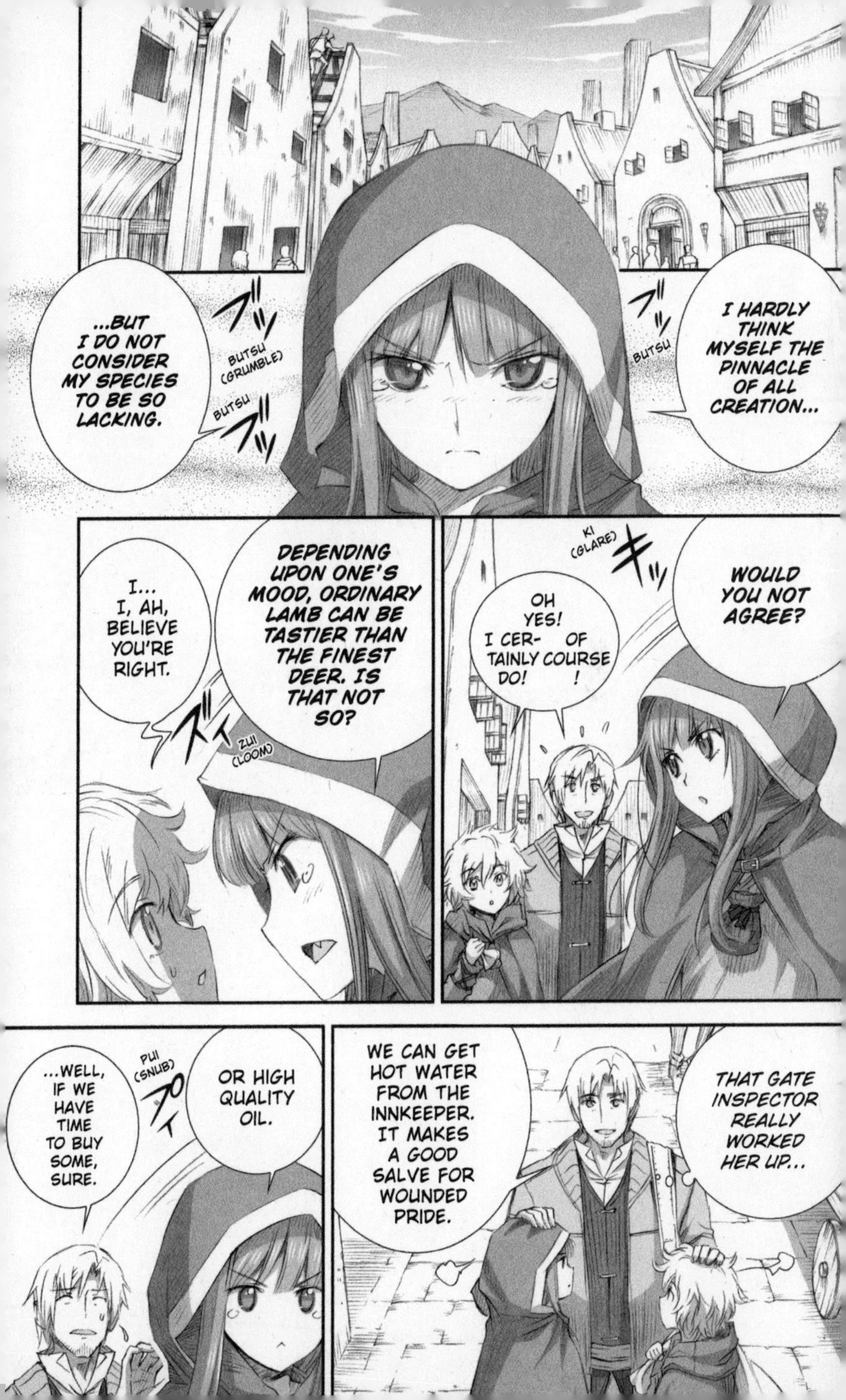

BUTSU
I HARDLY THINK MYSELF THE PINNACLE OF ALL CREATION...
BUTSU (GRUMBLE)
BUTSU
...BUT I DO NOT CONSIDER MY SPECIES TO BE SO LACKING.
WOULD YOU NOT AGREE?
KI (GLARE)
OF COURSE!
OH YES! I CERTAINLY DO!
DEPENDING UPON ONE'S MOOD, ORDINARY LAMB CAN BE TASTIER THAN THE FINEST DEER. IS THAT NOT SO?
ZUI (LOOM)
I... I, AH, BELIEVE YOU'RE RIGHT.
THAT GATE INSPECTOR REALLY WORKED HER UP...
WE CAN GET HOT WATER FROM THE INNKEEPER. IT MAKES A GOOD SALVE FOR WOUNDED PRIDE.
OR HIGH QUALITY OIL.
PUI (SNUB)
...WELL, IF WE HAVE TIME TO BUY SOME, SURE.

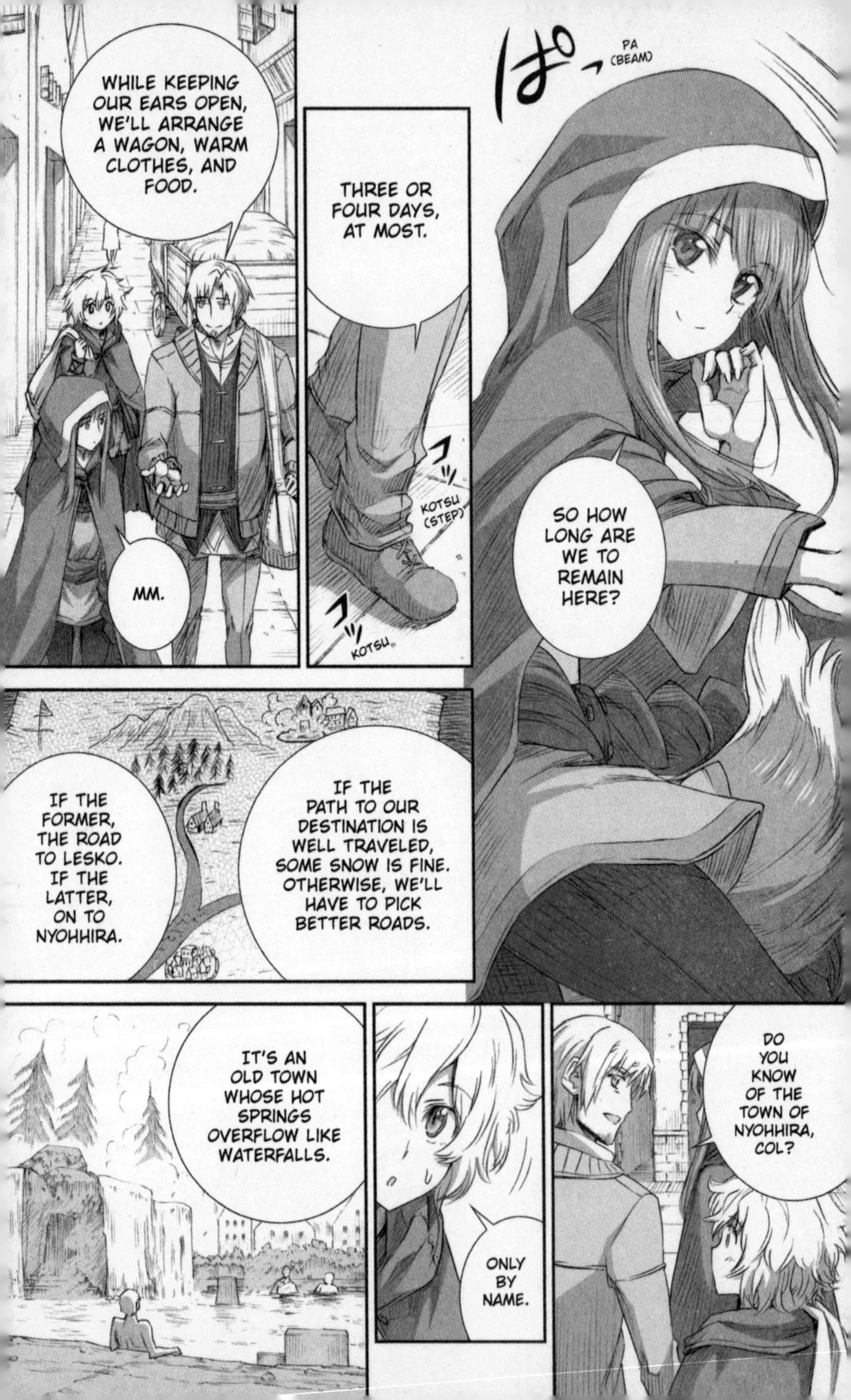
ぱっ
PA (BEAM)
SO HOW LONG ARE WE TO REMAIN HERE?
THREE OR FOUR DAYS, AT MOST.
KOTSU (STEP)
KOTSU
WHILE KEEPING OUR EARS OPEN, WE'LL ARRANGE A WAGON, WARM CLOTHES, AND FOOD.
MM.
IF THE PATH TO OUR DESTINATION IS WELL TRAVELED, SOME SNOW IS FINE. OTHERWISE, WE'LL HAVE TO PICK BETTER ROADS.
IF THE FORMER, THE ROAD TO LESKO. IF THE LATTER, ON TO NYOHHIRA.
DO YOU KNOW OF THE TOWN OF NYOHHIRA, COL?
ONLY BY NAME.
IT'S AN OLD TOWN WHOSE HOT SPRINGS OVERFLOW LIKE WATERFALLS.

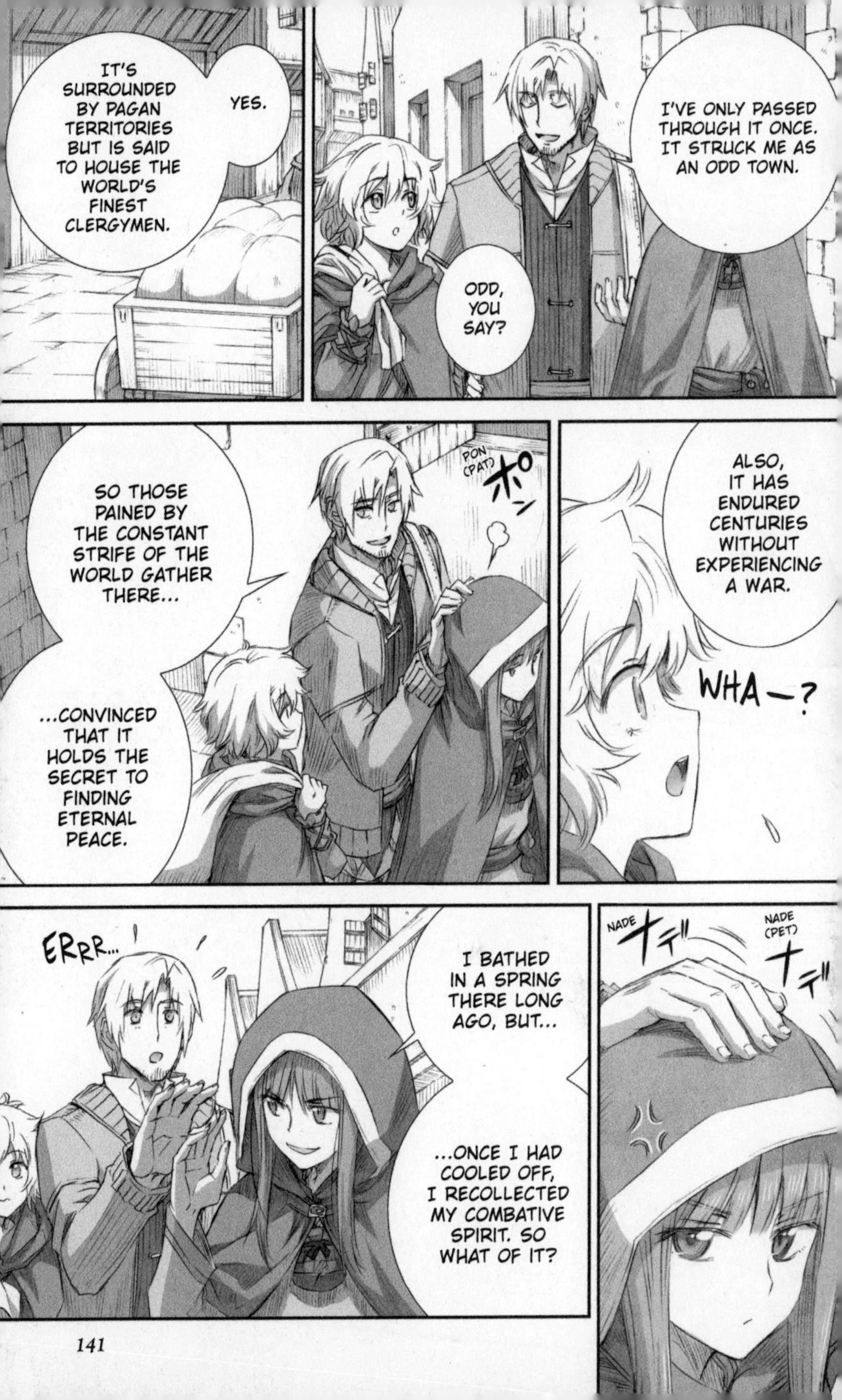
I'VE ONLY PASSED THROUGH IT ONCE. IT STRUCK ME AS AN ODD TOWN.
ODD, YOU SAY?
YES.
IT'S SURROUNDED BY PAGAN TERRITORIES BUT IS SAID TO HOUSE THE WORLD'S FINEST CLERGYMEN.
ALSO, IT HAS ENDURED CENTURIES WITHOUT EXPERIENCING A WAR.
WHA—?
PON (PAT)
SO THOSE PAINED BY THE CONSTANT STRIFE OF THE WORLD GATHER THERE...
...CONVINCED THAT IT HOLDS THE SECRET TO FINDING ETERNAL PEACE.
NADE
NADE (PET)
I BATHED IN A SPRING THERE LONG AGO, BUT...
...ONCE I HAD COOLED OFF, I RECOLLECTED MY COMBATIVE SPIRIT. SO WHAT OF IT?
ERRR...

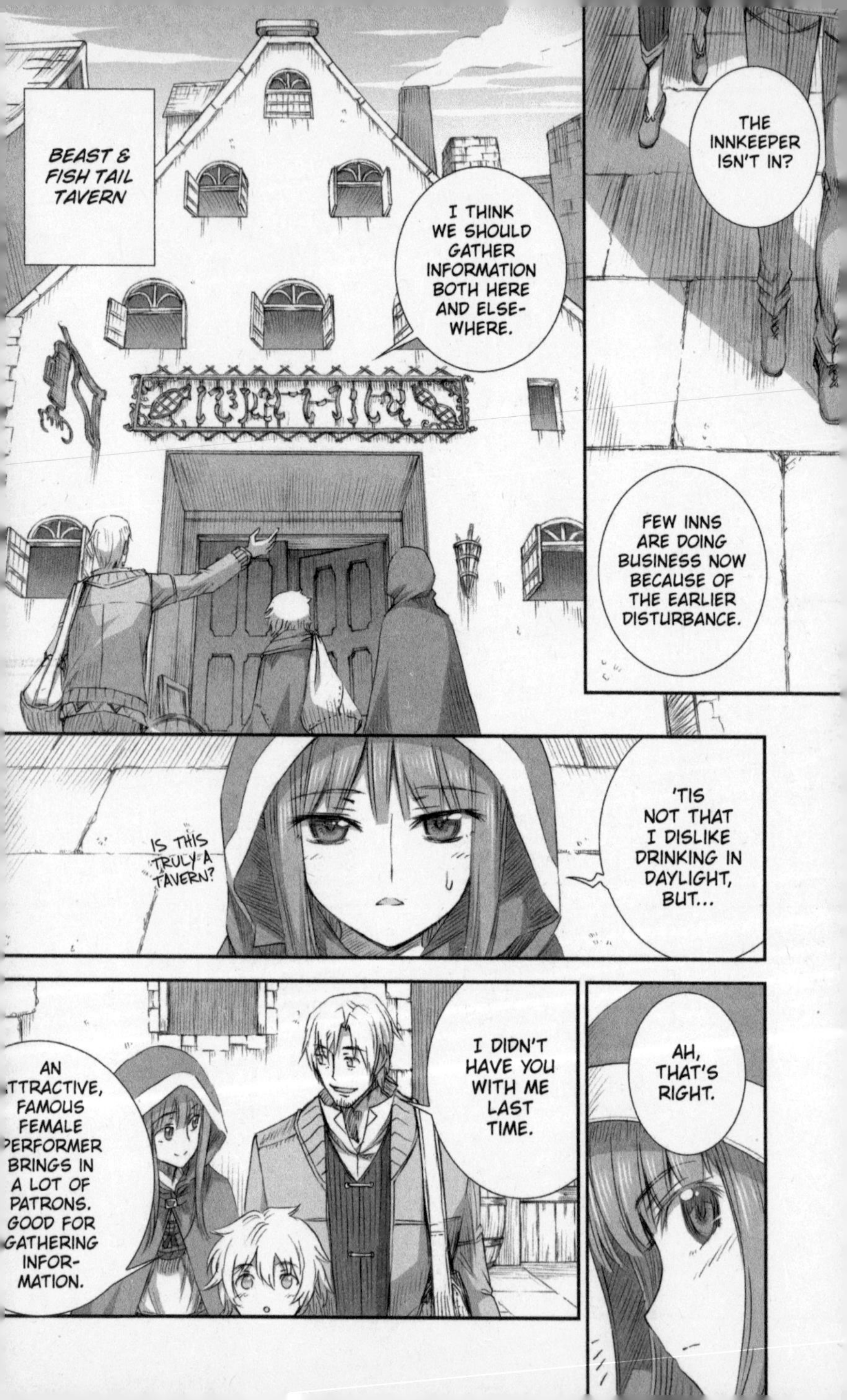
THE INNKEEPER ISN'T IN?
FEW INNS ARE DOING BUSINESS NOW BECAUSE OF THE EARLIER DISTURBANCE.
I THINK WE SHOULD GATHER INFORMATION BOTH HERE AND ELSE-WHERE.
BEAST & FISH TAIL TAVERN
'TIS NOT THAT I DISLIKE DRINKING IN DAYLIGHT, BUT...
IS THIS TRULY A TAVERN?
AH, THAT'S RIGHT.
I DIDN'T HAVE YOU WITH ME LAST TIME.
AN TTRACTIVE, FAMOUS FEMALE ERFORMER BRINGS IN A LOT OF PATRONS. GOOD FOR GATHERING INFOR-MATION.

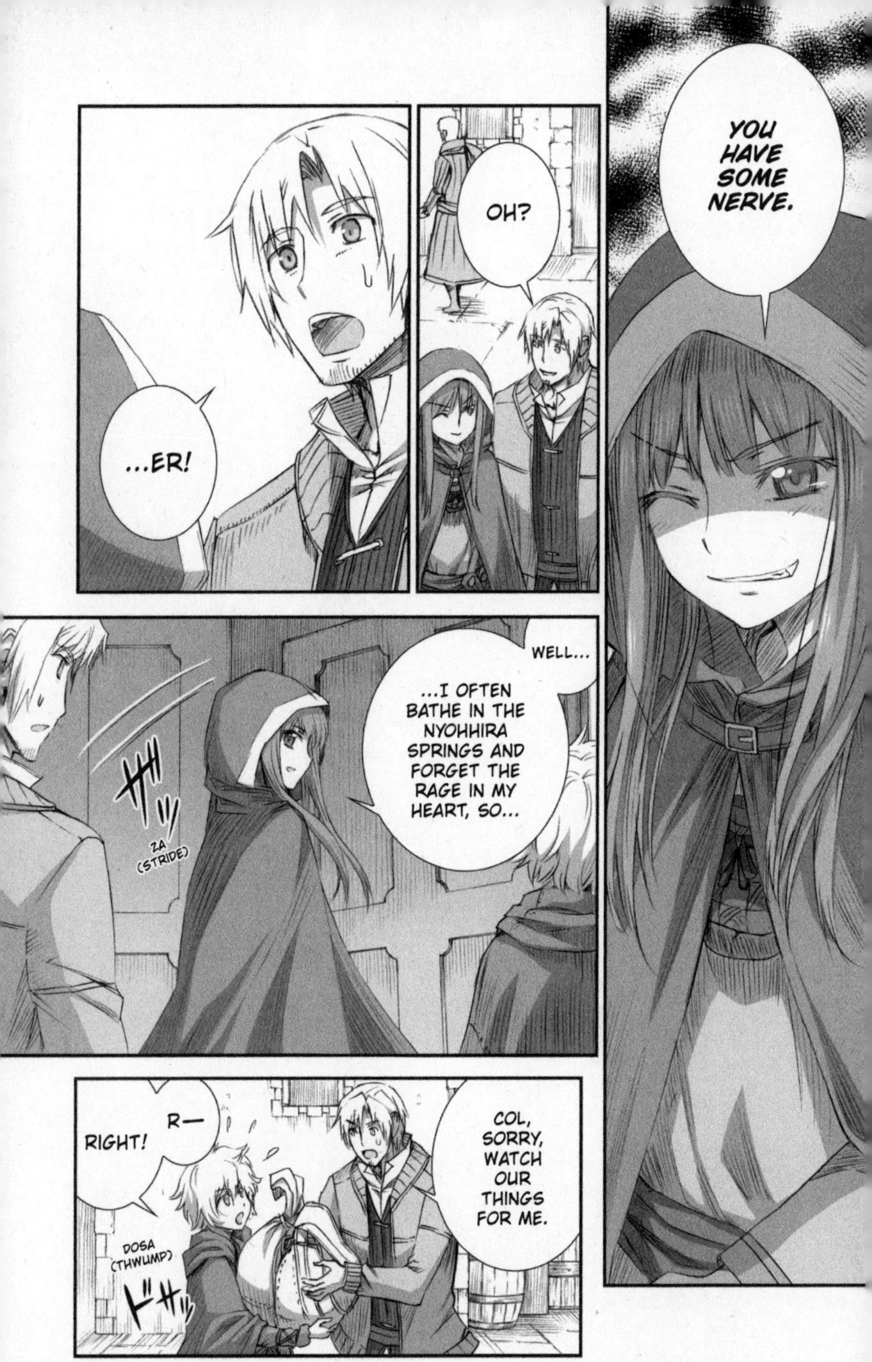
YOU HAVE SOME NERVE.
OH?
...ER!
WELL...
...I OFTEN BATHE IN THE NYOHHIRA SPRINGS AND FORGET THE RAGE IN MY HEART, SO...
ZA (STRIDE)
COL, SORRY, WATCH OUR THINGS FOR ME.
R— RIGHT!
DOSA (THWUMP)

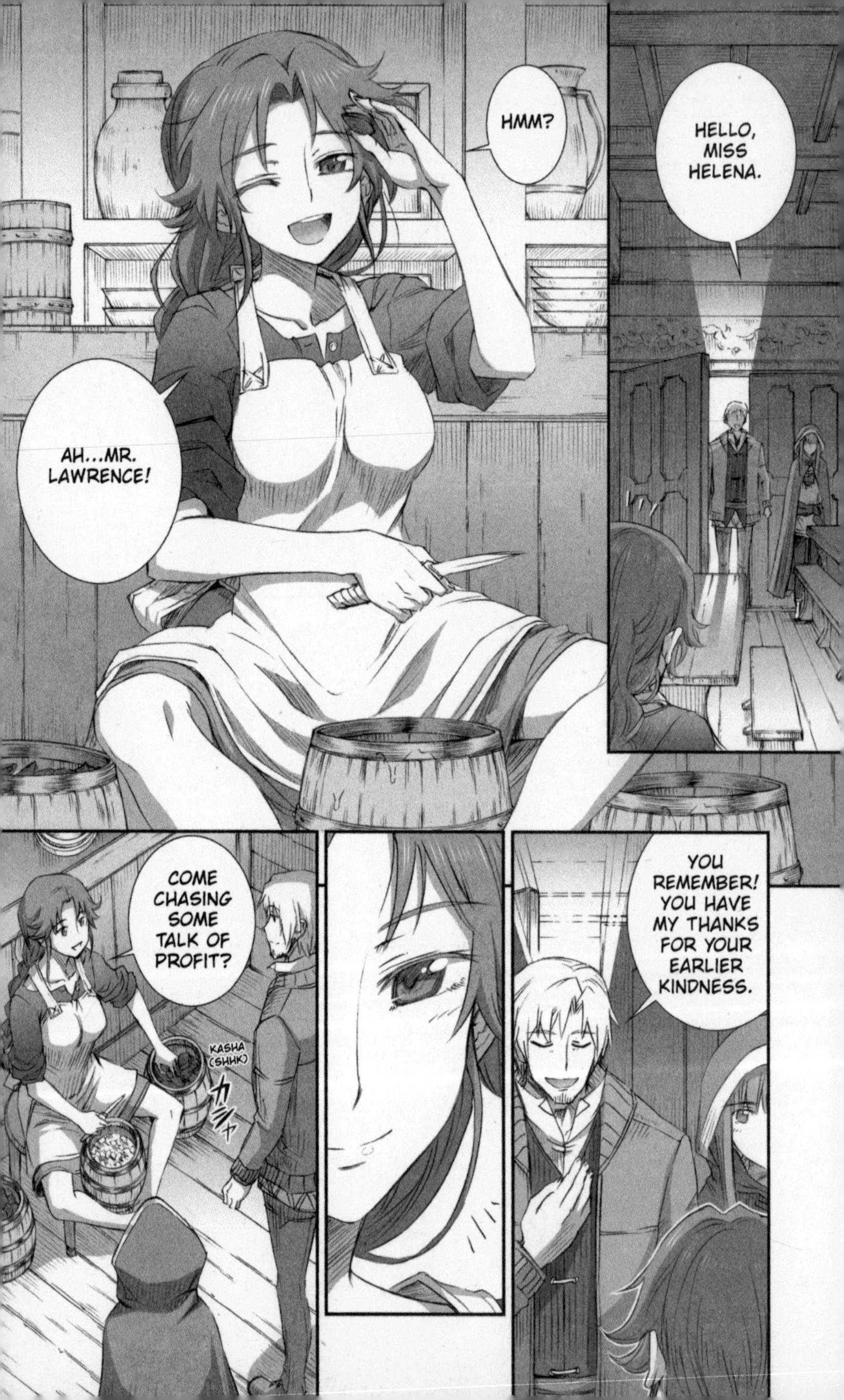
HELLO, MISS HELENA.
HMM?
AH...MR. LAWRENCE!
YOU REMEMBER! YOU HAVE MY THANKS FOR YOUR EARLIER KINDNESS.
COME CHASING SOME TALK OF PROFIT?
KASHA (SHHK)
カシャ

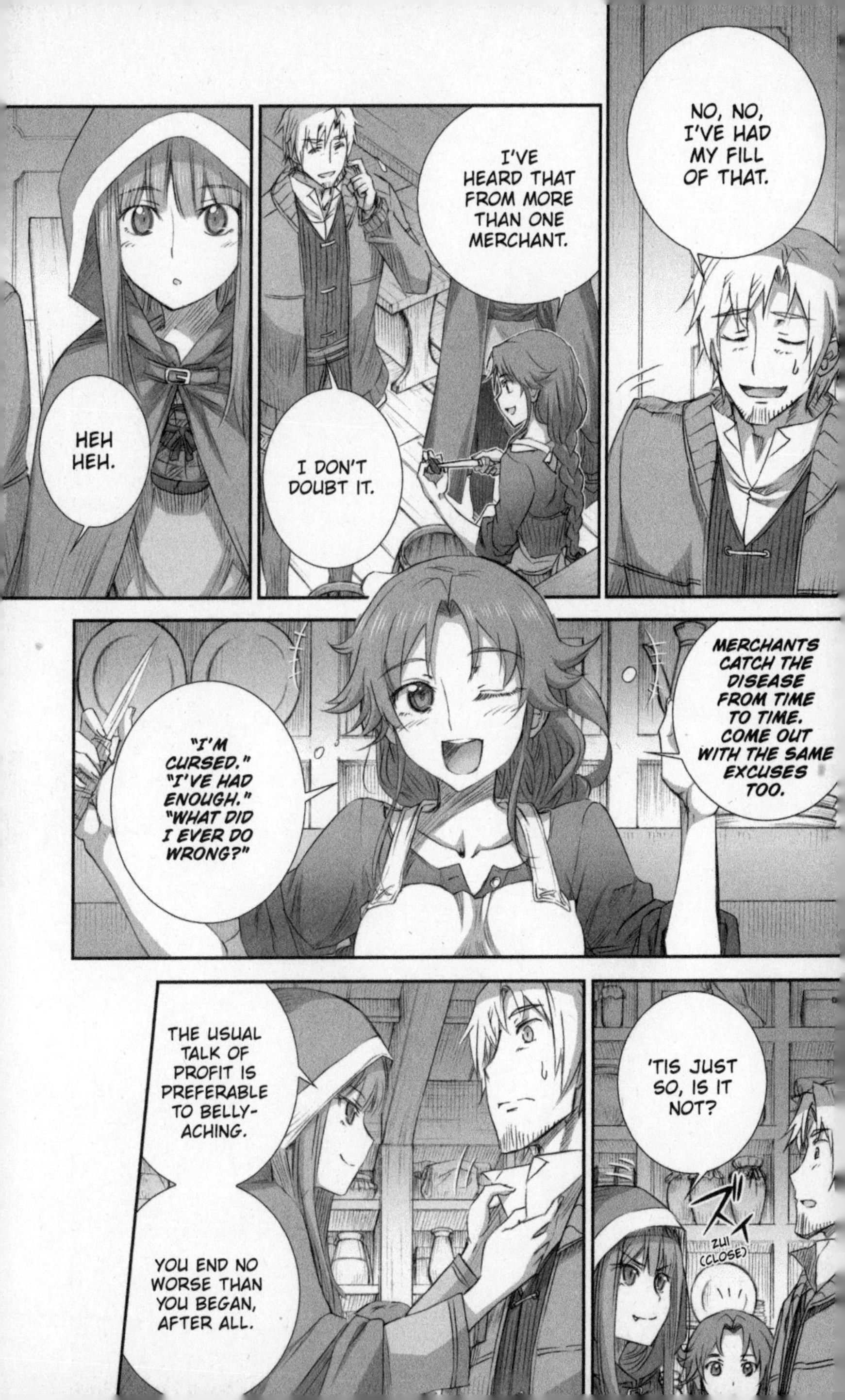

NO, NO, I'VE HAD MY FILL OF THAT.
I'VE HEARD THAT FROM MORE THAN ONE MERCHANT.
I DON'T DOUBT IT.
HEH HEH.
MERCHANTS CATCH THE DISEASE FROM TIME TO TIME. COME OUT WITH THE SAME EXCUSES TOO.
"I'M CURSED." "I'VE HAD ENOUGH." "WHAT DID I EVER DO WRONG?"
'TIS JUST SO, IS IT NOT?
ZUI (CLOSE)
THE USUAL TALK OF PROFIT IS PREFERABLE TO BELLY-ACHING.
YOU END NO WORSE THAN YOU BEGAN, AFTER ALL.

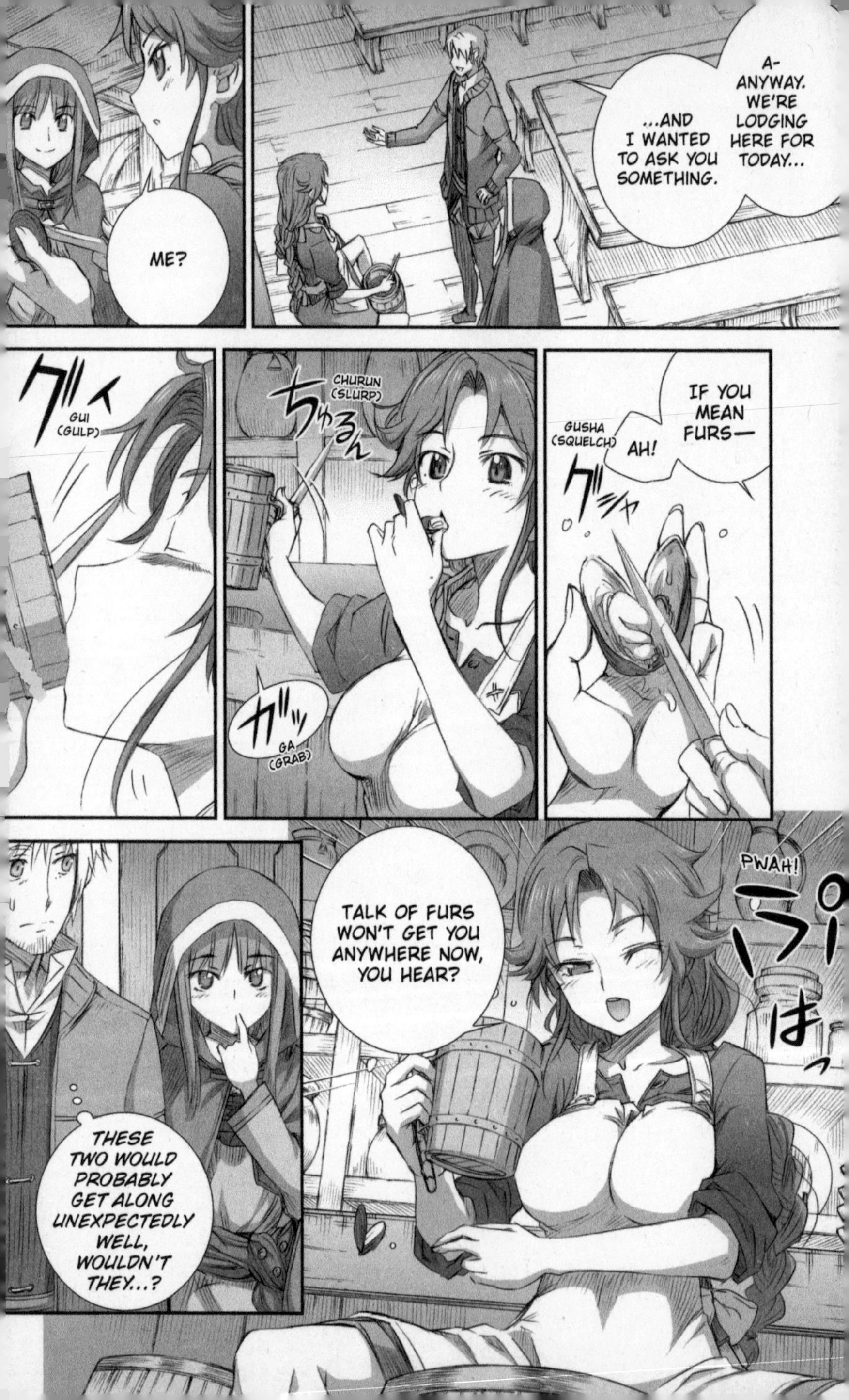
A- ANYWAY. WE'RE LODGING HERE FOR TODAY...
...AND I WANTED TO ASK YOU SOMETHING.
ME?
IF YOU MEAN FURS—
AH!
グシャ
GUSHA (SQUELCH)
ちゅるん
CHURUN (SLURP)
ガッ
GA (GRAB)
グイ
GUI (GULP)
ぷはっ
PWAH!
TALK OF FURS WON'T GET YOU ANYWHERE NOW, YOU HEAR?
THESE TWO WOULD PROBABLY GET ALONG UNEXPECTEDLY WELL, WOULDN'T THEY...?

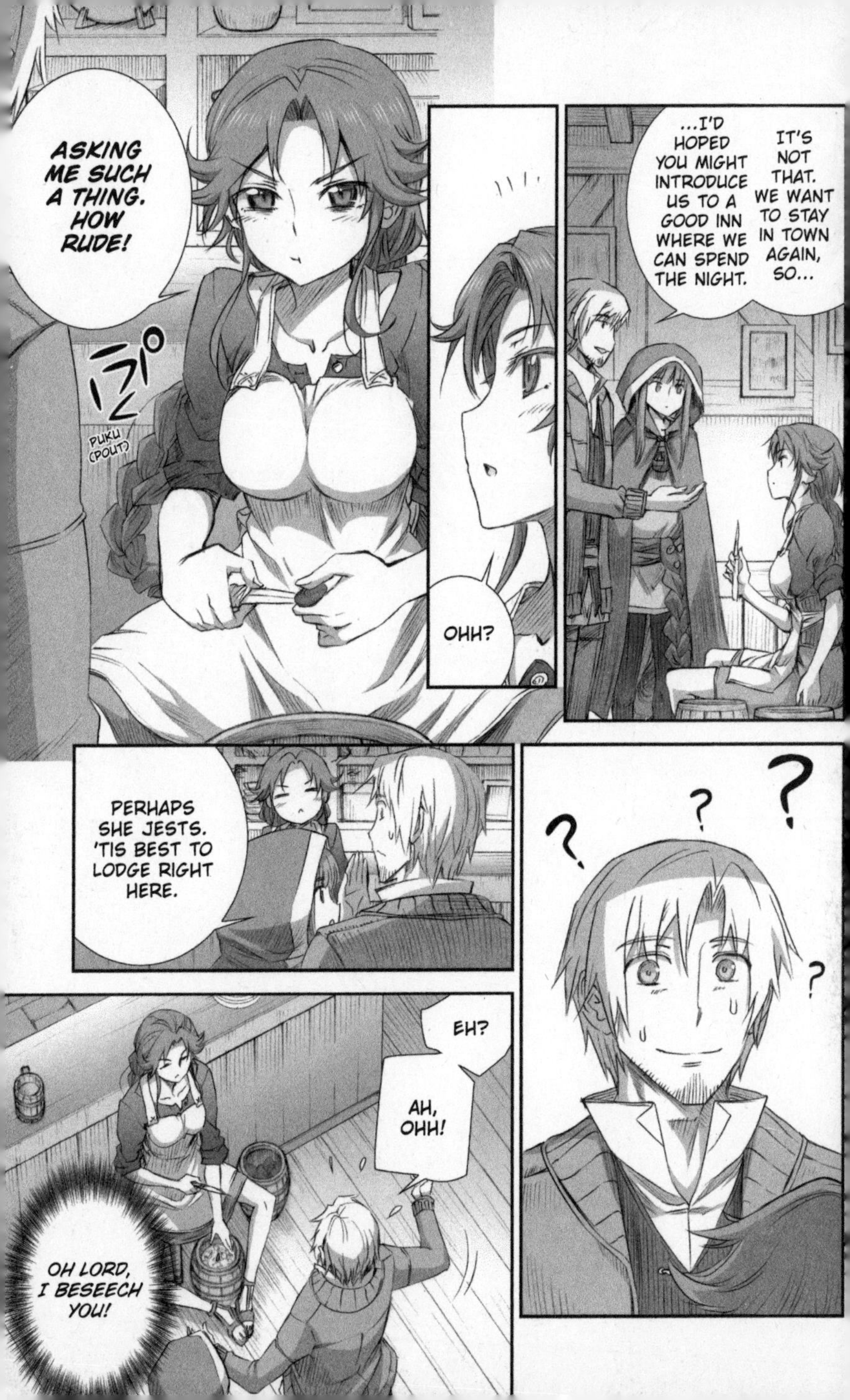

IT'S NOT THAT. WE WANT TO STAY IN TOWN AGAIN, SO...
...I'D HOPED YOU MIGHT INTRODUCE US TO A GOOD INN WHERE WE CAN SPEND THE NIGHT.
OHH?
ASKING ME SUCH A THING. HOW RUDE!
ぷくっ
PUKU (POUT)
? ? ? ?
PERHAPS SHE JESTS. 'TIS BEST TO LODGE RIGHT HERE.
EH?
AH, OHH!
OH LORD, I BESEECH YOU!

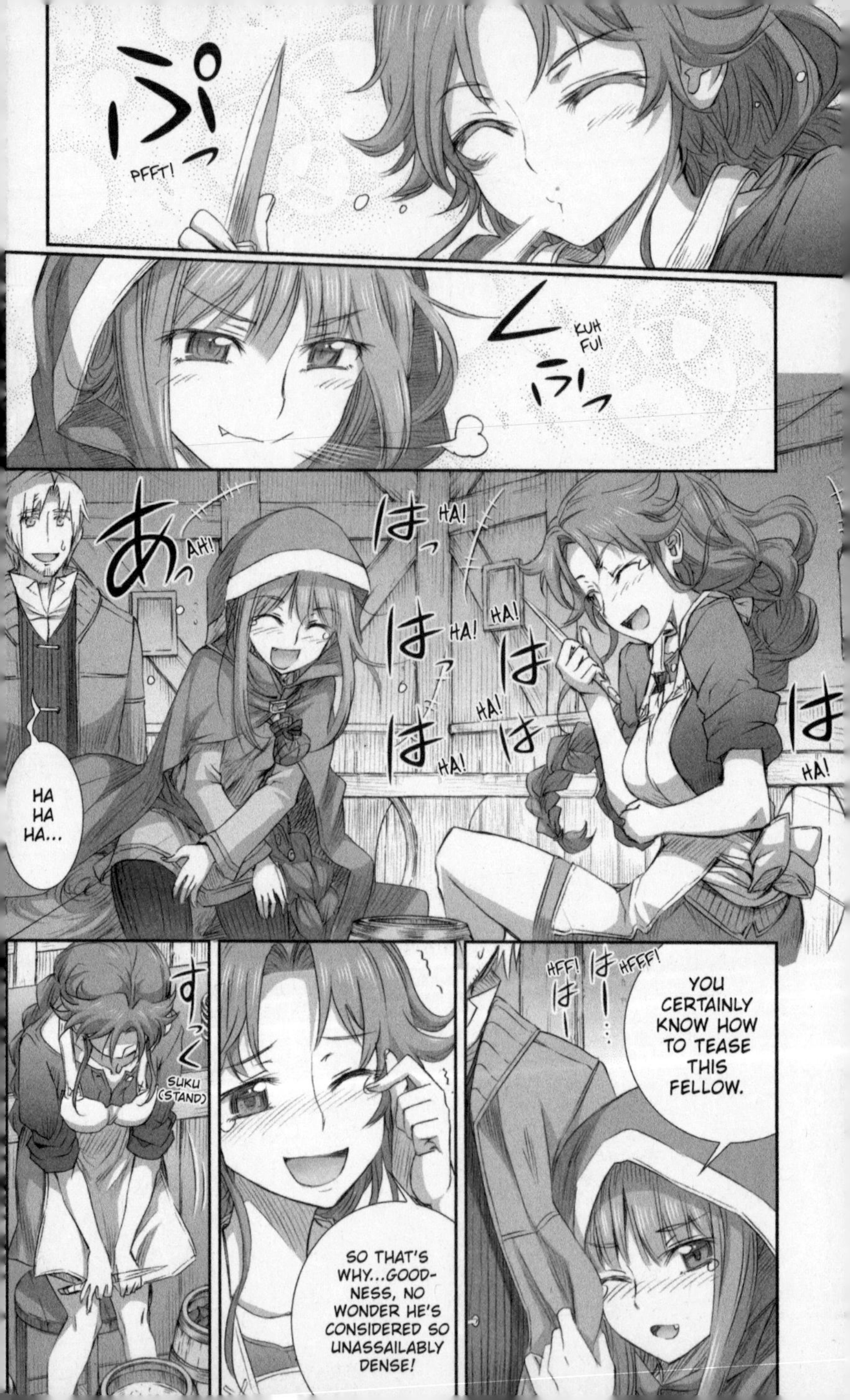
ぷっ
PFFT!
くふっ
KUH FU!
はっ
HA!
は
HA!
はっ
HA!
はっ
HA!
は
HA!
は
HA!
はっ
HA!
あっ
AH!
HA HA HA...
はーはー...
HFF! HFFF!
YOU CERTAINLY KNOW HOW TO TEASE THIS FELLOW.
SO THAT'S WHY...GOOD-NESS, NO WONDER HE'S CONSIDERED SO UNASSAILABLY DENSE!
すっく
SUKU (STAND)

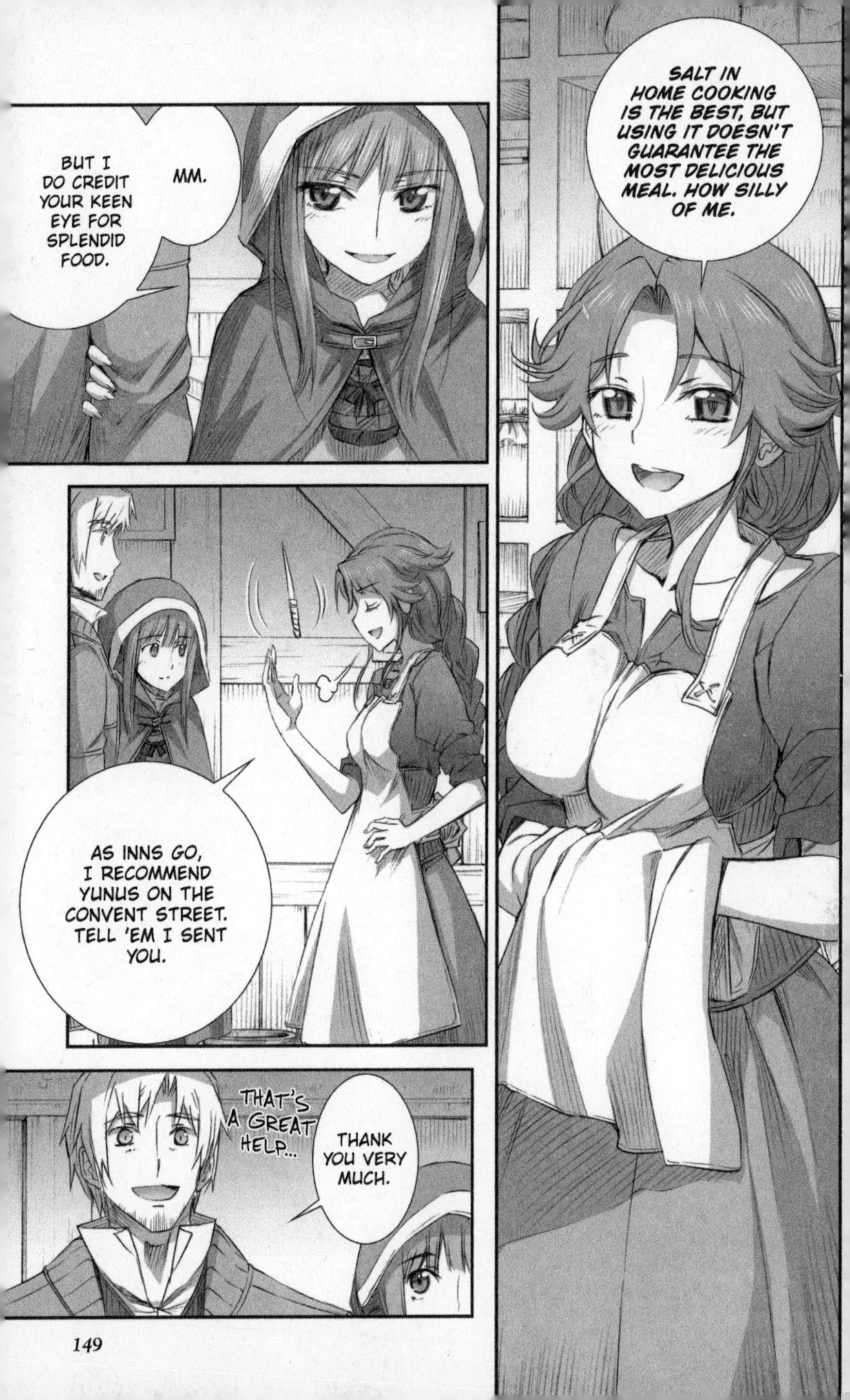
SALT IN HOME COOKING IS THE BEST, BUT USING IT DOESN'T GUARANTEE THE MOST DELICIOUS MEAL. HOW SILLY OF ME.
MM.
BUT I DO CREDIT YOUR KEEN EYE FOR SPLENDID FOOD.
AS INNS GO, I RECOMMEND YUNUS ON THE CONVENT STREET. TELL 'EM I SENT YOU.
THAT'S A GREAT HELP...
THANK YOU VERY MUCH.

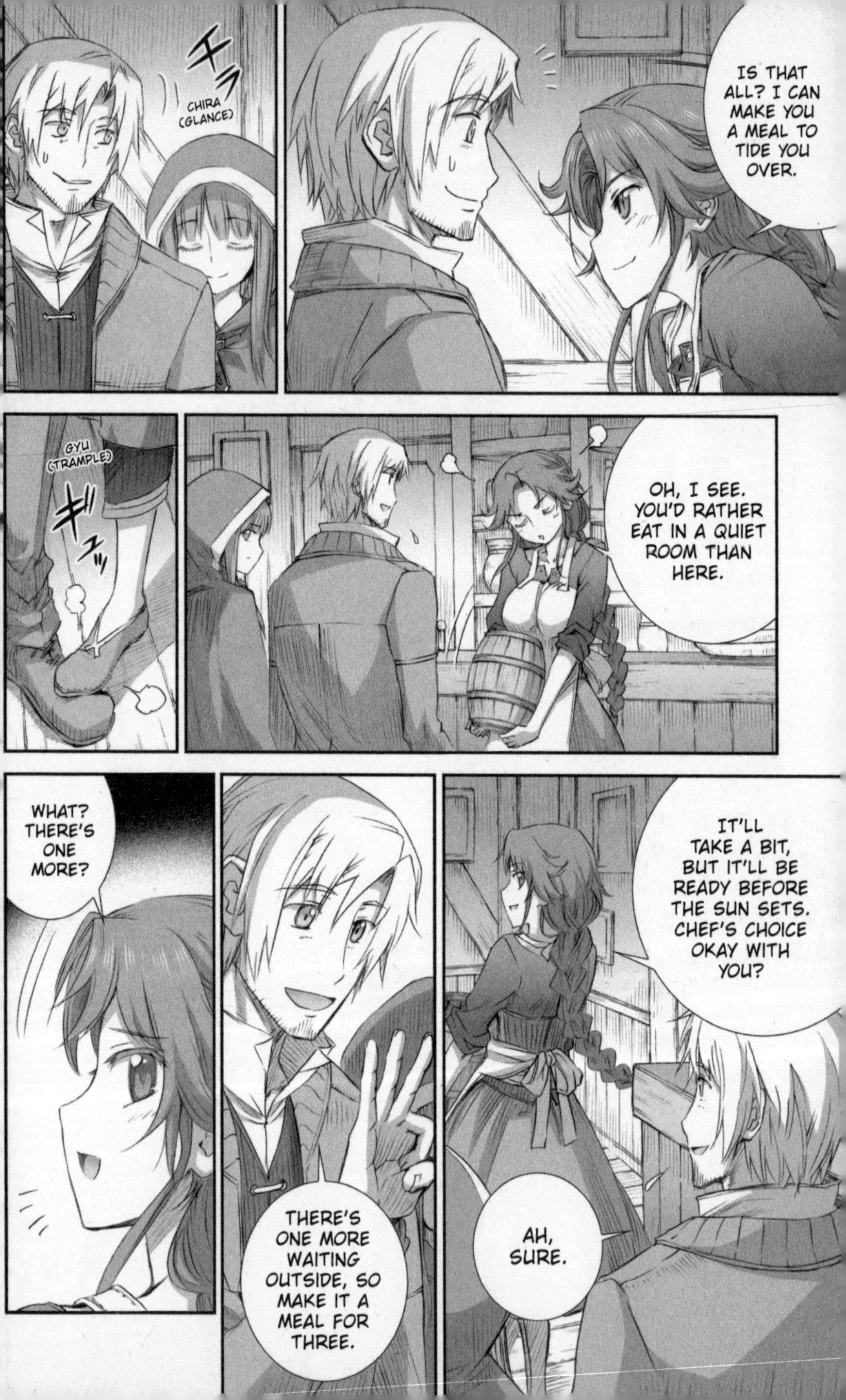
IS THAT ALL? I CAN MAKE YOU A MEAL TO TIDE YOU OVER.
チラ
CHIRA (GLANCE)
OH, I SEE. YOU'D RATHER EAT IN A QUIET ROOM THAN HERE.
GYU (TRAMPLE)
ギュッ
IT'LL TAKE A BIT, BUT IT'LL BE READY BEFORE THE SUN SETS. CHEF'S CHOICE OKAY WITH YOU?
AH, SURE.
THERE'S ONE MORE WAITING OUTSIDE, SO MAKE IT A MEAL FOR THREE.
WHAT? THERE'S ONE MORE?

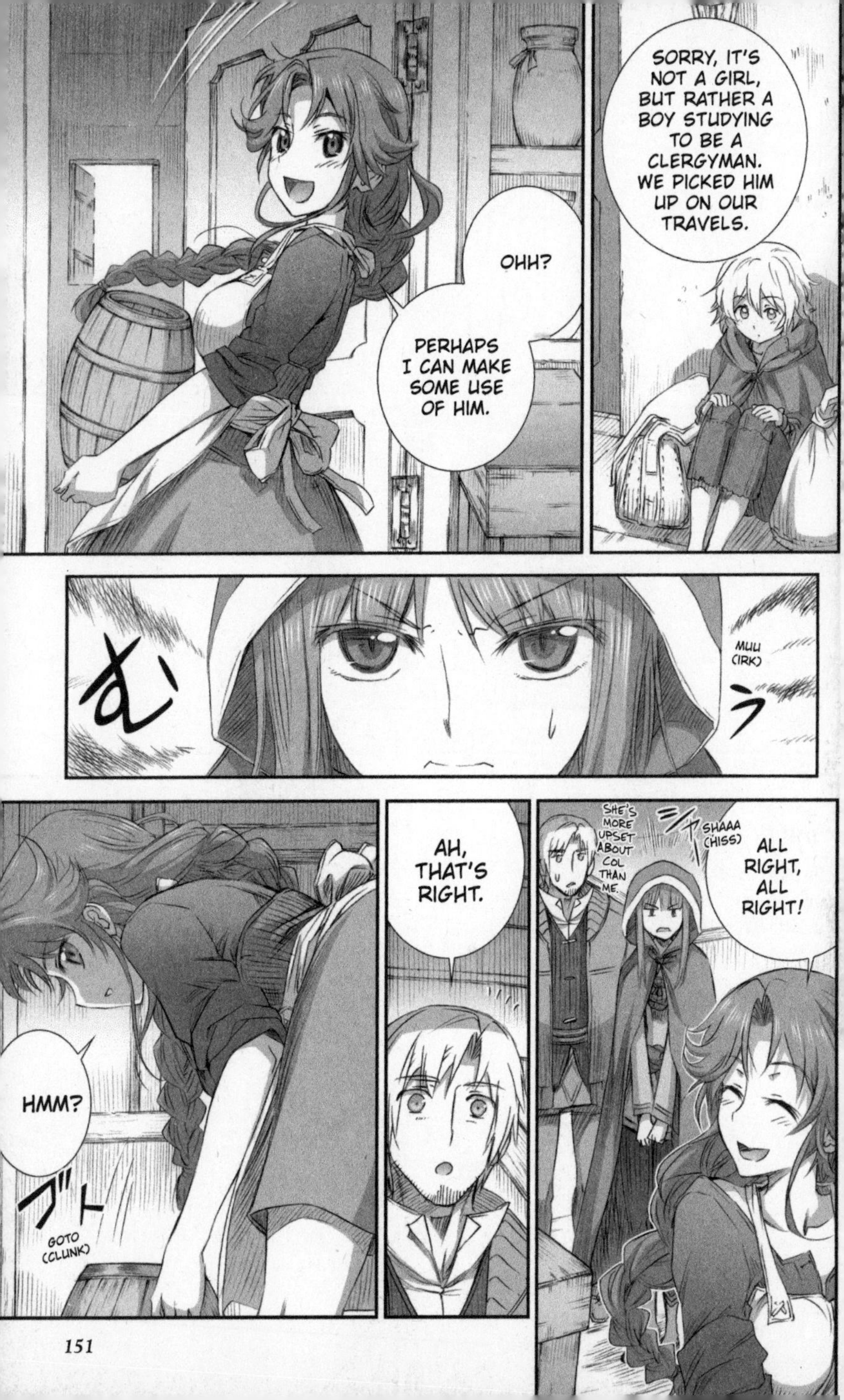
SORRY, IT'S NOT A GIRL, BUT RATHER A BOY STUDYING TO BE A CLERGYMAN. WE PICKED HIM UP ON OUR TRAVELS.
OHH?
PERHAPS I CAN MAKE SOME USE OF HIM.
ウ
MUU (IRK)
む
SHE'S MORE UPSET ABOUT COL THAN ME.
シャ
SHAAA (HISS)
ALL RIGHT, ALL RIGHT!
AH, THAT'S RIGHT.
HMM?
ゴト
GOTO (CLUNK)

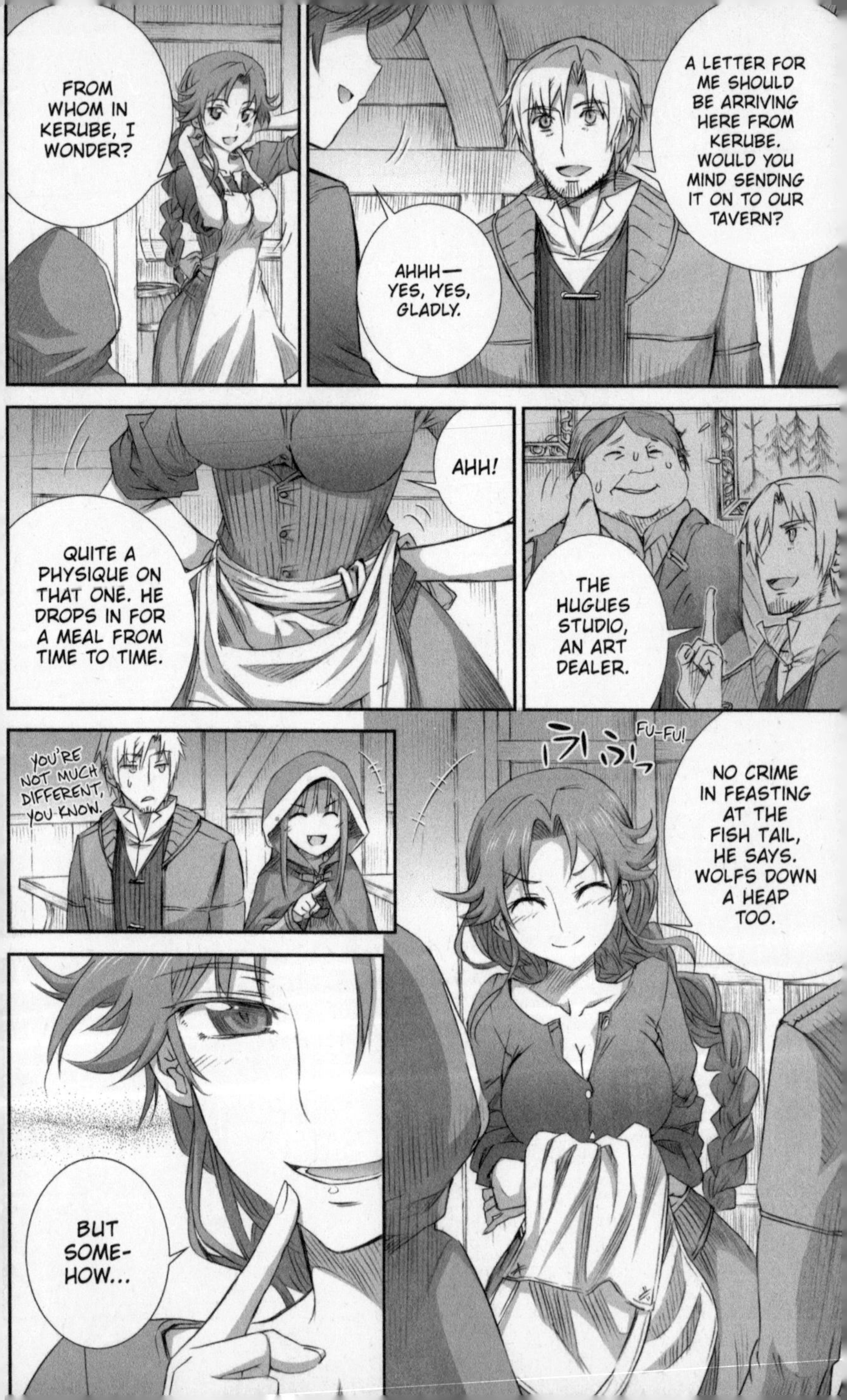
A LETTER FOR ME SHOULD BE ARRIVING HERE FROM KERUBE. WOULD YOU MIND SENDING IT ON TO OUR TAVERN?
AHHH— YES, YES, GLADLY.
FROM WHOM IN KERUBE, I WONDER?
THE HUGUES STUDIO, AN ART DEALER.
AHH!
QUITE A PHYSIQUE ON THAT ONE. HE DROPS IN FOR A MEAL FROM TIME TO TIME.
FU-FU!
NO CRIME IN FEASTING AT THE FISH TAIL, HE SAYS. WOLFS DOWN A HEAP TOO.
YOU'RE NOT MUCH DIFFERENT, YOU KNOW.
BUT SOME-HOW...

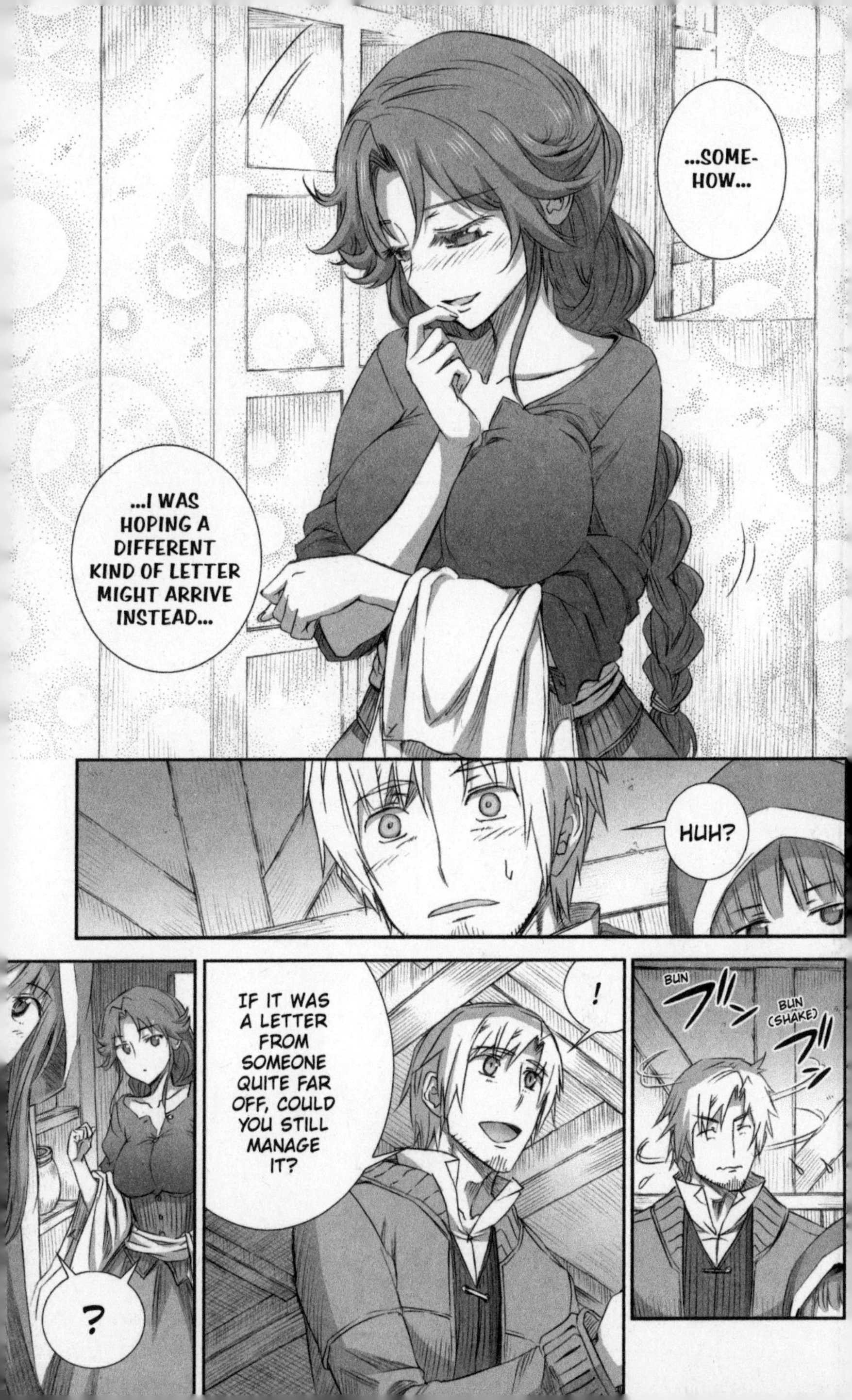
...SOME-HOW...
...I WAS HOPING A DIFFERENT KIND OF LETTER MIGHT ARRIVE INSTEAD...
HUH?
BUN
BUN (SHAKE)
!
IF IT WAS A LETTER FROM SOMEONE QUITE FAR OFF, COULD YOU STILL MANAGE IT?
?

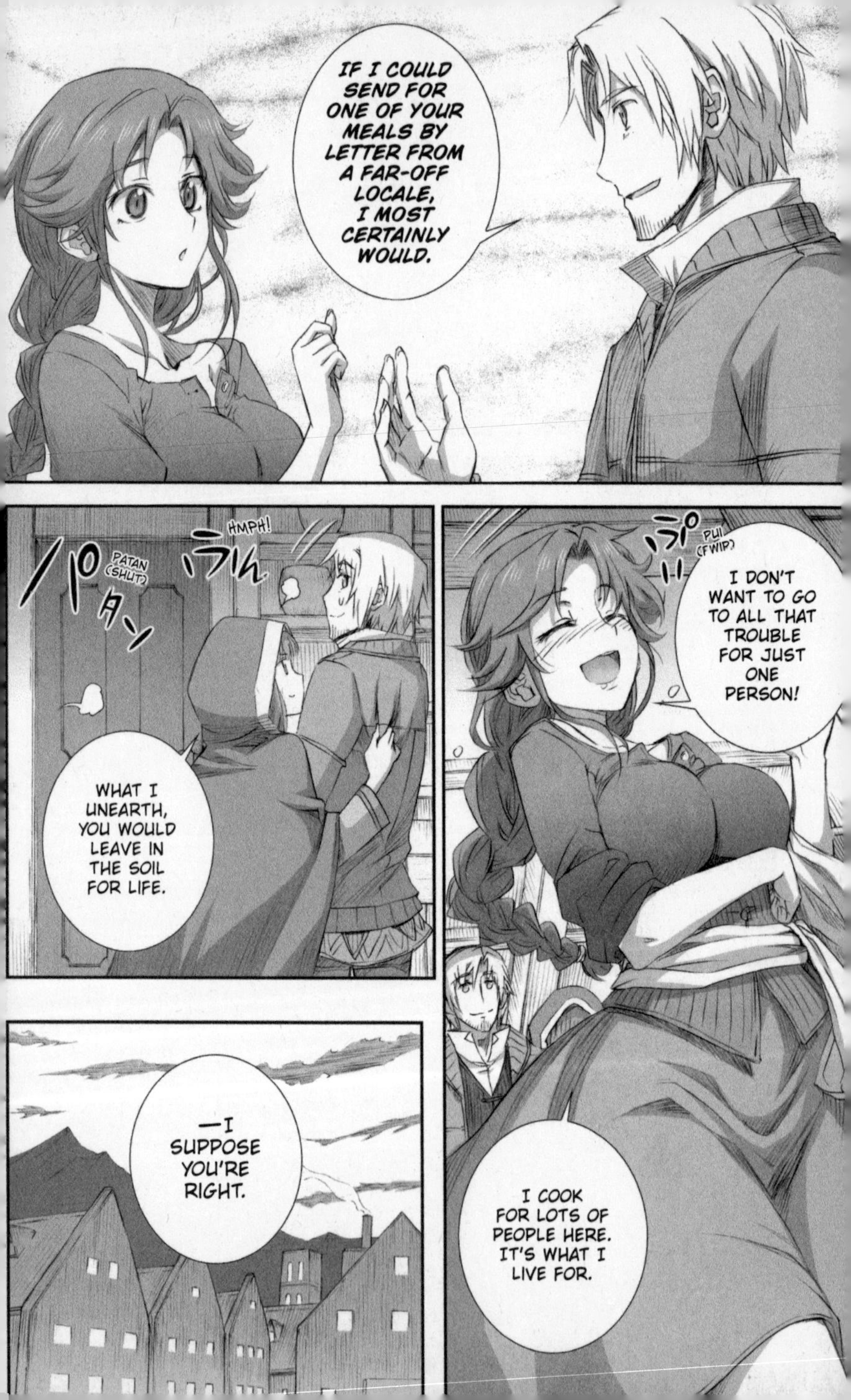
IF I COULD SEND FOR ONE OF YOUR MEALS BY LETTER FROM A FAR-OFF LOCALE, I MOST CERTAINLY WOULD.
PUI (FWIP)
I DON'T WANT TO GO TO ALL THAT TROUBLE FOR JUST ONE PERSON!
I COOK FOR LOTS OF PEOPLE HERE. IT'S WHAT I LIVE FOR.
PATAN (SHUT)
HMPH!
WHAT I UNEARTH, YOU WOULD LEAVE IN THE SOIL FOR LIFE.
—I SUPPOSE YOU'RE RIGHT.

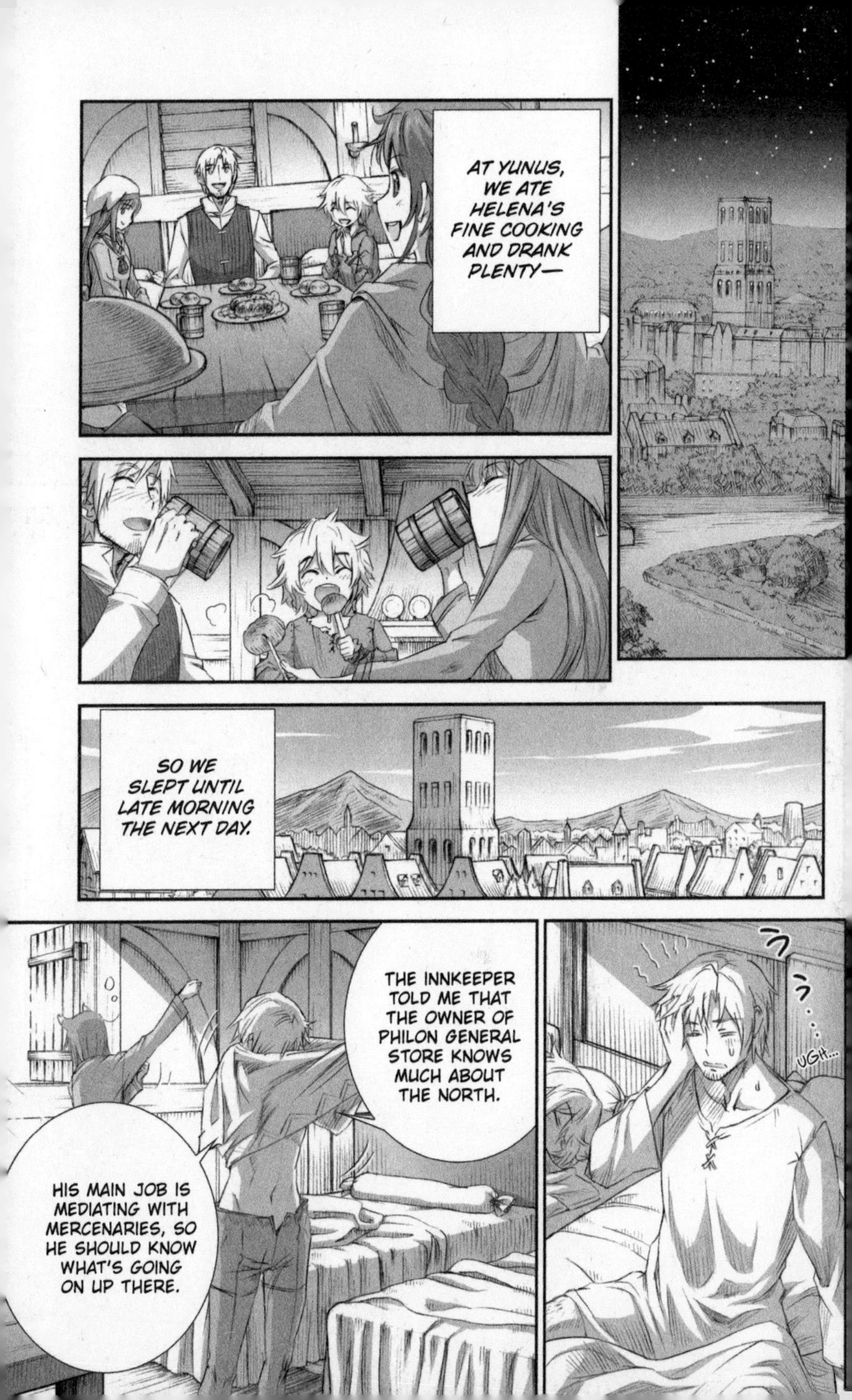
AT YUNUS, WE ATE HELENA'S FINE COOKING AND DRANK PLENTY—
SO WE SLEPT UNTIL LATE MORNING THE NEXT DAY.
UGH...
THE INNKEEPER TOLD ME THAT THE OWNER OF PHILON GENERAL STORE KNOWS MUCH ABOUT THE NORTH.
HIS MAIN JOB IS MEDIATING WITH MERCENARIES, SO HE SHOULD KNOW WHAT'S GOING ON UP THERE.

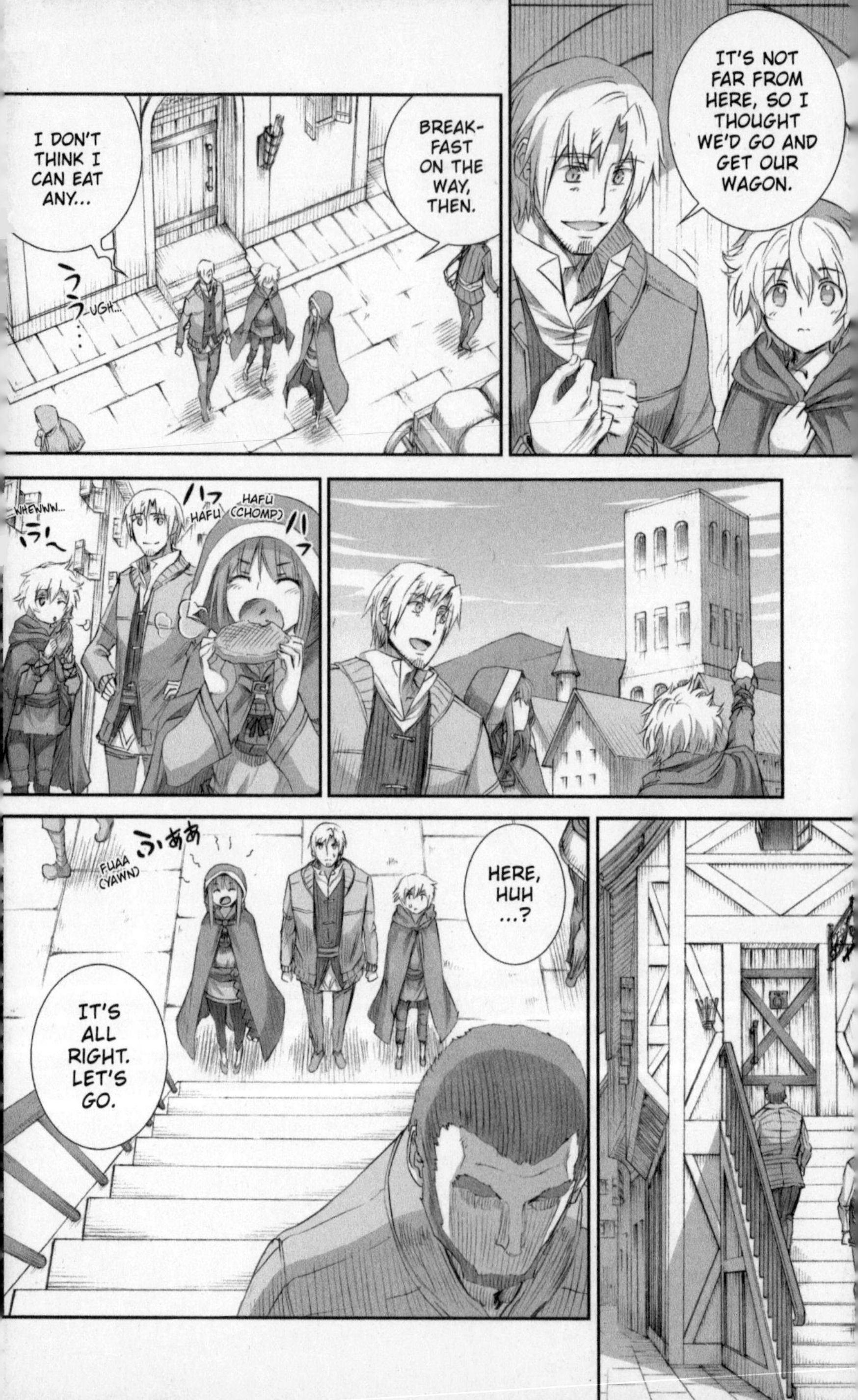
IT'S NOT FAR FROM HERE, SO I THOUGHT WE'D GO AND GET OUR WAGON.
BREAK-FAST ON THE WAY, THEN.
I DON'T THINK I CAN EAT ANY...
うう… UGH...
ハフ HAFU (CHOMP)
ハフ HAFU
ふへ WHEWWW...
ふあぁ FUAA (YAWN)
HERE, HUH ...?
IT'S ALL RIGHT. LET'S GO.

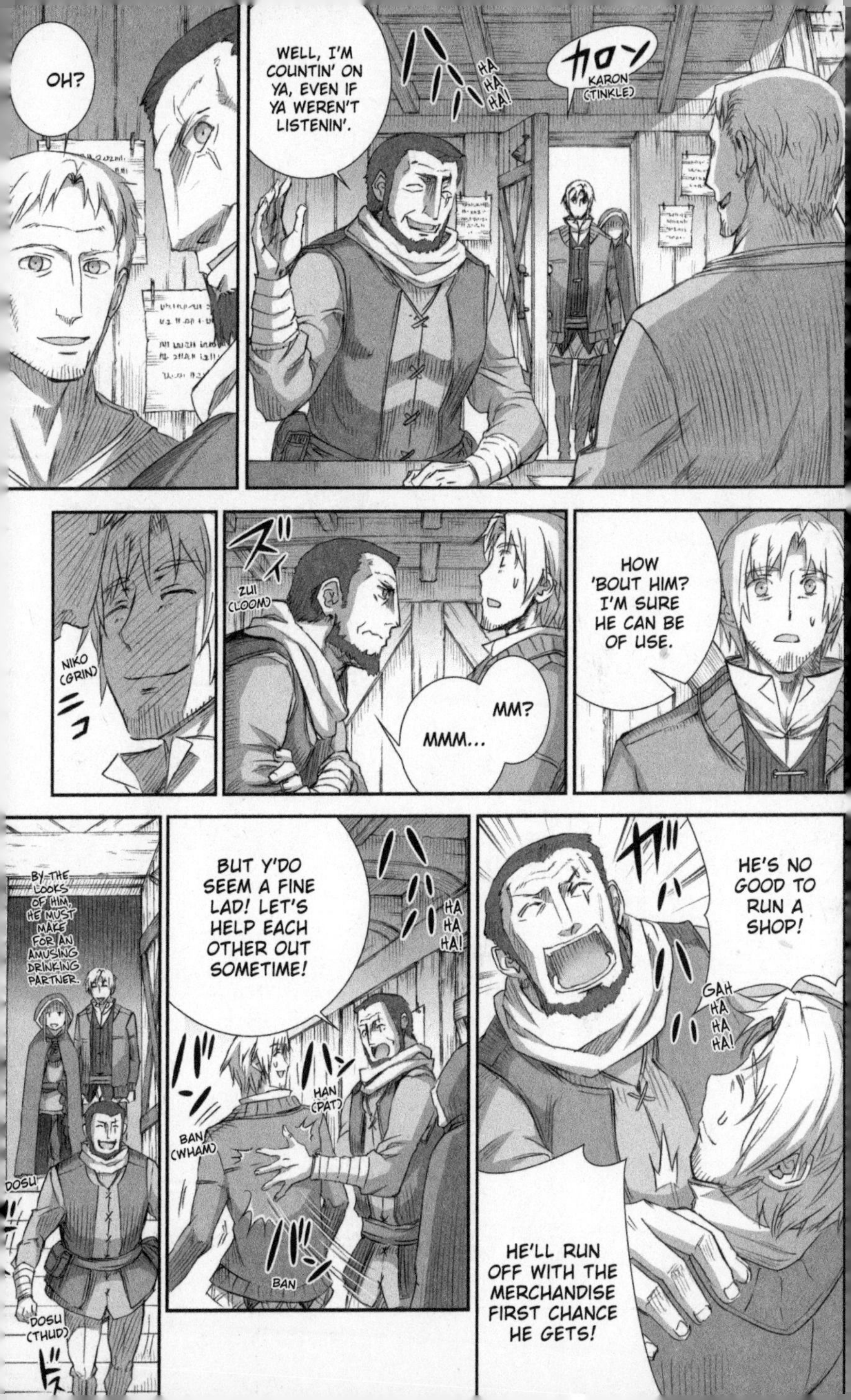
カロン
KARON (TINKLE)
HA HA HA!
WELL, I'M COUNTIN' ON YA, EVEN IF YA WEREN'T LISTENIN'.
OH?
HOW 'BOUT HIM? I'M SURE HE CAN BE OF USE.
ZUI (LOOM)
MM?
MMM...
NIKO (GRIN)
HE'S NO GOOD TO RUN A SHOP!
GAH HA HA HA!
HE'LL RUN OFF WITH THE MERCHANDISE FIRST CHANCE HE GETS!
BUT Y'DO SEEM A FINE LAD! LET'S HELP EACH OTHER OUT SOMETIME!
HA HA HA!
HAN (PAT)
BAN (WHAM)
BAN
BY THE LOOKS OF HIM, HE MUST MAKE FOR AN AMUSING DRINKING PARTNER.
DOSU
DOSU (THUD)

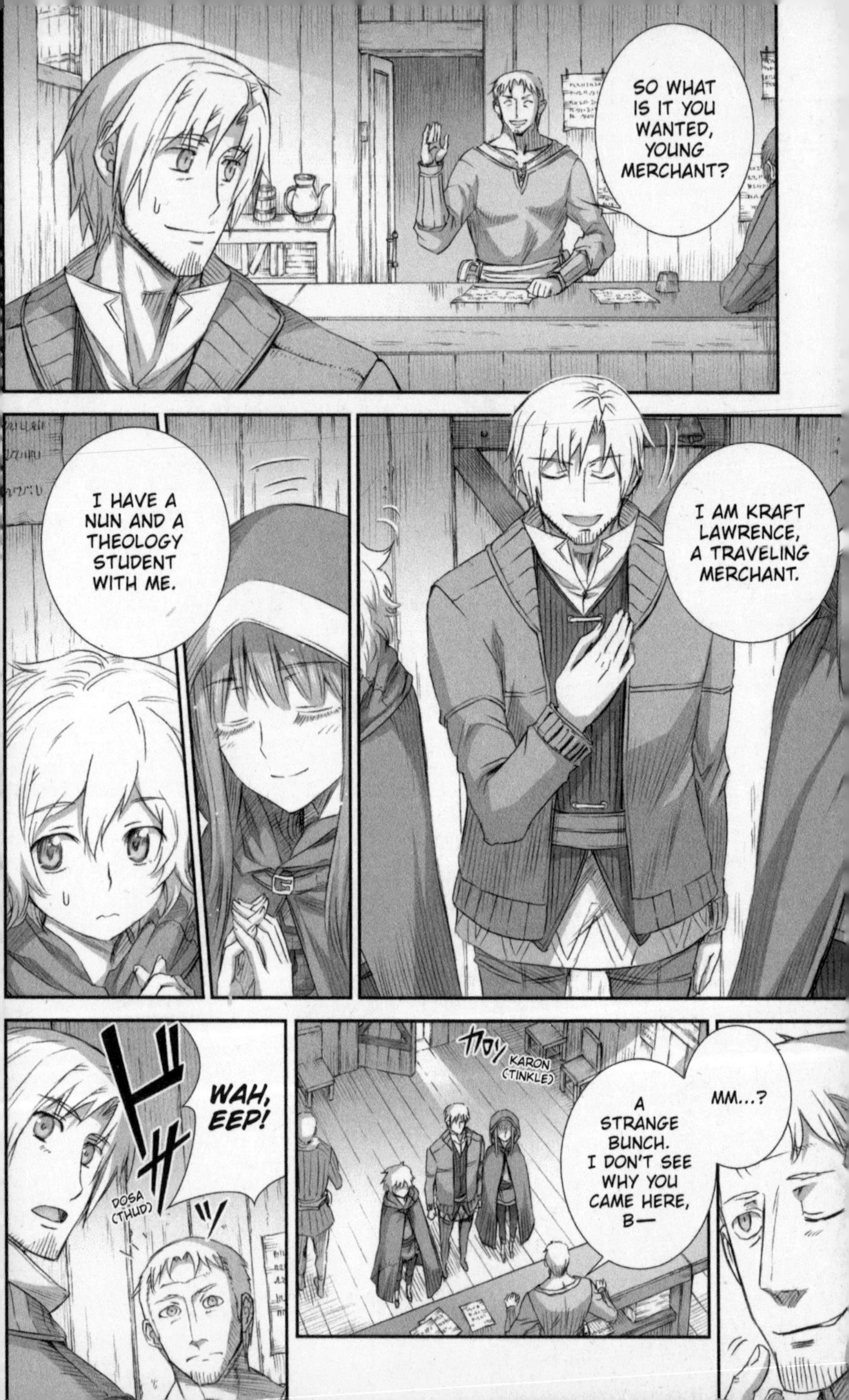
SO WHAT IS IT YOU WANTED, YOUNG MERCHANT?
I AM KRAFT LAWRENCE, A TRAVELING MERCHANT.
I HAVE A NUN AND A THEOLOGY STUDENT WITH ME.
MM...?
A STRANGE BUNCH. I DON'T SEE WHY YOU CAME HERE, B—
カロン
KARON (TINKLE)
WAH, EEP!
ドサ
DOSA (THUD)

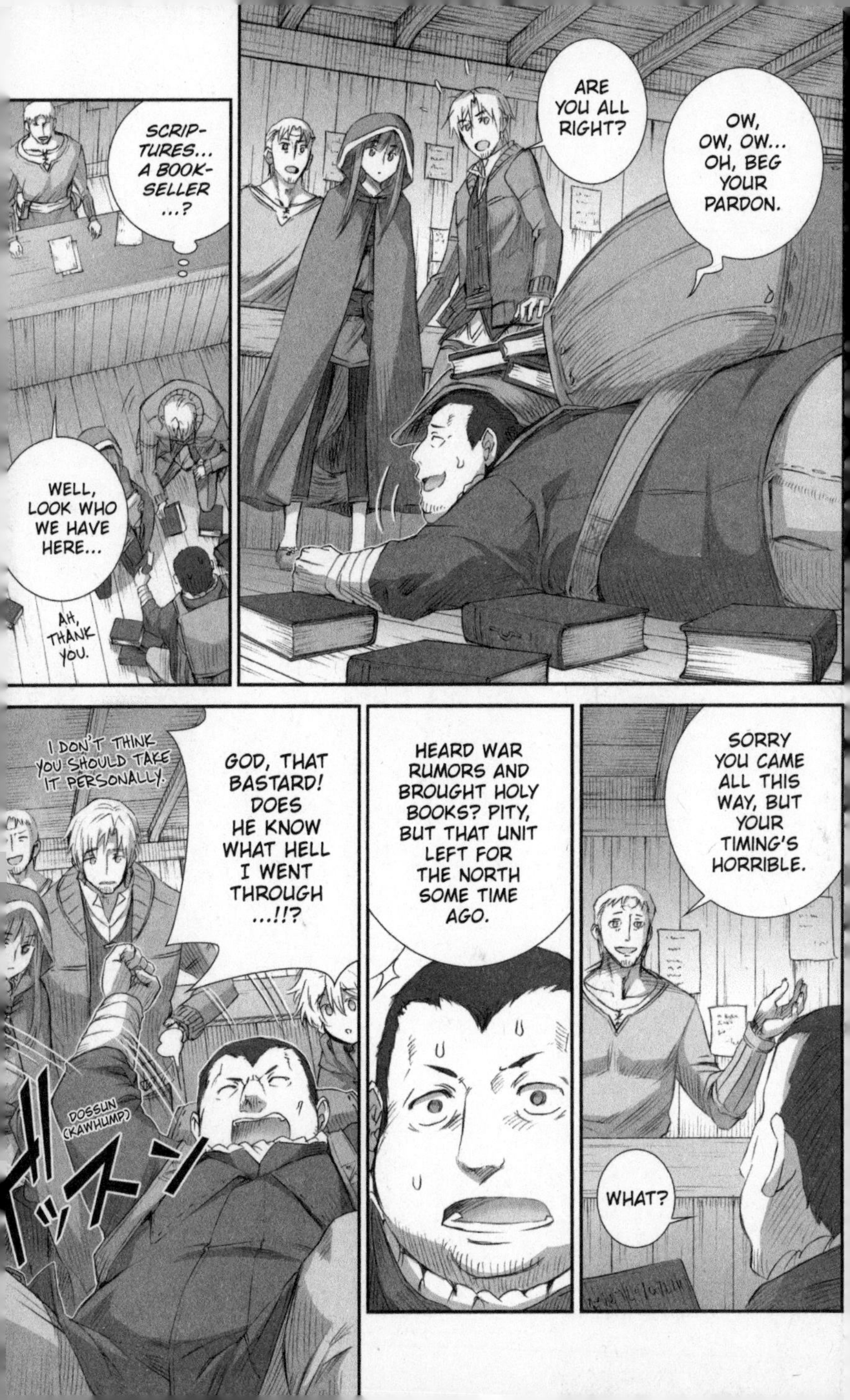
OW, OW, OW... OH, BEG YOUR PARDON.
ARE YOU ALL RIGHT?
SCRIPTURES... A BOOKSELLER ...?
WELL, LOOK WHO WE HAVE HERE...
AH, THANK YOU.
SORRY YOU CAME ALL THIS WAY, BUT YOUR TIMING'S HORRIBLE.
WHAT?
HEARD WAR RUMORS AND BROUGHT HOLY BOOKS? PITY, BUT THAT UNIT LEFT FOR THE NORTH SOME TIME AGO.
GOD, THAT BASTARD! DOES HE KNOW WHAT HELL I WENT THROUGH ...!!?
I DON'T THINK YOU SHOULD TAKE IT PERSONALLY.
DOSSUN (KAWHUMP)

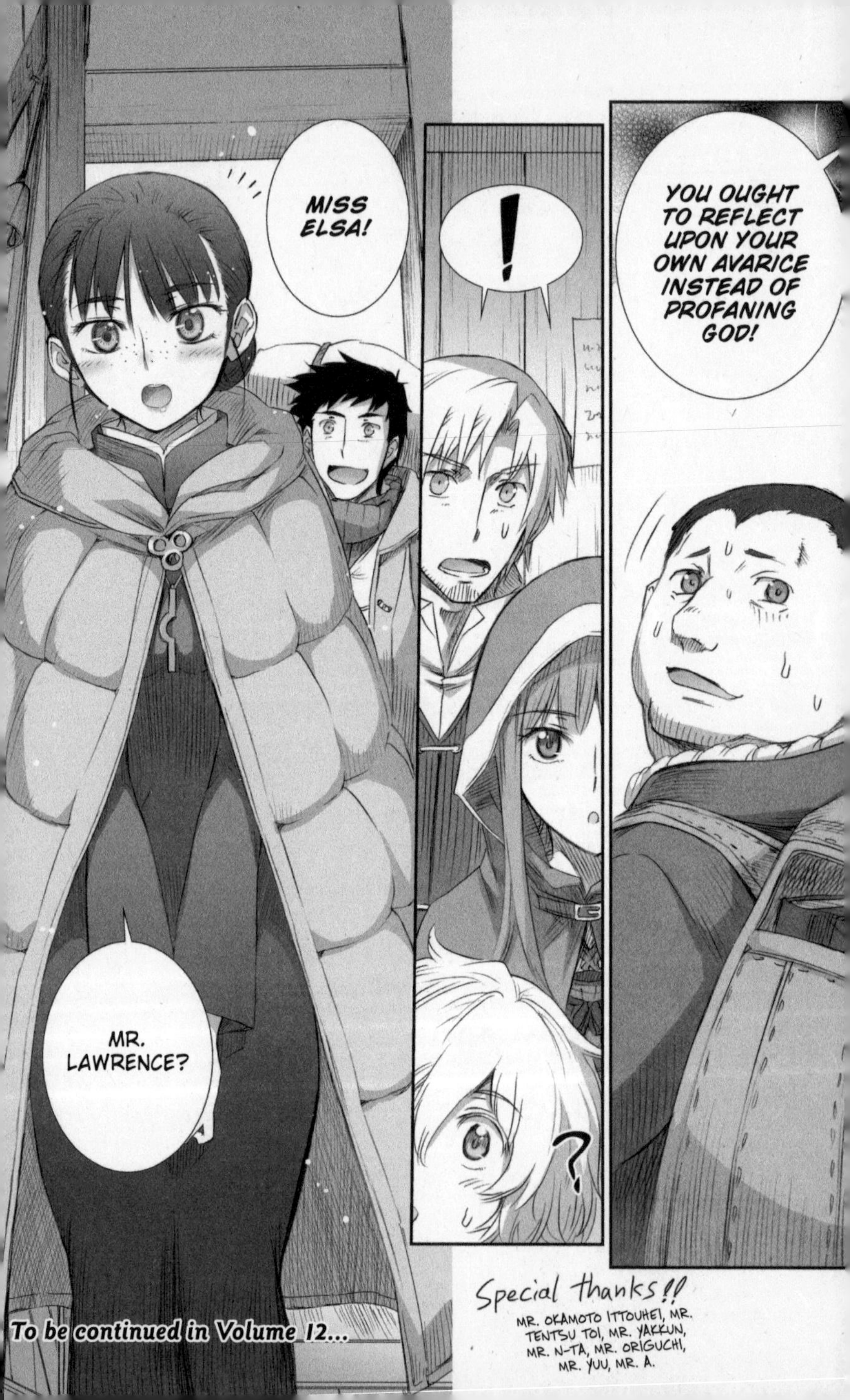
YOU OUGHT TO REFLECT UPON YOUR OWN AVARICE INSTEAD OF PROFANING GOD!
!
?
MISS ELSA!
MR. LAWRENCE?

To be continued in Volume 12...

Special thanks!!
MR. OKAMOTO ITTOUHEI, MR. TENTSU TOI, MR. YAKKUN, MR. N-TA, MR. ORIGUCHI, MR. YUU, MR. A.

Three cheers for Volume 11 being released! we're finally headed for the final conflict and a big climax! you simply must enjoy the developments to come! you don't want to disappoint cute little Holo do you? (^_^)

ISUNA HASEKURA

SPICE&WOLF

■ Three cheers for Volume 11's release! There's still more to come, so don't you dare look away!

JYUU AYAKURA

SPICE & WOLF ⑪

Isuna Hasekura
Keito Koume
Character design:
Jyuu Ayakura

Translation: Jeremiah Bourque

Lettering: Lys Blakeslee

OOKAMI TO KOUSHINRYOU Vol. 11
©Isuna Hasekura/Keito Koume 2014
Edited by ASCII MEDIA WORKS
First published in Japan in 2014 by
KADOKAWA CORPORATION, Tokyo.
English translation rights arranged with
KADOKAWA CORPORATION, Tokyo,
through Tuttle-Mori Agency, Inc., Tokyo.

Translation © 2015 by Hachette Book Group

Yen Press
Hachette Book Group
1290 Avenue of the Americas
New York, NY 10104

www.HachetteBookGroup.com
www.YenPress.com

Yen Press is an imprint of Hachette Book Group, Inc. The Yen Press name and logo are trademarks of Hachette Book Group, Inc.

The publisher is not responsible for websites (or their content) that are not owned by the publisher.

First Yen Press Edition: September 2015

ISBN: 978-0-316-30505-1

10 9 8 7 6 5 4 3 2

BVG

Printed in the United States of America